Quantifying Neighbourhood Effects

Many policies in several Western European countries and the U.S. aim to counter spatial concentrations of deprivation and create more socio-economically mixed residential areas. Such policies are founded on the belief that neighbourhoods have a strong and independent effect upon the well-being and life-chances of individuals. The adequacy of the evidence base to support this position has been the subject of spirited debate on both sides of the Atlantic. The primary purpose of this book is to contribute to this policy-relevant discussion by presenting new scholarship from many countries that rigorously quantifies various sorts of neighbourhood effects through the use of cutting-edge social scientific techniques.

The secondary purpose of this book is to introduce these techniques to a wider array of housing and planning researchers and to show how a variety of disciplines have offered insightful, synergistic perspectives. Over the last 15 years, research on neighbourhood effects has led to a body of knowledge extending far beyond the sociological urban research where it originated. The problem of quantifying neighbourhood effects and the use of associated methodologies (such as multi-level analysis, instrumental variables) has attracted scholars from criminology, sociology, social geography, economics and health science, and thus serves as a critical locus for interdisciplinary scholarship.

This book was previously published as a special issue of *Housing Studies*.

Jörg Blasius is Professor of Sociology at the Institute for Political Science and Sociology, University of Bonn, Germany. He currently serves as the president of RC33 (research committee of logic and methodology in sociology) of the International Sociological Association.

Jürgen Friedrichs is Professor Emeritus of the Research Institute for Sociology at the University of Cologne, Germany. He serves as senior editor of the Kölner Zeitschrift für Soziologie und Sozialpyschologie.

George Galster is the Clarence Hilberry Professor of Urban Affairs at the Department of Geography and Urban Planning, Wayne State University. His research has dealt with metropolitan housing markets, racial discrimination and segregation.

Quantifying Neighbourhood Effects

Frontiers and perspectives

Edited by Jörg Blasius, Jürgen Friedrichs
and George Galster

LONDON AND NEW YORK

First published 2009 by Routledge
2 Park Square, Milton Park, Abingdon, Oxon, OX14 4RN

Simultaneously published in the USA and Canada
by Routledge
270 Madison Avenue, New York, NY 10016

Routledge is an imprint of the Taylor & Francis Group, an informa business

© 2009 Edited by Jörg Blasius, Jürgen Friedrichs and George Galster

Typeset in Times by Value Chain, India
Printed and bound in Great Britain by MPG Books Ltd, Bodmin, Cornwall

All rights reserved. No part of this book may be reprinted or reproduced or utilised in any form or by any electronic, mechanical, or other means, now known or hereafter invented, including photocopying and recording, or in any information storage or retrieval system, without permission in writing from the publishers.

British Library Cataloguing in Publication Data
A catalogue record for this book is available from the British Library

ISBN10: 0-415-47809-X
ISBN13: 978-0-415-47809-0

Contents

1 Introduction: Quantifying Neighbourhood Effects
   Jörg Blasius, Jürgen Friedrichs & George Galster 1

2 What Mix Matters? Exploring the Relationships between Individuals' Incomes and Different Measures of their Neighbourhood Context
   Roger Andersson, Sako Musterd, George Galster & Timo M. Kauppinen 11

3 Mixed Tenure Communities and Neighbourhood Quality
   Ade Kearns & Phil Mason 35

4 Homeownership, Poverty and Educational Achievement: School Effects as Neighbourhood Effects
   Glen Bramley & Noah Ko. Karley 66

5 The Influence of Neighborhood Poverty During Childhood on Fertility, Education, and Earnings Outcomes
   George Galster, Dave E. Marcotte, Marv Mandell, Hal Wolman & Nancy Augustine 95

6 Internal Heterogeneity of a Deprived Urban Area and its Impact on Residents' Perception of Deviance
   Jörg Blasius & Jürgen Friedrichs 124

7 The Effects of Neighbourhood Poverty on Adolescent Problem Behaviours: A Multi-level Analysis Differentiated by Gender and Ethnicity
   Dietrich Oberwittler 152

8 The Socio-cultural Integration of Ethnic Minorities in the Netherlands: Identifying Neighbourhood Effects on Multiple Integration Outcomes
   Mérove Gijsberts & Jaco Dagevos 175

9 Intergenerational Neighborhood-Type Mobility: Examining Differences between Blacks and Whites
   Thomas P. Vartanian, Page Walker Buck & Philip Gleason 202

   Index 227

Introduction: Quantifying Neighbourhood Effects

JÖRG BLASIUS, JÜRGEN FRIEDRICHS & GEORGE GALSTER

The policy context

The prevailing thrust of housing and urban planning policy in several Western European countries, notably France, the Netherlands, Sweden and the UK, aims to create more socio-economically mixed residential environments (Andersen, 2002; Andersson, 2006; Musterd & Andersson, 2005; Kearns & Mason, this issue; Kintrea, 2007; Kleinhans, 2004; Meen *et al.*, 2005; Murie & Musterd, 2004; Musterd, 2003; Tunstall & Fenton, 2006). Although not enshrined as national policy in the US, many programmatic efforts aimed at reducing the economic segregation of neighbourhoods are underway nonetheless, and more comprehensive efforts have been strongly advocated (de Souza Briggs, 2004; Dreier *et al.*, 2004).

Regardless of the particular programmatic forms that this policy thrust has assumed internationally, all are founded on the belief that neighbourhoods have a strong and independent effect upon the well-being and life-chances of individuals. The adequacy of the evidence base to support this position has been the subject of spirited debates on both sides of the Atlantic (see Atkinson & Kintrea, 2001; Delorenzi, 2006; Friedrichs, 2002; Galster, 2007b; Galster & Zobel, 1998; Joseph, 2006; Kearns, 2002; Kleinhans, 2004; Musterd, 2003; Joseph *et al.*, 2006; Ostendorf *et al.*, 2001). Indeed, although large in volume, much of the literature quantifying neighbourhood effects can be challenged on methodological grounds (for reviews see: Ellen & Turner, 2003; Friedrichs, 1998; Friedrichs *et al.*, 2003; Galster, 2003; Gephart, 1997; Leventhal & Brooks-Gunn, 2000; Sampson *et al.*, 2002; Van Kempen, 1997). The primary purpose in this Special Issue is to contribute to this housing policy-relevant discussion by assembling papers that quantify various types of neighbourhood effects through the use of cutting-edge social scientific techniques.

Neighbourhood Effects Investigation as a Means of Cross-disciplinary Integration

The secondary purpose of this book is to introduce these techniques to a wider array of housing researchers and to show how a variety of disciplines have offered insightful, synergistic perspectives on a field of enquiry that is central to the scholarship on housing. It is noteworthy that over the last 15 years research on neighbourhood effects has led to a research tradition extending far beyond the sociological urban research where it originated. The problem of quantifying neighbourhood effects and the use of associated methodologies (such as multi-level analysis or instrumental variables) has attracted scholars from criminology, sociology, social geography, economics and health science.

Although typically unnoticed by each of the involved disciplines, neighbourhood effect research and research methodology have grown to constitute a common core of interdisciplinary and cumulative research effort. The differences among disciplines appear to vary only by the dependent variables investigated, such as crime rates, disorder, education, earnings or health impacts. A recent illustration was the inauguration of a joint workshop at the 2006 European Network for Housing Research conference that brought together the Poverty Neighbourhood and Health Effects Working Groups. Even at the risk of overstating the cumulative evidence from the last 15 years, it is thought that the study of neighbourhood effects has made an extremely important contribution to the integration of social sciences.

About this book

An important precursor to the effort here was the *Housing Studies* Special Issue: 'Life in Poverty Neighbourhoods, (vol. 18(6)' 2003) that we guest edited in collaboration with Sako Musterd. The papers pertained to different aspects of these deprived residential environments, such as social status mobility, residential mobility, social norms, and residents' bonds to the neighbourhood. Although suggestive, the papers often were descriptive in approach and did not utilize sophisticated, multivariate/multi-level methods to quantify the impact of poverty neighbourhoods. Indeed, the 2003 Special Issue also contained two papers that pointed to these shortcomings and offered directions for future research.

This book comprises a series of innovative responses to the challenges raised in our 2003 work. In contrast to the 2003 issue, contributions now focus on the multi-level problem: the impact of neighbourhood composition on the attitudes and behaviours of individual residents. Some of the chapters here use multi-level statistical techniques such as Hierarchical Linear Modelling (HLM), whereas others seek to explore these effects with techniques appropriate to small samples on the neighbourhood context level (correspondence analysis). One uses a comparison of siblings over time and another uses instrumental variables as a way to correct for selection bias associated with unmeasured parental effects. All studies provide a wealth of control variables applied in a multivariate statistical context, in an effort to isolate the independent contribution of neighbourhood context. As with the 2003 Special Issue, an international array of authors is presented here: England, Finland, Germany, Netherlands, Scotland, Sweden and the US are represented. Thus it is hoped that this book encourages continuities in the Trans-Atlantic dialogue. Below in this Introduction you will find a brief summary of the substantive results of the studies represented; the details of the statistical methods employed are supplied in the Appendix.

Andersson, Musterd, Galster & Kauppinen begin the Special Issue by addressing two fundamental questions: Which aspect of neighbourhood socio-economic environment is most strongly correlated with adult earnings outcomes? Does the answer depend on gender and metropolitan/non-metropolitan residence? Their analysis of Swedish social register data finds that the percentages of adult males with earnings in the lowest 30th and (to a lesser degree) the highest 30th percentiles hold greater explanatory power for all strata than domains of neighbourhood mix related to education, ethnicity or housing tenure, although the correlation is much stronger for men and for metropolitan residents.

Kearns & Mason also probe the question of which characteristics of the neighbourhood matter most to whom. They explore the relationship between different mixes of housing tenure in UK neighbourhoods and incidence of neighbourhood problems, resident-reported deficiencies, and the demand for improvements to local services and amenities. Their multivariate findings based on the Survey of English Housing indicate that the share of social renting in the area is a more important predictor of neighbourhood problems and service improvement desires than the degree of tenure mixing. Moreover, for both social renters and owner occupiers, the identification of problems in areas where social renting makes up around a quarter of the housing market is at least double than in areas where owner occupation comprises the vast majority of the housing market and social renting is at half this level or less, suggesting a social disadvantage threshold consistent with much US evidence (Galster, 2002).

Bramley & Karley address a closely related question: Is 'neighbourhood' better operationalized as school environment or residential environment? To find an answer, they use UK student achievement data merged with data on both the schools the students attend and the small-scale neighbourhoods in which they reside. Bramley & Karley find that the proportions of homeowners in both the school and (especially) the neighbourhood strongly explain better primary and secondary school attainment outcomes, although the distinct influences of poverty and homeownership are difficult to disentangle.

Galster, Marcotte, Mandell, Wolman & Augustine investigate the consequences for children of the proportion of poor residents in the neighbourhood where they were growing up. They employ the US Panel Study of Income Dynamics (PSID) to examine the cumulative childhood conditions of children born 1968–74, and a variety of fertility, educational and earnings outcomes that they experienced as young adults in 1999. Although their application of instrumental variables substantially attenuates the apparent neighbourhood effects, they nevertheless find that cumulative neighbourhood poverty over childhood has an independent, non-trivial relationship with high school attainment and earnings.

Blasius & Friedrichs shift the emphasis toward outcomes traditionally examined by sociologists. They uncover the sizeable differentiation within an infamous 'deprived area' in Cologne (Germany) and relate it to residents' perceptions of disorder, deviance and perceived risk. They conclude that perceived disorder, observed deviant behaviour and perceived risk are quite unrelated, and thus have distinct correlates. Neighbourhood-level collective efficacy and intergenerational closure are strongly related to the perceived extent of deviance, but social status heterogeneity is not. The proportion of residents with specific characteristics, such as single-heads of households, accounts for much of the variation of the dependent variables.

Oberwittler investigates a different set of outcomes related to psychological strain and delinquent behaviours, employing a cross-sectional survey of adolescents in 61 neighbourhoods in two German cities. He finds support for neighbourhood effects, but they appear strongly contingent on ethnicity and the spatial orientation of adolescents' routine activities and peer networks. For example, native German girls are particularly prone to react violently to neighbourhood disadvantage. Like Bramley & Karley, Oberwittler finds that both school and neighbourhood environments are important predictors (in this case, of delinquency).

Gijsberts & Dagevos explore a particularly sensitive dimension of neighbourhood context: the proportion of ethnic minority groups. Using two large-scale Dutch social surveys, they probe the degree to which non-Dutch concentrations are related to inter-ethnic contacts, language proficiency and mutual stereotypical attitudes. Their analysis shows that inter-ethnic contacts occur less frequently in neighbourhoods with non-Dutch concentrations, and that this inhibits minorities' attainment of Dutch language skills. Moreover, some mixing appears to have a positive influence on Dutch perceptions of the minorities, although a sudden and sizeable increase in the neighbourhood proportion of minorities apparently yields more negative Dutch attitudes toward minorities.

Finally, Vartanian, Buck & Gleason conduct the first investigation of intergenerational mobility across various types of neighbourhoods, using the US PSID. They are particularly interested in the extent to which children who grow up in disadvantaged neighbourhoods are likely to live in such neighbourhoods as adults. They find that whites who grow up in the most disadvantaged white neighbourhoods are far more likely to live in such places during adulthood than white children who grow up in even slightly better neighbourhoods. Although the relationship appears weaker for blacks, the estimated parameters indicate that had black children been raised in the most disadvantaged white (instead of black) neighbourhoods, their chances of living in these poorest neighbourhoods as adults would be dramatically lower.

Conclusions and Policy Implications

In sum, several threads of common findings emerge from the international body of methodologically sophisticated work contained in this book:

- All studies find support for non-trivial neighbourhood effects on a wide variety of outcomes for individuals, controlling for individual characteristics and (in some cases) selection effects.
- The strongest relationships involving many economic outcomes (e.g. earnings, education and mobility) and social-psychological outcomes (e.g. attitudes, perceptions, satisfactions, delinquencies) involve neighbourhood characteristics emphasizing absolute proportions of disadvantaged (in terms of income and/or social benefit-social housing status) households; other aspects of neighbourhoods (e.g. ethnic minority concentrations, collective efficacy) are also important for many outcomes.
- Both attributes of residential neighbourhood and school environments appear to be influential.
- Neighbourhood effects are contingent on an individual's gender, race-ethnicity, and the degree to which one's life is spent within particular types of neighbourhood.

These findings hold several implications for the aforementioned policy debates. First, the household mix of a neighbourhood indeed seems to matter, but policy makers must carefully specify the particular dimension of mix that a specific programme is intended to shape (e.g. tenure status, income, ethnicity, etc.) because different outcomes depend on these different dimensions. Second, administratively defined neighbourhoods can exhibit large internal variation, but the most powerful neighbourhood effects are related to smaller-scale environments (including schools). This implies that a policy to alter household composition must be finely grained in its spatial focus. Third, the evidence here suggests that it is not mix per se but the absolute proportion of a disadvantaged group (defined in various possible ways) that is the single most common and powerful predictor of negative neighbourhood effects. This may suggest more emphasis on (in the words of Kearns & Mason, this issue) a 'dispersal' of the disadvantaged among strong neighbourhoods, not a 'dilution' of concentrated areas of deprivation with a few upper-income homeowners. However, the optimal mix of advantaged and disadvantaged households (and the means to achieve this mix) will be defined quite differently in different national contexts, depending on the weighting of equity and efficiency concerns (Galster, 2007a). It is hoped that the papers presented here help focus and factually inform these policy discussions, as well as advance the science of quantifying neighbourhood effects of various sorts.

References

Andersen, H. S. (2002) Can deprived housing areas be revitalised? Efforts against segregation and neighborhood decay in Denmark and Europe, *Urban Studies*, 39, pp. 767–790.
Andersson, R. (2006) 'Breaking segregation': Rhetorical construct or effective policy? The case of the Metropolitan Development Initiative in Sweden, *Urban Studies*, 43, pp. 787–799.
Atkinson, R. & Kintrea, K. (2001) Area effects: what do they mean for British housing and regeneration policy?, *European Journal of Housing Policy*, 2, pp. 147–166.
Blasius, J. & Greenacre, M. (1994) Computation of Correspondence Analysis, in: M. Greenacre & J. Blasius (Eds) *Correspondence analysis in the social sciences*, pp. 53–78 (London: Academic Press).
Blasius, J. & Greenacre, M. J. (2006) Multiple correspondence analysis and related methods in practice, in: M. J. Greenacre & J. Blasius (Eds) *Multiple Correspondence Analysis and Related Methods*, pp. 3–40 (Boca Raton, FL: Chapman & Hall).
de Souza Briggs, X. (Ed.) (2004) *The Geography of Opportunity* (Washington DC: Brookings Institution Press).
Delorenzi, S. (2006) Introduction, in: S. Delorenzi (Ed.) *Going Places: Neighbourhood, Ethnicity and Social Mobility*, pp. 1–11 (London: Institute for Public Policy Research).
Dreier, P., Mollenkopf, J. & Swanstrom, T. (2004) *Place Matters*, 2nd edn (Lawrence, KS: University of Kansas Press).
Ellen, I. & Turner, M. (2003) Do neighborhoods matter and why?, in: J. Goering & J. Feins (Eds) *Choosing a Better Life? Evaluating the Moving to Opportunity Experiment*, pp. 313–338 (Washington, DC: Urban Institute Press).
Friedrichs, J. (1998) Do poor neighborhoods make their residents poorer? Context effects of poverty neighborhoods on their residents, in: H. Andress (Ed.) *Empirical Poverty Research in a Comparative Perspective*, pp. 77–99 (Aldershot: Ashgate).
Friedrichs, J. (2002) Response: contrasting US and European findings on poverty neighborhoods, *Housing Studies*, 17, pp. 101–106.
Friedrichs, J., Galster, G. & Musterd, S. (2003) Neighborhood effects on social opportunities: the European and American research and policy context, *Housing Studies*, 18, pp. 797–806.

Galster, G. (2002) An economic efficiency analysis of deconcentrating poverty populations, *Journal of Housing Economics*, 11, pp. 303–329.
Galster, G. (2003) Investigating behavioral impacts of poor neighborhoods: towards new data and analytic strategies, *Housing Studies*, 18, pp. 893–914.
Galster, G. (2007a) Neighbourhood social mix as a goal of housing policy: a theoretical analysis, *European Journal of Housing Policy*, 7, pp. 19–43.
Galster, G. (2007b) Should policy makers strive for neighborhood social mix? An analysis of the Western European evidence base, *Housing Studies*, 22(4), pp. 523–545.
Galster, G. & Zobel, A. (1998) Will dispersed housing programmes reduce social problems in the US?, *Housing Studies*, 13, pp. 605–622.
Gephart, M. (1997) Neighborhoods and communities as contexts for development, in: J. Brooks-Gunn, G. Duncan & J. Aber (Eds) *Neighborhood Poverty: Vol. I. Context and Consequences for Children*, pp. 1–43 (New York: Russell Sage Foundation).
Greenacre, M. (1984) *Theory and Application of Correspondence Analysis* (London: Academic Press).
Greenacre, M. (1993) *Correspondence Analysis in Practice* (London: Academic Press).
Joseph, M. (2006) Is mixed-income development an antidote to urban poverty?, *Housing Policy Debate*, 17, pp. 209–234.
Joseph, M., Chaskin, R. & Webber, H. (2006) The theoretical basis for addressing poverty through mixed-income development, *Urban Affairs Review*, 42, pp. 369–409.
Kearns, A. (2002) Response: from residential disadvantage to opportunity? Reflections on British and European policy and research, *Housing Studies*, 17, pp. 145–150.
Kintrea, K. (2007) Policies and programmes for disadvantaged neighbourhoods: recent English experience, *Housing Studies*, 22, pp. 261–282.
Kleinhans, R. (2004) Social implications of housing diversification in urban renewal: a review of recent literature, *Journal of Housing and the Built Environment*, 19, pp. 367–390.
Leventhal, T. & Brooks-Gunn, J. (2000) The neighborhoods they live in, *Psychological Bulletin*, 126, pp. 309–337.
Maas, C. J. M. & Hox, J. (2004) Robustness issues in multilevel regression analysis, *Statistica Nederlandica*, 58, pp. 127–137.
Marsh, L. & Cormier, D. (2001) *Spline Regression Models* (Thousand Oaks, CA: Sage).
Meen, G., Gibb, K., Goody, J., McGrath, T. & Mackinnon, J. (2005) *Economic Segregation in England* (York: Joseph Rowntree Foundation).
Murie, A. & Musterd, S. (2004) Social exclusion and opportunity structures in European cities and neighbourhoods, *Urban Studies*, 41, pp. 1441–1459.
Musterd, S. (2003) Segregation and integration: a contested relationship, *Journal of Ethnic and Migration Studies*, 29, pp. 623–641.
Musterd, S. & Andersson, R. (2005) Housing mix, social mix, and social opportunities, *Urban Affairs Review*, 40, pp. 1–30.
Ostendorf, W., Musterd, S. & de Vos, S. (2001) Social mix and the neighborhood effect: policy ambition and empirical support, *Housing Studies*, 16, pp. 371–380.
Sampson, R., Morenoff, J. & Gannon-Rowley, T. (2002) Assessing 'neighborhood effects': social processes and new directions in research, *Annual Review of Sociology*, 28, pp. 443–478.
Snijders, T. A. B. & Bosker, R. J. (1999) *Multilevel Analysis. An Introduction to Basic and Advanced Multilevel Modelling* (London: Sage).
Tunstall, R. & Fenton, A. (2006) *In the Mix: A Review of Mixed Income, Mixed Tenure and Mixed Communities* (York: Joseph Rowntree Foundation, English Partnerships, and the Housing Corporation).
Van Kempen, E. (1997) Poverty pockets and life chances, *American Behavioral Scientist*, 41, pp. 430–449.

APPENDIX

According to the focus of the book, in addition to the research questions, all papers deal with methodological problems. This Appendix briefly introduces the techniques used in the following papers.

Regression Models

Regression analysis is a well-known technique to explain a dependent metric scaled variable y by a set of m independent variables (x), i.e. $y_{ij} = \beta_0 + \beta_1 x_{1i} + \beta_2 x_{2i} + \ldots + \beta_m x_{mi} + e_i$, with the β's as regression coefficients and the error term e. To give an example, using a large Swedish dataset that covers almost the whole population, Andersson et al. (this issue) use multiple regression to explain the amount of individual income from work; as explanatory variables they use personal characteristics such as educational level and age, characteristics of the neighbourhood, of the local labour market and of the municipality of residence. To exclude the gender effect and to show differences between metropolitan and non-metropolitan areas they subdivided the sample into four groups ('males in metropolitan areas' and 'females in non-metropolitan areas').

Already at this level of multivariate analysis there are some methodological problems that might occur, for example, the correlation of the error term with the dependent variable, multicollinearity or endogeneity. Endogeneity occurs when the relationship between dependent and independent variables is either backwards or circular, i.e. changes in the dependent variable cause changes in the independent variable(s); the explanatory variables (or their covariates) are correlated with the error term. For example, average household income in different areas can have this property: if the household income increases the areas might improve (better shops, less deviant behaviour), but improving areas also attract households with higher income. There are several possibilities to avoid this problem, for example, using instrumental variables and/or applying two-step-least-squares regression.

Suppose there are a dependent variable y with an error term ϵ and an explanatory variable x_1 with an error term δ_1, where x_1 is recursively correlated with y and where there is an error correlation of δ_1 on y and/or of ϵ on x_1. For receiving consistent predictors one should replace x_1 by an instrumental variable z (or a set of variables z_j) that is (are) highly correlated with x_1, but not caused by y and not correlated with ϵ. In the second step x_1 has to be regressed on the instrumental variable z and the other variable(s) that are theorized to cause it recursively, i.e. $x_1 = \beta_0 + \beta_1 z + \beta_2 x_2 + \ldots + \beta_m x_m$. Save the predictions of x_1 ($= \text{pred}(x_1)$) and use them to predict y instead of the variables that are hypothesized to be recursively correlated with the dependent variable, i.e. $y = \alpha + \alpha_1 \text{pred}(x_1) +$ other explanatory variables that are not recursively connected with the dependent variable. Two-step-regression and instrumental variables are used by Galster et al. (this issue) to explain, among others, the relatively low annual earnings in poverty neighbourhoods.

If the dependent variable is dichotomous, one usually switches to logistic regression analysis, which estimates the probability of $y_i = 1$ (with $P(y_i = 1) = 1 - P(y_i = 0)$). The probability can be estimated by $P(y_i = 1) = \frac{e^{\beta_0 + \beta_1 x_{1i} + \beta_2 x_{2i} + \ldots + \beta_m x_{mi}}}{1 + e^{\beta_0 + \beta_1 x_{1i} + \beta_2 x_{2i} + \ldots + \beta_m x_{mi}}}$; the algorithm for estimating the β-coefficients requires the logarithm of the equation. As the solution we receive probabilities or log-odds, if the values are greater than 1 (or their logarithm greater than 0), the effect is positive. If the values are less than 1, then the effect is negative. Solutions from logistic regression are provided by Kearns & Mason (this issue) to describe different problems in the neighbourhood, for example, vandalism, graffiti and crime (reported is the presence/absence of these problems) by indicators such as housing (with categories 'social renter', 'private renter', and 'owner' serving as reference category) and proportion of social renter in the neighbourhood.

Another problem in regression analysis is abrupt changes in the data, which might be caused by certain events, for example, political changes or changes in taxes. An analytical approach designed to address this issue is spline regression. When applying spline regression models one is searching for points, or 'knots', in the data where (significant) changes occur (for an overview, see Marsh & Cormier, 2001). The method can be understood as a technique that is between smoothing and breaking the data into segments. Vartanian *et al.* (this issue) use spline models to estimate the likelihood that adults live in a neighbourhood with a certain quality, given the quality of their neighbourhood in childhood; thereby, the neighbourhood quality was categorized: 1 per cent worst, between 1 and 5 per cent worst, 5–10 per cent worst, ..., 1–5 per cent best, and 1 per cent best (1 per cent, 5 per cent, 10 per cent, ..., 95 per cent, 99 per cent are the knots).

Multi-level Analysis

Multi-level analysis or hierarchical linear modelling (HLM) can be understood as a special kind of regression analysis. The idea of this model is that there are nested data where the higher levels have an influence on the predicted variable. A typical application comes from school data; school achievement should be explained by individual characteristics such as hours spent for learning and educational background of the parents; these variables belong to the first level (level 1). However, there might be an influence of the characteristics of the teachers, for example, their motivational level; such characteristics belong to the second level (level 2). One might even think of a third level: an influence of the schools or of the neighbourhoods where the schools are located, for example, schools in rich areas might have more money for offering better learning conditions (faster computers, better equipment). These conditions may affect the characteristics of the schools and these in turn affect the educational achievements of pupils.

One basic idea of HLM is to decompose the variance according to the hierarchical levels. So, for example, we might seek to distinguish how much variation in school achievement can be explained by individual characteristics and how much variation is explained by the teachers (the schools).

Suppose a simple hierarchical model seeks to estimate the achievement y using one independent variable x (level 1) and a second level variable that only affects the intercept, i.e. the slope of the regression line is the same for each value of the second level variable. This model yields $y_{ij} = \beta_{0j} + \beta_1 x_{ij} + e_{ij}$, where i is the level-1 index and j the level-2 index. The model can be extended to slopes affected by the second level variable(s) and one can include higher level variables that have an impact on y. Supposing two variables on the first level (x_1 and x_2) and one variable (z) on the second level, the model is described by $y_{ij} = \beta_{0j} + \beta_{1j} x_{1ij} + \beta_{2j} x_{2ij} + \beta_3 z_j + e_{ij}$. Further extensions to more variables, more levels and other regression models, for example, the logistic regression model, are possible (for an overview, see Snijders & Bosker, 1999). However, the data demands of HLM models are quite stringent: the minimum number of cases on each level should be at least 10, but then no inferences about the population can be made (Snijders & Bosker, 1999, p. 44). Maas & Hox (2004) suggest 50 units are needed to have stable estimates of standard errors. Examples of the application of multi-level models are given by Oberwittler, as well as by Bramley & Karley, and Gijsberts & Dagevos (all in this issue).

Correspondence Analysis

In the models discussed above, the aim is to receive coefficients to explain the variation of a dependent variable, for example, household income. If the number of cases on level 2 is too low to apply HLM, one possibility is to visualize the results for different levels by means of correspondence analysis (CA). This technique is probably less familiar, so it is described in a little more detail.

The aim of CA is to visualize rows and columns of contingency tables. Given a simple example from a survey, there are two variables with I rows and J columns, for example, marital status with categories such as single and married, and employment status with categories such as full-time, part-time and retired. The cells n_{ij} of the table $\mathbf{N}$ contain the frequencies of the bivariate cross-tabulation, with $\sum_{ij} n_{ij} = n$. The relative marginals of the rows are then defined by $r_{i\cdot} = n_{i\cdot}/n$ and the relative marginals of the columns are $c_j = n_{\cdot j}/n$.

Under the assumption of independence from rows and columns yields: $\hat{n}_{ij} = r_i c_j$, also known as expected values. The data are centred by $p_{ij} - r_i c_j$, with $p_{ij} = n_{ij}/n$, and normalized through division by the square root of $r_i c_j$. Applying these transformations provides the matrix of standardized residuals:

$$\mathbf{S} = \mathbf{D}_r^{-1/2}(\mathbf{P} - \mathbf{r}\mathbf{c}^T)\mathbf{D}_c^{-1/2}, \text{ or in scalar notation } s_{ij} = (p_{ij} - r_i c_j)/\sqrt{r_i c_j}$$

Thereby $\mathbf{r}$ and $\mathbf{c}$ are the row and column vectors of the masses, and $\mathbf{D}_r$ and $\mathbf{D}_c$ are diagonal matrices. This is known from chi-square analysis, which is defined as: $\sum s_{ij}^2 = \chi^2 = \sum_{i=1}^{I} \sum_{j=1}^{J} \frac{(n_{ij} - \hat{n}_{ij})^2}{\hat{n}_{ij}}$, where $\hat{n}_{ij} = \frac{n_{i\cdot} \times n_{\cdot j}}{n}$ are the expected values under the assumption of independence. Dividing χ^2 by n provides us with $\frac{\chi^2}{n} = \sum_{i=1}^{I} \sum_{j=1}^{J} \frac{(p_{ij} - r_i c_j)^2}{r_i c_j}$, a coefficient that is called 'total inertia'. Applying singular value decomposition to the matrix of standardized residuals provides us with $\text{SVD}(\mathbf{S}) = \mathbf{U}\mathbf{\Sigma}\mathbf{V}^T$, where $\mathbf{\Sigma}$ is the diagonal matrix with singular values in descending order $\sigma_1 \geq \sigma_2 \geq \ldots \geq \sigma_S \geq 0$, and with $S = $ rank of the matrix ($\mathbf{S}$). The columns from $\mathbf{U}$ are the left singular vectors, the columns from $\mathbf{V}$ are the right singular vectors; it yields $\mathbf{U}^T\mathbf{U} = \mathbf{V}^T\mathbf{V} = \mathbf{I}$.

There is a close connection between SVD as used in correspondence analysis and the well-known canonical decomposition as, for example, applied for principal component analysis:

$$\mathbf{S}^T\mathbf{S} = \mathbf{V}\mathbf{\Sigma}\mathbf{U}^T\mathbf{U}\mathbf{\Sigma}\mathbf{V}^T = \mathbf{V}\mathbf{\Sigma}^2\mathbf{V}^T = \mathbf{V}\mathbf{\Lambda}\mathbf{V}^T, \text{ with } \mathbf{S}\mathbf{S}^T = \mathbf{U}\mathbf{\Sigma}\mathbf{V}^T\mathbf{V}\mathbf{\Sigma}\mathbf{U}^T = \mathbf{U}\mathbf{\Sigma}^2\mathbf{U}^T = \mathbf{U}\mathbf{\Lambda}\mathbf{U}^T$$

$$\lambda_1 \geq \lambda_2 \geq \ldots \geq \lambda_S \geq 0; \sum_s \lambda_s = \text{total inertia, since trace}(\mathbf{S}\mathbf{S}^T) = \text{trace}(\mathbf{S}^T\mathbf{S})$$

$$= \text{trace}(\mathbf{\Sigma}^2) = \text{trace}(\mathbf{\Lambda}).$$

For the graphical representation we use $\mathbf{F} = \mathbf{D}_r^{-1/2}\mathbf{U}\mathbf{\Sigma}$ providing the (principal) co-ordinates of the rows, and $\mathbf{G} = \mathbf{D}_c^{-1/2}\mathbf{V}\mathbf{\Sigma}$ providing the (principal) co-ordinates of the columns (for further details see Greenacre, 1984, 1993; for the algorithm to perform CA Blasius & Greenacre, 1994). The interpretation of CA is very similar to PCA, both methods provide eigenvalues and their explained variances, factor loadings and factor values. In general CA can be understood as a generalization of PCA to categorical data. However, CA is often used to show the similarities between rows and columns within a map. Further, CA also can be applied to any kind of tables, for example, to indicator and

Burt matrices—in this case the method is called multiple correspondence analysis—but also to rank, rating and metric data. Although not often done, the main advantage of applying CA instead of PCA is the visualization of the data in a low-dimensional space. An example of correspondence analysis is given by Blasius & Friedrichs (this issue).

They apply correspondence analysis to a table of aggregated data that consists of variables on different scales, which requires standardization because the values depend on the direction of the scales and the variables themselves have different ranges (for example, percentages, differences between percentages and standard normalized variables). It follows that the variables have, first, to be standardized to the same range and, second, to be 'doubled' (see also Greenacre, 1984, 1993).

The purpose of standardizing and doubling is to create two endpoints for each variable, one representing the positive endpoint and the other the negative endpoint. In the standardization-step Blasius & Friedrichs (this issue) first subtract from the single variables their minimum value that is given to any of the six natural areas, i.e. $x_i - x_{min}$, providing a lower bound of 0 and an upper bound of $x_{max} - x_{min}$. Then they divide these differences by the range of the single variables, i.e. $x_{max} - x_{min}$, receiving a value between '0' for the natural area that has the lowest value, and '1' for the natural area that has the highest value; they call these new variables 'images'. In the doubling-step they calculate the differences between 1 and the actual scale values; the resulting variables are the 'anti-images'. Input data for CA are therefore a matrix with 26 rows containing the images and anti-images and six columns containing the natural areas. In each column in their matrix of input data images and anti-images sum up to 1, resulting in a constant column sum (= 12, the number of indicators). Further, the sum of images and anti-images is constant (= 6, the number of natural areas). It follows that all variables (images and anti-images) and all natural areas have the same weight, i.e. the direction of the scales and the scaling of the indicators do not influence the CA solution. Thus, the differences in the amount of explained variance in the model are based on the differences between the natural areas according to the indicators in the model.

What Mix Matters? Exploring the Relationships between Individuals' Incomes and Different Measures of their Neighbourhood Context

ROGER ANDERSSON, SAKO MUSTERD, GEORGE GALSTER & TIMO M. KAUPPINEN

Research and Policy Context

Scholarly interest in the degree to which neighbourhood conditions affect the life chances of children, youth and adults has skyrocketed over the last 15 years, as evidenced by the upsurge of research papers, special issues of scholarly journals and reviews of the literature.[1] Although there seems to be an emerging consensus in the US that neighbourhood indicators typically do have non-trivial relationships with a range of outcomes related to childhood cognitive development, academic achievement and credential attainment, teen fertility and labour market consequences as adults, there remains debate about which precise indicators of neighbourhood conditions are the most predictive. There is even less consensus in Western European scholarship that *any* types of neighbourhood effects are prominent, let alone which indicator is most powerful (cf. Andersen, 2003; Kearns, 2002; Musterd, 2002; Musterd *et al.*, 2003; Musterd & Andersson, 2005, 2006; Ostendorf *et al.*, 2001; Van der Klaauw & Van Ours, 2003).

However, this lack of scholarly consensus has not slowed neighbourhood diversification policy initiatives on either side of the Atlantic (Friedrichs *et al.*, 2003; Galster & Zobel, 1998; Musterd *et al.*, 2003; Murie & Musterd, 2004).[2] A common guiding principle appears to be that concentrations of lower-income, disproportionately ethnic minority (typically immigrant in Europe) households need to be replaced by mixed residential environments that will provide superior social opportunities for the disadvantaged group. Although important differences remain between US and Western European approaches (cf. Goetz, 2002; Johnson *et al.*, 2002; Kearns, 2002; Musterd, 2002), this goal of enhancing the mix of social groups at the neighbourhood level has been sought through two common programmatic strategies. First, in Europe there have been large-scale investments aimed at restructuring large, homogeneous, post-war neighbourhoods and housing estates (through selective demolition, infill construction and the sale of social or public housing) so that they contain a greater diversity of housing types by price range and tenure (Murie *et al.*, 2003). Although smaller in scale, the redevelopment of US public housing developments as mixed-income complexes through the HOPE VI programme is strategically comparable. Second, it is now required in several jurisdictions in both Europe and the US that new, larger-scale residential developments must set aside a minimum share of the dwelling units for social (subsidized) housing.

What typically has been left implicit in this set of policy initiatives is what aspect of neighbourhood mix is deemed crucial for expanding opportunities. Is the domain of mix: socio-economic? National origin or ethnicity? Housing type and tenure? Within a domain, is it the percentage of a certain 'disadvantaged' group or the percentage of 'advantaged' groups that is more important? Or is it the balance of these two groups? Or is it diversity per se across all groups comprising a specific domain that is crucial?

In order to provide badly needed answers to these questions, this paper will explore the degree to which a wide variety of 1995 neighbourhood conditions in Sweden are statistically related to earnings for metropolitan and non-metropolitan men and women during the 1996–99 period, controlling for a wide variety of personal characteristics.

Alternative Mechanisms of Neighbourhood Effects and their Implications for what Household Mix Matters

There have been several comprehensive reviews of the potential theoretical links between neighbourhood processes and individual outcomes (in particular, see Atkinson *et al.*, 2001; Duncan *et al.*, 1997; Ellen & Turner, 2003; Friedrichs, 1998; Gephart, 1997; Haurin *et al.*, 2002; Jencks & Mayer, 1990; Sampson *et al.*, 2002). However, these theories often offer ambiguous or contradictory implications about what mix matters in neighbourhoods. The paper will describe these mechanisms only briefly here because they are well known, drawing out any implications for household mix. In organizing this summary the useful distinction introduced by Manski (1995, 2000) among endogenous, exogenous, and correlated neighbourhood effects is employed.

Endogenous Neighbourhood Effects

Endogenous neighbourhood effects are those that occur when the behaviours or attitudes of one neighbourhood resident have a direct influence on (at least a portion of) his or her neighbours' behaviours or attitudes. Numerous versions of endogenous effects have been forwarded:

- *Socialization:* Behaviours and attitudes of all individuals may be changed (for better or worse) by contact with role models or peers who may be neighbours. When these changes occur they are often referred to as 'contagion effects'. For example, the actions by some to informally police and clean common neighbourhood spaces may encourage all others in the area to do the same.
- *Epidemic/Social Norms:* This is a special subset of socialization effects that are characterized by a minimum threshold being achieved before noticeable consequences ensue. The need for some subset of the neighbourhood population to reach a critical mass before their social norms begin to influence others to conform is a case in point. Another is the influence of local acts of crime and violence: when neighbours finally perceive the neighbourhood as too dangerous they will restrict their activities outside the home.
- *Selective Socialization:* This process is another special type of socialization process wherein neighbours are not all equally affected by others. Employed residents are often viewed as positive role models encouraging (only) their unemployed neighbours to find work, for example. Conversely, secondary school dropouts may discourage only their same-age peers from attending school and have no impact on other residents.
- *Social Networks:* Although it may be said that socialization proceeds through social networks, this is specified as a distinct process involving the communication of information and resources. One set of residents may intensify the density and multi-nodal structure of their social networks (create 'strong ties') by spatial clustering, thereby increasing their sources of assistance in times of need. On the other hand, such situations may lack the 'weak ties' that offer the prospect of bringing new information and resources into the community, thereby increasing social isolation.
- *Competition:* Under the premise that certain local resources are limited and not pure public goods, this theory posits that groups within the neighbourhood will compete for these finite resources amongst themselves. Because the context is a zero-sum game, social conflict will arise as one group more successfully competes. The control of a local public park for one type of specialized group activities provides an example.
- *Relative Deprivation:* This mechanism suggests that residents who have achieved some socio-economic success will be a source of disamenities for their less-well off neighbours. The latter will view the successful with envy or will make them perceive their own relative inferiority as a source of dissatisfaction.

What do these endogenous mechanisms imply about which household mix in neighbourhoods matters? The socialization, epidemic/social norms and selective socialization theories generally imply that neighbourhoods with larger shares of residents who exhibit 'socially undesirable' behaviours will encourage less favourable outcomes and those with larger shares of residents who exhibit 'socially desirable' behaviours will encourage more favourable outcomes for (some or all of) their neighbours. But this tells us little about which characteristics of the populace—demographic, socio-economic, ethnic, housing tenure—serve as the best proxies for these behaviours or what sort of mixing of groups is appropriate. The social networks theory is even more ambiguous in its implications, torn as it is between the potential benefits of strong ties fostered by own-group homogeneity versus those of extra-group weak ties, whose balance varies depending on the circumstance (Granovetter, 2005; Ionnides & Datcher Loury, 2004). The competition and relative deprivation theories are perhaps the most clear, suggesting that to mix socio-economically advantaged and disadvantaged residents in the same neighbourhood will further harm the latter group.

Exogenous Neighbourhood Effects

Exogenous neighbourhood effects occur if the behaviours or attitudes of one neighbour depend on the exogenous (or predetermined, fixed) characteristics of the individual's neighbours, such as ethnicity, religion or race. Here, for example, a recent immigrant may feel a special comfort and security because of proximity to another from the same national background, what is often termed 'ethnic solidarity'. As an illustration, Murie & Musterd (2004) note:

> Social homogeneity of a peripheral estate may offer an (temporary) asset, instead of a burden. Homogeneity may help to stimulate interaction and mutual support, which is especially important for newly arrived immigrants, who still have to learn their way in the place of settlement. (p. 1454)

Or, expressed in a less positive version, a person may have an aversion to proximity to certain prospective neighbours because of racial or religious differences and may therefore behave differently if confronted by them in the neighbourhood context. Yet another version of this mechanism may be termed 'social cohesion': the notion that residential contact among groups that differ in their exogenous characteristics will increase their social interactions and thereby reduce inter-group prejudices and misapprehensions, providing benefits not only to themselves but also to the larger society beyond the neighbourhood.

For analytical purposes here, exogenous neighbourhood effects are similar to the endogenous mechanisms described above, inasmuch as in both cases the characteristics of the households in the neighbourhood affect individual outcomes. Unfortunately, the exogenous theories are equally ambiguous in providing guidance as to what mix matters and in what direction.

Correlated Neighbourhood Effects

Correlated neighbourhood effect mechanisms do not vary by alterations in neighbourhood household composition, but rather are determined by larger structural forces in the metropolitan area, like locations of jobs and geographic disamenities and the structures of local government. These external forces may impinge differentially on different neighbourhoods, but within any given neighbourhood they affect all residents roughly equally, producing thereby correlations in neighbours' outcomes. Several such mechanisms have been forwarded in the literature:

- Spatial mismatch: certain neighbourhoods have little accessibility (in either spatial proximity or as mediated by transportation networks) to job opportunities appropriate to the skills of their residents.
- Local institutional resources: certain neighbourhoods have access to few private, non-profit, or public institutions and organizations.
- Public services: certain neighbourhoods are located within local political jurisdictions that offer inferior services and facilities.
- External stigma: certain neighbourhoods may be stigmatized regardless of their current population because of their history, environmental or topographical disamenities, style, scale and type of dwellings, or condition of their commercial districts and public spaces.

These correlated effect mechanisms may be important,[3] but they will not be the subject of this paper. Rather, the focus is on the issue of neighbourhood population mix, and therefore on the endogenous and exogenous effect mechanisms arising from the household composition of the neighbourhood. It might be hypothesized that neighbourhood effects in a welfare state of the Swedish kind would be less pronounced compared to many other countries. This can be true but there are at least three reasons for the choice of Sweden here. First, the country has a legacy of anti-segregation policy within the framework of a redistributive welfare state. Such institutional arrangements may reduce the correlated effects but are they also effective in relation to endogenous and exogenous effects? Second, the segregation issue is high up the political agenda in Sweden, and the issue of social and ethnic mix is regarded as a crucial vehicle for avoiding the development of divided cities (Andersson, 2006). Finally, Sweden offers unique types of data, i.e. comprehensive longitudinal and geocoded information on all residents.

Previous Research on Neighbourhood Household Composition and Impacts on Individuals

Previous empirical research offers scant bases for answering the question of what mix matters. Although there have been numerous multivariate statistical studies attempting to quantify the relationship between indicators of neighbourhood household composition and a variety of outcomes for children, youth and adults (as reviewed in the articles cited above), relatively few have experimented with alternative measures of neighbourhood household composition in ways that permit meaningful comparisons of magnitudes and statistical significance of observed relationships. The results have been inconsistent, with some contingencies based on gender and race.

Most work has examined educational attainment. Corcoran *et al.* (1987) and Duncan (1994) found that measures of neighbourhood disadvantage (percentages of male unemployment, in poverty or using public assistance) were the strongest neighbourhood predictors, although the measures' strength depended on gender. Haveman & Wolfe (1994) and Ginther *et al.* (2000) found that neighbourhood rates of not completing secondary school were the strongest correlates of an individual not completing secondary school. However, contrary results were produced by Crane (1991), Brooks-Gunn *et al.* (1993) and Ensminger *et al.* (1996), that emphasized the role played by affluent neighbours, at least for many gender-race categories.

Other studies have focused on teen sexual activity as the main outcome, generally finding that neighbourhood affluence was more predictive than neighbourhood disadvantage. Brewster's (1994) study determined that the share of advantaged neighbours was positively related to girls' use of contraception, but not boys'. Crane (1991) and Brooks-Gunn *et al.* (1993) found that a larger share of affluent neighbours reduced the likelihood of female teens' risk of bearing a child, but differed on whether the relationships were stronger for white or black female teens. However, the findings of South & Crowder (1999) were the opposite: the share of disadvantaged neighbours had a stronger relationship with teen childbearing outside marriage, as least for black women.

Finally in the area of labour market outcomes, Weinberg *et al.* (2004) discovered that several alternative measures of neighbours' social status were related to individuals' annual hours of work. In descending order of strength, these measures were rates of: public assistance, male employment, female employment, poverty and dropping out of secondary school. The impacts of neighbours' social status proved stronger for less-educated and Hispanic youth, although not for black (compared to white) youth. Dawkins *et al.* (2005) found that the percentage of poor neighbours was more predictive for individuals' duration of unemployment than either the percentage of secondary school dropouts or percentage of whites, although the coefficient was only statistically significant for blacks, not whites. However, they did not test the impact of affluent neighbours. Hoynes (2000) reported that the percentage of women in the postal code area who have never been married is a stronger predictor of individual women's entrances into and exits from public assistance in California than median household incomes. Van der Klaauw & Van Ours' (2003) study found native Dutch transition rates from welfare into work in Rotterdam were predicted by unemployment rates in the neighbourhood, but not a wide variety of other neighbourhood characteristics.

The extant work thus leaves a circumscribed and cloudy picture. Although most studies conclude that an individual's educational attainments and teenage fertility are best explained by the percentage of the 'advantaged' population in the neighbourhood (alternatively measured by professional-managerial occupations or high income), several find that characteristics of the 'disadvantaged' population (those on public assistance or not completing high school) are more important. However, labour market outcomes (annual hours of work, duration of unemployment), seem better explained by measures of 'disadvantaged' neighbours. Most studies stress the contingency of impacts based on race and gender. Moreover, to the authors' knowledge a comparison of alternative neighbourhood indicators has not been carried out in the realm of labour market earnings. Finally, the evidence thus far has been almost exclusively American. The study reported here hopes to contribute to filling this large gap in the literature by examining the statistical relationship between a large variety of neighbourhood characteristics and the subsequent earnings of Swedish men and women in both metropolitan and non-metropolitan settings, controlling for personal attributes and labour market characteristics.

Empirical Approach

Data Sources

Most of the variables employed were constructed from data contained in the Statistics Sweden *Louise* files, which are produced annually. These files contain a large amount of information on all individuals age 15 and above and represent compilations of data assembled from a range of statistical registers (income, education, labour market and population). The current study merged selected information about individuals from annual *Louise* files to create a longitudinal database 1991–99 for all individuals present in Sweden in 1991. The other sources of information used were the Statistics Sweden real estate and property registers, from which the study obtained data on housing type and tenure that were used to construct certain neighbourhood characteristic variables.

It must be emphasized that the dataset includes observations of virtually the *entire population* within the desired adult age range, not a sample. Thus, the *t*-statistics presented below should not be interpreted as guides for prospective errors involving inferences from a sample to the larger population.

Model for Conducting Empirical Tests

The outcome of interest here is the average annual income from work (during 1996–99) for working-age individuals (ages 20–60 in 1996) who were residents of Sweden in 1991 and present each year 1995–99.[4] Since this indicator encapsulates educational credentials, labour force participation, employment regularity and hourly compensation, it is thought to be the most comprehensive single measure of an individual's economic worth. Descriptive statistics for this outcome variable are presented for males in Table 1 and for females in Table 2, both stratified by metropolitan/non-metropolitan place of residence in 1995.

The study models income as a gender- and place-specific, log-linear function of personal characteristics, characteristics of the neighbourhood in which they reside at the beginning of the period, municipality of residence at the beginning of the period, and local labour market conditions at the end of the period in question.[5] Symbolically:

$$\ln(I_{96-99ij}) = \alpha + \beta[P_{96-99ij}] + \gamma[P_{95ij}] + \theta N_{95ij} + \mu[M_{95ij}] + \phi[L_{95-99ij}] + \epsilon \quad (1)$$

where:

- I_{96-99} = cumulative income from work (annualized) observed for individual during period 1996–99.[6]
- $[P_{96-99}]$ = observed personal characteristics that can vary over time (e.g. marital or fertility status, educational attainment).
- $[P_{95}]$ = observed personal characteristics that do not vary after 1995 (e.g. year and country of birth, experiences prior to 1995).
- N_{95} = observed characteristics of neighbourhood where individual resides in 1995 (a variety of characteristics will be modelled).
- $[M_{95}]$ = municipality of residence in 1995.
- $[L_{95-99}]$ = observed characteristics of local labour market(s) in which individual resides at 1995 and 1999 (e.g. mean earnings).
- ϵ = a random error term with the usual assumed statistical properties
- i = gender
- j = metropolitan or non-metropolitan place

Table 1. Descriptive statistics for outcome and control variables[a]: males

	Metro residence		Non-Metro residence	
	Mean	Std. dev.	Mean	Std. dev.
Outcome Variable				
Annual mean labour income, 1996–99 (SEK100)	2175.54	1839.08	1893.63	1222.39
Control Variables				
No. children under age 7, 1995	0.31	0.66	0.32	0.68
Some sick leave during 1995 (1 = yes)	0.13	0.34	0.15	0.35
Pre-retired during 1995 (1 = yes)	0.05	0.22	0.06	0.23
Parental leave during 1995 (1 = yes)	0.17	0.38	0.19	0.39
Studying during 1995 (1 = yes)	0.05	0.22	0.03	0.17
No. years with pre-retirement, 1996–99 (1 = yes)	0.27	0.96	0.29	1.01
No. child-years under 7, 1996–99	1.12	2.28	1.09	2.27
No. years studying, 1996–99	0.16	0.62	0.12	0.55
No. years with parental leave, 1996–99	0.63	1.23	0.64	1.24
No. years with sick leave, 1996–99	0.44	0.95	0.53	1.04
Immigrants w/ < 5 years in Sweden (1 = yes)	0.008	0.089	0.004	0.061
Western country of birth (1 = yes)	0.07	0.25	0.04	0.21
Eastern European country of birth (1 = yes)	0.03	0.16	0.01	0.11
Non-Western country of birth (1 = yes)	0.06	0.24	0.02	0.14
No formal education (1 = yes)	0.01	0.11	0.01	0.07
< 10 years education (1 = yes)	0.09	0.29	0.16	0.36
10 years education (1 = yes)	0.13	0.34	0.14	0.34
13 years, some post-secondary (1 = yes)	0.10	0.30	0.07	0.25
14+ years, but no PhD (1 = yes)	0.20	0.40	0.13	0.34
PhD attained (1 = yes)	0.017	0.130	0.004	0.066
Education rose LT 11–12 to 11–12+ (1 = yes)	0.005	0.071	0.003	0.054
Education rose 11–12 to higher (1 = yes)	0.01	0.10	0.01	0.10
Age in years	40.96	10.28	41.64	10.33
Age more than 50 years (1 = yes)	0.22	0.42	0.24	0.43
Single 1995 but couple 1999 (1 = yes)	0.08	0.27	0.06	0.24
Couple 1995 but single 1999 (1 = yes)	0.06	0.24	0.06	0.24
Single 1991 but couple 1995 (1 = yes)	0.09	0.29	0.08	0.27
Couple 1991 but single 1995 (1 = yes)	0.09	0.28	0.08	0.27
Mean income in local labour market, 1999	1769.72	144.21	1550.79	90.16
N	847162		1236095	

Note: [a] The listed variables were used in the model runs. Omitted variables, e.g. 11–12 years of education, are reference categories. For Metro males, 45 per cent belong to the educational reference category. For Non-Metro males the corresponding value is 49 per cent.

All Greek letters represent parameters to be estimated through OLS multiple regression techniques, with each regression stratified for a particular gender/place stratum.

The study will compare the magnitudes of the (standardized) coefficients θ and their statistical significance across various specifications of N within each of four strata as the empirical test. All other control variables in (1) shall remain the same in these trials.

Table 2. Descriptive statistics for outcome and control variables[a]: females

	Metro residence		Non-Metro residence	
	Mean	Std. dev.	Mean	Std. dev.
Outcome Variable				
Annual mean labour income, 1996–99 (SEK100)	1520.57	1024.81	1293.88	819.39
Control Variables				
No. children under age 7, 1995	0.35	0.69	0.37	0.70
Some sick leave during 1995 (1 = yes)	0.19	0.39	0.20	0.40
Pre-retired during 1995 (1 = yes)	0.07	0.25	0.09	0.28
Parental leave during 1995 (1 = yes)	0.28	0.45	0.29	0.45
Studying during 1995 (1 = yes)	0.07	0.26	0.05	0.22
No. years with pre-retirement, 1996–99 (1 = yes)	0.35	1.09	0.43	1.20
No. child-years under 7, 1996–99	1.23	2.36	1.18	2.34
No. years studying, 1996–99	0.28	0.79	0.27	0.78
No. years with parental leave, 1996–99	0.98	1.52	0.96	1.51
No. years with sick leave, 1996–99	0.66	1.07	0.75	1.14
Immigrants w/ < 5 years in Sweden (1 = yes)	0.008	0.086	0.004	0.061
Western country of birth (1 = yes)	0.08	0.27	0.05	0.22
Eastern European country of birth (1 = yes)	0.03	0.18	0.01	0.12
Non-Western country of birth (1 = yes)	0.05	0.21	0.02	0.13
No formal education (1 = yes)	0.007	0.086	0.003	0.058
< 10 years education (1 = yes)	0.08	0.27	0.12	0.33
10 years education (1 = yes)	0.12	0.32	0.12	0.33
13 years, some post-secondary (1 = yes)	0.06	0.24	0.03	0.17
14+ years, but no PhD (1 = yes)	0.28	0.45	0.21	0.41
PhD attained (1 = yes)	0.005	0.074	0.001	0.034
Education rose LT 11–12 to 11–12 + (1 = yes)	0.004	0.065	0.003	0.057
Education rose 11–12 to higher (1 = yes)	0.02	0.13	0.02	0.13
Age in years	41.01	10.33	41.95	10.32
Age more than 50 years (1 = yes)	0.22	0.42	0.25	0.43
Single 1995 but couple 1999 (1 = yes)	0.07	0.25	0.05	0.22
Couple 1995 but single 1999 (1 = yes)	0.06	0.24	0.06	0.24
Single 1991 but couple 1995 (1 = yes)	0.08	0.28	0.08	0.26
Couple 1991 but single 1995 (1 = yes)	0.08	0.27	0.07	0.25
Mean income in local labour market, 1999	1770.51	144.18	1550.22	87.74
N	842542		1181080	

Note: [a] The listed variables were used in the model runs. Omitted variables, e.g. 11–12 years of education, are reference categories. For Metro females, 45 per cent belong to the educational reference category. For Non-Metro females the corresponding value is 52 per cent.

Variables

Measures of neighbourhood composition. In this study 'neighbourhood' is operationalized as the area delineated by a SAMS defined by Statistics Sweden. The SAMS classification scheme is designed to identify relatively homogeneous areas by taking into account housing type, tenure and construction period. There are approximately 9000 SAMS in Sweden, each with an average population of approximately 1000 inhabitants; SAMS in metropolitan areas are considerably smaller geographically than those in non-metropolitan areas, prompting the study to stratify the analyses by place so that geographic scale of neighbourhood can be made more comparable across individuals being analyzed.[7]

It is important to test for three aspects of neighbourhood composition: (1) 'absolute' share of a 'particular' group, (2) 'relative' shares of two 'particular' groups; and (3) 'overall' diversity among 'all' groups. The study measures the: (1) absolute share as percentages of the 'advantaged' and 'disadvantaged' categories; (2) the relative share as the ratio of the percentages of these two categories; and (3) overall diversity as an entropy index based on all categories of data available. The entropy index measures the extent to which a population is *evenly* distributed among the specified categories (Theil, 1972) and is calculated as:

$$E = \sum_{m=1}^{M} \pi_m \ln\left(\frac{1}{\pi_m}\right),$$

where π_m denotes the proportion of individuals in category m in the neighbourhood. The entropy index ranges between 0 and $\ln M$: 0 when all individuals are members of a single category; $\ln M$ when individuals are evenly distributed among the M categories. E is divided by its maximum value $\ln M$ to set the upper bound to 1. The theoretical and empirical superiority of this measure of inequality has been demonstrated by Reardon & Firebaugh (2002).

These three versions of composition measures are computed in four domains for each SAMS in Sweden in 1995:

- *Education:* (1) percentage aged 20 years and older with 'low' (less than 12 years of schooling) or 'high' (14 or more years) educational attainment; (2) the ratio of these; (3) entropy based on seven educational attainment groups (see Appendix Table 1A).
- *Ethnicity:* (1) percentage of foreign-born and percentage native-born Swedes; (2) the ratio of these; (3) entropy based on four regional places of birth: Swedes, Western, East European, other/non-Western.
- *Income:* (1) percentage lowest income males (0–29th percentiles), percentage high-income males (70th percentile or higher); (2) ratio of these; (3) entropy based on all male income deciles.
- *Housing tenure:* (1) percentage households living in public rental housing,[8] percentage in owner-occupied units; (2) the ratio of these; (3) entropy based on four housing type categories: those above, plus cooperatives and private rental.

Sweden has pursued a social mix neighbourhood policy since the mid-1970s. Its efficiency may be questioned (Musterd & Andersson, 2005) and its rather vague goal formulation but there is no doubt that the primary instrument has been tenure mix and that the idea has been to avoid segregation by getting a mix in terms of households' social class positions and (later) also ethnic origin (Bergsten & Holmqvist, 2007). Hence, the choice here of the four dimensions is of policy relevance but it is also relevant from the perspective of existing theory concerning endogenous and exogenous neighbourhood effects.

In computing neighbourhood population characteristics, all 1995 residents of the SAMS age 20–65 years are used; in computing housing characteristics, all housing units in the SAMS in 1995 are used.

Control variables. The personal characteristics of individuals [$P_{96-99ij}$] and [P_{95ij}] are operationalized with a set of variables describing their demographic and household characteristics, educational attainments, nativity and immigrant status and features of their employment during the period that will affect their income, but are probably not related to neighbourhood context (such as parental leave or pre-retirement status). [M_{95ij}] is operationalized with a set of dummy variables representing each municipality of residence in 1995 and [L_{99ij}] with the mean earnings for the local labour market area in which the individual resided in 1999. Descriptive statistics for these control variables are presented for males in Table 1 and for females in Table 2, both stratified by metropolitan/non-metropolitan place of residence in 1995.

Results

Relationships among Neighbourhood Mix Measures

Although the aforementioned variables for neighbourhood household mix are distinct conceptually, they may prove not to be in practice. If it proved the case that all measures were highly correlated the question of what mix matters would be rendered moot. This clearly is not the case here, as shown by the bivariate correlation coefficients in Table 3. As expected, some are of course highly correlated, in particular those related to the ethnic composition; high proportions of natives means of course low presence of immigrants, and vice versa. However, in general correlations are low or modest.

Patterns of Neighbourhood Mix in Sweden

Neighbourhood characteristics are displayed for all groups separately in Table 4 (metropolitan) and Table 5 (non-metropolitan). The metropolitan subset contains all neighbourhoods in the Stockholm, Gothenburg and Malmö labour market regions, comprising 35 per cent of the SAMS areas and about 41 per cent of the population in the selected age groups (aged 20–64 in 1995). Hence, Table 5 shows the neighbourhood characteristics for the rest of Sweden. Values for the mean, standard deviation, 1st percentile, and 99th percentile are presented for the four subsets.

Entropy values for incomes and education are very compressed (mean approximately 0.9), indicating highly diverse neighbourhoods in the country in terms of class compositions (Musterd & Andersson, 2005). This is to be expected, given the long-standing Swedish policy of building developments with a mix of housing types and providing social housing benefits to a large share of the households. Also as expected, values for ethnic and housing tenure entropies show wider ranges (means 0.25–0.40 and around 0.51 respectively), with lower means for the ethnic entropies in non-metropolitan areas.

The range of values is much greater for other measures. Immigrants are more often found in metropolitan regions, resulting both in higher averages and higher values for the 99th percentile in metropolitan regions. Also as expected, the top values for percentage high-income males and percentage highly educated are found in metropolitan regions. Homeownership is more common in non-metropolitan areas (60/40), but entropy measures as well as percentage values for tenure forms show substantial variation across neighbourhoods in both types of regional settings.

Table 3. Correlations between the neighbourhood characteristics: Swedish males

		1	2	3	4	5	6	7	8	9	10	11	12	13	14	15	16
1	Ethnic entropy		0.76	−0.95	0.67	−0.25	0.49	−0.21	0.11	0.02	0.23	−0.11	0.17	0.31	0.53	−0.58	0.33
2	% non-Western 1995	0.79		−0.79	0.95	−0.25	0.57	−0.29	0.18	0.02	0.13	−0.01	0.09	0.24	0.53	−0.56	0.43
3	% Swedes 1995	−0.92	−0.93		−0.76	0.30	−0.55	0.25	−0.15	0.03	−0.25	0.13	−0.20	−0.24	−0.50	0.53	−0.35
4	Ratio % non-Western / % Swedes	0.53	0.86	−0.78		−0.29	0.53	−0.28	0.18	−0.02	0.17	−0.05	0.14	0.15	0.44	−0.45	0.36
5	Income entropy	−0.03	−0.17	0.18	−0.30		0.03	−0.43	−0.22	0.10	0.12	−0.26	0.02	0.22	−0.09	−0.07	−0.17
6	% in lowest 3 male income deciles	0.67	0.72	−0.75	0.59	−0.02		−0.69	0.36	−0.21	0.21	−0.14	0.23	0.28	0.44	−0.55	0.39
7	% in highest 3 male income deciles	−0.55	−0.54	0.58	−0.41	−0.44	−0.81		−0.23	0.28	−0.52	0.52	−0.46	−0.26	−0.28	0.36	−0.24
8	Ratio % lowest 3 / % highest 3 income deciles	0.34	0.46	−0.50	0.61	−0.33	0.56	−0.40		−0.21	0.03	0.05	0.07	0.04	0.17	−0.14	0.17
9	Educational entropy	0.10	0.05	−0.04	0.00	0.32	−0.14	−0.07	−0.10		−0.24	0.40	−0.59	0.01	−0.08	0.02	−0.08
10	% low educated	0.46	0.52	−0.54	0.47	0.17	0.41	−0.64	0.31	0.28		−0.85	0.85	−0.09	0.08	0.11	0.04
11	% high educated	−0.28	−0.26	0.29	−0.22	−0.31	−0.11	0.47	−0.12	−0.43	−0.88		−0.77	0.07	−0.02	−0.12	0.03
12	Ratio % low education / % high education	0.41	0.46	−0.49	0.43	0.07	0.40	−0.57	0.31	−0.05	0.90	−0.76		−0.07	0.08	0.07	0.05
13	House type entropy	0.13	0.04	−0.06	−0.01	0.34	0.16	−0.22	0.02	0.04	−0.10	0.13	−0.11		0.26	−0.69	0.05
14	% public rental	0.60	0.58	−0.57	0.39	0.10	0.53	−0.52	0.23	0.09	0.38	−0.23	0.32	0.04		−0.56	0.56
15	% owner occupied	−0.61	−0.44	0.52	−0.26	−0.34	−0.62	0.63	−0.22	0.02	−0.12	0.00	−0.13	−0.52	−0.51		−0.34
16	Ratio % public rental / % owner occupied	0.35	0.47	−0.42	0.44	0.02	0.35	−0.28	0.16	0.03	0.18	−0.04	0.15	0.12	0.47	−0.35	

Note: The coefficients below the diagonal are for metropolitan males and the coefficients above the diagonal are for non-metropolitan males.

Table 4. Descriptive statistics for neighbourhood variables in metropolitan areas

	Mean	Std. dev.	Percentiles 1	Percentiles 99
Males				
Ethnic entropy	0.405	0.186	0.110	0.885
% non-Western 1995	0.062	0.095	0.000	0.525
% Swedes 1995	0.859	0.110	0.415	0.974
Ratio % non-Western / % Swedes	0.127	0.388	0.000	1.981
Income entropy	0.900	0.068	0.669	0.975
% in lowest 3 male income deciles	0.307	0.129	0.140	0.762
% in highest 3 male income deciles	0.345	0.141	0.050	0.636
Ratio % lowest 3 / % highest 3	1.574	4.314	0.242	13.519
Educational entropy	0.910	0.053	0.692	0.979
% low educated	0.231	0.096	0.062	0.503
% high educated	0.312	0.145	0.093	0.697
Ratio % low / % high	1.107	1.048	0.087	4.953
House type entropy	0.518	0.291	0.000	0.986
% public rental	0.187	0.279	0.000	1.000
% owner occupied	0.398	0.392	0.000	1.000
Ratio % public rental / % owner occupied	213.6	613.7	0.0003	3465.0
Females				
Ethnic entropy	0.403	0.183	0.114	0.879
% non-Western 1995	0.061	0.091	0.000	0.525
% Swedes 1995	0.861	0.105	0.432	0.973
Ratio % non-Western / % Swedes	0.119	0.360	0.000	1.981
Income entropy	0.900	0.067	0.684	0.975
% in lowest 3 male income deciles	0.300	0.120	0.138	0.710
% in highest 3 male income deciles	0.352	0.139	0.055	0.638
Ratio % lowest 3 / % highest 3	1.452	3.839	0.242	12.337
Educational entropy	0.911	0.052	0.704	0.978
% low educated	0.228	0.094	0.062	0.503
% high educated	0.315	0.144	0.094	0.692
Ratio % low / % high	1.076	1.018	0.088	4.799
House type entropy	0.520	0.292	0.000	0.986
% public rental	0.186	0.278	0.000	1.000
% owner occupied	0.400	0.391	0.000	0.978
Ratio % public rental / % owner occupied	211.0	601.1	0.0003	2572.5

Multivariate Regression Results

Table 6 shows the results of the regression analyses for the neighbourhood variables in metropolitan areas and Table 7 shows the results in non-metropolitan areas. The conclusions to be made here are based mainly on the standardized regression coefficients (Std. Beta) that show how many standard deviations (along the natural log scale) the dependent variable changes when the neighbourhood variable increases by one standard deviation. Statistical significance of the effects is not shown, because given the size of the dataset, the p value for all effects is below 0.001, except for educational entropy

Table 5. Descriptive statistics for neighbourhood variables in non-metropolitan areas

	Mean	Std. dev.	Percentiles 1	Percentiles 99
Males				
Ethnic entropy	0.257	0.150	0.051	0.746
% non-Western 1995	0.022	0.038	0.000	0.209
% Swedes 1995	0.923	0.066	0.646	0.987
Ratio % non-Western / % Swedes	0.029	0.069	0.000	0.330
Income entropy	0.933	0.042	0.782	0.982
% in lowest 3 male income deciles	0.284	0.099	0.122	0.621
% in highest 3 male income deciles	0.277	0.107	0.061	0.558
Ratio % lowest 3 / % highest 3	1.500	5.391	0.261	8.691
Educational entropy	0.905	0.038	0.799	0.971
% low educated	0.285	0.084	0.108	0.475
% high educated	0.207	0.093	0.072	0.501
Ratio % low / % high	1.819	1.299	0.220	5.867
House type entropy	0.511	0.224	0.000	0.961
% public rental	0.107	0.181	0.000	0.886
% owner occupied	0.593	0.311	0.000	0.998
Ratio % public rental / % owner occupied	21.4	121.4	0.0004	702.0
Females				
Ethnic entropy	0.258	0.149	0.052	0.746
% non-Western 1995	0.023	0.037	0.000	0.199
% Swedes 1995	0.923	0.065	0.653	0.987
Ratio % non-Western / % Swedes	0.029	0.067	0.000	0.328
Income entropy	0.933	0.041	0.783	0.982
% in lowest 3 male income deciles	0.281	0.094	0.122	0.594
% in highest 3 male income deciles	0.281	0.107	0.068	0.564
Ratio % lowest 3 / % highest 3	1.390	3.314	0.251	7.395
Educational entropy	0.906	0.037	0.802	0.972
% low educated	0.283	0.084	0.109	0.471
% high educated	0.210	0.094	0.074	0.500
Ratio % low / % high	1.777	1.268	0.225	5.722
House type entropy	0.512	0.225	0.000	0.961
% public rental	0.108	0.181	0.000	0.886
% owner occupied	0.594	0.309	0.000	0.999
Ratio % public rental / % owner occupied	21.0	119.6	0.0004	702.0

for metropolitan males ($p = 0.579$). The common list of control variables used in all models can be seen in Appendix Table 1A, which also shows the coefficients for these variables in one representative model (effect of the proportion in lowest three male income deciles for females in non-metropolitan areas).[9]

If the strength of neighbourhood effects is compared across the four strata, it can be seen that the effects are generally stronger in metropolitan than in non-metropolitan areas and stronger for males than for females, regardless of indicator. However, it is specifically the extremes of the income distribution in the neighbourhood that matter most, while the mix

Table 6. Effects of neighbourhood characteristics[a] in metropolitan areas when added to a model controlling for individual, municipality and labour market characteristics

	B	Std. Beta	Exp(B)	R squared
Males				
Ethnic entropy	−0.8062	−0.067	0.45	0.456
% non-Western 1995	−1.5451	−0.065	0.21	0.456
% Swedes 1995	1.5548	0.076	4.73	0.457
Ratio % non-Western / % Swedes	−0.3044	−0.053	0.74	0.455
Income entropy	−0.1557	−0.005	0.86	0.453
% in lowest 3 male income deciles	−2.1475	−0.124	0.12	0.466
% in highest 3 male income deciles	1.6957	0.107	5.45	0.463
Ratio % lowest 3 / % highest 3	−0.0305	−0.059	0.97	0.456
Educational entropy	−0.0206	0.000	0.98	0.453
% low educated	−1.4476	−0.062	0.24	0.456
% high educated	0.6047	0.039	1.83	0.454
Ratio % low / % high	−0.1159	−0.054	0.89	0.455
House type entropy	−0.1254	−0.016	0.88	0.455
% public rental	−0.3818	−0.048	0.68	0.457
% owner occupied	0.4144	0.073	1.51	0.459
Ratio % public rental / % owner occupied	−0.0001	−0.032	1.00	0.454
Females				
Ethnic entropy	−0.5572	−0.048	0.57	0.452
% non-Western 1995	−1.3602	−0.057	0.26	0.453
% Swedes 1995	1.2787	0.063	3.59	0.454
Ratio % non-Western / % Swedes	−0.3175	−0.053	0.73	0.453
Income entropy	0.4758	0.015	1.61	0.451
% in lowest 3 male income deciles	−1.4066	−0.078	0.24	0.456
% in highest 3 male income deciles	0.8997	0.058	2.46	0.454
Ratio % lowest 3 / % highest 3	−0.0273	−0.049	0.97	0.453
Educational entropy	0.2456	0.006	1.28	0.451
% low educated	−1.1583	−0.051	0.31	0.453
% high educated	0.3642	0.025	1.44	0.451
Ratio % low / % high	−0.1020	−0.048	0.90	0.452
House type entropy	−0.0264	−0.004	0.97	0.452
% public rental	−0.2774	−0.036	0.76	0.453
% owner occupied	0.1773	0.032	1.19	0.452
Ratio % public rental / % owner occupied	−0.0001	−0.029	1.00	0.452

Note: [a]The 16 neighbourhood variables are in the model with the control variables one at a time. This Table is thus the result of 32 runs where only the neighbourhood variable is exchanged.

in the domains of housing tenure, ethnicity and education have progressively weaker effects. Indeed, variables measuring the share of both low-income and high-income males in the neighbourhood have the strongest effects in both metropolitan and non-metropolitan areas and for both sexes. The standardized beta coefficients for percentage low-income range from −0.124 for metropolitan males to −0.054 for non-metropolitan females; the comparable figures for percentage high-income are 0.107 and 0.053.

When the effects of different mix measures of each domain are compared, it can be seen that the proportions of specific groups have stronger effects than either general diversity

Table 7. Effects of neighbourhood characteristics[a] in non-metropolitan areas when added to a model controlling for individual, municipality and labour market characteristics

	B	Std. Beta	Exp(B)	R squared
Males				
Ethnic entropy	−0.6102	−0.044	0.54	0.460
% non-Western 1995	−2.5430	−0.046	0.08	0.460
% Swedes 1995	1.5245	0.048	4.59	0.460
Ratio % non-Western / % Swedes	−1.2747	−0.042	0.28	0.460
Income entropy	−0.6216	−0.013	0.54	0.459
% in lowest 3 male income deciles	−1.9630	−0.093	0.14	0.466
% in highest 3 male income deciles	1.7606	0.090	5.82	0.465
Ratio % lowest 3 / % highest 3	−0.0051	−0.013	0.99	0.459
Educational entropy	1.0698	0.019	2.91	0.459
% low educated	−1.4961	−0.060	0.22	0.460
% high educated	1.0794	0.048	2.94	0.460
Ratio % low / % high	−0.0717	−0.045	0.93	0.460
House type entropy	−0.1713	−0.018	0.84	0.459
% public rental	−0.3381	−0.029	0.71	0.460
% owner occupied	0.3019	0.045	1.35	0.460
Ratio % public rental / % owner occupied	−0.0004	−0.026	1.00	0.459
Females				
Ethnic entropy	−0.4229	−0.029	0.66	0.458
% non-Western 1995	−1.9960	−0.034	0.14	0.458
% Swedes 1995	1.1756	0.035	3.24	0.458
Ratio % non-Western / % Swedes		−0.034	0.34	0.459
Income entropy	−0.1590	−0.003	0.85	0.458
% in lowest 3 male income deciles	−1.2448	−0.054	0.29	0.460
% in highest 3 male income deciles	1.0663	0.053	2.90	0.460
Ratio % lowest 3 / % highest 3	−0.0111	−0.017	0.99	0.458
Educational entropy	1.0198	0.018	2.77	0.458
% low educated	−1.3660	−0.053	0.26	0.459
% high educated	0.8872	0.038	2.43	0.458
Ratio % low / % high	−0.0704	−0.041	0.93	0.459
House type entropy	−0.0684	−0.007	0.93	0.458
% public rental	−0.2293	−0.019	0.80	0.458
% owner occupied	0.1319	0.019	1.14	0.458
Ratio % public rental / % owner occupied	−0.0004	−0.020	1.00	0.458

Note: [a] The 16 neighbourhood variables are in the model with the control variables one at a time. This Table is thus the result of 32 runs where only the neighbourhood variable is exchanged.

as measured by the entropy indices, or ratio of disadvantaged and advantaged groups (although this is less clear for education). Of the entropy measures, only ethnic entropy has an effect comparable to the effect of the proportion variable. However, in the Swedish context, high ethnic entropy actually means high proportion of immigrants, while low ethnic entropy can be observed mainly in neighbourhoods with mostly Swedish population. This means that the entropy measure may actually capture the effect of the proportion of immigrants in the neighbourhood. This may also explain why ethnic entropy has the strongest effect of the entropy measures.

Table 8. Predicted incomes in different neighbourhood conditions

Cut-point of the neighbourhood variable	% lowest 3 male income deciles at the cut-point	Predicted average labour income 1996–99 (SEK100)	% non-Western 1995 at the cut-point	Predicted average labour income 1996–99 (SEK100)
Males, metropolitan				
5th percentile	16.7	2855	0.3	2318
Mean − std. dev.	17.8	2788	<0	–
Mean	30.7	2114	6.2	2114
Mean + std. dev.	43.5	1603	15.7	1827
95th percentile	58.9	1152	23.7	1614
Females, metropolitan				
5th percentile	16.5	1902	0.3	1701
Mean − std. dev.	18.0	1862	<0	–
Mean	30.0	1573	6.1	1573
Mean + std. dev.	42.0	1329	15.1	1390
95th percentile	54.1	1120	22.9	1250
Males, non-metropolitan				
5th percentile	15.9	2562	0.0	2121
Mean − std. dev.	18.5	2433	<0	–
Mean	28.4	2004	2.2	2004
Mean + std. dev.	38.3	1650	6.0	1820
95th percentile	46.8	1396	8.1	1725
Females, non-metropolitan				
5th percentile	15.8	1605	0.0	1441
Mean − std. dev.	18.6	1550	<0	–
Mean	28.1	1378	2.3	1378
Mean + std. dev.	37.5	1225	5.9	1280
95th percentile	45.7	1106	8.1	1227

A further inspection of the effects of the proportions of specific groups reveals that it is mostly the proportion of the disadvantaged group rather than the proportion of the advantaged group that has the stronger effect, although the differences are not large. For the income and education variables the proportion of the disadvantaged group has the stronger effect in all strata. However, for the housing tenure and ethnic variables there is no clear pattern.

The magnitudes of estimated relationships between selected neighbourhood variables and individuals' subsequent labour earnings can be seen in more concrete terms in Table 8, which is based on the multivariate analyses. It shows the predicted labour income for an average individual when the proportion in three lowest male income deciles and the proportion of foreign born vary between their extremes. These predicted incomes are calculated for a hypothetical individual with mean characteristics, whose average yearly labour income in 1996–99 would be the median income in his/her stratum when living in an average neighbourhood in terms of proportion of low-income or non-Western neighbours. The ratios of predicted incomes between different neighbourhood conditions would be the same as in Table 8 for other types of individuals, too.

The main observation from Table 8 is that the differences in the predicted labour income between the extreme neighbourhood conditions (represented by the 5th and 95th percentiles of the variables) are huge, especially in metropolitan areas. Because using these extremes might overemphasize the strength of the effects, the effects of one-standard-deviation deviations from the average values are also shown. The differences in the predicted labour incomes are large nevertheless, even when these cut-points are used. As an illustration, for the largest apparent effect of percentage of low-income in a neighbourhood (males in metropolitan areas), a difference is seen in the 1996–99 average labour income of SEK118 000 (56 per cent of the median) associated with 1995 residence in neighbourhoods that are one standard deviation above and below the mean, respectively. For the smallest apparent effect of percentage of low-income in a neighbourhood (females in non-metropolitan areas) the comparable figures are SEK32 000 (24 per cent of the median).

A final comment is offered to provide the context in interpreting these perhaps unexpectedly large differences in predicted incomes. It should be noted that, although large in magnitude, the neighbourhood variables do not add much to the proportion of explained variance in the models.[10] This means that although there are large differences between predicted incomes associated with neighbourhood income variations, this effect is far from deterministic. There is much variation around the predicted values depending on individual characteristics and other contextual factors (many of which are unmeasured), such as family background. This issue of omitted variables is returned to below.

Extensions of the Analysis

To further probe the issue of what mix matters, the basic model was extended to examine how two measures of neighbourhood composition would perform in the *same* regression. There was particular interest in exploring whether the similarity in coefficients for the percentage of low-income and percentage of high-income males in the neighbourhood would persist when they were both entered into the regression. It was found that they diverged substantially in importance for all subsets (Table 9). For all four strata, the effect of low-income residents proved to be larger than the effect of high-income residents in the neighbourhood. For metropolitan females, the effect of high-income males was slightly

Table 9. Effects of the proportions of low- and high-income residents when simultaneously in the model

	B	Std. Beta	Exp(B)	R squared
Males, metropolitan				
% in lowest 3 male income deciles	−1.8437	−0.106	0.16	0.466
% in highest 3 male income deciles	0.3428	0.022	1.41	
Females, metropolitan				
% in lowest 3 male income deciles	−1.6157	−0.090	0.20	0.456
% in highest 3 male income deciles	−0.2213	−0.014	0.80	
Males, non-metropolitan				
% in lowest 3 male income deciles	−1.3926	−0.066	0.25	0.466
% in highest 3 male income deciles	0.7167	0.037	2.05	
Females, non-metropolitan				
% in lowest 3 male income deciles	−0.8874	−0.039	0.41	0.460
% in highest 3 male income deciles	0.4263	0.021	1.53	

negative in this model, but for the other strata the effect of high-income males stayed positive and the effect of low-income males negative.

Econometric Issues

The data are organized across multiple spatial levels: the individual, the SAMS, the municipality and the local labour market. It is recognized that the use of OLS under such circumstances is inefficient and produces standard errors that are biased downward. Nevertheless, the *t*-statistics are incredibly robust and therefore the authors are confident that they are not drawing improper inferences by using them.

All models were also checked for multicollinearity, and it was found that none used standard benchmarks for tolerance and variance inflation factors (Belsey *et al.*, 1980).

Finally, the issue of potential selection bias is addressed. The coefficients of neighbourhood characteristics may not be fully appropriate estimates of causal effects insofar as unobserved individual characteristics that affect labour income may also affect their choice of neighbourhood (Galster, 2003). Although the direction of this potential bias cannot be ascertained with certainty, it is acknowledged that the point estimates cannot be interpreted as indicative of purely causal influences emanating from the neighbourhood environment. Nevertheless, it can be argued that this should not detract from the tests being performed in this paper. Whatever the unobserved selection bias, it should affect equally the coefficients of all the estimated neighbourhood mix variables. Therefore, conclusions regarding the rank ordering of which measure provides the greatest explanatory power should be unaffected by selection bias.

Conclusions and Caveats

It is recognized that neighbourhood household mix itself typically is not the desired end by policy makers, and that indicators of mix may be poor proxies for the neighbourhood social processes that we probably do care about (such as collective efficacy, bridging social capital networks, community cohesion, etc.). Although there are correlations between neighbourhood population mix and some underlying processes (Cook *et al.*, 1997; Sampson, 1997; Sampson *et al.*, 1999), this is not the point here. Rather, it is that policy makers (especially in countries like Sweden, Denmark and the Netherlands) are taken at their word—that they are aiming for mix as a proximal outcome. In this context it is perfectly appropriate to test the extent to which such proximal mix indicators in fact correlate with a widely accepted measure of economic success: labour income.

The study found that how household mix is operationalized does indeed matter. The extremes of the neighbourhood income distribution in 1995, operationalized by the percentages of adult males with earnings in the lowest 30th and the highest 30th percentiles, hold greater explanatory power for average labour income in 1996–99 than domains of household mix related to education, ethnicity or housing tenure. This holds for both genders residing in either metropolitan or non-metropolitan areas of Sweden. By contrast, diversity per se (as measured by entropy) has a much weaker relationship with economic outcomes.

Without doubt and in principle, the findings here support two types of policy interventions already on the agenda in some Western European countries. In Sweden and the Netherlands, for example, the presumed existence of neighbourhood effects at least implicitly underpins urban area-based programmes launched to support residents in deprived neighbourhoods (Andersson & Musterd, 2005). Such programmes do have different points of departures and rationales but if it is proved that people residing in neighbourhoods having a high concentration of low-income people are indeed negatively affected by their residency as such, politicians can argue that extra resources have to be added in order to compensate for the negative effects. Furthermore, these two countries, but also the UK, Finland and others, have active housing and social mix programmes as an important part of their current housing policies. However, such programmes seldom make clear what mix is desirable and appropriate, only that mix is good. Therefore, clarifying what mix matters is seen here as an important task for social science research. According to research findings in a recently finished EU-funded project, Urban Governance, Inclusion and Sustainability (UGIS), both area-based policies and most mix policies are now partly driven by the fear of ethnic clustering (Andersson, 2003; Beaumont et al., 2003). The findings of the current study do not support the hypothesis that the ethnic dimension is the most crucial one. On the contrary, the study finds that the socio-economic composition of neighbourhoods is the most important dimension, at least in terms of individuals' incomes.

It must be emphasized that the findings should not be misinterpreted as advocating for a particular sort of neighbourhood intervention strategy or what socio-economic mix of neighbourhoods is optimal. Such an analysis requires a much deeper consideration of the social equity and efficiency bases of the mixing policy (Galster, 2005, 2007a, 2007b), which is beyond the scope of this paper.

It is recognized that more nuanced investigations will be required before it is possible to answer completely the question of what mix matters. First, this study has investigated only one outcome, labour income, and there is widespread belief that different indicators of neighbourhood conditions may possess different explanatory power depending on which outcome is being considered (Brooks-Gunn et al., 1997; Leventhal & Brooks-Gunn, 2000). Second, the study has investigated outcomes for adults only, and different household mix characteristics may prove more efficacious in predicting outcomes for children and youth (Ellen & Turner, 2003). Third, the analysis has considered additive, linear relationships between alternative indicators of household mix; more refined analyses should include checking for non-linearities in the neighbourhood effects and for interactions between an individual's characteristics (like educational or ethnic background) and the neighbourhood variables (Galster, 2003). It is hoped that the present paper's results are sufficiently provocative to stimulate such advances.

Notes

[1] For example, see the two volume *Neighbourhood Poverty*, (Eds) Brooks-Gunn et al. (1997); the reviews in Dietz (2002); Duncan & Raudenbush (1999); Ellen & Turner (1997, 2003); Friedrichs (1998); Friedrichs et al. (2003); Leventhal & Brooks-Gunn (2000); Robert (1999); Sampson et al. (2002); and the special issue of *Housing Studies*, 18(6), 2003.

[2] In Western Europe the issue links up with ongoing discussions over 'social exclusion'. Although not typically seen as a cause of social exclusion, it can serve as a mediator that can deepen or weaken it (Murie & Musterd, 2004). In the US the issue is linked with 'concentrated poverty', articulated most prominently by Wilson (1987) and Jargowsky (1997).

[3] For example, see Van Kempen (1997) and Bauder (2001). For a recent Swedish contribution to the study of spatial mismatch, see Åslund et al. (2007).

⁴ The analysis intentionally excludes recent (after 1991) immigrants to Sweden because it is thought that their labour market experience is neither indicative of their longer-term economic value nor reflective of their initial neighbourhood environments when they enter Sweden. The authors are conducting a companion analysis that focuses on neighbourhood effects for immigrants.

⁵ The log-linear transformation is not only appropriate given the positive skew of the income distribution, but also has sound grounding in economic theory, implicitly suggesting that income is an interactive (not additive) function of personal, neighbourhood, municipality and labour market characteristics.

⁶ Formally, income from work is computed here as the sum of: cash salary payments, income from active businesses and tax-based benefits that employees accrue as terms of their employment (sick or parental leave, work-related injury or illness compensation, daily payments for temporary military service or giving assistance to a handicapped relative).

⁷ There remains some unavoidable inter-urban variation in SAMS scale nevertheless. At the extremes, the average SAMS in Gothenburg has a population of about 500 but in Stockholm it contains over 10 times as many people.

⁸ Public rental in Sweden means almost entirely multi-family dwellings owned by municipal housing companies. These companies have emerged over a period of 60 years and they now possess about 20 per cent of all dwelling units (local variations). Public rental is not means tested and allocation is normally arranged in the form of waiting lists. Sweden does not have condominiums so owner occupation means single housing. Close to 50 per cent of the population live in owner-occupied houses. Urban residential segregation processes primarily sort people between home ownership and rental housing. See for example Musterd & Andersson (2005, note (i)) for more information on housing and residential segregation in Sweden.

⁹ The control variables' coefficients vary little across the alternative neighbourhood mix specifications.

¹⁰ R-squared value from a model with the control variables but without any neighbourhood variables is 0.455 for metropolitan males, 0.452 for metropolitan females, 0.459 for non-metropolitan males and 0.458 for non-metropolitan females.

References

Andersson, R. (2003) Urban development programmes in a Scandinavian welfare state: a top-down approach to bottom-up planning?, in: P. de Decker, J. Vranken, J. Beaumont & I. Nieuwenhuyze (Eds) *On the Origins of Urban Development Programmes in Nine European Countries*, pp. 165–181 (Antwerpen-Apeldoorn: Garant).

Andersson, R. (2006) Breaking segregation—Rhetorical construct or effective policy? The case of the metropolitan development initiative in Sweden, *Urban Studies*, 43, pp. 787–799.

Andersson, R. & Musterd, S. (2005) Area-based policies: a critical appraisal, *Tijdschrift voor economische en sociale geografie*, 96, pp. 377–389.

Åslund, O., Östh, J. & Zenou, Y. (2007) How important is access to jobs? Old question, improved answer, in: J. Östh (Ed.) *Home, Job and Space. Mapping and Modeling the Labor Market*. Geografiska Regionstudier No. 72 (Uppsala: Uppsala University).

Atkinson, R., Kintrea, K., Austin, M. D. & Baba, Y. (2001) Disentangling area effects: the contributions of place to household poverty, *Urban Studies*, 38, pp. 2277–2298.

Bauder, H. (2001) You're good with your hands, why don't you become an auto mechanic: neighborhood context, institutions and career development, *International Journal of Urban and Regional Research*, 25, pp. 593–608.

Beaumont, J., Burgers, J., Decker, K., Dukes, T., Musterd, S., Staring, R. & Van Kempen, R. (2003) Urban policy in the Netherlands, in: P. de Decker, J. Vranken, J. Beaumont & I. Nieuwenhuyze (Eds) *On the Origins of Urban Development Programmes in Nine European Countries*, pp. 119–137 (Antwerpen-Apeldoorn: Garant).

Belsley, D., Kuh, E. & Welsch, R. (1980) *Regression Diagnostics* (New York: Wiley).

Bergsten, Z. & Holmqvist, E. (2007) Blanda olika befolkningsgrupper fortfarande en målsättning—En undersökning av kommunala planeringsavdelningarnas och allmännyttiga bostadsföretags planeringsmål och strategier (Gävle: IBFs rapportserie).

Brewster, K. (1994) Race differences in sexual activity among adolescent women: the role of neighborhood characteristics, *American Sociological Review*, 59, pp. 408–424.

Brooks-Gunn, J., Duncan, G. J., Klebanov, P. K. & Sealand, N. (1993) Do neighbourhoods influence child and adolescent development?, *American Journal of Sociology*, 99, pp. 353–395.

Brooks-Gunn, J., Duncan, G. J. & Aber, J. L. (Eds) (1997) *Neighborhood Poverty: Vol. 1 Context and Consequences for Children* (New York: Russell Sage Foundation).

Cook, T. D., Shagle, S. C., Degirmencioglu, S. M., Coulton, C. J., Korbin, J. E. & Su, M. (1997) Capturing social process for testing mediational models of neighborhood effects, in: J. Brooks-Gunn, G. J. Duncan & L. Aber (Eds) *Neighborhood Poverty: Vol. 2 Policy Implications in Studying Neighborhoods*, pp. 94–119 (New York: Russell Sage Foundation).

Corcoran, M., Gordon, R., Laren, D. & Solon, G. (1987) Intergenerational transmission of education, income and earnings. Unpublished manuscript (Ann Arbor: University of Michigan).

Crane, J. (1991) The epidemic theory of ghettos and neighborhood effects on dropping out and teenage childbearing, *American Journal of Sociology*, 96, pp. 1226–1259.

Dawkins, C. J., Shen, Q. & Sanchez, T. W. (2005) Race, space, and unemployment duration, *Journal of Urban Economics*, 58, pp. 91–113.

Dietz, R. (2002) The estimation of neighborhood effects in the social sciences, *Social Science Research*, 31, pp. 539–575.

Duncan, G. J. (1994) Families and neighbors as sources of disadvantage in the school decisions of white and black adolescents, *American Journal of Education*, 103, pp. 20–53.

Duncan, G. J., Connell, J. P. & Klebanov, P. K. (1997) Conceptual and methodological issues in estimating causal effects of neighborhoods and family conditions on individual development, in: J. Brooks-Gunn, G. J. Duncan & J. L. Aber (Eds) *Neighborhood Poverty: Vol. 1 Context and Consequences for Children*, pp. 219–250 (New York: Russell Sage Foundation).

Duncan, G. & Raudenbush, S. (1999) Assessing the effect of context in studies of child and youth development, *Educational Psychology*, 34, pp. 29–41.

Ellen, I. & Turner, M. (1997) Does neighborhood matter? Assessing recent evidence, *Housing Policy Debate*, 8, pp. 833–866.

Ellen, I. & Turner, M. (2003) Do neighborhoods matter and why?, in: J. Goering & J. Feins (Eds) *Choosing a Better Life? Evaluating the Moving to Opportunity Experiment*, pp. 313–338 (Washington DC: Urban Institute Press).

Ensminger, M. E., Lamkin, R. P. & Jacobson, N. (1996) School leaving: a longitudinal perspective including neighborhood effects, *Child Development*, 67, pp. 2400–2416.

Friedrichs, J. (1998) Do poor neighbourhoods make their residents poorer? Context effects of poverty neighbourhoods on their residents, in: H. Andress (Ed.) *Empirical Poverty Research in a Comparative Perspective*, pp. 77–99 (Aldershot: Ashgate).

Friedrichs, J., Galster, G. & Musterd, S. (2003) Neighbourhood effects on social opportunities: the European and American research and policy context, *Housing Studies*, 18, pp. 797–806.

Galster, G. (2003) Investigating behavioural impacts of poor neighbourhoods: towards new data and analytic strategies, *Housing Studies*, 18, pp. 893–914.

Galster, G. (2005) *Neighbourhood Mix, Social Opportunities, and the Policy Challenges of an Increasingly Diverse Amsterdam* (Amsterdam: University of Amsterdam, Department of Geography, Planning, and International Development Studies). Available at: http://www.fmg.uva.nl/amidst/object.cfm/objectid = 7 C149E7C-EC9F-4C2E-91DB7485C0839425.

Galster, G. (2007a) Neighbourhood social mix as a goal of housing policy: a theoretical analysis, *European Journal of Housing Policy*, 7, pp. 19–43.

Galster, G. (2007b) Should policymakers strive for neighbourhood social mix? An analysis of the Western European evidence base, *Housing Studies*, (forthcoming).

Galster, G. & Zobel, A. (1998) Will dispersed housing programmes reduce social problems in the US?, *Housing Studies*, 13, pp. 605–622.

Gephart, M. A. (1997) Neighborhoods and communities as contexts for development, in: J. Brooks-Gunn, G. J. Duncan & J. L. Aber (Eds) *Neighborhood Poverty: Vol. 1 Context and Consequences for Children*, pp. 1–43 (New York: Russell Sage Foundation).

Ginther, D., Haveman, R. & Wolfe, B. (2000) Neighbourhood attributes as determinants of children's outcomes: how robust are the relationships?, *Journal of Human Resources*, 35, pp. 603–642.

Goetz, E. G. (2002) *Clearing the Way* (Washington DC: Urban Institute Press).

Granovetter, M. (2005) The impact of social structure on economic outcomes, *Journal of Economic Perspectives*, 19, pp. 33–50.

Haurin, D. R., Dietz, R. D. & Weinberg, B. A. (2002) *The impact of neighborhood homeownership rates: a review of the theoretical and empirical literature*. Working paper (Columbus, OH: Department of Economics, Ohio State University).

Haveman, R. & Wolfe, B. (1994) *Succeeding Generations: On the Effects of Investments in Children* (New York: Russell Sage Foundation).

Hoynes, H. W. (2000) Local labor markets and welfare spells, *Review of Economics and Statistics*, 82, pp. 351–368.

Ionnides, Y. M. & Datcher Loury, L. (2004) Job information networks, neighborhood effects, and inequality, *Journal of Economic Literature*, 42, pp. 1056–1093.

Jargowsky, P. (1997) *Poverty and Place* (New York: Russell Sage Foundation).

Jenks, C. & Mayer, S. (1990) The social consequences of growing up in a poor neighborhood, in: L. E. Lynn & M. F. H. McGeary (Eds) *Inner-city Poverty in the United States*, pp. 111–186 (Washington DC: National Academy Press).

Johnson, M., Ladd, H. & Ludwig, J. (2002) The benefits and costs of residential mobility programmes for the poor, *Housing Studies*, 17, pp. 125–138.

Kearns, A. (2002) Response: from residential disadvantage to opportunity? Reflections on British and European policy and research, *Housing Studies*, 17, pp. 145–150.

Leventhal, T. & Brooks-Gunn, J. (2000) The neighborhoods they live in, *Psychological Bulletin*, 126, pp. 309–337.

Manski, C. F. (1995) *Identification Problems in the Social Sciences* (Cambridge, MA: Harvard University Press).

Manski, C. F. (2000) Economic analysis of social interactions, *Journal of Economic Perspectives*, 14, pp. 115–136.

Murie, A., Knorr-Siedow, T. & Van Kempen, R. (2003) *Large Housing Estates in Europe: General Developments and Theoretical Backgrounds* (Utrecht: Restate).

Murie, A. & Musterd, S. (2004) Social exclusion and opportunity structures in European cities and neighbourhoods, *Urban Studies*, 41, pp. 1441–1459.

Musterd, S. (2002) Response: mixed housing policy: a European (Dutch) perspective, *Housing Studies*, 17, pp. 139–144.

Musterd, S. & Andersson, R. (2005) Housing mix, social mix and social opportunities, *Urban Affairs Review*, 40, pp. 761–790.

Musterd, S. & Andersson, R. (2006) Employment, social mobility and neighbourhood effects, *International Journal for Urban and Regional Research*, 30, pp. 120–140.

Musterd, S., Ostendorf, W. & De Vos, S. (2003) Environmental effects and social mobility, *Housing Studies*, 18, pp. 877–892.

Ostendorf, W., Musterd, S. & de Vos, S. (2001) Social mix and the neighbourhood effect: policy ambition and empirical support, *Housing Studies*, 16, pp. 371–380.

Reardon, S. F. & Firebaugh, G. (2002) Measures of multigroup segregation, *Sociological Methodology*, 32, pp. 33–67.

Robert, S. (1999) Socioeconomic position and health: the independent contribution of community socioeconomic context, *Annual Reviews of Sociology*, 25, pp. 489–516.

Sampson, R. J. (1997) Collective regulation of adolescent misbehavior: validation results for eighty Chicago neighborhoods, *Journal of Adolescent Research*, 12, pp. 227–244.

Sampson, R. J., Morenoff, J. D. & Earls, F. (1999) Beyond social capital: spatial dynamics of collective efficacy for children, *American Sociological Review*, 64, pp. 633–660.

Sampson, R., Morenoff, J. & Gannon-Rowley, T. (2002) Assessing 'neighborhood effects': social processes and new directions in research, *Annual Reviews of Sociology*, 28, pp. 443–478.

South, S. & Crowder, K. (1999) Neighborhood effects on family formation: concentrated poverty and beyond, *American Sociological Review*, 64, pp. 113–132.

Theil, H. (1972) *Statistical Decomposition Analysis: With Applications in the Social and Administrative Sciences* (Amsterdam: North-Holland).

Van der Klaauw, B. & Van Ours, J. C. (2003) From welfare to work: does neighborhood matter?, *Journal of Public Economics*, 87, pp. 957–985.

Van Kempen, E. (1997) Poverty pockets and life chances, *American Behavioral Scientist*, 41, pp. 430–449.

Weinberg, B. A., Reagan, P. B. & Yankow, J. J. (2004) Do neighborhoods affect work behavior? Evidence from the NLSY79, forthcoming, *Journal of Labor Economics*, 24, pp. 891–924.

Wilson, W. J. (1987) *The Truly Disadvantaged* (Chicago, IL: University of Chicago Press).

Appendix

Table 1A. Regression results for control variables

Parameter	B	Std. Error	t
Intercept	6.6893	0.0569	117.52
No. children under age 7, 1995	−0.1873	0.0040	−46.66
Some sick leave during 1995 (1 = yes)	0.0880	0.0042	21.18
Pre-retired during 1995 (1 = yes)	−2.3630	0.0123	−192.44
Parental leave during 1995 (1 = yes)	0.1378	0.0052	26.63
Studying during 1995 (1 = yes)	−0.2201	0.0075	−29.32
No. years with pre-retirement, 1996–99 (1 = yes)	−0.5234	0.0030	−175.72
No. child-years under 7, 1996–99	−0.0862	0.0013	−65.70
No. years studying, 1996–99	−0.3575	0.0022	−159.96
No. years with parental leave, 1996–99	0.1439	0.0018	80.82
No. years with sick leave, 1996–99	0.1622	0.0015	110.26
Immigrants w/ < 5 years in Sweden (1 = yes)	−0.6511	0.0253	−25.75
Western country of birth (1 = yes)	−0.2763	0.0068	−40.73
Eastern European country of birth (1 = yes)	−0.5297	0.0123	−42.89
Non-Western country of birth (1 = yes)	−1.1387	0.0122	−93.56
No formal education (1 = yes)	−2.0446	0.0264	−77.48
< 10 years education (1 = yes)	−0.6330	0.0051	−123.61
10 years education (1 = yes)	−0.4369	0.0047	−92.49
13 years, some post-secondary (1 = yes)	0.3777	0.0091	41.59
14 + years, but no PhD (1 = yes)	0.4780	0.0039	122.76
PhD attained (1 = yes)	1.0229	0.0435	23.52
Single 1991 but couple 1995 (1 = yes)	−0.0434	0.0066	−6.59
Couple 1991 but single 1995 (1 = yes)	−0.1053	0.0061	−17.39
Education rose LT 11–12 to 11–12+(1 = yes)	0.4107	0.0262	15.66
Education rose 11–12 to higher (1 = yes)	0.4143	0.0123	33.70
Age in years	0.0016	0.0003	5.91
Age more than 50 years (1 = yes)	−0.2989	0.0052	−57.04
Single 1995 but couple 1999 (1 = yes)	−0.0922	0.0075	−12.24
Couple 1995 but single 1999 (1 = yes)	−0.1029	0.0063	−16.40
Mean income in local labour market, 1999	0.0003	0.0000	8.02

Note: [a]Results are shown for female-non-metropolitan stratum. The model also included the percentage of low-income males and the municipality dummies. All p-values are below 0.001.

Mixed Tenure Communities and Neighbourhood Quality

ADE KEARNS & PHIL MASON

Introduction: Policies for Mixed Communities

There is a clear emphasis within both urban policy and neighbourhood renewal policies in the UK upon the creation of 'mixed communities'. As Kleinhans (2004) shows, this focus upon mixed communities can be traced back to the early 1990s in Britain (see DoE, 1991, 1995) following a public debate about the need to have 'balanced communities' (Page, 1993), whilst a similar policy thrust has existed since 1997 in Dutch renewal programmes. In Britain, during the post-1997 New Labour Government, mixed communities policy first received explicit expression in the report of the Urban Task Force under the Chairmanship of Lord Richard Rogers:

> Whether we are talking about new settlements or expanding the capacity of existing urban areas, a good mix of incomes and tenures is important ... (Urban Task Force, 1999, p. 65)

In its later policy statement for urban development, the government included the following as a key requirement of 'sustainable communities':

> A well-integrated mix of decent homes of different types and tenures, to support a range of household sizes, ages and incomes. (ODPM, 2003, p. 5)

The broader definition of sustainable communities of which 'mixed communities' is a key component is relevant not only to the new urban growth areas declared by the government for the South-East of England, but also to its Market Renewal Programme to redevelop areas of low housing demand in the Midlands and the North. In its consultation on changes to planning policies to support mixed communities (ODPM, 2005), the government emphasised two key objectives to which housing mix could contribute, namely sustainability and social inclusion. In relation to the former, the document repeated the earlier (2003) statement above. Others have explained that the contribution to sustainability comes both from the: "longevity of resident and community stability" associated with home ownership and from the ability of an area "to meet the changing needs and aspirations of those who live in it through changing life stages, household shapes and sizes or changes in income" (Tunstall & Fenton, 2006, p. 21).

In relation to social inclusion, the consultation paper stated that "the Government does not consider that different types of housing and tenures make bad neighbours"; indeed its current definition of sustainable communities includes not only "sufficient range, diversity, affordability and accessibility of housing within a balanced housing market" (DCLG, 2006)[1] but also that such communities are 'fair, tolerant and cohesive' with "tolerance, respect and engagement with people from different cultures, backgrounds and beliefs". Of course, the government is not explicit in making any firm connections between the different elements of its sustainable communities vision, but the implication from these two documents is that socially inclusive communities founded upon diversity of housing are desirable and can be cohesive.

Whilst the government's main explication of its neighbourhood renewal policy by the Social Exclusion Unit (SEU) (2001) also included a statement about 'Encouraging Mixed Communities' (p. 41), it was less explicit about what this would mean in deprived areas and tended to focus upon the use of more balanced social housing lettings policies, rather than on the issue of housing tenure. However, even cursory observation of areas undergoing regeneration in the UK would indicate that tenure mixing was part of the renewal package, and the government's summary of what is required in deprived areas stated that: "... communities function best when they contain a broad social mix ... " (SEU, 2000, p. 53).

Furthermore, the evaluation of the government's central programme for neighbourhood renewal, New Deal for Communities (NDC), highlights the significance of housing tenure mix. The evaluation report for 2003, for example, makes reference to the mixed community definition that emerged from the ODPM as one of a number of policy developments that will impact upon renewal areas. It also points out that owner occupation in NDC areas is low at 32 per cent, and shows how the creation of successful, mixed communities is crucial to the future of renewal areas with its finding that among households with mobility intentions, owner occupiers are more likely to seek to move outside the locality (Lawless, 2003). Therefore, the challenge for deprived areas is both to increase levels of home ownership and to provide residential environments which attract and retain owners.

There are at least three important questions to ask about the policy notion of 'mixed communities'. First, is tenure mix an end in itself or simply a means to achieve greater income mix within communities? An alternative expression of the latter objective is that of 'deconcentrating poverty populations', which has particularly achieved policy attention in the US. Through deconcentrating poverty, or greater income mix, there are supposed to be benefits for both individual households, in terms of longer-term incomes and positive attitudes, and poor communities in terms of a reduction in 'problem behaviours' and the development of community social norms. However, as Galster (2002) points out in a US review, there is little attempt to examine the external effects upon origin and destination communities or moving poor people around, and "the empirical evidence is exceedingly sparse" to support the overall net social benefit from this policy.

In the UK, a recent review also concluded that "the available UK evidence for special neighbourhood effects of concentrated poverty is weak, and the case is not proven" (Tunstall & Fenton, 2006, p. 11). Nonetheless, UK policy has tended to equate mixed tenure areas with mixed income communities, largely due to the fact that "housing policies and trends in the 1980s in particular led to a 'residualisation' of social housing" (Tunstall & Fenton, 2006, p. 12). Thus:

> much central and local government policy tends to conflate income and tenure and assumes that by achieving mixed tenure, a range of incomes will also be represented in any particular development. (Bailey *et al.*, 2006, p. 18)

However, Tunstall & Fenton (2006) conclude that although mixing tenures "usually reduces the concentration of income poverty and disadvantage ... the range of incomes will vary, as the connection between tenure and income is not perfect" (p. 12).

However, if housing mix is to be a means to achieve income mix, the portents are not good. In a study of 9200 statistical neighbourhoods (Sams units) in Sweden, Musterd & Andersson (2005) concluded that "the association between housing mix and social mix is not very strong, despite the fact that Sweden has had such a political goal since at least the mid-1970s" (p. 786). They showed that "a fair share of the heterogeneous housing areas [defined by tenure and household-type dwelling] is characterised by a homogenous social profile" (p. 786).

In the UK context, it can be argued that tenure mixing is not only a means to achieve income mixing for the reasons stated above, but is also an end in itself, for at least three reasons. First, the social inclusion goals of sustainable communities (closely allied to the Home Office's goal of community cohesion) stress the aim of helping people in British society to 'get along' with others from backgrounds other than their own; mixing housing tenures is a means to achieve greater social integration of diverse and advantaged/ disadvantaged groups. Second, New Labour's social exclusion policy agenda has associated problematic behaviours (anti-social behaviour in UK terms) with residualised social housing estates: the 'worst estates' are described as a phenomenon that "no civilised society should tolerate" (Social Exclusion Unit, 1998, Cmd 4045, p. 7), so that tenure mixing is seen as a way to break up housing-based collectivities with deviant norms. Third, again allied to the social exclusion agenda, tenure mixing is seen as a way of tackling the problem of area stigmatisation or poor reputation that has developed in the UK in relation to social housing estates (see Dean & Hastings, 2000). It is for these reasons, as well as for the reason that UK policy more commonly focuses on housing tenure rather than income, that the paper proceeds to examine housing tenure mix and its effects.

The second question about mixed communities policy relates to the benefits, and specifically to whether it can be assumed that everyone gains. The majority of the focus on social gains from mixing relates to the advantages for low income and social renter households of living in an area with owner and higher-income residents, but there are at least three potential caveats to this. First, if Wilkinson's (1996) argument about the negative health effects of social inequalities applies at a local scale, then it could be expected that poor households may be negatively impacted in psychological and physical (stress-related) terms by their observation and interaction with higher-status households holding positions and enjoying privileges to which they themselves could not aspire. This is akin to what is sometimes called a 'relative deprivation' neighbourhood effect (although not often discussed as such) that results in feelings of envy and inferiority among poorer households. Second, higher-income, owner households may be negatively affected by living in neighbourhoods with high numbers of poor, social renter households. For example, their children may be influenced to engage in anti-social behaviours; problematic behaviours could be reduced for some whilst being exacerbated for others. Third, if particularly problematic residents are moved out of deprived areas into more affluent neighbourhoods in accord with a mixed communities policy, the receiving community could suffer a general detriment as a result, should problematic behaviours be continued in the new location.

The third question to be asked of mixed communities policy is whether it applies to all neighbourhoods and communities. In theory it should, given the sustainability and social inclusion goals noted above, but in practice policy in the UK is mostly applied to deprived areas undergoing regeneration and to private housing developments of significant size. This lack of application to high- and middle-income neighbourhoods is problematic for the policy in that mixed-tenure, mixed-income communities are not perceived to be the norm in the UK, and thus may undermine the longevity of policy-induced mixed communities. As Meen *et al.* (2005) point out, "there is no reason why mixed communities should be stable, and therefore sustainable" (p. 5) since social interactions and dynamics tend to produce segregated rather than integrated communities. Nonetheless, there are neighbourhoods in the UK that are mixed tenure by default (through the unplanned impacts of market forces and social policies over a long period of time) as well as those mixed by intention (or policy).

Across housing policy, urban policy and neighbourhood renewal policy, a government has three broad strategies and a range of policy instruments available to it in order to try to create communities that are more mixed in housing tenure terms. These three strategies, which are not always mutually exclusive, are defined below. Note that the paper here describes these approaches in terms of housing tenure, although they could apply to income as well as tenure (especially in other policy contexts).

Dilution: This represents an attempt to reduce marginally the significance of social rented housing within an existing neighbourhood or locality. This may be done by the sale of rented homes to tenants, as under the Right to Buy policy in the UK, or by the development of homes for market sale. The latter is often done at below-market prices through the sale of spare land on social housing estates to private developers during regeneration programmes. In most cases to date, social renting remains the largest tenure in areas subject to dilution policies.

Diversity: This strategy aims to ensure that all new housing developments or new communities have a reasonable proportion of social rented homes included within them. This is often referred to as 'planning gain' and involves a negotiated outcome between planning control officers and developers. A recent study of this process in the UK concluded that the two sides involved often failed to understand one another's objectives, with the result that the system delivered fewer 'affordable homes' in new housing developments than the official record declared (see Crook *et al.*, 2002).

Dispersal: An alternative approach to dilution, this strategy consists of using a variety of policy instruments to relocate residents of deprived areas to non-poverty neighbourhoods. Examples of this strategy in the US are the Moving to Opportunity programme (see Orr *et al.*, 2003), and the earlier Gatreaux Assisted Housing Programme and the use of Section 8 vouchers. However, the ability of such dispersal programmes to contribute a net overall gain to society in the reduction of social problems has been questioned (Galster & Zobel, 1998).

Some programmes combine elements of more than one of the above. For example, at the extreme end of the spectrum of dilution policies lie attempts to completely redevelop social housing estates by rebuilding them as mixed-tenure neighbourhoods, as in the HOPE VI programme in the US (see Popkin *et al.*, 2004). But this programme also includes an element of dispersal in that a proportion of the original estate residents are given vouchers to relocate to rented homes in the private market. Overall, it has been observed that UK governments have been keener to use policies of dilution and diversity than they have to use policies of dispersal (Kearns, 2002).

Mixed Community Benefits and Mechanisms

Mixed communities, and in particular communities of mixed income and housing tenure, are intended and alleged by their advocates to have a range of beneficial effects upon neighbourhoods and their residents (see Atkinson & Kintrea, 2000 for a review). These effects of mixed communities are summarised in Figure 1, covering four main areas, hereafter described. First, there should be better public and private services and, related to the latter, more local economic activity and increased local employment. Second, the

Economic & Service Impacts	Community-Level Effects
Better quality public services	Increased social interaction
Improved quality & quantity of private services	Enhanced sense of community and place attachment
Enhanced local economy	Reduction in mobility and greater residential stability
Increased rates of employment	
Social & Behavioural Effects	**Overcoming Social Exclusion**
Reduction in anti-social behaviour	Reduction in area stigma
Better upkeep of properties and gardens	Increased connectivity with other places
Raised aspirations	Enhanced social networks
Enhanced educational outcomes	

Figure 1. The expected benefits to disadvantaged neighbourhoods of greater income mixing

behaviours of residents previously living in excluded social housing areas should improve, both in relation to crime and anti-social behaviour and in terms of the upkeep of housing and the local environment. Impacts upon behaviours and aspirations should feed into enhanced educational outcomes for local young people. Third, community-level effects would include an enhanced sense of community and place attachment, partly stemming from increased social interaction among neighbours who no longer fear public space occupied by anti-social neighbours. There would also be greater housing opportunities within the local area and a consequent reduction in residential turnover and its disruptive effects. Finally, mixed communities would be less socially excluded in that the stigma associated with mono-tenure estates would be lessened; neighbourhoods would be reconnected to their surrounding areas and the wider urban area; and information and useful intelligence, for example, about employment opportunities and other relevant developments, would be passed between residents with different connections and knowledge.

Looking behind these expected benefits, it is possible to identify a number of potential mechanisms at work within mixed communities to bring these benefits about. The paper describes four types of effect on which policy makers appear to be relying.

Resource Effects

One of the anticipated consequences of providing neighbourhoods of mixed tenure is a result of broadening the class base of the residential population, in contrast to the situation where a residualised state housing sector has increasingly accommodated only residents of the lowest social classes. A more middle-class resident group would bring income into the local area and thus help to sustain a better range of private retail outlets and services. In addition, these middle-class residents are also expected to contribute to the raising of standards of public service provision by their stronger 'voice' and advocacy skills. This is important as it has long been argued that deprived areas, those areas most in need, tend to receive worse services than other areas. In their longitudinal study of 12 deprived areas in the UK, nine of which were council estates, the Centre for the Analysis of Social Exclusion, describing the position of these areas in the late 1990s, stated:

> The problem was not that the [public] services were absent ... More often, neighbourhood services were beset by two other problems. One was that they were insufficient to keep up with demand; the other that they struggled to provide the quality of services that was needed and that residents in other areas could expect to receive. (Lupton, 2003, p. 99)

The (some would say condescending) argument for mixed tenure neighbourhoods is that the middle classes would be less likely to put up with this situation, or, slightly differently, that with a more mixed neighbourhood, public servants would not try to get away with providing a lower quality of service. Of course, one of the reasons for these effects is that the middle classes have better means, through a mixture of social and cultural capital, to bring about resolutions or improvements to problems with services, and to gain the most from existing provision. This reflects Bourdieu's argument that cultural capital, for example in the nuances of language and symbolic expression of aesthetic preferences, enables the middle classes to appear as 'insiders' in society's institutions rather than as outsiders (see Lauglo, 2000).

Role Model Effects

Again, the mixing of tenures is expected to bring benefits via the diversification of the resident group, in particular through the provision of role models for deprived, excluded groups to follow. Behavioural changes might be seen in several areas: in social behaviours, i.e. in how one relates to others and in whether one engages in anti-social behaviour; in personal behaviours, i.e. in how one exercises control over one's own family members and in how one cares for one's own property; and in aspirational behaviours, i.e. in what one seeks to achieve, for example, in employment, education or leisure pursuits. These role model effects might arise through peer pressure influences, emulation or as a result of a higher expectation of reprimand and sanction following unwelcome behaviours in a mixed tenure situation. Notwithstanding this policy theory, there is every possibility that interactions between neighbours from different housing tenures may be negative rather than positive. Qualitative research among residents of mixed-tenure estates in Scotland, for example, indicated that the closer the physical proximity between tenures, the greater the social tensions between residents from different backgrounds (Beekman *et al.*, 2001).

Community Effects

Communities may change as a result of tenure mixing and any compositional changes may result in due course in cultural changes, such as placing greater value on employment or on living a healthy lifestyle. It is expected that tenure mixing will enhance a community's social capital, embracing all three components of networks, norms and trust (Putnam, 2001). By this means, there should be better local outcomes, for example, in terms of reduced anti-social behaviour as a result of a shift in norms, and through enhanced well-being via strengthened community social networks (Gilchrist, 2004). But there should also be wider benefits due to a shift from relying mainly on bonding social capital, towards a greater utilisation of both bridging and linking social capital (Woolcock, 2001). In this way, communities will be 'getting ahead' through wider networking and accessing influence and opportunity, rather than just 'getting by' through solidaristic emotional and material support (see Briggs, 1998). The instrument of mixed tenure housing policy is just one example of the British Government's interest in, and reliance upon, social capital as a means to improve circumstances for deprived communities (Kearns, 2003).

Transformation Effects

The image of poor areas has been difficult to change because such places not only have poor reputations, but the problem is compounded by the stigma attached to social housing (Dean & Hastings, 2000). In order to change the future destiny of communities that have been stuck at the bottom of the heap for some time, there is a need for wholesale transformation, rather than incremental improvements. This has to be real, tangible and visible for both residents and outsiders (visitors and observers). Only in this way will residents acquire a sense of change and a degree of optimism about their own and their neighbourhood's future, and will outsiders begin to talk about and treat certain areas differently. Housing tenure mixing is seen as a key element in convincing people that areas are changing, visibly in terms of the quality of the built environment, socially in terms of the type of people who live there, and economically in terms of the viability of the local housing market.

Available Evidence to Support Mixed Communities Policy

There is not enough space in this paper to review comprehensively all the available research evidence either on neighbourhood effects (i.e. the problems that mixing might reduce), or on the outcomes of mixed community strategies (i.e. the additional benefits that neighbourhood mixing might deliver). However, the paper will briefly highlight some of the salient points made about this evidence from recently published reviews of the field. It is worth noting that much of the evidence that informs policy prescriptions in the UK and Europe comes from multivariate analysis and experimental studies carried out in the US which, whilst welcome, can itself be an issue, as will be seen.

In a review of research into the effects of the main housing mobility or dispersal programmes in the US, Atkinson (2005) highlights evident gains to poor households from relocation to non-poor, socially mixed areas in terms of neighbourhood quality and residential satisfaction, feelings of safety and improved educational outcomes (both in terms of school performance and college entrance). The evidence on employment effects is more mixed, with research on the Gatreaux Assisted Housing Programme showing employment gains for black adults (Rosenbaum, 1995), whilst research on scattered site public housing residents showed no gains in terms of employment opportunity (Briggs, 1998) and little use of social networks to gain information about, or access to jobs (Briggs, 1998; Kleit, 2001).

Berube (2005) reviews US evidence specifically to inform UK policy on mixed communities. He stresses the effects upon children living in high-poverty neighbourhoods of absent sanctions and low opportunity costs of crime, together with peer-group effects promoting involvement in crime. He summarises research on the Movement to Opportunity (MTO) experiment to show that youths in suburban situations are less involved in violent crime (see Ludwig *et al.*, 2001), and in low-poverty neighbourhoods children experience less violence and disorder and show improved mental health, with better community facilities such as schools and parks playing a part in these outcomes (Leventhal & Brooks-Gunn, 2003).

Berube (2005) also cites work by Brophy & Smith (1997) on mixed-income housing to argue that the success of mixed communities depends upon how it is done. Two issues are crucial: a wide income gap between subsidised and 'market-rate' residents may cause tensions in developments; second, full spatial integration of higher-income and lower-income residents "has important positive effects on the overall functioning of developments" (p. 31), since clustering of low-income households results in stigma and disorder. Similar points about the advantages of 'pepper-potting' owner occupied and social rented housing have been made in the UK context by Page & Boughton (1997) and Atkinson & Kintrea (1998).

Galster's (2005) review of US and European research is much wider ranging, but the paper will highlight just a few key points relevant to the question of mixing tenure groups. The neighbourhood context seems particularly important for child and adolescent outcomes, but these links are stronger in relation to neighbourhood socio-economic status than for racial or ethnic variations. However, the evidence from Europe is less consistent than that for the US, and shows neighbourhood effects of smaller magnitude. The US evidence indicates that affluent households can have positive effects on their less well-off neighbours, but again the evidence is more mixed (sic) in the European context. Galster's judgement on the implications of the research for US policy is that disadvantaged households should be kept below a threshold of 20 per cent in any neighbourhood, and that advantaged households should be kept in the majority. For Europe, he says that the message is not as clear-cut, and echoes the earlier point that mixing groups that are very different in income terms may have detrimental effects upon those on lower incomes.

The research evidence in Britain and the Netherlands, two European countries pursuing similar housing tenure mix strategies in urban renewal, was recently reviewed by Kleinhans (2004). He found consistent evidence to support the notion of benefits to the neighbourhood environment through the behaviours of owner occupiers but mixed evidence on whether tenure mixing improved an area's reputation. His review did not support the idea that there is significant social interaction between residents in different tenures and partly for this reason he also did not find evidence for role model effects, whilst acknowledging the argument of Friedrichs & Blasius (2003) that role models may be available outside the neighbourhood. Two conclusions pertinent to the research here were, first, that owners can benefit all neighbourhood residents through complaining to local authorities about neighbourhood problems and developing local associations as a prevention strategy (based on Jupp's (1999) research on mixed tenure estates in the UK), and second, that many mixed tenure neighbourhoods exhibit social conflicts and tensions due to increased exposure between residents who do not have shared values and lifestyles.

Across the piece, more extensive and more consistent evidence can be seen emerging from the US than in Europe on the effects of deprived areas and on the impacts of mixed-income and mixed-tenure neighbourhoods. Furthermore, the use of large datasets to examine these issues is less common in Europe, although growing in the Netherlands and Scandinavia, and to a lesser extent in the UK. Much of the UK evidence to date has come from small case-study research or multi-site studies of mixed-tenure estates, both regenerated social housing estates and private housing developments containing low-income housing. In what follows, the paper seeks to add to this evidence base through the use of household survey data from a representative sample of neighbourhoods in England.

Research Aims and Objectives

The overall aim of the research here is to examine whether the empirical evidence across all types of neighbourhood in England provides support for the notion of creating 'mixed communities'. This aim can be elaborated as a series of research questions as follows:

(1) How does the pattern of incidence of perceived neighbourhood deficiencies (i.e. the incidence of neighbourhood problems and the demand for improvements to local services and amenities) vary according to the level and mix of housing tenures across localities?
(2) How do housing tenure mix and the level of social renting in an area compare in terms of their relationships with neighbourhood quality (defined as perceived neighbourhood deficiencies)?

(3) Do the occupants of all housing tenures appear to have similar or different experiences in mixed tenure situations?
(4) Does the evidence indicate the existence of any critical levels of particular housing tenures within an area that are associated with either rapid increases or reductions in the incidence of neighbourhood deficiencies?

Analytical Approach

Data Source

The main data source used for this research is the Survey of English Housing (SEH), which is the primary general-purpose housing survey commissioned by the Department for Communities and Local Government (DCLG), that part of government which has responsibility for housing, regeneration and urban policy in England.

The SEH is a continuous household survey designed to achieve a nationally representative sample of around 20 000 household interviews per year, roughly 1 in 1000 households across the country. Two dozen addresses are randomly selected for each of 1176 postcode sectors spread across the metropolitan and non-metropolitan regions of England, with the achieved response rate being 72 per cent (for more information see http://www.communities.gov.uk/seh). For the purposes of this paper, two years' worth of data were combined from the survey, 2001/02 and 2002/03, giving a total sample size of 39 175 respondents (approximately 1 in 530 households in England). The interviews were conducted with the 'householder' or his/her partner.

Neighbourhood Variables

The study has concentrated on two sets of questions asked in the SEH, one about neighbourhood problems and the other about improvements required to services and facilities in the neighbourhood. The wording of these questions is as follows. First, on neighbourhood problems:

> I am going to read out a list of things that can cause problems for people in their areas. I would like you to tell me whether each of them is a problem in this area

This is a pre-coded question with the available response categories being: not a problem; a problem, but not serious; and a serious problem. Ten types of problem are asked about (see Table 6). Second, on neighbourhood improvements:

> Please look at a list of aspects of your area which might be improved ... could you tell me which, if any, of the aspects of your area would you like to see improved

This is a multiple-response question, with respondents being able to select up to 10 items for improvement (see Table 10).

However, first there is a look at two other questions about neighbourhood asked in the survey. Respondents were asked a standard neighbourhood satisfaction question with a five-fold Likert response scale ranging from very satisfied to very dissatisfied:

How satisfied are you with this area as a place to live?

Finally, respondents were asked about neighbourhood change:

On the whole, do you think that over the past two years this area has got better or worse as a place to live?

The response categories for this question are: 'area has got better'; 'area has got worse'; 'area has not changed much'; 'has lived here less than two years'.

Spatial Unit of Analysis

The primary sampling unit for the SEH is postcode sectors, which are similar in size to wards, the spatial unit traditionally used in geographical analysis in the UK. Housing tenure statistics for wards have been extracted from the UK Census 2001 and have been attached to the SEH data-file by the ODPM, linking through by means of the full postcodes of the respondents (which were allocated to wards for this purpose). This procedure preserved the confidentiality of the data.

There are 7970 wards in England, with a median population size of 5132 persons (mean 6195) and a minimum size of 1003. The two-year data-file here contains respondents living in 4296 wards in England, or 54 per cent of all wards.

Measuring Tenure Mix

Achieving a sensible overall measure of the degree of housing tenure mixing within an area is not easy. Past UK research, such as that by Hiscock (2002), has utilised pre-set categories of tenure mixing with handy descriptors of each category. For example, the Hiscock classification system describes places where owner occupation is 70 per cent or more of the market as 'heavily dominated by owning' and places where owner occupation is between 30–70 per cent, but private renting and social renting are each below 30 per cent as 'mixed, but more owned than rented'. Some use is made of this classification system in the analysis, but it is recognised that whilst on the one hand it is simple and straightforward, on the other hand the categories are merely intuitive.

Thus, the study investigated using three different measures of the degree to which all three main housing tenures are present in the mix within each ward, i.e. owner occupation, social renting and private renting. In the end, the Shannon-Weaver Equitability Index was adopted, which is a standardised measure of entropy. This measure, from information science, is commonly used for measuring biological diversity (Magurran, 1988), combining information on numbers of species and their relative abundance, and is calculated as follows:

$$E_H = \frac{-\sum_{i=1}^{S} p_i \ln p_i}{\ln S},$$

where, for the purposes here, i is the tenure category and S is the total number of tenure categories. The numerator corresponds to an absolute measure of diversity (or entropy), which is standardised upon division by ln S. In the case here, the number of 'species' of tenure type is the same in all comparisons, so the index varies solely as a function of their relative proportions in each ward, providing a measure of the evenness of proportions, from 0 (where only one housing tenure is present in a ward) to 1 (where all three tenures are equally present). Thus, the higher the value of E_H, the more similar are the proportions of each tenure type.

In addition to the equitability index, use is made of measures of the actual percentage of each housing tenure within each ward. In this way, the relative importance of the prevalence of any one tenure can be assessed against the degree to which there is equal mixing of tenures (or 'balanced communities').

Analyses

The study commences by describing the pattern of housing tenures across wards in England in order to see to what extent localities in England can be considered to be of mixed tenure in current circumstances. This first part of the study also examines the general pattern of neighbourhood conditions as assessed by residents, seeing to what extent there are perceived to be neighbourhood problems or deficiencies in local services and facilities.

In turn, neighbourhood problems and neighbourhood improvements are then considered. First their incidence is examined according to the level and mix of housing tenures within wards. This is done by plotting the incidence of problems and improvements against percentiles of social renting and owner occupation, and by using the archetypal tenure-mix categorisations devised for the UK by Hiscock (2002). The consequences of polarised or extreme tenure situations are then assessed by contrasting the responses, first of social renters living in wards in the highest quintile of owner occupation, with, second, the responses of owner occupiers living in wards in the highest quintile of social renting.

Subsequently, binomial logistic regression modelling is used to assess the impact of each housing tenure and of the housing tenure mix (using the equitability index) upon the likelihood of each neighbourhood problem and improvement being cited by respondents. These models included the covariates of age, sex and employment status. Models were built by forward selection, with a significance level of $p<0.01$ for inclusion and rejection. These stricter criteria were imposed because of the large number of models being tested in this study. Characteristically for such a large dataset, it is common for parameter estimates to be highly significant even though they are of low magnitude, and for the proportion of the total variation explained by the model to be small: in the analyses presented here, values of Nagelkerke's R^2 seldom exceeded 0.1. A cursory inspection of many of the other variables in the SEH (results not shown) suggests this low explanatory power is not especially characteristic of those that are examined here, but reflects the large amount of variation in the data that cannot be simply explained by a small number of variables of major effect.

Investigating Non-Linearities

In recent years, there has been much interest in the question of whether the impacts of neighbourhood environments or context upon social problems are non-linear, in other words whether 'threshold effects' exist. Much of the theoretical basis for this contention lies in the consideration of 'neighbourhood effects' as a form of social interaction (see Manski, 2000). Either as a result of collective socialisation, social contagion or gaming behaviour, there are critical levels at which social problems 'explode' or 'take off' (see Galster, 2003 and Meen et al., 2005).[2] In the case of collective socialisation, it is argued that the ability to ensure conformity to collective norms of behaviour increases rapidly after the sanctioning group grows beyond a certain size in an area. In the case of social contagion, it is argued that problematic behaviours are spread more rapidly through peer influence after the social 'epidemic' in question reaches a particular prevalence. Gaming models contend that only after individuals observe a certain level of prior behaviour by others do they consider that the potential payoff to themselves is great enough to warrant the adoption of the behaviour concerned. However, Galster (2002) found few studies which provided empirical evidence that there were threshold-type relationships between neighbourhood conditions and either income or problematic behaviours.

In the case here, the question arises as to whether the incidence of neighbourhood problems or service deficiencies grows or declines rapidly after the level of one or more of the housing tenures reaches a certain critical point. If this were the case, it would warrant a different approach to the statistical modelling of the outcomes, such as using spline-type regression models wherein the relationship between the neighbourhood characteristic (in this case the level of one of the housing tenures) and the incidence of neighbourhood problems is divided into a series of steps or linear segments divided by breakpoints, rather than being considered as one continuous linear trend (see Galster et al., 2000 for a worked example). However, one of the difficulties is in deciding where the breakpoints in the spline model should be placed along the distribution of the neighbourhood characteristic in question under conditions where the hypothesis includes no prior expectation of their location.

Given the theoretical interest in threshold effects, or non-linearities, two approaches were taken to investigate the existence of these in the data. First, and most importantly, the apparent existence of non-linearities was explored through plotting techniques that might then be tested through appropriate statistical approaches. Plots were examined for each individual neighbourhood problem and improvement (not shown here) as well as for the aggregate number of problems and improvements cited across the full range of levels of social renting and owner occupation within wards, using tenure percentiles.[3] This provides a good picture of whether the relationship between tenure levels and neighbourhood problems and deficiencies shows any signs of substantial thresholds or breaks, which in fact it did not (see below).

Second, in the course of developing the regression models, examination of the residuals of the fitted models suggested that there *may* be non-linearities in the correspondence between the continuous independent variables (proportions of tenure type, equitability index) and the probability of citing an item as a serious problem. An attempt to account for these was made by fitting a polynomial series of independent terms of tenure proportions. While these additional terms indeed generally yielded a better fit to the data, they failed to explain substantially more of the variation in the data. It was concluded that it would not be wise to include them in the final models for several reasons. First, there was no prior hypothesis to justify the incorporation of higher-order polynomial terms in the models. Second, there was no consistency among the models of the number and order of the additional polynomial terms that gave the best fits. Finally, the greater complexity of these models undermines the interpretative value of the approach here. In any case, and as already indicated, exploratory analyses did not suggest any of the abrupt changes that indicate threshold effects, for example of the type described by Galster (2005).

Limitations

There are a number of limitations to the analysis that should be highlighted to the reader. First, the dataset is cross-sectional and therefore it is not possible to tell what impacts the introduction of housing tenure mix might have on a community over time; nor whether other unmeasured changes would have an impact alongside tenure mix (such as investment in public services during a regeneration programme). Second, the dataset is national in coverage and thus includes the views of residents in both 'evolved' mixed neighbourhoods and 'created' mixed neighbourhoods, which cannot be distinguished.

Third, and related to the last point, the dataset does not contain any measure of income for the respondents and thus it is not possible to control for the selection-bias problem which bedevils neighbourhood effects research (Galster, 2003). In relation to this research, those owners who live in areas of more mixed housing tenure are likely to be of lower income than those living in more homogeneous owner-occupied areas and it is suggested that they are therefore less likely to identify neighbourhood deficiencies than other owners. This would have the effect of giving a more positive impression of the impacts of housing tenure mix than would otherwise be the case, if the same types of owners were involved in both mixed and non-mixed situations.

Finally, the research is limited by the spatial scale of analysis. Wards are probably larger than neighbourhoods understood as familiar home areas (see Kearns & Parkinson, 2001), containing several smaller neighbourhoods, although the way in which housing tenures are mixed within wards in terms of spatial configuration will vary greatly. Nevertheless, wards are important for two reasons: (1) spatial planning for urban development within British towns and cities often considers the housing profile and needs of wards and (2) political arrangements are such that many decisions about local public services are taken at the ward level. Thus, there is some merit in knowing the effects of housing tenure mix at ward level, even if this leaves unanswered the question of housing tenure impacts at the true neighbourhood level.

The problem of spatial scale is similar to that faced by US neighbourhood effects research, where census tracts which are fairly homogeneous areas of around 4000 people are used as the spatial unit of analysis. An overview of this field of research stated that "such tracts might be too large in scale to measure accurately the variables of 'local neighbourhood' that actually are affecting residents" (Friedrichs *et al.*, 2003, p. 800). In the present case, while it would have been preferable to use a smaller spatial unit of analysis, this was not possible at the time. However, the authors would intend to return to this line of enquiry using the smaller Census Super Output Area, which is roughly a quarter the size of a ward, in future.

Neighbourhood Conditions and Housing Tenure in England

As Table 1 shows, most people in England are satisfied with their neighbourhood, with fewer than 1 in 10 people dissatisfied. However, the response to this question paints a rather too rosy picture of the situation. Parkes *et al.* (2002) expressed their suspicions about the interpretation of the unusual 'fairly satisfied' response category, which would

Table 1. Overall assessment of neighbourhoods, 2001/02 and 2002/03

	%	%
Neighbourhood satisfaction:		
Very satisfied	48.9	–
Fairly satisfied	36.8	–
Neither	4.9	–
Slightly dissatisfied	6.0	–
Very dissatisfied	3.4	–
	($n = 38\ 297$)	
Neighbourhood change:		
Area has got better	8.6	9.7
Area has got worse	23.8	26.9
Area has not changed much	56.3	63.4
Lived here for < 2 years	11.3	($n = 33\ 892$)[a]
	($n = 38\ 206$)	

Note: [a] Omitting those who have lived in the neighbourhood for less than two years.

lead one to believe that only the 'very satisfied', around half the sample, are truly happy with their neighbourhood. As Table 1 also shows, whilst most people consider that their neighbourhood has not changed in the past two years, nearly three times as many people think their neighbourhood has got worse than think it has got better. Furthermore, regional analysis across three years of the SEH shows wide variations in neighbourhood satisfaction, with 57 per cent of people in the South West being very satisfied with their neighbourhood, compared with only 37 per cent in London (see ODPM, 2004).

Tables 2 and 3 show the overall perceptions of neighbourhood problems and improvements as cited in 2001/02–2002/03. The most prevalent neighbourhood problem is crime, followed by traffic, litter and vandalism. Most of the problems are less prevalent than they were a decade earlier when the survey started in 1992. This is particularly true of crime, which was cited by 22 per cent of people as a serious problem in their area in 1992 (see Bates et al., 2001), compared with 15 per cent in 2001–03. The most frequently

Table 2. Neighbourhood problems, 2001/02 and 2002/03

	Serious problem (%)	Problem but not serious (%)	Total (problem) (%)
Vandalism and hooliganism	11.3	32.8	44.1
Graffiti	5.7	19.5	25.2
Crime	15.0	41.5	56.5
Dogs	8.6	18.3	26.9
Litter and rubbish in the streets	15.1	29.7	44.8
Neighbours	3.7	9.2	12.9
Racial harassment	1.0	3.0	4.0
Noise	5.9	18.6	24.5
Traffic	17.6	28.8	46.4
Other harassment	1.2	4.3	5.5

Note: Minimum sample 37 988, apart from 'other harassment' where $n = 18\ 909$.

Table 3. Neighbourhood improvements, 2001/02 and 2002/03

	Improvement desired (%)
Amount and quality of housing	13.1
Availability of jobs	11.5
Crime and vandalism	23.0
Local amenities, parks and leisure facilities	19.8
Local health services	11.8
Opportunities and facilities for children and young people	25.7
Public transport service	20.9
Quality of environment	13.5
Schools and colleges	7.7
Shopping and commercial facilities	15.8

Note: Sample size 39 042.

demanded improvements to local neighbourhoods are better facilities for children and young people and reduction in crime and vandalism, each required by around a quarter of respondents; then better public transport and better parks and leisure facilities, both demanded by around a fifth of respondents. Despite the impression given that local schooling is a preoccupation in England, fewer than 1 in 10 people considered improvements to their local schools to be desirable (although this response comes from non-parents as well as parents).

Housing tenure in England has changed dramatically over the past two decades. Owner occupation has grown from 57 per cent in 1981 to 70 per cent in 2001 (see Bates *et al.*, 2001; ODPM, 2003). The other two tenures have reduced accordingly: private renting has not changed very much, from 11 per cent to 10 per cent, but social renting has declined by a third from 32 per cent in 1981 to 20 per cent in 2001. Within social renting, council housing has fallen by three-fifths, whilst housing association tenure has tripled, so that they comprise 13 and 7 per cent respectively in 2001. What this means for the residential environments in which people live is shown in Table 4, which gives the distribution of SEH respondents across the tenure mix categories devised by Hiscock. Two-thirds of people live in wards heavily dominated by owner occupation (over 70 per cent owners), with a further 1 in 6 living in wards where owner occupation, although not so dominant, is still much more common than each of the other two tenures. Only 1 in 7 people live in mixed tenure

Table 4. Respondents by ward tenure mix

Ward description	Category definition	% Respondents
Heavily dominated by owner occupation	O/O >70%	67.4
Mixed, more owned than rented	O/O 30–70%; SRS < 30%; PRS < 30%	16.1
Mixed, owned and social rented	O/O 30–70%; SRS 30–50%; PRS < 30%	10.4
Mixed, owned and private rented	O/O 30–70%; SRS <30%; PRS 30–70%	3.4
Dominated by social rented	SRS >50%	2.3
Other mix	None of the above	0.5
		(*n* = 39 175)

Table 5. Tenure deciles for wards in England, 2001

Decile	Proportions (%s) of each tenure defining the deciles		
	Owner occupation	Social renting	Private renting
1	≤53.2	≤3.5	≤4.1
2	53.2–62.4	3.5–5.4	4.1–5.0
3	62.4–68.5	5.4–7.3	5.0–5.9
4	68.5–73.2	7.3–9.5	5.9–6.8
5	73.2–77.4	9.5–11.8	6.8–8.0
6	77.4–80.4	11.8–14.7	8.0–9.5
7	80.4–83.4	14.7–19.0	9.5–11.6
8	83.4–86.2	19.0–24.4	11.6–14.9
9	86.2–90.0	24.4–33.3	14.9–21.4
10	90.0+	33.3+	21.4+

wards where owner occupation is on a par with one or other of the two remaining tenures. Notwithstanding the public representation of widespread problems of social housing, just 1 in 50 people live in wards where the housing tenure is majority social rented.

Another way of describing the pattern of housing tenures on the ground in England is to examine the distribution of wards by deciles of each housing tenure proportion within wards. This is given in Table 5 and shows that over 90 per cent of wards have a majority of owner occupiers, and 40 per cent of wards have fewer than 1 in 10 social renters. On the other hand, 1 in 10 wards comprise over a fifth of private renters and 1 in 5 wards comprise a quarter or more social renting. Social renting appears the most unevenly distributed tenure across wards in England.

Neighbourhood Problems and Tenure Mix

Respondents in the SEH were asked about 10 potential problems in their neighbourhood. The change in mean number of problems cited across the ward tenure percentiles is greater for the citation of serious problems than it is for all problems (serious and minor combined), and thus Figure 2 examines the former. It can be seen that as the percentiles of

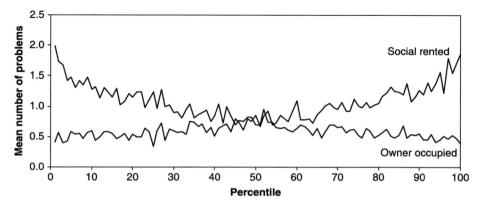

Figure 2. Mean number of serious problems cited for all households by percentile of proportion of social-rented and owner-occupied tenures (private-rented values not shown)

social renting and private renting increase, so does the mean number of serious problems cited, roughly tripling across the range, whereas the opposite is true for owner occupation. The mean number of serious problems cited by private renters (not shown, for clarity) increases, but by only about two-thirds. Inspection of the plotted values raises the possibility that the change in the average number of problems cited by residents deviates slightly from a uniform linear relationship, but there is no suggestion of abrupt changes that would imply the existence of threshold effects.

If the identification of neighbourhood problems is examined according to the pre-set tenure mix categories described earlier, it can be seen that with the exception of traffic, every problem is cited most often in wards dominated by social renting. Interestingly, for 7 of the 10 problems, the second lowest rate of incidence of problems, after that in wards dominated by owner occupation, is in wards where owning and private renting are roughly equivalent in size, rather than in wards where owning is still by far the largest tenure.

By comparing the views of owners and renters living in wards where the opposite tenure is towards the height of its presence, the effects of policies can be seen which try either to diversify housing tenure in social housing areas by introducing owner occupiers, or conversely (as in mobility schemes in the USA) try to disperse social renters to more affluent neighbourhoods. These contrasts are shown in Table 7. Here it will be seen that all serious problems are cited most often in the same rank ordering of residential circumstances: mostly by social renters in high-social-renting wards; then by owner occupiers in high-social-renting wards; then by social renters in high-owner-occupation wards; and least often by owner occupiers in high-owner-occupation wards. The only exception to this rule is the high frequency of citation of problems with traffic by owner occupiers in both high-social-renting and high-owner-occupation wards.

From the final column of the Table it is possible to get a sense of the impact upon people of living in different circumstances whilst remaining in the same housing tenure themselves. It can be seen that for owner occupiers, the incidence of problems is usually tripled if they live in high-social-renting wards compared with living in high-owner-occupation wards. For social renters, problems are usually at least double in incidence if they live in high-social-renting wards compared with high-owner-occupation wards,

Table 6. Neighbourhood problems by tenure mix categories

	% Within each tenure mix category citing problem				
	Owner dominated	Mixed, more owned	Mixed owned & social rent	Mixed owned & private rent	Social dominated
Vandalism	38.9	51.8	60.0	45.1	67.1
Graffiti	20.2	32.4	38.4	32.5	47.4
Crime	52.0	63.2	69.3	61.6	75.1
Dogs	25.4	29.2	31.9	25.7	35.8
Litter	38.7	55.3	60.9	53.0	66.3
Neighbours	10.5	16.6	19.2	16.8	22.2
Racial harassment	2.3	6.7	7.3	5.9	17.6
Noise	20.9	30.5	31.2	36.3	40.1
Traffic	46.0	49.2	41.1	56.5	46.7
Other harassment	4.0	7.2	10.5	5.9	14.4
n	(26 388)	(6310)	(4085)	(1317)	(896)

Table 7. Serious neighbourhood problems in contrasting circumstances, and relative loss due to living in high social renting wards compared with high owner occupied wards

	A. In high owner wards (%) [a]	B. In high social renting wards (%) [b]	Ratio B/A (losses)
Owner Occupiers			
Vandalism	5.0	17.2	3.4
Graffiti	2.6	9.4	3.6
Crime	7.1	24.0	3.4
Dogs	6.1	10.4	1.7
Litter	7.2	23.6	3.3
Neighbours	1.5	4.6	3.1
Racial harassment	0.2	1.6	8.0
Noise	3.3	7.2	2.2
Traffic	17.2	18.3	1.1
Other harassment	0.4	1.7	4.3
	(n = 6836)[c]	(n = 3647)	
Social Renters			
Vandalism	10.3	27.9	2.7
Graffiti	2.7	14.2	5.3
Crime	9.9	32.3	3.3
Dogs	7.3	14.4	2.0
Litter	11.6	29.1	2.5
Neighbours	4.3	9.1	2.1
Racial harassment	0.5	2.8	5.6
Noise	4.5	11.2	2.5
Traffic	11.6	17.0	1.5
Other harassment	0.0	3.6	?
	(n = 435)	(n = 3320)	

Notes: [a] Defined as the top quintile of owner wards, where owner occupation is 86% or more of the housing tenure.
[b] Defined as the top quintile of social renting wards, where social renting is 24% or more of the housing tenure.
[c] All 'n' are minimum sample sizes, excluding 'other harassment', for which sample sizes are typically halved.

or conversely halved, or more than halved, in the latter. For 5 of the 10 items, the proportionate losses due to living in a high-social-renter ward rather than a high-owner-occupation ward are greater for owners than for renters. The biggest impact upon owners of living in high-social-renting areas is in the increase in incidence of racial harassment as a problem. For social renters, the biggest gains from living in high-owner-occupation areas are reductions in the incidence of harassment and graffiti as problems.

Table 8 gives the results of the logistic regression modelling of each neighbourhood problem, showing the significant odds ratios ($p < 0.01$, in bold) for the tenure variables included in each model. Conclusions should be drawn with care from these models (and of those presented in Table 12) since the high correlation between the variables examined and their low explanatory capacity (as indicated by Nagelkerke's R^2) mean that different combinations of terms can produce equally good models, judged on purely statistical criteria.

With regard to the covariates of age, sex and employment status (terms not shown here for reasons of space), it was found that women were 10 per cent more likely than men to identify vandalism, crime and litter as serious problems in the neighbourhood. In the case

Table 8. Predictors of serious problems in the neighbourhood (odds ratios)

	Vandalism	Graffiti	Crime	Dogs	Litter	Neighbours	Racial harassment	Noise	Traffic	Other harassment
Tenure: Social renter (SR)	*1.066*	*0.791*	**1.251**	**1.165**	**0.603**	**5.224**	**0.346**	**1.367**	*1.177*	**1.710**
Tenure: Private renter (PR)	*0.981*	*0.466*	*0.993*	**0.592**	*0.778*	*0.924*	**0.182**	*1.113*	*0.860*	*0.881*
Proportion SR (0–100%)	**32.828**	**9.848**	**9.441**	**4.419**	**4.999**	–	–	**0.363**	**0.144**	–
Equitability (0–1)	**5.997**	**4.030**	**5.981**	–	**5.591**	**7.250**	–	–	–	–
Proportion OO (0–100%)	**3.910**	*0.663*	*1.243*	–	*0.634*	–	**0.006**	**0.065**	**0.156**	**0.055**
Proportion OO by tenure SR	**1.954**	**2.355**	–	–	**2.483**	–	**11.838**	–	**0.555**	–
Proportion OO by tenure PR	*1.148*	*2.292*	–	–	*1.245*	–	**14.587**	–	*1.074*	–
Equitability by tenure SR	–	–	–	–	–	**0.324**	–	–	–	–
Equitability by tenure PR	–	–	–	–	–	*0.873*	–	–	–	–
Nagelkerke's R^2	0.095	0.072	0.096	0.028	0.074	0.075	0.111	0.040	0.011	0.063

Notes: Controlling for age, sex and economic status.
*Odds Ratios (exp(B)) in bold are significant, $p \leq 0.01$; in normal type are significant, $p \leq 0.05$; in italic, n.s. (highlighted; consider removing from model). Values for tenure categories are relative to owner occupiers.

of half the items, the odds of citing a serious problem reduced by 1 or 2 per cent for every year that age increased—this was true for graffiti, dogs, neighbours and both forms of harassment. Being employed part-time, being retired or being a student each increased the odds of citing a serious problem for a minority of items. However, being long-term sick or disabled increased the odds of citing every problem by between 50 and 80 per cent, and in the case of harassment other than by race, more than doubled the odds of a serious problem.

In general, renters are less likely than owner occupiers to complain about racial harassment (reflecting the fact that ethnic minorities have a greater presence in the rented tenures than the white majority). In particular, social renters are more likely than owners to identify crime, dogs, neighbours, noise and other harassment as problems, although they are less likely to cite litter as a problem. Private renters are less prone to citing dogs as being a problem than are owners. As the proportion of social renting in an area increases, so does the likelihood of residents citing five of the 10 items as being serious problems. This is especially the case for vandalism, which, curiously, also becomes more prevalent (although to a far lesser degree) as the proportion of owner occupation increases. The odds of two of the problems being cited (noise and traffic) reduces as social renting in an area increases.

However, in general, the likelihood of there being serious neighbourhood problems reduces as the proportion of owner occupation in an area increases, although the results are only statistically significant for the two harassment items and for the environmental issues of noise and traffic. It is worth noting from the interaction terms that for three items (vandalism, graffiti and litter) social renters are more likely to identify serious problems as the proportion of owner occupation increases. Although it is not possible to tell why this is the case, it may be that social renters have higher residential expectations once they live in predominantly owner occupied areas, or that social renters are clustered in poorer quality 'ghettos' when located in areas of owner occupation. However, the largest interaction effects are that both private and social rented tenure respondents are far more likely than others to cite racial harassment as a serious problem as the proportion of owner occupation increases. This could be as a result of ethnic differences between renters and owners, with the latter more likely to be white British in origin.

The results for the equitability index indicate that as one moves towards tenure mixing or evenness in an area, the likelihood that anti-social behaviour (i.e. vandalism, crime, graffiti and neighbours) and litter will be serious problems increases, although the effects for the more serious problems of vandalism, graffiti and crime are less than the effects of increasing social renting, and the propensity to cite neighbours as a problem as equitability increases is somewhat ameliorated in social renters compared with owners.

The relative effects of each of the tenure measures within the logistic regression model are illustrated in Table 9, which shows the impact of a 10 percentage point increase in the presence of social renting, owner occupation and of equitability between the tenures on the odds ratio for each item being cited as a serious problem by respondents. It is seen that only equitability has consistent effects, with a 10-point increase in equitability increasing the odds of serious problems by 19 per cent on average for five of the items. Increasing social renting is associated with slightly greater increases in the odds of a serious problem for five items, on average by 25 per cent, but it is also associated with a reduction in the odds of noise and traffic being serious problems. Increasing owner occupation is generally associated with a reduction in the incidence of serious problems (apart from vandalism and

Table 9. Effects of 10-point increase in tenure measures within areas upon incidence of serious problems

Dependent variable (serious)	Odds ratio exp(B)/10		
	% Owner occupation	Equitability index	% Social renting
Vandalism	1.146	1.196	1.418
Graffiti	0.960	1.150	1.257
Crime	1.022	1.196	1.252
Dogs	–	–	1.160
Litter	0.955	1.188	1.175
Neighbours	–	1.219	–
Racial harassment	0.600	–	–
Noise	0.761	–	0.904
Traffic	0.830	–	0.824
Other harassment	0.748	–	–

Note: Derived from the model in Table 8, controlling for age, sex and economic status. Includes both significant and non-significant terms.

crime). A 10-point increase in owner occupation has a small effect on reducing the incidence of graffiti and litter, resulting in an average reduction in the odds of a serious problem of 4 per cent. However, increasing owner occupation by 10 per cent is associated with much larger reductions in the odds of racial or other harassment and environmental issues (noise and traffic) being serious problems, by over 25 per cent. The effect of increasing owner occupation upon the odds of vandalism being a serious problem is less than for increases in mixing (equitability) or social renting.

Neighbourhood Service and Amenity Improvements and Tenure Mix

The paper now examines the responses given to questions about the desire for improvements to nine local services and amenities (leaving out the question about crime and vandalism here as those issues have already been dealt with above). Figure 3 shows

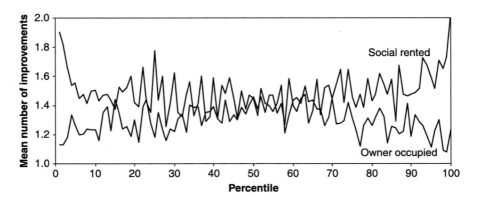

Figure 3. Mean number of desired improvements cited for all households by percentile of proportion of social-rented and owner-occupied tenures (private-rented values not shown)

the mean number of improvements desired by people living in wards within each percentile of social rented and owned housing tenures (private rented not shown for clarity). It can be seen that the number of neighbourhood improvements desired tends to rise with the percentiles of social renting; there is an approximate 1.4-fold increase between the first and last percentiles. The pattern for owner occupation is the opposite of that for social renting, falling by a similar factor, while the change for private renters (graph not shown) is negligible. As with the total number of problems, no striking threshold effects are apparent.

Table 10 shows that there is a much more even pattern of desire for service improvements across places with different tenure mixes than in the case of neighbourhood problems. There are two clear patterns evident in the Table. First, the demand for improvements is most often highest in areas dominated by social rented housing—this is true for seven of the nine items. Second, the lowest demand for improvements is usually in areas of mixed owning and private renting with social renting the smallest tenure—this is true for six of the nine items. Thus, areas where owner occupation and private renting are *both* large tenures perform well in terms of the quality of local services and amenities, echoing the findings reported earlier for the incidence of neighbourhood problems, where this type of area performed second best after areas dominated by owner occupation. Areas where owner occupation is by far the largest tenure (> 70 per cent) appear to offer the best quality of housing and local environment, but are the worst performers in terms of public transport.

The effects upon people of living in contradictory or contrasting circumstances are not as great in relation to service improvements as they are for neighbourhood problems. Table 11 shows that owner occupiers living in areas with high levels of social rented housing cite a desire for improvements to the environment and quality of housing at twice the rate of owners in areas with the highest levels of owner occupation, and at one-and-a-half times the rate in the case of the availability of jobs. Contrasts on the other items are less notable, although owners in areas of high social renting are less likely to identify a need to improve public transport. This last item is reflected in the lower half of the Table in relation to social renters, who are more likely to desire improvements in public transport if

Table 10. Neighbourhood improvements by tenure mix categories

	% Within each tenure mix category desiring improvement				
	Owner dominated	Mixed, more owned	Mixed owned & social rent	Mixed owned & private rent	Social dominated
Housing (amount/quality)	10.5	16.7	19.6	15.9	28.1
Jobs (availability)	11.5	11.9	12.3	7.3	12.2
Amenities / parks	19.4	20.1	23.0	14.3	24.2
Health services	11.9	11.4	11.6	10.9	14.0
Facilities for the young	24.7	27.0	30.5	19.8	33.0
Public transport	22.6	18.6	16.2	18.6	16.6
Quality of environment	11.0	17.5	19.3	16.0	24.0
Schools & colleges	7.2	8.3	9.3	5.6	13.0
Shopping	15.6	16.3	16.0	13.3	19.4
n	(26 388)	(6310)	(4085)	(1317)	(896)

Table 11. Neighbourhood improvements in contrasting circumstances

	A. In high-owner wards (%)[a]	B. In high social renting wards (%)[b]	Ratio B/A (losses)
Owner occupiers			
Housing (amount/quality)	6.5	12.2	1.9
Jobs (availability)	9.0	13.2	1.5
Amenities / Parks	19.7	22.8	1.2
Health Services	12.1	11.6	1.0
Facilities for the Young	23.0	28.9	1.3
Public Transport	22.7	16.9	0.7
Quality of Environment	9.7	20.5	2.1
Schools & Colleges	7.6	10.1	1.3
Shopping	13.7	18.2	1.3
	($n = 6956$)	($n = 3761$)	
Social renters			
Housing (amount/quality)	13.1	26.1	2.0
Jobs (availability)	7.9	12.1	1.5
Amenities / Parks	16.7	23.4	1.4
Health Services	8.6	11.0	1.3
Facilities for the Young	27.0	33.0	1.2
Public Transport	22.3	15.5	0.7
Quality of Environment	6.3	18.0	2.9
Schools & Colleges	2.3	8.4	3.7
Shopping	14.4	16.2	1.1
	($n = 444$)	($n = 3438$)	

Notes: [a] Defined as the top quintile of owner wards, where owner occupation is 86% or more of the housing tenure.
[b] Defined as the top quintile of social renting wards, where social renting is 24% or more of the housing tenure.

they live in areas with the highest levels of owner occupation. However, for all other services and amenities, social renters appear to gain from living in areas of high owner occupation, requiring improvements to services less frequently, with the gains being particularly large in the case of schools and colleges and environmental quality.

Table 12 gives the results of the logistic regression modelling of the desire for neighbourhood improvements. It can be seen that being a social renter increases the odds of wanting housing, health services and youth facilities improved, but reduces the odds that someone wants an improved environment. The desire for improved housing and health services is even more pronounced among private renters, although they are less likely to cite local amenities, youth facilities and environment as requiring improvement than are owners. However, the effects of the proportion of social renting within an area are greater and more common, increasing the odds that six of the nine items are deemed to need improvement, especially local parks, amenities and leisure facilities. Social and private renters are even more likely than owners to desire improved housing as the proportion of social renting within an area increases. Private renters alone are also more likely than owners to desire environmental improvements but less anxious for job improvements as the proportion of social renting rises.

Four items (jobs, local amenities, youth facilities and shopping facilities) are also more likely to be cited as needing improvement as owner occupation increases in an area,

Table 12. Predictors of the desire for neighbourhood improvements (odds ratios)

	Housing	Jobs	Amenities	Health services	Children/youth facilities	Public transport	Environment	Schools / colleges	Shopping
Tenure: Social renter (SR)	**3.038**	*0.955*	*1.057*	**1.788**	**1.213**	–	**0.830**	*1.264*	–
Tenure: Private renter (PR)	**6.055**	*1.117*	**0.715**	**2.153**	**0.738**	–	**0.498**	*0.499*	–
Proportion SR (0–100%)	*0.510*	**9.379**	**15.701**	–	**8.130**	**0.235**	**2.319**	**2.166**	**3.956**
Equitability (0–1)	**6.543**	**4.028**	–	–	–	–	**2.316**	–	–
Proportion OO (0–100%)	–	**16.779**	**7.785**	*1.191*	**3.562**	–	*0.485*	*0.810*	**2.164**
Proportion SR by tenure SR	**4.419**	*0.710*	–	–	–	–	*0.764*	–	–
Proportion SR by tenure PR	**6.872**	**0.106**	–	–	–	–	**3.827**	–	–
Proportion OO by tenure SR	–	–	–	**0.304**	–	–	–	**0.386**	–
Proportion OO by tenure PR	–	–	–	**0.338**	–	–	–	*1.249*	–
Equitability by tenure SR	**0.378**	–	–	–	–	–	–	–	–
Equitability by tenure PR	**0.127**	–	–	–	–	–	–	–	–
Nagelkerke's R^2	0.087	0.023	0.052	0.008	0.049	0.012	0.038	0.065	0.006

Note: Controlling for age, sex and economic status.
*Odds Ratios (exp(B)) in bold are significant, $p \leq 0.01$; in normal type are significant, $p \leq 0.05$; in italic, n.s. (highlighted; consider removing from model). Values for tenure categories are relative to owner occupiers.

Table 13. Effects of 10-point increase in tenure measures within areas upon the demand for neighbourhood improvements

Dependent variable	Odds ratio exp(B)/10		
	% Owner occupation	Equitability index	% Social renting
Housing (amount/quality)	–	1.207	0.935
Jobs (availability)	1.326	1.149	1.251
Amenities / parks	1.228	–	1.317
Health services	1.018	–	–
Facilities for the young	1.135	–	1.233
Public transport	–	–	0.865
Quality of environment	0.930	1.088	1.088
Schools & colleges	0.979	–	1.080
Shopping	1.080	–	1.147

Note: Derived from the model in Table 12, controlling for age, sex and economic status. Includes both significant and non-significant terms.

although to a lesser degree than for increasing social renting for local amenities, youth facilities and shopping facilities (the relationship is reversed in the case of jobs). All renters become less desiring of improved health services, and social renters alone are less concerned about improved schools and colleges as the proportion of owners in an area increases.

Increasingly, equitability between the tenures only has a significant effect upon three of the items, increasing the odds that housing, jobs and the local environment need improvement. There are no instances where increasing equitability reduces the odds that services need improvement overall, although the effects on the desire for improvements to housing are ameliorated for social and private renters as the equitability of tenure increases.

The relative size of impact of the different tenure measures in the logistic regression model is shown in Table 13. A 10-point rise in all three tenure measures increases the odds that improvements are desired for between three and six items. The effect is greatest for social renting, with an average increase in odds of about 19 per cent, than for owner occupation (average 16 per cent increase in odds), and least for equitability (an average 15 per cent increase in the odds). Whereas an increase in social renting reduces the odds of two items (housing and public transport) needing improvement, and owner occupation reduces the odds for two items (environment and schools), equitability does not reduce the odds of improvement for any item.

Conclusions

Returning to the four main research questions, the main messages and implications of the analysis can be summarised. First, with regard to patterns of neighbourhood deficiency, it was found that areas dominated by social rented housing perform the worst both in terms of identified neighbourhood problems and desired improvements to facilities and services. Furthermore, areas where social renting and owner occupation are both sizeable (30–50 per cent each) are the next-worst performers. In contrast, areas with an overwhelming proportion of owner occupied housing have the lowest incidence of neighbourhood problems, but areas with substantial proportions of both owner occupation and private renting also perform reasonably well in terms of neighbourhood problems and perform best in terms of having the lowest desire for improvements to local services and amenities. Thus, the findings show that dominance by owner occupation is not the only tenure structure associated with neighbourhoods of reasonable quality that meet people's needs and expectations.

From the multivariate modelling, it was found that housing tenure mixing, if taken to mean evenness between tenures (or 'balanced communities' in earlier parlance) is associated with an increase in the identification of five out of 10 neighbourhood problems and in the desire for improvements in three out of nine local services and amenities. Tenure mixing is not associated with a reduction in the citation of any neighbourhood deficiencies. Similarly, as the presence of social renting in an area increases, so does the likelihood that residents will identify five out of 10 neighbourhood problems and desire six out of nine improvements to local services and amenities. Where tenure mixing and social renting are similarly related to increases in the identification of neighbourhood problems, the effects of social renting appear to be slightly greater than for mixing/equitability. On the other hand, increases in social renting are also associated with reductions in the identification of noise and traffic as problems, and a decrease in the demand for public transport improvements. Thus, many social housing estates may in fact provide quiet residential environments rather than the disruptive environments that they are often portrayed as. Overall, therefore, three conclusions could be drawn: the level of social renting is the more important factor determining the incidence of problems; 'balanced communities' in tenure terms offer no guarantee that neighbourhood problems will be reduced; and there are some respects in which social renting can offer satisfactory, quiet environments.

In relation to the third research question, it is noted that the examination of residents in contrasting circumstances offers more support for dispersal policies than for dilution policies, since social renters appear to gain a great deal in neighbourhood environment terms from living in areas of high owner occupation, whereas owner occupiers appear to have a lot to lose from living in areas with an above-average proportion of social renting. This is relevant to the issue raised by Galster (2002) as to whether or not there are net social benefits to be had from 'social mixing' if we take into account the impacts upon both high-poverty and low-poverty individuals and communities. Indeed, in the present case, the ratio of losses to owners and renters in contrasting tenure circumstances suggests a potential zero sum gain if both dispersal and dilution policies were pursued simultaneously. A further complication is added by the findings here that as owner occupation in an area increases, social renters are more likely to identify some anti-social behaviour problems (such as vandalism, graffiti, litter and racial harassment) whilst being less likely to desire improvements to health services and schools. Therefore, again, deriving an aggregate measure of the gains from dispersal policies will not be straightforward as different kinds of gains and losses are involved.

Finally, in relation to the fourth research question, the study has not, at least at ward level, identified a critical level of social renting or of owner occupation which either exacerbates or reduces the incidence of neighbourhood deficiencies. Rather, the identification of neighbourhood problems and the desire for neighbourhood improvements appear to rise consistently with an increase in the proportion of social renting and decrease consistently as owner occupation increases. Having said that, it is known that for both social renters and owner occupiers, the identification of problems in areas where social renting makes up around a quarter of the housing market is double or treble that in areas where owner occupation comprises the vast majority of the housing market and social renting is at half this level or less. Whilst not all social renters are disadvantaged, it is worth noting that this finding is similar to Galster's (2005) conclusion from US research that better outcomes are achieved in neighbourhoods where disadvantaged households make up less than 20 per cent of the population.

It is not possible to use the data and analysis to say anything concrete about the operation of neighbourhood effect mechanisms because the study has no measures of social interaction between residents in different tenures. Combining observations from this study on differential impacts on different tenure groups with Galster's (2005) conclusion that "different [neighbourhood effect] mechanisms lead to radically different conclusions regarding desired neighbourhood household mix on either equity or efficiency grounds" (p. 39), it could be argued that 'mixed communities' as a guiding principle for regeneration and urban policy is too crude a mantra, and is not founded upon knowledge of which neighbourhood processes operate in what circumstances, nor on how the positive gains to some people and communities are weighed against the dis-benefits that mixed communities may bring to others, depending on how it is operationalised.

There are several ways in which the present analysis could be extended. First, it must be asked whether the findings would hold true at a lower spatial scale than the ward. There is a strong argument that wards represent the 'locality' within which someone lives, a spatial scale that affects the provision of services and amenities in particular, but that neighbourhoods interpreted as more familiar areas of more regular day-to-day use and social interaction, are somewhat smaller than wards (see Kearns & Parkinson, 2001). However, getting the spatial scale right is difficult; earlier research in the UK concluded that a 'balanced community' or tenure diversity was difficult to operationalise, partly because one had to look at a spatial scale *larger* than any one estate to see the implications of 'balance' (Cole *et al.*, 1997). Nonetheless, it would be worth repeating the analysis here in later research at the smaller spatial scale of the census super output area (a quarter the size of a ward). This would also make it possible to examine further the question of whether there are non-linearities in the relationships between neighbourhood characteristics and social outcomes. The latter would also be aided by using a continuous dependent variable (rather than the dichotomous categorical responses examined here), such as the small area poverty rate and other measures used in the study by Galster *et al.* (2000) of neighbourhood thresholds.

Moreover, some important aspects of neighbourhoods have not been included and assessed for influence here, most importantly the nature of the built environment, design and layout of neighbourhoods; and the location of a neighbourhood within urban space, which could be expected to affect not only neighbourhood problems but also the range and quality of services available. It is difficult to measure these features across the entire UK, but this should be attempted in future research if possible.

Finally, the study has focused on housing tenure mix as the key contextual variable, but neighbourhoods are obviously mixed in other ways which may also influence the quality of the social, service and physical environments. In particular, it would be worth studying similar issues in relation to the social composition of residential neighbourhoods: this should cover income, employment and social class mix on the one hand, and forms of demographic mix (household type and ethnicity) on the other.

Notes

[1] DCLG, Department for Communities and Local Government, formerly the ODPM, Office of the Deputy Prime Minister.
[2] There is also a preference model pertaining to out-migration behaviours (see Galster *et al.*, 2000), but here we are interested in within-neighbourhood behaviours or problems.
[3] The proportions of each tenure within each ward in England exhibit the following ranges: owner occupation, 13–99 per cent; social renting, 0–77 per cent; private renting, 1–72 per cent.

References

Atkinson, R. (2005) *Neighbourhoods and the Impacts of Social Mix: Crime, Tenure Diversification and Assisted Mobility*, CNR Paper 30. Available at www.neighbourhoodcentre.org.uk.
Atkinson, R. & Kintrea, K. (1998) *Reconnecting Excluded Communities: Neighbourhood Impacts of Owner Occupation* (Edinburgh: Scottish Homes).
Atkinson, R. & Kintrea, K. (2000) Owner occupation, social mix and neighbourhood impacts, *Policy and Politics*, 28, pp. 93–108.
Bailey, N., Haworth, A., Manzi, T., Paranagamage, P. & Roberts, R. (2006) *Creating and Sustaining Mixed Income Communities. A Good Practice Guide* (Coventry: Chartered Institute of Housing, Joseph Rowntree Foundation, Housing Corporation and Town and Country Planning Association).
Bates, B., Joy, S., Roden, J., Swales, K., Grove, J. & Oliver, R. (2001) *Housing in England 1999/00* (London: DTLR).
Beekman, T., Lyons, F. & Scott, J. (2001) *Improving the Understanding of the Influence of Owner Occupiers in Mixed Tenure Neighbourhoods*. Report 89 (Edinburgh: Scottish Homes).
Berube, A. (2005) *Mixed Communities in England: A US Perspective on Evidence and Policy Proposals* (York: Joseph Rowntree Foundation).
Briggs, X. (1998) Brown kids in white suburbs: housing mobility and the many faces of social capital, *Housing Policy Debate*, 9, pp. 177–221.
Brophy, P. & Smith, R. (1997) Mixed-income housing: factors for success, *Cityscape*, 3(2), pp. 3–31.
Cole, I., Gidley, G., Ritchie, C., Simpson, D. & Wishart, B. (1997) *Creating Communities or Welfare Housing? A Study of New Housing Association Developments in Yorkshire/Humberside* (Coventry: Chartered Institute of Housing).
Crook, T., Currie, J., Jackson, A., Monk, S., Rowley, S., Smith, K. & Whitehead, C. (2002) *Planning Gain and Affordable Housing: Making it Count* (York: York Publishing Services).
Dean, J. & Hastings, A. (2000) *Challenging Images: Housing Estates, Stigma and Regeneration* (Bristol: The Policy Press).
DCLG (Department of Communities and Local Government) (2006) The components of a sustainable community. Available at http://www.communities.gov.uk/index.asp?id=1139866.
DoE (Department of the Environment) (1991) *New Life for Local Authority Estates: Guidance for Local Authorities on Estate Action and Housing Action Trusts and Links with Related Programmes* (London: DoE).
DoE (1995) *Our Future Homes: Opportunities, Choices, Responsibilities. The Government's Housing Policies for England and Wales* (London: The Stationery Office).
Friedrichs, J. & Blasius, J. (2003) Social norms in distressed neighbourhoods: testing the Wilson hypothesis, *Housing Studies*, 18, pp. 807–826.
Friedrichs, J., Galster, G. & Musterd, S. (2003) Neighbourhood effects on social opportunities: the European and American research and policy context, *Housing Studies*, 18, pp. 797–806.
Galster, G. (2000) Neighbourhood mix, social opportunities, and the policy challenges of an increasingly diverse Amsterdam, Wibaut Lecture (Amsterdam: Department of Geography and Planning, University of Amsterdam).
Galster, G. (2002) An economic efficiency analysis of deconcentrating poverty populations, *Journal of Housing Economics*, 11, pp. 303–329.
Galster, G. (2003) Investigating behavioural impacts of poor neighbourhoods: towards new data and analytic strategies, *Housing Studies*, 18, pp. 893–914.
Galster, G. (2005) Neighbourhood mix, social opportunities, and the policy challenges of an increasingly diverse Amsterdam, Wibaut Lecture (Amsterdam: Department of Geography and Planning, University of Amsterdam).

Galster, G., Quercia, R. & Cortes, A. (2000) Identifying neighborhood thresholds: an empirical exploration, *Housing Policy Debate*, 11, pp. 701–732.

Galster, G. & Zobel, A. (1998) Will dispersed housing programmes reduce social problems in the US?, *Housing Studies*, 13, pp. 605–622.

Gilchrist, A. (2004) *The Well-Connected Community: A Networking Approach to Community Development* (Bristol: The Policy Press).

Hiscock, R. (2002) Mixing tenures: is it good for social wellbeing. Paper presented to the European Network for Housing Research conference, Vienna, 1–5 July (Stockholm: Family Medicine Stockholm Karolinska Institutet).

Jupp, B. (1999) *Living Together. Community Life on Mixed Tenure Estates* (London: Demos).

Kearns, A. (2002) Response: from residential disadvantage to opportunity? Reflections on British and European policy and research, *Housing Studies*, 17, pp. 145–150.

Kearns, A. (2003) Social capital, regeneration and urban policy, in: R. Imrie & M. Raco (Eds) *Urban Renaissance? New Labour, Community and Urban Policy* (Bristol: The Policy Press).

Kearns, A. & Parkinson, M. (2001) The significance of neighbourhood, *Urban Studies*, 38, pp. 2103–2110.

Kleinhans, R. (2004) Social implications of housing diversification in urban renewal: a review of recent literature, *Journal of Housing and the Built Environment*, 19, pp. 367–390.

Kleit, R. G. (2001) The role of neighbourhood social networks in scattered-site public housing residents" search for jobs, *Housing Policy Debate*, 12(3), pp. 541–573.

Lauglo, J. (2000) Social capital trumping class and cultural capital? Engagement with school among immigrant youth, in: S. Baron, J. Field & T. Schuller (Eds) *Social Capital: Critical Perspectives*, pp. 142–167 (Oxford: Oxford University Press).

Lawless, P. (2003) *New Deal for Communities. The National Evaluation. Annual Report 2002/3* (London: Neighbourhood Renewal Unit).

Leventhal, T. & Brooks-Gunn, J. (2003) Moving to opportunity: an experimental study of neighbourhood effects on health, *American Journal of Public Health*, 93, pp. 1576–1582.

Ludwig, J., Hirschfield, P. & Duncan, G. (2001) Urban poverty and juvenile crime: evidence from a randomized housing-mobility experiment, *Quarterly Journal of Economics*, 116, pp. 665–679.

Lupton, R. (2003) *Poverty Street: The Dynamics of Neighbourhood Decline and Renewal* (Bristol: The Policy Press).

Magurran, E. (1988) *Ecological Diversity and its Measurement* (Princeton, NJ: Princeton University Press).

Manski, C. F. (2000) Economic analysis of social interactions, *Journal of Economic Perspectives*, 14(3), pp. 115–136.

Meen, G., Gibb, K., Goody, J., McGrath, T. & Mackinnon, J. (2005) *Economic Segregation in England: Causes, Consequences and Policy* (Bristol: The Policy Press).

Musterd, S. & Andersson, R. (2005) Housing mix, social mix, and social opportunities, *Urban Affairs Review*, 40, pp. 761–790.

ODPM (Office of the Deputy Prime Minister) (2003) *English House Condition Survey 2001* (London: ODPM).

ODPM (2004) *Survey of English Housing Sub-Regional Results* (London: ODPM).

ODPM (2005) *Sustainable Communities: Building for the Future* (London: ODPM).

Orr, L., Feins, J. D., Jacob, R., Beecroft, E., Sanbonmatsu, L., Katz, L. F., Liebman, J. B. & Kling, J. R. (2003) *Moving to Opportunity Interim Impacts Evaluation* (Washington DC: US Department of Housing and Urban Development).

Page, D. (1993) *Building For Communities: A Study of New Housing Association Developments* (York: Joseph Rowntree Foundation).

Page, D. & Boughton, R. (1997) *Mixed Tenure Housing Estates. A Study Undertaken for Notting Hill* (London: Notting Hill Housing Association).

Parkes, A., Kearns, A. & Atkinson, R. (2002) What makes people dissatisfied with their neighbourhoods?, *Urban Studies*, 39, pp. 2413–2438.

Popkin, S., Katz, B., Cunningham, M. K., Brown, K. D. & Gustafson, M. A. T. (2004) *A Decade of HOPE VI: Research Findings and Policy Challenges* (Washington DC: Urban Institute).

Putnam, R. (2001) Social capital: measurement and consequences, *ISUMA Canadian Journal of Policy Research*, 2, pp. 41–52.

Rosenbaum, J. (1995) Changing the geography of opportunity by expanding residential choice: lessons from the Gatreaux Program, *Housing Policy Debate*, 6, pp. 231–269.

Social Exclusion Unit (1998) *Bringing Britain Together: A National Strategy for Neighbourhood Renewal.* Cmd 4045 (London: Social Exclusion Unit).
Social Exclusion Unit (2000) *National Strategy for Neighbourhood Renewal: A Framework for Consultation* (London: Cabinet Office).
Social Exclusion Unit (2001) *A New Commitment to Neighbourhood Renewal: National Strategy Action Plan* (London: Cabinet Office).
Tunstall, R. & Fenton, A. (2006) *In the Mix. A Review of Mixed Income, Mixed Tenure and Mixed Communities* (London: English Partnerships, Joseph Rowntree Foundation and Housing Corporation).
Urban Task Force (1999) *Towards an Urban Renaissance. Final Report of the Urban Task Force Chaired by Lord Rogers of Riverside* (London: DETR).
Wilkinson, R. (1996) *Unhealthy Societies: The Afflictions of Inequality* (London: Routledge).
Woolcock, M. (2001) The place of social capital in understanding social and economic outcomes, *ISUMA Canadian Journal of Policy Research*, 2, pp. 11–17.

Homeownership, Poverty and Educational Achievement: School Effects as Neighbourhood Effects

GLEN BRAMLEY & NOAH KOFI KARLEY

Introduction

Deprived neighbourhoods are characterised by the clustering of social problems—crime, joblessness, poor health—and it is clear that this applies also to the under-achievement of children at school, and to popular perceptions of school quality and performance in such areas. At the same time, concentrations of poor households facing material and other deprivations are clearly bound up with the operation of the housing market and tenure systems. In most countries, such neighbourhoods comprise predominantly rented housing, and in Britain they are increasingly associated with social rented housing (Hills, 2007).

If the housing system is substantially responsible for socio-economic segregation and polarisation of neighbourhoods, could different housing policies produce more benign effects? If the effects of housing outcomes spill over into other areas of social policy, such as education, and threaten the achievement of societal goals, the case for different approaches may be strengthened. Governments in the UK and elsewhere have shown increased interest in promoting wider homeownership, for a variety of reasons including the spread of asset-holding and the fostering of neighbourhood social capital. Could better educational performance be an additional rationale for such policies?

This paper examines the proposition that homeownership improves educational attainment. It is likely that the children of homeowners themselves tend on average to do better in school, but it is an open question how far homeownership adds anything to the effect of associated characteristics such as income and occupation of parents. Beyond this, homeownership may have neighbourhood effects, on culture, behaviour and expectations, which have wider effects on school attainment. What is less clear is how far these effects operate in the residential neighbourhood and how far within the school itself, what the relevant scale of neighbourhood is, and again how far it is homeownership rather than the associated characteristics which matter.

The paper presents the results of analyses of school attainment outcomes in England and Scotland, designed to test these propositions while shedding broader light on the drivers of school performance. As a prelude to that analysis, relevant literature is reviewed by examining the way school and other factors affect educational attainment and the specific role of housing tenure. In the third section the methodology adopted for modelling attainment is then discussed, explaining the rationale of the approach and the data sources and case study areas employed. The next section describes the modelling results for England, which build on earlier work. In particular it is shown how homeownership and other related individual, neighbourhood or school-level factors impact when introduced into the model. It goes on to consider possible interactions with these other variables, the relative roles of clustering at school versus neighbourhood levels, non-linearities and the possible impact of school-level ownership on non-owners' children. The following section reports broadly comparable results for Scotland, including an examination of the impact of changes in neighbourhood tenure mix. The final section draws conclusions based on this evidence and discusses policy implications, while pointing the way to further research questions and possibilities.

Review of Factors Affecting Educational Attainment

Both school and non-school factors influence children's educational attainment. School factors include the structural characteristics and human, physical and financial resources of schools as institutions, as well as more qualitative attributes such 'ethos' and 'management'. Non-school factors are those that relate especially to the background of the child, such as the child's personal character and innate abilities, and the socio-economic and educational background of parents, but also wider environmental and cultural factors. Each of these dimensions represents an input towards educational attainment and is considered important in its own right.

Some researchers (e.g. Reynolds *et al.*, 1996; Thomas & Mortimer, 1996) suggest that non-school factors are a more important source of variation in educational attainment than differences in the quality of education received. Nevertheless, the paper begins with a brief discussion of school factors.

School Factors

School resources include quantity and quality of teaching, facilities and management, which may be more or less well-represented by expenditure measures. The debate on effects of school resources on attainment is on-going. In the mid-1980s Hanushek (1986) concluded that there is no strong and consistent relationship between school resources and performance. However, after reanalyses of the same sample, Hedges *et al.* (1994) showed a consistent and positive relationship between resources and educational attainment. A recent study by Bramley *et al.* (2005) also shows positive relationships between educational spending per pupil and attainment level at pupil and school levels in England.

The role that school management plays towards overall school progress and educational attainment is often deemed as vital. The inspection agency Ofsted (2001) suggests that deprived socio-economic context does not in itself determine school failure, and that an important (sometimes dominant) explanation for poor quality of schools in disadvantaged areas has been internal problems, mainly accounted for by poor management and professional practice. This naturally reflects the orientation of an inspectorial service, but also builds on earlier work such as Rutter (1979) which pointed to the importance of leadership, ethos and organisation. However, while poor school management could pose a potential constraint to educational attainment, deprivation and lack of finance can make schools harder to manage. Even where the essentially subjective ratings of the inspection service are included in the analysis, these may not contribute greatly to the explanation (Bramley & Evans, 2002).

Non-school Factors

Associations between non-school factors and low levels of educational attainment have long been recognised in the sociological and education literature. Sparkes & Glennerster (2002) provide a list of key non-school factors that influence educational attainment: pupils' characteristics such as prior attainment and gender; socio-economic position of parents such as employment and housing condition; parents' educational attainment; family structure; ethnicity; and other parental interest. Thomas & Smees (1997) established that among non-school factors, prior attainment explains the greatest proportion of variance in educational attainment at pupil level and indicated a high correlation between socio-economic variables and prior attainment.

It has long been known that social class, and associated factors such as parental educational background, are important factors in affecting educational attainment. Over time, the causation runs both ways, as better educational attainment feeds through to improve the occupational outcomes and class position of later generations. There is also of course a strong association between tenure and socio-economic class.[1] This suggests that changing the tenure mix of neighbourhoods and schools is likely to be associated with better attainment outcomes in those schools. Whether this is more than a simple mix effect, and whether there are more virtuous spillover effects in neighbourhoods and schools, to the benefit of children from poorer and lower socio-economic backgrounds, is a more open question.

Townsend's definition of poverty as to "the lack of resources to obtain access to conditions of life that allows people to participate as members of society" (1979, p. 915). Parsons (1999) has revealed that childhood poverty and educational experiences are very powerful influences on an individual's life course. Poverty is in itself a barrier to equal educational opportunity. A hungry or malnourished child is unlikely to be good at concentrating on work at school; limited finances may mean parents may not be able to afford the toys, books, sports equipment, home computers and other learning resources that can aid success; and children from poor backgrounds may not be able to afford to pay to attend major trips and other enrichment activities (Middleton & Asworth, 1997). Psycho-social effects of poverty may be even more significant (see below).

Much research provides evidence on the effect of poverty on education attainment and shows that concentrated poverty tends to aggravate poor performance. Clark *et al.* (1999), Gewirtz (1998) and Ofsted (2000) have shown that concentrated poverty has an impact on what schools do, as well as directly on what pupils achieve. The Social Exclusion Unit (SEU, 1998) found that five times as many secondary schools in 'worst neighbourhoods' had serious weaknesses than was typically the case, and children drawn from poorer family origins were more likely to have been in the lowest quartile of the educational tests compared to wider counterparts. Evidence from Glennerster (2002) shows from a study in England that, at Key Stage 3 (age 14), the median for schools with more than 40 per cent Free School Meals (FSM) (the most common measure of poverty for school pupils), was that no pupil achieved the expected performance level in English, compared with 83 per cent in schools with less than 5 per cent FSM. West *et al.* (2001) argue that poverty was the best single predictor of school performance. Bramley *et al.* (2005, ch. 3) showed that key attainment in 2001/02 increased from the most deprived wards of residence through to most prosperous wards. Yet these statistical relationships do not necessarily reveal the dynamics of how these factors actually operate in practice (Farrington, 1997).

The links between poverty and the likelihood of school failure may derive from the psychological and emotional outcomes of poverty and its effect on domestic and social lives. The level of a child's emotional well-being could affect interest in learning; for example, a charged emotional environment may cause children to be anxious, traumatised, unhappy, jealous or angry. Beresford *et al.* (1999) explored the way poverty generates psychological pressures and stresses, which affect the quality of relationships, and reveals how financial pressure contributes to the social isolation of families and curtails their participation in community activities. Middleton (1994) also gave insights into how social pressures resulting from poverty impact upon children's ability to concentrate upon school. In a recent research, Lupton (2004) described how pupils from deprived backgrounds often have severely disturbed behaviour and on many occasions are aggressive towards other pupils and staff, finding it difficult to concentrate or get through the school day on a regular basis. This picture is strongly supported by a recent qualitative study of children on the margins of school exclusion by Hilton (2005).

Effect of Exclusion

It is clear that the characteristics of a social environment in which one lived as a child have lifelong effects on behaviour and ability (Hobcraft, 1999, 2000). Hobcraft established that educational failure is strongly associated with the process of social exclusion from interaction in community networks. Lack of access to such networks and activities can lead to children lacking the vital capabilities that become manifest in cognitive development and educational achievement.

Some research highlights the link between access to finance and educational attainment (Koba & Paxton, 2002). The consequence of financial exclusion includes decreased security and little or no access to mainstream credit. A family experiencing financial difficulties may face a charged emotional environment at home, which could affect children. Groups at risk of financial exclusion are heavily concentrated in communities with high levels of overall deprivation, which in Britain tend increasingly to be associated with social renting.

Role of Housing Tenure

One obvious condition to satisfy to avoid social exclusion is a place to live. However, the terms on which housing is occupied may have deeper effects. Homeownership is, for example, associated with financial inclusion because of the implied financial stake in the occupied residence (Haurin et al., 2002). Most aspire to be homeowners because of perceived benefits, including more choice, better investment opportunities and greater ability to borrow against future income (Whitehead, 1979). Several recent studies, particularly in the US (Aaronson, 2000; Boehm & Schlottman, 1999; Green & White, 1997; Harkness & Newman, 2001), have also found that homeownership has positive effects on children's educational attainment and development. In a comprehensive review, Dietz & Haurin (2003) found "solid studies that report positive direct and indirect effects of homeownership on child outcomes" (p. 439), while warning of the analytical pitfalls associated with omitted variables and sample selection biases.

Galster (1987) finds different standards of home maintenance and repairs between owner occupants and absentee owners, which could affect children's health, cognitive and school development differently. A recent study by Harkness & Newman (2002) arrived at a similar conclusion. Green & White (1997) and Boehm & Schlottmann (1999) cited Do it Yourself home repairs, negotiation with plumbers, and seeking refinance as examples of the skills children of homeowners could potentially learn from parents. Aronson (2000) in particular emphasised the lower rate of mobility associated with homeownership, and this is also relevant to neighbourhood effects. Haurin et al. (2002) underlined that the financial stake in the property/neighbourhood implies a greater motivation to regulate the behaviour of one's own children and, insofar as this is possible, other children. A more general hypothesis might be that families seeking and attaining homeownership have a greater and more optimistic future orientation, associated with a greater interest in and commitment to investing in human capital. As Dietz & Haurin (2003, p. 431) stated, "personal responsibility and a willingness to invest" may be key to both homeownership and good parenting. However, if this reflects a predisposition, rather than something which results from or is reinforced by homeownership, then there is a potential case of bias associated with unmeasured or selection effects.

It is also argued that homeownership helps to build 'social capital' in a neighbourhood. DiPasquale & Glaeser (1999) argued that homeownership is predicted in theory (derived from human capital theory) to be positively associated with social capital, particularly because of its lower mobility rate. They also found that US and German empirical evidence on group memberships supports this and other predictions of the theory.

They found a particularly strong link between homeownership and social capital measures (group affiliations) linked to education.

The major alternative tenure in the UK is social renting. In a recent comprehensive review Bramley & Evans (2002) cite evidence from Hobcraft (2002) and Sigle-Rushton (2004) that growing up in social housing has been increasingly associated with adverse outcomes in later life, including having no qualifications, low earnings or unemployment.

This discussion suggests that there are reasons and evidence to expect homeownership to be associated with better educational outcomes. This would be first and foremost an individual household effect, but it may have a neighbourhood/community dimension to it, following the 'social capital' argument. Linking back to the discussion of school factors, there may also be a collective dimension to this associated with the school as an institution. A greater share of homeownership in a school's pupil intake may assist in the creation of a supportive ethos for learning.

At the same time, the characterisation of owner occupation here has placed some emphasis on financial advantages and inclusion. This is open to the counter-argument that what is really being measured is income and wealth, and that this is the common underlying driver of both homeownership and educational performance. Ultimately, whether there is a tenure effect that is partially independent of the income/wealth effect is a matter for empirical testing. There are limitations in the data available for fully separating these effects, but some of the studies mentioned above do make this separation. Further observations can be made that the income profile of owner occupation in Britain today is increasingly diverse (Burrows & Wilcox, 2000), and that the background attributes which affect education are clearly not just about income, for example, the role of parental educational level.

The most interesting policy question is whether households with relatively poor or middling economic circumstances would benefit from more opportunities to enter owner occupation, and whether their children would thereby achieve more at school. Homeownership is a potential source of assets, a growing focus for social policy, and this together with its other attributes could help reduce the poverty risk and benefit children's development, particularly their educational performance. Some have suggested that programmes that help families become homeowners might better serve to improve children's educational attainment and other outcomes than certain other programmes, for example, those involving relocation (Harkness & Newman, 2002).

Neighbourhood Effects

From the point of view of social capital accumulation, homeownership may impact on children's educational attainment through benefits derived from neighbourhoods of homeowners. Harkness & Newman (2002) argued that these benefits manifest in three main ways: directly through parenting practices, physical environment, residential stability and wealth; indirectly through positive neighbourhood externalities via its effect on physical and/or social capital; and interactively through interplay of factors that result from the direct and indirect effects mentioned earlier. Because homeowners normally live in the same dwelling/location longer than those renting, social networks among homeowning families in a neighbourhood are likely to be more stable than that of those renting. Arguably, greater stability would help strengthen the neighbourhood's social network, and a stronger network enables a variety of positive social outcomes, including participation in local collective organisations such as parent teacher associations (PTAs), that could lead to progress in children's education. This overlaps with the 'social capital' argument cited above (DiPasquale & Glaeser, 1999).

Stronger local social networks may also counter negative neighbourhood effects, for example, crime, vandalism, drug abuse and other anti-social behaviour, through informal mechanisms of social control, peer group effects and alternative role models. In an influential set of studies, Morenoff *et al.* (1999) posited that greater neighbourhood stability promotes greater 'collective efficacy' of communities in resisting criminal and anti-social behaviour patterns by the young. This occurs because children staying longer in a neighbourhood tend to be well known by adults in the area, which could in effect make the children more disciplined and well behaved. This can also be linked to the argument of Haurin *et al.* (2002) that having a financial stake will motivate stronger efforts at such control.

If the rate of homeownership is higher, it would be expected that the neighbourhood's social network would be stronger and the outcome would be a positive effect, although that would depend on a variety of factors such as length of time in the area, age etc. (for rather mixed evidence, see Atkinson & Kintrea, 2001, but also Bramley & Morgan, 2003). This literature distinguishes 'strong' and 'weak' social ties; while homeownership, or mixed tenure, may promote weak ties more than strong ones, these may still be relevant to collective efficacy.

Neighbourhood image can also affect children's educational attainment. Hawarth (2002) demonstrated that living in a stigmatised neighbourhood can engender low esteem. Educational attainment in such areas is often low. For example, in a study of social exclusion and neighbourhoods in England, Lupton (2004) showed that attainment at school is low in stigmatised areas (see also Gibson & Asthana, 1998). Stigmatised neighbourhoods in Britain tend to be associated with social rented housing, and a broader tenure mix may help to lessen stigma.

Schools are associated with neighbourhoods. Most of the British, and especially the Scottish, education system is based on the concept of schools serving a local community with a defined catchment area. Alternative principles, entailing either selection, specialisation, religious affiliation or parental choice, compete with this concept, particularly in England and at secondary level. Whatever the formal policy, processes of self-selection (including the choice to opt out and go private) may operate to produce the result that schools are not a perfect mirror of their catchment areas; they may be more or less polarised in socio-economic or ethnic terms (Burgess & Wilson, 2004). For this reason, it is worth investigating the effects of different clustering of background characteristics at school level, as a distinct arena for the operation of collective processes affecting attainment.

The central theme of educational attainment literature is that the main problem pertains to poverty and exclusion, but also that some school factors play a part. Given the attributes of homeownership, it can arguably help education attainment of poorer areas and people in at least two ways. First, more households could become owner occupiers, given the right opportunities, and this would (over time) influence their attitudes, behaviour, stability and security so that their children would be more likely to succeed. Second, more mixing of tenures, with non-owner occupiers in previously poor areas, should influence neighbourhood peer group values/behaviour and within-school ethos, process and expectations so that attainment is improved for both owner occupiers' children and other children.

Modelling School Attainment

Background to Modelling Attainment

There has been extensive research that seeks to use statistical modelling to unpick the determinants of school effectiveness and school outcomes, in the UK, US and elsewhere. This body of research is developing rapidly as better data become available and policy interest intensifies. A useful recent review of this literature is provided by Dolton & Vignoles (2000). They found that much of the research is inadequate in terms of theoretical background, over-aggregation of data, and not using the most appropriate statistical techniques, although some recent studies are better. These authors argue for the commissioning of substantial further research with a longitudinal element linking pupil level records of attainment and background, school/class level resource measurement, and area level background. This study attempts to follow this guidance, within the limits of data and time resources. It builds on previous work by one of the present authors (Bramley, 1989; Bramley & Wyatt, 1998; Bramley & Evans, 2002), while also reflecting insights from other recent UK work (Burgess *et al.*, 2001; Bynner *et al.*, 1997; Bynner & Steedman, 1995; Goldstein, 1995; Goldstein & Sammons, 1997; Yang *et al.*, 1997).

The conceptual framework adopted, implicitly or explicitly, in most of this work is that of 'educational production functions'. This derives from micro-economic theory, originally developed to analyse firms and industries but subsequently extended into other areas including households and public services, which seeks to explain outputs as a function of the quantities of various inputs applied. In the education context, the outputs of greatest interest are the attainment levels achieved by pupils, which would more generally be termed 'outcomes'. Schools may be conceived as firms or plants, but this approach has always recognised that the range of inputs is broader than in the industrial context, including critically the 'quasi-inputs' supplied by households in the form of varying degrees and types of support to children in the educational process. This level of support has been shown by much previous research to be strongly related to such factors as poverty/affluence, parental educational level, family type and size, housing circumstances etc. Children vary in their innate abilities or specific learning difficulties, and may also be affected by cultural differences that may be related to ethnicity, class, or neighbourhood peer group effects.

The production function approach draws attention to issues of the functional form of relationships. In particular, key inputs may be subject to increasing or decreasing returns, implying a need to consider non-linear or interactive relationships; the study here tests for non-linearity in some key relationships, including those relating to school-level concentrations of poverty, school resources and school size. Non-linearity with respect to social composition of schools may be potentially significant in policy terms, because it implies that changing the distribution of pupils with different backgrounds between schools may have a net effect on the average level of attainment (Galster, 2002).

Attainment at one level will be strongly conditioned by prior experiences and attainment earlier in the school or pre-school career of the pupils involved. Allowing for prior attainment can be seen as in part controlling for innate ability. This study uses longitudinal relationships with prior outcomes where available (when modelling secondary attainment in England and 'Higher' attainment in Scotland), but otherwise relies mainly on the indirect approach.

Much earlier research focused on quite aggregated data, for example, for local authorities or schools. However, this is open to the criticism of 'ecological fallacy', whereby an aggregate correlation may not actually represent a direct influence at the individual level. Some of the relationships of interest are clearly individual, for example, from specified learning difficulties or language background to learning outcomes. However, other relationships apply at a higher level of aggregation, for example, the influence of concentrations of poverty within schools or neighbourhoods on outcomes. Ideally, a modelling strategy should be followed which enables both types of influence to be separately identified. The general term for such a strategy is 'multi-level modelling' (Goldstein, 1995; Hepple & Rees, 1998; Sniders & Bosker, 1999). This study adopts this strategy to some degree, although it does not follow its full ramifications.

Structure of Models

Specifically, the study models individual pupil outcomes in England at primary age 11 (in England) and secondary age 15–16 (both England and Scotland) as a function of the following classes of factor:

(a) Individual pupil attributes, such as gender, ethnicity, language, learning difficulty (assessed as having Special Educational Needs (SEN)) and poverty (proxied by Free School Meals eligibility (FSM)).
(b) Structural characteristics of schools attended, such as size, occupancy, age range, denominational status, special classes.
(c) Spending resources of schools.
(d) The concentration of pupils with particular attributes in each school (i.e. aggregated average scores of variables from (a) above, or (e) below).
(e) Socio-demographic attributes of the neighbourhoods in which pupils live.

The variables may also be classified in terms of 'levels', at each of which there are different numbers of units in the English sample:

1. Individual pupil (or household) level ((a) above) ($n = 20\,495$ primary cohort or 16 626 secondary cohort).
2. School level ((b), (c) and (d) above) ($n = 677$ primary schools or 232 secondary schools).
3. Micro-neighbourhood scale of Census Output Area (COA), typically with populations of $c.100$ households ($n = 6052$).
4. Larger neighbourhood scale of Ward, typically with $c.2500$ households ($n = 229$).

Socio-demographic variables of type (e) above are derived from the 2001 Census and may be represented at either level 3 (COA) or level 4 (Ward). However, specific poverty/deprivation indicators from the Index of Multiple Deprivation (IMD) are only available at the larger Ward scale, although the pupil poverty measure (FSM), available at levels 1 and 2, is related through its eligibility rules to the IMD low-income measure. Homeownership rate is available at levels 3 or 4, and can be aggregated from level 3 to level 2, but is not available as an individual attribute. Level 1 nests within level 2; level 1 also nests within level 3 which nests within level 4.

The models are multi-level in the sense that they combine data from the individual level with data from two distinct but overlapping higher levels, the school and the neighbourhood, and they permit the separate identification of relationships operating at these different levels. This is more clearly so in relation to the school level, where aggregated individual characteristics are included alongside their individual-level effects. With regard to the neighbourhood variables, these combine the influence of these factors both at individual and area level (the pupil datasets do not identify these attribute values for individual pupils' families, other than poverty and ethnicity). However, there is some choice about the geographical level of neighbourhood which is used (levels 3 vs. 4 above). In formal terms, the models are hierarchical random-effects models, an appropriate choice given the authors' interest in group-level effects (Snijders & Bosker, 1999, p. 43). The option of including Local Education Authority-level dummy variables (fixed effects) was considered but rejected, but these would have disguised the influence of factors such as expenditure which vary significantly between local authorities (and the number of authorities at this level would be small, only five in the English sample).

It is recognised that certain variables are endogenous; this applies specifically to school expenditure/resources, which are determined by funding formulae that reflect pupil and school characteristics which are in the model. An Instrumental Variables approach is adopted in a limited way to the treatment of the expenditure variable, noting that this is a school-level variable modelled at this higher level. It can be argued that other school-level social composition variables are also endogenous, as an outcome of the selection processes affecting which school pupils attend. This perspective is reflected in the final models reported, which also extend this approach to the school-level FSM measure. Variables capturing these characteristics enter the models as predicted values.

As discussed above, previous literature testifies to the important influence of the socio-economic characteristics of pupils' backgrounds, and provides some pointers to particular aspects of this that may be more important. For example, it suggests that the educational level (qualifications) of parents may be important. However, this particular variable poses the problem of possible spurious correlation (reverse causation), in cross-sectional models, because low attainment areas will tend to reproduce low-qualified populations.

There is also a further general problem, that these socio-economic background variables may be quite strongly correlated with one another, particularly at the aggregated level of schools or neighbourhoods. This multicollinearity problem reduces the statistical significance of particular coefficients and can lead to unstable results. Typical solutions to this problem involve either selecting a small number of variables from this larger set, or creating composite variables using principal components or factor analyses. For the main results reported here the study relies on the first of these strategies, retaining in the model the variable of particular interest (owner occupation) and a few other measures believed, on the basis of previous research, to be important in their own right. A variant approach is also tested based on a factor analysis of school-level social variables. However, the problem remains a real source of uncertainty about the results, because it is clear that homeownership is closely correlated with a group of other variables relating to income. The view that the model results for homeownership may reflect mainly an income effect cannot be refuted, although an attempt has been made to tease out any additional effect of variations in ownership allowing for the general effect of ownership-and-income together.

Datasets which link individual pupil attainment to individual social attributes may better enable the influence of particular factors to be separated. One such dataset, made available to the authors during this research, is the Scottish School Leavers Survey (SSLS). Analysis of these data reported in Bramley & Karley (2005) showed that individual owner occupation tenure was strongly associated with better secondary school attainment and other outcomes; the effect was nearly as large as the most important parental attribute, qualifications. This finding reinforced the view here that it was reasonable to hypothesise and test for an independent effect of homeownership in attainment modelling. However, this analysis is not discussed further in this paper because the SSLS source does not enable the analysis to reflect school and neighbourhood level effects.

Attainment Measures

At both primary and secondary level in England two different measures of attainment are modelled: the average score per pupil in the cohort, and the binary variable of achieving the most widely used thresholds at two levels (Level 4 in the three main tests at Key Stage 2; achieving five or more grades A–C at General Certificate of Secondary Education (GCSE) level). In Scotland, the data are roughly comparable to the 'score' measures at secondary level in England (the Scottish 'Standard Grade' and 'Higher Grade' examinations are roughly equivalent to GCSE and AS levels in England). For the score indicators, which are continuous, ordinary least squares linear regression is used. For the binary level indicators, the study uses logistic regression fitted using maximum likelihood.

Prior attainment for the same individual pupils at an earlier key stage is available in some cases—for secondary pupils in England, referring back to their attainment at the end of primary education five years earlier; and for Scottish pupils taking 'Highers', referring back to their Standard Grade attainment one year earlier. The attainment data are contained within general pupil databases which integrate individual attributes such as free meals, ethnicity and special needs with school attributes and home postcodes.

When extending this research to Scotland, the dataset provided included Datazone codes (Datazones are a new smaller area Census geography, with populations in the range 500–1000). Both this linkage and the linkage to school codes were subject to 'record-swapping' procedures which introduced some random noise into the dataset.

Areas Studied

The English pupil dataset is derived from a previous project (Bramley *et al.*, 2005), concerned with the drivers of school attainment variations, in particular the roles of deprivation and education expenditure. The previous study focused on five areas in England: Bradford, the London Borough of Brent, East Kent, Liverpool and Nottingham. This selection is somewhat biased towards relatively deprived localities, but taken as a whole it represents a range of regions, urban and rural conditions, deprivation profiles and patterns of educational provision. In Scotland, pupil data have been analysed for three large local authorities: Edinburgh, Fife and North Lanarkshire.

Data were obtained from the local authorities on school budgets and spending (for appropriate years), and these were linked to data from the first available set of the National Pupil Database (NPD). Other data were derived from the 1991 and 2001 Censuses, Neighbourhood Statistics and IMD 2000 sources, chiefly at Ward level.

Results for England

Attainment Model for Pupils in England

The attainment models for English pupils reported here are a development of Bramley *et al.* (2005, chapter 3). The models are built up sequentially by the introduction of different classes of variable at different levels. Model performance is summarised in Table 1, which compares the adjusted r-squared statistics. Individual-level variables are introduced first and tend to have the strongest effects in the models; this applies particularly to those relating to special needs (SEN Stage), poverty (FSM) and language (English not spoken at home). At secondary level this category also includes pupils' prior educational attainment, accounting for the higher overall r-squared. At the next stage structural school characteristics like size, special classes and spending are introduced, adding a modest additional level of explanation.

Social Effects at Different Levels

The primary interest here is the influence of 'social' variables, including homeownership, and the level at which they are included. Moving down the Table, the impact of adding a group of social characteristics (e.g. health, qualifications, car ownership, unemployment)[2] is compared to the model with the impact of adding homeownership alone, and then the combination of these characteristics and ownership. Finally, the effect is shown of including poverty at school level as well. Going across the Table, the performance is compared when variables representing social characteristics and homeownership are included at school, ward or COA levels.

Reading down Table 1 suggests that homeownership on its own could account for or proxy quite a lot, but not all, of the social effects. Homeownership adds a little to the explanatory power, over and above that offered by the other social variables, except in the

Table 1. Summary comparison of models including different combinations of variables at different levels (adjusted r-squared)

Variables included	Level of social variables		
	School level	Ward level	COA level
Primary			
Indiv pupil only	0.317		
Indiv & school structure	0.330		
Social characteristics	0.349	0.347	0.348
Homeownership	0.345	0.335	0.339
Social + ownership	0.351	0.347	0.349
Including school poverty	0.351	0.352	0.353
Secondary			
Indiv pupil only	0.445		
Indiv & school structure	0.482		
Social characteristics	0.491	0.489	0.496
Homeownership	0.486	0.485	0.492
Social + ownership	0.494	0.489	0.498
Including school poverty	0.494	0.491	0.499

models focused on Ward level effects. Clearly, a great deal of any homeownership effect overlaps with the effects of other social factors. The Table may suggest that social and tenure factors do not add much to the basic model. However, the basic model includes individual pupil level poverty, special needs, etc.

Reading across Table 1, it can be said that at primary level aggregation of social effects at school level provides a slightly better explanation, with aggregation at the broader ward level providing a poorer explanation. At secondary level, aggregation at the micro-neighbourhood level appears to give the best explanation, but again ward level is poorest. It is possible to help to account for these patterns by observing that (a) COAs are very small units which come closer to capturing an individual effect as well as a neighbourhood effect, while (b) secondary schools are much larger than primary schools.

Horizontal comparisons in Table 1 indicate that aggregating social composition variables at school level gives a better model than aggregating them at ward level. This finding suggests that, so far as school attainment is concerned, the crucial 'area effects' are in part school effects rather than just area-of-residence effects. In other words, the processes involved which create these effects are either happening within the schools or, if outside the school gates, they are still related to the social relationships associated with particular schools. From these data it cannot be said exactly what these processes are, although some were suggested in the literature review. Nevertheless, this does provide some justification for the sub-title of this paper: in other words, school effects may be a particular type of neighbourhood effect.

The optimal model, in the light of this discussion, may be one that includes an appropriate mix of school-level and COA-level inputs. Such models are illustrated in Table 2.

The primary attainment (Key Stage 2 (KS2)) OLS model shown in Table 2 explains about 35 per cent of the variance in scores at individual level using 20 variables drawn from the five groups (a) to (e) identified above. The secondary attainment OLS model (Key Stage 4 (KS4)), also shown in Table 2, explains approximately 50 per cent of the variance in scores, using a similar number of variables (22). The higher level of explanation of secondary attainment is mainly due to the ability to include prior attainment in this model, and this is indeed the most powerful single explanatory factor.

Only the most significant and salient features of these models are highlighted here before the impact of homeownership is considered. The models are parsimonious in their inclusion of social factors at school/area level, reflecting the issues of multicollinearity discussed earlier, the particular focus on homeownership, and some of the findings of other research.

Even though prior attainment is controlled for in the secondary (KS4) model, most of the other factors such as poverty continue to exert a powerful influence on the gain in attainment at secondary level, in a similar fashion to their impact in the primary sector. Poverty is strongly negative at individual level, for example, although the apparent effect at school-level is marginally positive (in this model, which also includes ownership, IMD and qualifications). However, there are some detailed differences in respect of gender, ethnicity and language variables.

These models also allow for school-level factors, including expenditure (modest positive impact), size (non-linear effects, differing between primary and secondary), denominational status, special classes and special policy designations. Greater school

Table 2. Regression models for attainment scores in primary and secondary sectors (OLS models for point scores at KS2 and KS4 in 2001/2 in five English authorities)

	Primary (KS2)			Secondary (KS4)		
	Coeff B	Std Coeff Beta	t-stat	Coeff B	Std Coeff Beta	t-stat
(Constant)	11.434		32.2	27.315		4.7
Level 1						
Girl	−0.232	−0.037	−6.4	3.150	0.083	14.9
Black	0.038	0.003	0.5	−1.934	−0.023	−3.9
Asian	0.496	0.031	4.8			
Not English spoken	−0.880	−0.104	−16.0	5.345	0.103	15.6
Free meal eligible	−0.671	−0.094	−15.0	−4.011	−0.088	−14.4
SEN stage	−1.606	−0.527	−73.6	−4.376	−0.208	−25.9
Statement of SEN	0.958	0.037	5.5	15.540	0.097	13.6
Attends in own LEA				−3.688	−0.043	−6.6
Prior attainment KS2 96/7				2.483	0.437	68.3
Level 2						
Voluntary sector controlled	−0.532	−0.044	−6.8	1.755	0.013	2.1
Religious/denominational	0.560	0.082	10.8			
Special classes				2.747	0.030	5.2
School size pupils	−1.064	−0.074	−2.4	−14.873	−0.613	−6.2
Size squared/mean	0.642	0.063	2.1	1.871	0.398	5.5
Reciprocal size				−17.362	−0.152	−4.7
Pupils < 5	0.424	0.014	2.1			
Pupils > 16	0.299	0.054	4.6	27.974	0.099	12.5
Pred expend/pupil	0.743	0.058	8.2	1.600	0.066	6.9
School SEN stage	1.257	0.062	2.0	−3.874	−0.061	−7.9
Pred school FSM	−0.004	−0.021	−1.5	2.900	0.024	1.1
School-ward IMD	0.015	0.022	3.5	0.126	0.105	7.5
School-ward private pupils				0.349	0.057	8.2
School no. qualifs	−0.037	−0.118	−8.9	−0.271	−0.124	−7.6
School owners %	0.025	0.135	8.2	0.208	0.145	9.6

	Dep Var: score at KS2: 7.7		Points at KS4: 15.5	
Level 3				
COA owners % diff	0.007	0.044	0.077	0.088
Model fit				
Mean		11.342		36.392
S D		3.283		19.392
Adj r-sq		0.353		0.501
S E Est		2.556		13.481
F ratio		560.6		759.4

expenditure per pupil is associated with moderately higher attainment scores in both primary and secondary sectors.

In this preferred model formulation, area effects are treated as school-level effects. Most deprivation effects are probably captured by poverty (FSM), qualifications and homeownership variables, accounting for the weaker effect of IMD. Proxies for a strong interest in education, qualifications and private schooling, remain statistically significant as expected. However, some caution is in order with regard to the significance of school-level effects, as discussed further below.

Comparable logistic regression models have been run for the binary variables for attaining Level 4 at Key Stage 2 (primary) and five or more good GCSEs (grades A–C) at Key Stage 4. The full detail of these models is not reported. Their results are more or less consistent across most variables.

Effect of Homeownership into the Model

Two homeownership variables are used in these models: the value based on the micro-neighbourhood (COA), and the average percentage of owners at school level. The former can be expressed as the difference from the school mean; this approach ('mean differencing') is common practice in multi-level modelling to help clarify the difference in effect at these two levels. The models reported in Table 2 include both ownership variables. It can be seen that both are positive and significant at both primary and secondary level in the OLS models. Interestingly, the school-level effect is larger in magnitude. These positive effects also apply in the comparable logit models. Thus, the basic hypothesis of an independent positive effect of homeownership on attainment is supported, as is the second hypothesis that this effect is partly an area effect expressed through the school level.

The significance of school-level ownership, and other variables at this level, may be somewhat inflated because the number of schools is much less than the number of pupils, although the numbers are still quite substantial—up to 677 primary and 232 secondary. To allow for this models estimated using OLS regression have also been compared with estimation (in Stata) of regression (a) using robust standard errors allowing for the clustering by school; and (b) using a Generalised Least Squares random effects model, again allowing for clustering at school level. The models compared are slightly more parsimonious than those shown in Table 2. These tests indicate that, in the primary sector, school-level ownership (and the other school-level variables) are still statistically significant at the 1 per cent level (or, in the GLS test, the 5 per cent level).

To give a feel for the magnitude of these effects, based on the models in Table 2, the implied impact of being a primary school age child of an individual owner (based on a 100 per cent difference in the homeownership variable) would be to raise the KS2 score by 6.6 per cent and the probability of achieving Level 4 by 22.7 per cent at the mean. An increase of 20 percentage points in the school-level owner occupation rate would raise KS2 scores by 4.3 per cent and the probability of achieving Level 4 by 12.1 per cent at the mean. Expressed in this way both the quasi-individual and the school-level effects appear quite sizeable. Clearly, for the same percentage increase, the school-level effect is bigger.

The magnitudes of the ownership effects appear to be larger in secondary schooling than those for primary schooling, in the Table 2 models, and this is particularly true for the COA-level effect. On points scores, an individual from a wholly homeowning COA would have a 21 per cent higher GCSE score and a 55 per cent higher chance of attaining five good GCSE grades, with other variables at mean values. A 20 percentage point rise in school-level owner occupation would increase scores by 11.4 per cent at the mean, while raising the probability of gaining five good grades by 18.7 per cent. It should be noted that these effects are partial, holding everything else constant.

However, the tests for robust standard errors indicate that more caution is in order about additional school-level ownership effects in the secondary case, reflecting the smaller number of secondary schools. These tests indicate that any additional school-level effect is not statistically significant.

Alternative Formulations

Owner occupation is inevitably related to a number of other variables in the model, for example poverty, unemployment or social class. This may mean that, while the owner occupation variables may show up as significant, they may also displace some of the explanation previously provided by other variables in the model. There is, as already noted, evidence that this is occurring: the overall fit of the models does not increase markedly when owner occupation is included. For most of the key variables the study is interested in there are not large changes in the estimated coefficients and the basic model is relatively stable. However, the variables where there appears to be substantial interaction are school-level poverty (as already noted) and special needs, and school/Ward level deprivation.

Another response to the correlation of social variables is to construct a composite variable using principal components or factor analysis. The results of a variant approach of this kind can be reported. Twelve school-level social variables (including homeownership, free meals and average SEN Stage) were subject to a principal components analysis, with the factors then being rotated (varimax rotation with Kaiser normalisation) to aid interpretation. The first three factors capture general dimensions of variation in social composition and conditions:

Factor 1: per cent homeownership (-ve), per cent lone parents, per cent FSM, per cent unemployment.
Factor 2: per cent in poor health, per cent with long-term illness, IMD index, per cent with no car.
Factor 3: per cent working (-ve), per cent adults with no qualifications.

It appears that homeownership is closely associated, at school level, with the dimension of income poverty-affluence; however, it is less closely associated with a dimension of general deprivation, which is more related to poor health, and a further dimension more related to work and qualifications. The next two factors are more specific to single variables—SEN Stage and private pupils—so it is suggested that these should remain in the model in their original form. The factor analysis for the secondary sector is similar but not identical. Factors 1 and 2 are reversed, and FSM loads more evenly across these two factors, while homeownership is even more strongly loaded on the composite factor.

Table 3 presents OLS models similar to those in Table 2, but with the three composite factors substituted for the relevant social variables. School-level ownership and FSM variables are included as residuals from regressions of these variables on Factor 1 above. This is to see whether they have an additional effect over and above the 'common' effect

Table 3. Regression models for attainment scores using factors (OLS models for point scores at KS2 and KS3 in 2001/2 in five English authorities)

	Primary			Secondary		
	Coeff B	Std Coeff Beta	t-stat	Coeff B	Std Coeff Beta	t-stat
(Constant)	11.465		47.7	30.017		5.5
Level 1						
Girl	−0.232	−0.036	−6.4	3.190	0.084	15.1
Black	0.090	0.007	1.2	−0.554	−0.007	−1.1
Asian	0.462	0.029	4.5			
Not English spoken	−0.787	−0.093	−13.0	7.452	0.143	20.8
Free meal elig	−0.663	−0.093	−14.6	−3.899	−0.086	−14.0
SEN stage	−1.610	−0.529	−73.8	−4.385	−0.208	−26.0
Statement of SEN	0.978	0.038	5.6	15.763	0.098	13.8
Attends in own LEA				−3.953	−0.046	−7.2
Prior attain KS2 96/7				2.453	0.432	67.3
Level 2						
Voluntary controlled	−0.475	−0.039	−6.1	2.620	0.019	3.1
Denominational	0.464	0.068	10.2			
Special classes				2.801	0.031	5.3
School size pupils	−1.102	−0.076	−2.5	−13.342	−0.550	−5.5
Size squared/mean	0.712	0.070	2.3	1.764	0.375	5.1
Reciprocal size				−13.201	−0.115	−3.6
Pupils < 5	0.290	0.010	1.4			
Pupils > 16				30.948	0.110	14.5
Pred expend/pupil	0.432	0.077	8.2	2.156	0.089	10.3
School SEN stage	0.419	0.033	3.4	−6.530	−0.102	−7.2
School-ward priv pup	0.031	0.047	7.6	0.415	0.067	9.2
PCA factors Level 2						
Fac1 pov/low own	−0.418	−0.132	−14.5	−2.525	−0.127	−12.9
Fac2 bad health/depr	−0.137	−0.043	−3.2	−0.094	−0.005	−0.4
Fac3 noqual/workless	−0.280	−0.091	−8.4	−0.828	−0.043	−3.2
Resid school owners	0.010	0.023	1.8	−0.197	−0.065	−3.6
Resid school FSM	0.227	0.008	0.6	−8.385	−0.058	−3.4

Level 3

	COA owners % diff	Dep Var ks2scor1		ks4point	
	0.008		7.7	0.078	
Mean		0.045			0.090
S D		11.342			15.7
		3.283			36.392
Adj r-sq		0.353			19.392
S E Est		2.556			0.503
F ratio		532.9			13.453
					732.5

Model fit: Adj r-sq, S E Est, F ratio

of the composite variable. The composite variable closely related to (low) homeownership and poverty ('Factor 1') at school level has a strong, statistically significant negative effect in both primary and secondary sectors. The third factor, relating to no qualifications and worklessness is also significantly negative. The second factor, poor health/deprivation, has a less strong effect and is not significant in the secondary model.

The COA-based ownership variable (difference from school mean) continues to have a significant positive effect in both models. However, the residual school ownership variable now has only a modest positive effect in the primary sector which is of marginal statistical significance. In the secondary sector this variable has an apparently negative effect. The residual school FSM variable is not statistically significant in the primary sector, but significantly negative in secondary.

The logit models for attainment of key thresholds are not shown, but in both primary and secondary the same broad findings apply with respect to the factors. The factor associated with ownership is noticeably the strongest social factor in the primary logit model, and the only one of the three to be statistically significant in the secondary model. However, the residual ownership variable is not statistically significant in either case.

From this alternative model, using factor analysis, it can be concluded that homeownership is closely related to other social composition factors, particularly poverty, and that, although this common factor is the most important social predictor of attainment, it is difficult to demonstrate any additional specific school-level ownership effect beyond this. However, the micro-neighbourhood (COA-based) ownership factor remains a significant explanatory factor in this alternative model. It should be noted that the common factor is more closely identified with homeownership in the secondary sector, whilst in the primary sector it is also closely related to school poverty (FSM).

Another way of looking at this impact of owner occupation issue is to recognise that, if an attempt were made to simulate the impact of a change in owner occupation in certain types of areas, particularly deprived areas, this would probably be associated with corresponding changes in poverty and other factors which are significant in the models. This would mean that the overall impact of such tenure changes could be substantially larger than those direct (partial) effects quoted above, given the general pattern of the effects associated with such variables as poverty and qualifications.

Of course, it can still be argued that, at individual/household level, the causality may run from poverty or lack of qualifications to both homeownership and attainment. The poorest families will find it difficult to attain or sustain homeownership. A policy of tenure diversification may be seen as an exercise in reshuffling the pack, in terms of social mix within schools. It may be expected to raise attainment levels in hitherto disadvantaged schools, but how far this spills over to benefit all pupils is unclear. As noted in an earlier section, this may be affected by non-linearities in the relationships.

Non-linearity

It is clear that non-linearity might be significant in its policy implications (Galster, 2002). What is more difficult, given the data and models worked with in this study, is to reach strong conclusions about possible non-linearity in the key relationships. The multicollinearity problem makes it difficult to test for this by adding further related variables such as quadratic terms. It is easier to perform an initial, exploratory test using the factors version of the model. A version of the models is tested in Table 3, where the effect of Factor 1 is hypothesised to be piecewise linear, with break points at -1 and $+1$ standard deviations. The results are statistically significant, at least for the higher end of the range on this composite variable, in the case of primary attainment scores.

Figure 1 shows the resulting relationship across the range of observed values on Factor 1. Basically, this diagram shows that non-ownership/poverty has a stronger negative effect in the middle range of primary schools, with a lesser impact in the higher range (and probably, although with less confidence, in the lowest range). For example, increasing non-ownership/poverty from the mean to $+1$ standard deviation reduces KS2 score by 0.475 points (4.1 per cent); increasing from $+2$ to $+3$ s.d. reduces the score by only 0.250 (2.4 per cent) points. It is not quite clear what this implies for policy. It appears to suggest that changing the social composition of the worst schools would have less impact than changing the composition of those in the middle range. This is perhaps a less convenient finding than would have been the case if the effects had been stronger in the higher range.

Applying the same approach to the secondary sector model yields coefficients that are not statistically significant for both high and low ranges.

Impact of Owner Occupation on Non-owners at School Level

The other related question posed was whether it was possible to use the data to test to see if school-level owner occupation affects the attainment level of non-owner children as well as the children of owners. It is difficult to do this in a satisfactory way, because measures at the COA scale are being used. The result is that there are very few pupils in the English sample who come from COAs containing no or virtually no owners. In order to perform a test with a reasonably large sample it is necessary to set the cut-off quite high. The results are now reported of applying the model to that subset of pupils who live in COAs containing less than 50 per cent owner occupation.

Table 4 shows the key results in terms of the coefficients for the two ownership variables and their significance in four models, two OLS models for scores at primary and secondary level, and two logistic regression models for attainment of target levels in primary and secondary. The analyses encompass the full range of variables set out in Table 2, and are based upon the variables in their original form rather than composite factors.

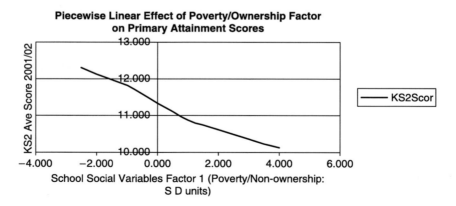

Figure 1. Piecewise linear effect of poverty/ownership factor on primary attainment scores

In the primary school case, the COA level homeownership variable shifts from a statistically significant positive effect to a marginally significant negative effect. It would be expected that this effect would weaken, because the range of variation in this variable has been sharply reduced within this sub-sample. The study is much more interested in the coefficient on the school-level homeownership variable. This reduces somewhat in size in both OLS and logit models, and remains statistically significant in the OLS while becoming just insignificant at the 10 per cent level ($p = 0.108$) in the logit case. The considerably smaller sample tends to lower significance levels in the low homeownership model. Nevertheless, the school-level ownership variable is still statistically significant using robust standard errors in Stata. As noted earlier, these effects are quite sizeable. This provides some positive evidence that having more children of owners in a primary school raises the attainment of pupils who are 'probably not' owners themselves.

The results in the secondary sector provide less support for the proposition. The COA-level homeownership variable drops in size and significance, while the school-level ownership variable becomes marginally insignificant positive (in the OLS case) or clearly insignificant negative (in the logit case). It could be said that there is a hint of support in the OLS model, which might be clearer with a larger sample.

Analysis of Pupil Data for Scotland

The Scottish data refer to all state secondary school pupils at two levels, S4 and S5, within three large local authorities, Fife, Edinburgh and North Lanarkshire. Although the study is aiming at broad comparability with the English models for secondary attainment, there are many detailed differences in the data available and hence in the model setup. No attainment data were available at primary level so the analysis focuses solely on

Table 4. Comparison of impact of owner occupation variables in models for all cases and those from low ownership output areas (5 English localities 2001–02)

	Primary all cases	Primary low own	Secondary all	Secondary low own
OLS model for Key Stage scores				
Coefficient % owners (COA)	0.007	−0.006	0.077	0.028
t-statistic	7.7	−1.9	15.5	1.7
Significance	0.000	0.052	0.000	0.097
Coefficient % owners (School)	0.025	0.017	0.208	0.057
t-statistic	8.2	2.7	9.6	1.3
Significance	0.000	0.000	0.000	0.192
Logistic Regression model for level				
Coefficient % owners (COA)	0.006	−0.004	0.010	0.004
Exp(B)	1.006	0.996	1.010	1.004
Significance	0.000	0.108	0.000	0.215
Coefficient % owners (school)	0.015	0.008	0.016	−0.003
Exp(B)	1.015	1.008	1.016	0.997
Significance	0.000	0.108	0.000	0.681

secondary schooling. Standard Grade at S4 is roughly equivalent to GCSE at Key Stage 4 in England. Higher Grades are taken in the following year, S5, by pupils remaining in the system beyond the compulsory leaving age. The Scottish pupil data focus on secondary pupils in 2003/04, with a sample of 11 888 pupils taking 'Standard Grades' (approximately equivalent to GCSE) at end of year S4, and 9346 taking 'Higher Grades' at end of year S5.[3] For the second of these groups, there are prior attainment data for the previous year. The dependent variables are the number of passes gained at specified levels, and the models reported in detail are fitted using OLS (although logit models are also compared). The individual pupil attributes that are recorded are similar to those for the English models but the ways of classifying special needs are different. School-level variables are similar in scope. Small area socio-demographic variables are based on Datazones (DZ), areas with population between 500 and 1000, larger than COAs but smaller than wards. This is the smallest area for which homeownership rates and other socio-demographic indicators can be calculated, and there is in effect only one neighbourhood scale considered in the Scottish analysis.

The overall fit of the Standard Grade model is poorer than the English model, mainly due to the lack of a prior attainment variable. As in England, both school-level and neighbourhood-level attributes significantly enhance the explanation beyond that obtained from individual factors alone. Adding in the homeownership variables only marginally improves the fit, beyond this level. However, if homeownership variables were added before the other neighbourhood factors, they would raise the explanatory power quite substantially.

The Higher Grade model only applies to those pupils who stay on at secondary school into Year 5, and the prior attainment score dominates this model while also raising its overall performance greatly. Neighbourhood variables seem to add more than school variables in this case. However, homeownership does not add much beyond that.

Table 5 shows the preferred OLS regression models for attainment at these two stages in the Scottish areas. Variables insignificant in both models are generally omitted. As in the English models, school expenditure and school-level FSM rates are predicted values from reduced form equations (i.e. recognising their endogeneity), while the ownership variable is again split into a school-level value and the difference of the 'individual' (Datazone) value from the school mean.

Poverty (FSM) is significantly negative at individual and school levels in the Standard Grade model; in the Higher model it is significant at the school level but not the individual level. These results are broadly consistent with England. The expenditure variable is negative for Standard Grade but positive for Higher level attainment. This may be explained by the greater tendency of school funding in these Scottish authorities to be skewed towards deprived areas. At Higher level, this may be offset by the tendency of per pupil funding to rise with staying-on rates.

A somewhat different set of neighbourhood (DZ) level social variables is found to be statistically significant in Scotland. Qualifications still have a powerful effect, negative from 'no qualifications' on Standard Grade and positive from 'higher qualifications' on Higher attainment. The percentage of flats is negative for Standard Grade. The proportion of higher education students living in the DZ is positive in both models; this may capture areas such as those near universities which have a higher concentration of academically-oriented families. Rather surprisingly, both general deprivation (SIMD score) and long-term illness have apparently positive associations with attainment, but this is in models which also contain poverty (FSM) and homeownership variables. In other words, multicollinearity affects this group of variables.

Table 5. Regression models for secondary school attainment in Scotland (OLS models for number of good passes at Standard and Higher Grade, all secondary schools in Edinburgh, Fife and North Lanarkshire)

Explanatory Variables	Standard grade			Highers		
	Coeff B	Std Coeff Beta	t-stat	Coeff B	Std Coeff Beta	t-stat
Level 1						
(constant)	10.045		11.1	−1.884		−4.0
No. of SCQF5s				0.378	0.663	85.0
Girl	0.605	0.100	12.3	0.091	0.026	3.6
Black				0.350	0.011	1.6
Indiv poverty (FSM)	−1.252	−0.146	−17.0	−0.039	−0.007	−0.9
Record of needs	−0.689	−0.024	−2.5			
Indiv educ prog	−1.671	−0.091	−9.5	0.105	0.007	1.0
Level 2						
School size 000	−0.849	−0.103	−5.6	0.091	0.019	1.2
Integ SEN unit	−0.181	−0.030	−3.0	−0.066	−0.019	−2.1
Denominational	0.178	0.021	2.4	0.132	0.028	3.6
Pred school FSM	−0.031	−0.080	−2.8	−0.013	−0.055	−2.3
Pred expend/pupil	−0.0009	−0.129	−6.0	0.00014	0.035	1.9
School owners %	−0.006	−0.022	−1.1	0.0039	0.024	1.4
Level 3						
SIMD score	0.0055	0.029	1.2	0.0072	0.063	3.3
Flats %	−0.0050	−0.044	−3.7			
No. qualif %	−0.058	−0.242	−10.9			
High qualif %	0.347	0.101	8.9	0.019	0.136	10.6
Students term %	0.019	0.043	2.9	0.058	0.030	2.9
Long-term ill %	0.016	0.103	5.6	0.0092	0.035	2.9
Owner % diff				0.0063	0.071	4.7
Dep Var SCQF5	Mean	2.903		SCQF6 Mean	1.380	
	S D	3.030		S D	1.790	
Model fit	Adj r-sq	0.219		Adj r-sq	0.531	
	S E Est	2.677		S E Est	1.223	
	F ratio	209.1		F ratio	663.0	

In the models at both levels homeownership is strongly and statistically significantly positive at the small neighbourhood level. However, school-level ownership is negative and insignificant in the Standard Grade model. In the Highers model it is positive but not quite significant. It is also relevant to report at this point that logit models have also been tested for the binary odds of achieving five or more good Standard Grades at S4 and three or more Highers at S5. These confirm the key findings here: small neighbourhood homeownership is significantly positive, school-level homeownership is statistically insignificant in both models.

Thus, it cannot be said that the Scottish findings on homeownership fully replicate those found in England, insofar as the school-level effect seems to be weak. However, it should be remembered that the models are not fully comparable, because ownership is measured for small neighbourhoods (Datazones) rather than for COAs. The Scottish results suggest that small neighbourhood of residence may be more important than clustering at school level, so far as the tenure effect is concerned. At the same time, the previously reported finding from individual SSLS data analysis should be remembered—that individual level homeownership is apparently very significant. It may be that, as with other social variables, measuring them at DZ level is capturing more of the individual effect as well as the area effect. A further factor underlying the apparent lack of school-level homeownership effects in Scotland is that, across the secondary schools in this sample, this variable is closely correlated with key school-level social variables included in the model: FSM, SIMD score and no qualifications. This is more the case in Scotland than in England.

The magnitudes of the ownership effect are similar to those reported in England: homeownership being 20 percentage points higher at DZ level would raise attainment by 10.8 per cent (SG) and 9.2 per cent (HG) at the mean. Allowing for the second order effect via the prior qualifications variable in the second model would raise this second figure to 17.8 per cent.

One further test of a variant of the model has been carried out, which takes account of neighbourhood change over the decade 1991–2001. In this variant the owner occupation rate (for the pupil's Datazone) in 1991 is entered, and the change in the owner occupation rate (1991–2001) in percentage points, and the net change in total households in the area (proxying new development or decline/demolition) are entered separately. The general pattern is that the 1991 owner occupation rate remains strongly positive in both models, while the increase in owner occupation is smaller and not quite statistically significant in the SG case. However, in the Highers model the second coefficient is still positive, of the same size and significant. It was hypothesised that 'new owner occupiers' (whether owner occupiers in new housing developments or former public tenants in Right to Buy properties) might be less supportive of good educational attainment than established owners. However, this hypothesis receives only limited support from the SG result, and is rejected in the case of Highers. The policy implication here is more positive: seeking to increase ownership rates in low-ownership/low-attainment areas, through planning or regeneration policies, should yield positive outcomes in educational attainment.

Concluding Discussion

School attainment has attracted increasing policy and research attention, recognising its wider impact on later life chances. Research on school attainment shows that non-school factors tend to be the dominant drivers of attainment, including factors such as gender, ethnicity and class, but arguably with poverty the most important factor. This can impact on children through lack of material resources and support in the home, through stresses leading to behavioural difficulties, and through wider psycho-social processes of expectation, stigma and subculture which operate more at neighbourhood level.

Some have gone on recently to argue that housing tenure is an independent factor impacting on school attainment, seeing owner occupation in particular as a positive factor. Most of this recent literature has been American. Homeownership is suggested to be influential because of its association with better housing conditions, more residential and household stability, avoidance of financial exclusion and insecurity, and its effects on wider attitudes and behaviour (sometimes bracketed as 'social capital'). Policies to promote homeownership reflect these and other concerns.

This paper has taken this hypothesis and subjected it to some initial testing in a UK context. It has utilised data from relatively new sources, national pupil databases, linked to Census data and other data on both schools and neighbourhoods. Analyses based on these sources carried out separately for areas in England and Scotland provide a degree of support for the hypothesis, although with substantial qualifications and provisos. The analysis is based on a general modelling framework, consistent with the emerging paradigm in school attainment research, which recognises that attainment reflects individual, family/household, neighbourhood and school-level influences. However, the available data place limits on the ability of the study to fully separate the effect of attributes such as homeownership at individual, neighbourhood and school levels.

The key finding is that homeownership does appear to have an additional, independent and positive impact on school attainment. Homeownership appears to have significant and sizeable positive effects on attainment at both primary and secondary levels in England. It appears to work both at a micro-neighbourhood and at a school level, although the additional school-level effect is not statistically robust in the secondary sector. In Scotland, using somewhat different data and models, the effect is mainly concentrated at the level of small neighbourhoods, without much apparent extra school effect.

The apparent school-level homeownership effect in England is difficult to separate from school-level poverty. Combining these in a single factor gives a powerful explanatory factor. It is certainly clear that changing an area's (and a school's) homeownership profile would be likely to also change substantially its profile in terms of other key variables, including poverty and parental qualifications, and hence its attainment record.

A general caution to be sounded about all of these findings is that there may be selection effects at work, involving unobserved predisposition factors whereby certain households have a particularly strong orientation to supporting their children's education. Such households may seek out 'good schools' as well as reinforcing their better performance. They may also have a greater predisposition to invest in owner occupation. For such households, the underlying causal factor is the predisposition, with owner occupation being as much a consequence as school attainment.

It may be argued that potential non-linearities in these relationships may be important in policy terms, because they may support policies to change the social composition of schools which could generate net improvements in attainment across the whole system, as opposed to just 'shuffling the pack'. However, a limited examination of this issue is inconclusive and it is difficult to pursue it further within the limits of the data available to this study.

A stronger test of the homeownership hypothesis is to see whether schools with more homeowner children help all their pupils to do better, including children who are probably not from homeowning families. Although the attempt here to test this is not very robust, it does appear to support the hypothesis in the primary sector, but not in the secondary sector.

It is not surprising that children from owner-occupier backgrounds do better, other things being equal. Recent individual survey analysis for Scotland strongly confirms that this is the case. The school-level effects are more interesting. They suggest that homeownership has effects on factors which operate at school level, such as ethos, expectations, parental involvement and behaviour. There is a strong analogy with the effects of poverty, which the models show to be also powerful at school level as well as at individual level (although the two factors are closely related and difficult to separate). They may also operate similarly at the neighbourhood level, in terms of culture, behaviour, interactions and expectations outside the school gates, but in ways which impact on achievement within schools. That is why this paper is termed to be about 'school effects as neighbourhood effects'; they operate in closely analogous ways, and indeed schools are key social institutions which are associated with neighbourhoods.

Ultimately, the case for owner occupation rests not just on these collective school or area-level effects, but also on possible causal linkages at the individual household level. Some argue that the act of becoming an owner occupier, which may be facilitated by policies which widen such opportunities, impacts over time on household attitudes, behaviour and outcomes in such arenas as saving, labour market participation and community involvement. Recent US work on 'social capital' suggests that such effects may operate. The data did not permit the testing of these hypotheses directly, although one might begin to approach this by looking at tenure changes and their relationship with migration. Initial tests in Scotland suggest that 'new owner occupiers' are associated with better educational attainment almost as much as established owners, but this requires further investigation. At the same time, it must be remembered the potential selection effects, which may imply causality running in a different direction.

Notes

[1] Analyses of the Scottish Household Survey data for 1999/00 show that 85.7 per cent of people in the highest social class in Scotland are homeowners compared to only 46.1 per cent in the lowest social class (2001/02 data are similar).
[2] The variables included vary slightly at different geographical levels according to data availability; for example, IMD low income is available at ward level but not at COA level
[3] There are a number of differences between the Scottish and English datasets. Scottish data are for 2003/04 (two years later); Scottish qualifications are not precisely comparable with the English; Scottish data supplied have been subject to a degree of random 'record-swapping' in respect of the neighbourhood and school link codes; neighbourhood is based on Datazone, rather than a combination of Output Areas and wards as in the English data; categories of special educational need used in Scotland are different; Scottish schools' budgets are based on FTE teacher numbers; Scottish attainment scores continuous, numbers of subjects passed at threshold levels.

References

Aaronson, D. (2000) A note on the benefits of homeownership, *Journal of Urban Economics*, 47, pp. 356–369.
Atkinson, R. & Kintrea, K. (2001) Disentangling area effects: evidence from deprived and non-deprived neighbourhoods, *Urban Studies*, 38(12), pp. 2277–2298.
Beresford, P., Green, D., Lister, R. & Woodward, K. (1999) *Poverty First Hand: Poor People Speak for Themselves* (London: Child Poverty Action Group).

Boehm, T. P. & Schlottman, A. M. (1999) Does homeownership by parents have economic impact on their children?, *Journal of Housing Economics*, 8, pp. 217–222.

Bramley, G. (1989) A model of educational outcomes at local level with implications for local expenditure needs, *Environment & Planning C: Government and Policy*, 7, pp. 37–58.

Bramley, G. & Evans, M. (2002) *Neighbourhood Spending and Outcomes: A Study of Education and Employment Outcomes in Three English Cities*. CRSIS Research Paper (Edinburgh: Heriot-Watt University). Available at www.crsis.hw.ac.uk.

Bramley, G. & Karley, N. K. (2005) Home-Ownership, Poverty and Educational Achievement: individual, school and neighbourhood effects, Report to Scottish Executive Education Department. Available at: www.crsis.hw.ac.uk.

Bramley, G. & Morgan, J. (2003) Building competitiveness and cohesion: the role of new housing in central Scotland's cities, *Housing Studies*, 18(4), pp. 447–471.

Bramley, G. & Wyatt, G. (1998) *The Use of Non-Expenditure Information in Standard Spending Assessments*. Report of Research to the Department of the Environment, Transport and the Regions (Local Government Research Unit).

Bramley, G., Evans, M. & Noble, M. (2005) *Mainstream Services and Neighbourhood Deprivation*. Neighbourhood Renewal Unit. Available at www.neighbourhoods.gov.uk.

Burgess, S., Gardiner, K. & Propper, C. (2001) *Growing Up: School, Family and Area Influences on Adolescents' Later Life Chances*. CASE Paper 49 (London: London School of Economics).

Burgess, S. & Wilson, D. (2004) *Ethnic Segregation in England's Schools*, CASE Paper 79 (London: London School of Economics).

Burrows, R. & Wilcox, S. (2000) *Half the Poor: Homeowners with Low Incomes* (London: Council of Mortgage Lenders).

Bynner, J. (1997) in: J. Bynner, E. Ferri & P. Shepherd (Eds) *Twenty-something in the 1990s: Getting On, Getting By, Getting Nowhere* (Aldershot: Ashgate).

Bynner, J. & Steedman, J. (1995) *Difficulties with Basic Skills* (London: Basic Skills Agency).

Clark, J., Dyson, A. (1999) *Housing and Schooling—A Case Study in Joined Up Problems* (York: Joseph Rowntree Foundation).

Dietz, R. & Haurin, D. (2003) The social and private micro-level consequences of homeownership, *Journal of Urban Economics*, 54, pp. 401–450.

DiPasquale, D. & Glaeser, E. (1999) Incentives and social capital: are homeowners better citizens?, *Journal of Urban Economics*, 45, pp. 354–384.

Dolton, P. & Vignoles, A. (2000) The effects of school quality on pupil outcomes: an overview, in: H. Heijke & J. Muyksen (Eds) *Education, Training and Employment in the knowledge-based economy* (London: MacMillan).

Gewirtz, S. (1998) Can all schools be successful? An exploration of the determinants of school 'success', *Oxford Review of Education*, 24, pp. 439–457.

Galster, G. (1987) *Homeowners and Neighbourhood Reinvestment* (Durham, NC: Duke University Press).

Galster, G. (2002) An economic efficiency analysis of deconcentrating poverty populations, *Journal of Housing Economics*, 11, pp. 303–329.

Gibson, A. & Asthana, S. (1998) School performance, school effectiveness and the 1997 White Paper, *Oxford Review of Education*, 24(92), pp. 195–210.

Glennerster, H. (2002) United Kingdom education 1997–2001, *Oxford Review of Economic Policy*, 18, pp. 120–137.

Goldstein, H. (1995) *Multilevel Statistical Models*, Kendall's Library of Statistics 3. 2nd edn (London: Edward Arnold).

Goldstein, H. & Sammons, P. (1997) The influence of secondary and junior schools on sixteen year examination performance: a cross-classified multilevel analysis, *School Effectiveness and Performance*, 8, pp. 219–230.

Hanushek, E. (1986) The economics of schooling, production and efficiency in public schools, *Journal of Economic Literature*, 24, pp. 114–117.

Green, R. & White, M. (1997) Measuring the benefits of home owning: effects on children, *Journal of Urban Economics*, 41, pp. 441–461.

Harkness, J. & Newman, S. J. (2001) *The Differential Effects of Homeownership on Children form Low-income and High Income Families* (Baltimore, MD: Johns Hopkins University, Institute for Policy Studies).

Harkness, J. & Newman, S. J. (2002) Homeownership for the poor in distress neighbourhoods: does it make sense?, *Housing Policy Debate*, 13, pp. 597–630.

Haurin, D. R., Parcel, T. L. & Haurin, R. J. (2002) Does homeownership affect child outcomes?, *Real Estate Economics*, 30, pp. 635–666.

Hawarth, C. (2002) So you're from Brixton? The struggle for recognition and esteem in a stigmatised community, *Ethnicities*, 2, pp. 231–254.

Hedges, L. V., Laine, R. D. & Greenwald, R. (1994) Does money matter? A meta-analyses of studies of the effects of differential school inputs on student outcomes, *Educational Researcher*, 23(3), pp. 5–14.

Hepple, L. & Rees, H. (1998) *Standard Spending Assessments and Multilevel Modelling*, Report to DETR (Local Government Research Unit) by Geoeconomic Research.

Hills, J. (2007) *Ends and Means: The Future Roles of Social Housing in England*, CASE Report 34. ESRC Research Centre for the Analysis of Social Exclusion (London: London School of Economics).

Hilton, Z. (2005) Outside the Mainstream School: young people's perspectives on disaffection, exclusion, support and change, CRSIS Research Briefing No 6. Available at: www.crsis.hw.ac.uk.

Hobcraft, J. (1999) *Intergenerational and Life-Course Transmission of Social Exclusion: Influences of Childhood Poverty, Family Disruption, and Contact with the Police*, CASE Paper 15 (London: London School of Economics).

Hobcraft, J. (2000) *The Roles of Schooling and Educational Qualifications in the Emergence of Adult Exclusion*, CASE Paper 43 (London: London School of Economics).

Hobcraft, J. (2002) Social exclusion and the generations, in: J. Hills, J. Le Grand & D. Piachaud (Eds) *Understanding Social Exclusion* (Oxford: Oxford University Press).

Koba, C. & Paxton, W. (Eds) (2002) *Asset based Welfare and Poverty: Exploring the Case for and Against Asset-Based Welfare Policies* (London: IPPR).

Lupton, R. (2004) *Schools in Disadvantaged Areas: Recognising Context and Raising Quality*, CASE Paper 76 (London: ESRC Research Centre Report).

Middleton, S. (1994) *Family Fortunes: Pressures on Parents and Children in the 1990s* (London: Child Poverty Action Group).

Middleton, S. & Asworth, K. (1997) *Small Fortunes: Spending on Children, Poverty and Parental Sacrifice* (York: Joseph Rowntree Foundation).

Morenoff, J. D., Sampson, P. J. & Earls, F. (1999) Beyond social capital: spatial dynamics of collective efficacy for children, *American Sociological Review*, 64(5), pp. 633–660.

Ofsted (2000) *Improving City Schools* (London: Ofsted).

Ofsted (2001) *National Summary Data Report for Secondary Schools*, 2001 Data (London: Ofsted). Available at www.ofsted.gov.uk.

Parsons, C. (1999) *Education, Exclusion and Citizenship* (London: Routledge).

Reynolds, D., Sammons, P., Stoll, P., Barber, M. & Hillman, J. (1996) School effectiveness and school improvement in the United Kingdom, *School Effectiveness and School Improvement*, 7, pp. 133–158.

Rutter, M. (1979) *Fifteen Thousand Hours* (Harmondsworth: Penguin).

Sigle-Rushton, W. (2004) *Intergenerational and Life-Course Transmission of Social Exclusion in the 1970 British Cohort Study*, CASE Paper 78 (London: London School of Economics).

Sniders, T. & Bosker, R. (1999) *Multilevel Analysis: An Introduction to Basic and Advanced Multilevel Modelling* (London: Sage).

Social Exclusion Unit (SEU) (1998) *Bringing Britain Together: A National Strategy for Neighbourhood Renewal* (London: SEU).

Sparkes, J. & Glennerster, H. (2002) Preventing social exclusion: education's contribution, in: J. Hills, J. Le Grand & D. Piachaud (Eds) *Understanding Social Exclusion* (Oxford: Oxford University Press).

Thomas, S. & Mortimer, P. (1996) Comparison of Value Added Models for secondary school effectiveness, *Research Papers in Education*, 11/1, pp. 279–295.

Thomas, S. & Smees, R. (1997) Dimensions of school effectiveness: comparative analyses across regions. Paper presented at the 10th International Congress for School Effectiveness, London.

Townsend, P. (1979) *Poverty in the United Kingdom* (Harmondsworth: Penguin).

Townsend, P. (1993) *The International Analysis of Poverty* (Milton Keynes: Harvester Wheatsheaf).

West, A., Pennell, H., Travers, T. & West, R. (2001) Financing school-based education in England: poverty, examination results and expenditure, *Environment & Planning C*, 19, pp. 461–471.

Whitehead, C. M. E. (1979) Why owner-occupation?, *CES Review*, 5–6, pp. 33–41.

Yang, M., Goldstein, H., Rath, T. & Hill, N. (1997) *The use of assessment data for school improvement purposes. Unpublished Research Report* (Institute of Education, University of London, and Hampshire CC).

The Influence of Neighborhood Poverty During Childhood on Fertility, Education, and Earnings Outcomes

GEORGE GALSTER, DAVE E. MARCOTTE, MARV MANDELL, HAL WOLMAN & NANCY AUGUSTINE

Introduction and Context

Much recent literature—emanating both from the US and Europe—has focused our attention on the plight of children growing up in neighborhoods of concentrated socio-economic disadvantage. From a policy perspective, it is critical for the guidance of urban revitalization initiatives and assisted housing programs designed to increase access to a wider range of locations to ascertain the degree to which neighborhood characteristics affect children's developmental context (Galster, 2002, 2005; Galster *et al.* 2003).

The research here is designed to advance understanding of the extent to which the success of children in young adult life (measured by a variety of indicators) is related to the characteristics of their neighborhoods while controlling for characteristics of their families (education, income, attitudes, values, family structure), parents' homeownership status and residential mobility history. This paper focuses on the relationship between one particular aspect of the child's developmental environment, the cumulative neighborhood poverty rate experienced during the first 18 years of life, and three outcomes: teen fertility, educational attainment and earnings. This establishes the focus for the literature review, theoretical development and discussion of findings, with the other background characteristics of young adults essentially being treated here as control variables.

The statistical literature seeking to identify the predictors of various social, economic, behavioral and psychological outcomes for children and adults is voluminous and has been subject to several recent comprehensive reviews (Earls & Carlson, 2001; Ellen & Turner, 2003; Galster, 2005; Leventhal & Brooks-Gunn, 2000; Robert, 1999; Sampson *et al.*, 2002). It is sufficient to note in summary that the bulk of this literature (e.g. Brooks-Gunn *et al.*, 1997; Furstenberg *et al.*, 1999) examines factors affecting outcomes measured during childhood, ranging from pre-school to adolescence. However important such outcomes are, it is also crucial to examine childhood factors that account for later success as adults. In this regard there is an established literature examining negative adult outcomes, such as welfare usage (e.g. Gottschalk *et al.*, 1994; Gottschalk, 1996; Moffitt, 1992; Pepper, 2000; Vartanian, 1999), school dropouts (e.g. Clark, 1992; Gleason & Vartanian, 1999; Mayer, 1997; Sawhill & Chadwick, 1999), crime (e.g. Freeman, 1991; Grogger, 1997; Peeples & Loeber, 1994; Sullivan, 1989), teen childbearing (e.g. Barber, 2001; Furstenberg *et al.*, 1990; Haurin, 1992; McLanahan & Bumpass, 1988; Sawhill & Chadwick, 1999), acceptance of deviant behavior (Friedrichs & Blasius, 2003), mental illness (Wheaton & Clarke, 2003), and economic idleness (Haveman & Wolfe, 1994; Mayer, 1997; Payne, 1987; Sawhill & Chadwick, 1999). The literature that examines childhood factors that account for economic success as adults is sparse by comparison (but see Corcoran *et al.*, 1992; Haveman & Wolfe, 1994; Holloway & Mulherin, 2004; Vartanian, 1999) and does not adequately address the methodological challenges with which we are concerned.

As will be explained below, previous studies attempting to estimate the relative importance of a child's family, neighborhood, residential stability and homeownership status characteristics on outcomes as an adult must be treated with caution because they have: (1) treated these background variables as though they were independent, and (2) employed inadequate methods to control for household selection effects (Galster, 2003a). The study offers what it is hoped will be advances in both areas. First, it treats the aforementioned key explanatory variables above as endogenously determined. Second, to deal both with endogeneity and selection problems, a variant of two-stage least squares is employed to derive an instrumental variable (IV) for childhood values of the neighborhood poverty and it is used to estimate relationships with young adult fertility, educational and earnings outcomes.

Data from the US Panel Study of Income Dynamics (PSID) that are matched with Census tract data are analyzed, thereby permitting documentation of a wide range of family background and neighborhood circumstantial characteristics. For children born between 1968 and 1974, an analysis is made of data on their first 18 years and various outcomes in 1999 when they are between 25 and 31 years of age. The study finds that, all else equal, the average rate of neighborhood poverty experienced by children during ages 0–18 is strongly related to their fertility, educational attainment and earnings, although only the latter outcomes are robust to IV procedures.

The paper is organized as follows. It first offers a holistic framework for understanding how children's neighborhood environment might influence outcomes when they are young adults. This is then employed as a vehicle for evaluating a range of previous work and establishing a foundation for the modeling efforts. Second, there is a description of the two pre-eminent challenges that must be overcome if accurate measurements are to be gained of the above relationship: selection and endogeneity. Third, there is a description of the dataset and the multi-step IV estimation procedure employed to meet the aforementioned challenges. Fourth, statistical results are presented of the key relationships between a child's neighborhood poverty rate and subsequent fertility, education and earnings outcomes. The final section discusses conclusions, implications and directions for further research.

How Might Children's Neighborhoods Influence their Outcomes as Young Adults?

Potential Causal Mechanisms

Neighborhood mechanisms are thought to operate through various individual, family, school, peer and community-level processes. Scholars have proposed various theoretical models, typically highlighting different underlying processes, to explain potential pathways of neighborhood influences (Jencks & Mayer, 1990; Leventhal & Brooks-Gunn, 2000; Sampson *et al.*, 2002). Prior empirical research has thus far been unable to sort out definitively these competing hypotheses (Brooks-Gunn *et al.*, 1997; Dietz *et al.*, 2002; Duncan & Raudenbush, 2001; Ellen & Turner, 1997, 2003; Friedrichs *et al.*, 2003; Leventhal & Brooks-Gunn, 2000; Sampson *et al.*, 2002). It is thought that several not-mutually exclusive possibilities may explain why highly disadvantaged neighborhood conditions experienced during childhood could influence young adult outcomes related to fertility, educations and earnings:

- Lower-quality public schools and other institutional infrastructure (health clinics, recreational areas, family support services, etc.) that offer less skill-building resources for their students to complete high school and move successfully into either post-secondary education or higher-paying employment.
- Higher levels of exposure to violence, which lead to stresses inhibiting ability to concentrate on their studies or work.
- Social norms that are less supportive of educational attainment and regular employment, and more supportive of teen fertility.
- Seemingly attractive forms of income generation through illegal and quasi-legal activities in the neighborhood that require little educational credentialing or participation in the mainstream labor force.
- Less information about and geographic access to places of higher-quality, post-secondary education and higher-wage employment.
- Spatial stigmatization of residents in disadvantaged neighborhoods by prospective employers and gatekeepers of post-secondary educational institutions.

98 *Quantifying Neighbourhood Effects*

Prior Statistical Work and Its Shortcomings

How neighborhood context affects children and adults has been a burgeoning field of empirical enquiry internationally, as evinced by several recent comprehensive and methodologically critical reviews of the literature (Dietz, 2001; Duncan *et al.*, 1997; Duncan & Raudenbush, 1999; Earls & Carlson, 2001; Ellen & Turner, 1997, 2003; Friedrichs *et al.*, 2003; Galster, 2003a, 2005; Gephart, 1997; Leventhal & Brooks-Gunn, 2000; Robert, 1999; Sampson *et al.*, 2002). There will be no attempt to duplicate these reviews here, but the methodological critiques that motivate the current paper will be noted. Few studies consider young adult outcomes or collect information over the entirety of childhood that may be used to predict such outcomes. Many omit key parental control variables, thereby biasing the apparent impacts of neighborhood. None meet fully the fundamental statistical challenges posed by selection and endogeneity, a topic which is now examined.

A Holistic Framework

In order to provide a framework for both illustrating the limitations of previous studies and guiding the efforts in this study, a model is presented and is portrayed in Figure 1. It is posited that young adult outcomes of interest (shown on the right panel of Figure 1) are

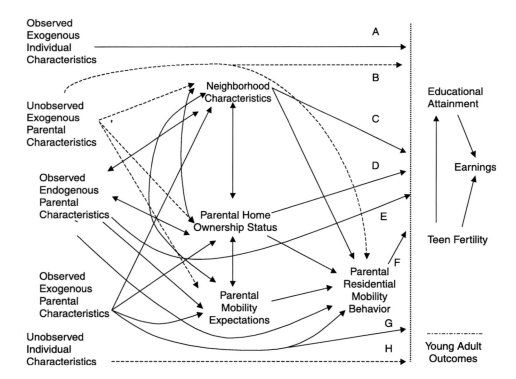

Figure 1. A structural model of young adult outcomes

determined by four sets of exogenous or predetermined variables: observed characteristics of individual children (path A: e.g. gender, race), unobserved characteristics of individual children (path H: e.g. intelligence), observed parental characteristics (path G: e.g. education, age), and unobserved parental characteristics (path B: e.g. ambition, present orientation, concern for their children's future). These unobserved parental factors (shown as dotted lines in Figure 1) are the source of omitted variables bias associated with selection, which will be discussed below. Young adult outcomes are also influenced by a set of parental characteristics that may more properly be modeled as endogenous to the childhood residential context (path E: e.g. parental employment and income history). Finally, it is seen that young adult outcomes are influenced by a set of intervening endogenous variables: neighborhood characteristics (path C), parental homeownership status (path D), and parental mobility expectations mediated by actual mobility behavior (path F).

The key innovation of the model is the specification of the intervening variables neighborhood location / homeownership status / mobility expectations / household socio-economic status as 'mutually causal phenomena'. It is argued that accurately measuring the relationship of 'any one of these phenomena' with young adult outcomes requires that its relationship 'with all the others' be taken into account, a key point to which will be returned to below. Brief, heuristic rationales are offered for these bi-directional causal relationships portrayed in Figure 1; supportive evidence is summarized in the aforementioned reviews:

- *Neighborhood and homeownership status*: If economic status, ethnicity or other factors constrain a household to a set of neighborhoods that are afflicted with numerous social problems and concomitant expectations of property value deflation, there will be little motivation to buy a home there; on the other hand, if a household would like to buy, certain neighborhoods may not be selected if they hold the prospect for little property appreciation.
- *Neighborhood and homeownership status* AND *mobility expectations* (expected duration of stay): If someone expects to remain long in a dwelling, given their employment and life-cycle stage situation, they may be more willing to bear the high transactions costs of buying *and* will try harder to avoid declining neighborhoods; in turn, if someone is willing and able to purchase a home, and succeeds in doing so in a good neighborhood, they will probably expect to move less in the future.
- *Homeownership status and parental characteristics*: Income, stability of employment and non-housing wealth will influence the ability to purchase a home; homeownership, in turn, may provide a sense of security and control over environment that promotes parental efficacy and marital stability, as well as a key financial resource for furthering children's education.
- *Neighborhood and parental characteristics*: Parental income and non-housing wealth will influence which neighborhoods can feasibly be chosen; neighborhood location with respect to potential employment and job information networks, social milieu and environmental features can influence, in turn, parents' health, employment and stigmatization by potential employers and, thereby, their income and wealth subsequently.

The foregoing relationships can be summarized in the following set of equations:

$$HO = f(N, ME, H, [X_1]) \qquad (1)$$

$$N = f(HO, ME, H, [X_2]) \qquad (2)$$

$$ME = f(HO, N, M, H, [X_3]) \qquad (3)$$

$$M = f(N, H, ME, [X_4]) \qquad (4)$$

$$H = f(N, HO, [X_5]) \qquad (5)$$

where:
HO = homeownership status (own or rent)
N = neighborhood poverty rate
ME = expectations regarding potential move during next year
M = actual mobility observed during the year
H = endogenous household economic characteristic (poverty status)
$[X_i]$ = vector of exogenous or predetermined predictors appropriate to equation i, to be presented in more detail below.

The holistic framework not only underscores the forthcoming econometric specification, but it provides a context for comprehending the difficult challenges faced by investigators of neighborhood effects. The paper now turns to a discussion of these challenges.

Challenges in Measuring Determinants of Young Adult Outcomes

The holistic framework portrayed in Figure 1 suggests that there are two pre-eminent challenges in obtaining accurate measurements of the relationship between young adult outcomes and key childhood predictors of interest, such as neighborhood, homeownership status, mobility and certain parental characteristics. These challenges involve selection and endogeneity.

The Challenge of Selection

Bias in the neighborhood-outcome relationship due to household selection is now a well-known challenge. The basic issue is that some parents who have certain (unmeasured) motivations and skills related to their children's upbringing would move to select neighborhoods. Any observed relationship between neighborhood conditions and child or young adult outcomes may therefore be biased because of this systematic spatial selection process, even if all the observable characteristics of parents are controlled (Dietz, 2001; Duncan *et al.*, 1997; Duncan & Raudenbush, 1999; Manski, 1995, 2000). Ordinary least squares regression provides biased estimates of the effect of neighborhood on outcomes because the neighborhood variable is correlated with the disturbance term in the regression. The problem can be formulated as omitted variables bias. Is the observed statistical relationship between outcomes and neighborhood indicative of neighborhood's independent effect, or merely unmeasured characteristics of parents that truly affected child outcomes but also led to neighborhood choices as well?[1] The implicit omitted variables' relationships in this selection problem are portrayed as dashed lines in Figure 1.

When analyzing a sample of households who have chosen their neighborhoods through the private market process, this selection bias is likely severe indeed (Manski, 1995; Tienda, 1991). A variety of econometric techniques, including sibling studies and instrumental variables, have been employed in an attempt to overcome this neighborhood selection bias, but with incomplete success and/or limited general applicability thus far (see review in Galster, 2003a, 2005). In addition, a few studies have attempted to model explicitly the selection process into owner and rental tenures (Green & White, 1997; Haurin *et al.*, 2002a, 2002b).

Analysis of data on outcomes that can be produced by an experimental design whereby individuals or households are randomly assigned to different neighborhoods has often been seen as the preferred method for avoiding biases from selection. In this regard, the US Moving To Opportunity (MTO) demonstration has been touted conventionally as *the* study from which to draw conclusions about the magnitude of neighborhood effects. Although the MTO research design randomly assigns those public housing residents who volunteer to one of three experimental groups, it does not fully control the assignment of neighborhood characteristics of the two experimental groups receiving tenant-based rental subsidies (Sampson *et al.*, 2002). Of course, the group that receives only a rental subsidy with no mobility counseling and no geographic restrictions can select from a wide range of neighborhoods. However, even the treatment group receiving intensive mobility counseling and assistance, although programmatically constrained to move initially to a neighborhood with less than 10 per cent poverty rates, has the ability nevertheless to choose neighborhoods varying on their school quality, homeownership rates, racial composition, local institutional resources, etc. Moreover, subsequent to their initial, constrained location they are free to move to different, higher-poverty neighborhoods should they choose (as many have; see Goering *et al.*, 2002). Thus, even studies based on MTO data cannot fully finesse the selection bias issue.

However, the challenge is even deeper. If Figure 1 was adopted as a working premise, the selection process would become much more complicated than merely the parents' 'independent' selection of neighborhood. It is the view of the authors of this study that the holistic challenge embodies the 'interdependent' selections of neighborhood, homeownership status and expected mobility.

The Challenge of Endogeneity[2]

Previous statistical studies have taken only a partial view of the causal patterns embodied in Figure 1 and Equations (1)–(5); virtually all have omitted one or more of the intervening variables. To the extent that these variables are mutually causal they will be correlated with the neighborhood variable. Under these circumstances, the coefficient will be a biased estimate of the effect of neighborhood on outcomes because the neighborhood variable is correlated with the disturbance term in the regression. As in the case of selection there is an omitted variables bias problem, but here it is due to the neighborhood variable's causal relationships with other, uncontrolled variables that affect outcomes as well.

However, the solution to this challenge may not be as straightforward as including all intervening variables in the outcome equation. If the causal relationships are as strong as has been posited above, these intervening variables may be so highly correlated that multicollinearity may arise as a new econometric challenge.

Meeting the Challenges through an Instrumental Variables Approach

It is thought that a promising strategy in response to *both* selection and endogeneity challenges in an analysis of households sampled from non-experimental circumstances is the application of instrumental variable techniques (IV).[3] The current study employs a variant of the well-known two-stage least squares technique for producing IVs (Murray, 2006). In the first stage of this technique, the endogenous variable in question (e.g. a neighborhood characteristic) is regressed on one or more other exogenous variables that, hopefully, are highly correlated with the endogenous variable but uncorrelated with the disturbance term. In a model such as (1)–(5), the explanatory variables in this first-stage regression include all exogenous or predetermined variables that appear on the right-hand sides of any of these Equations ([X]). The predicted values for the endogenous variable yielded by this first-stage regression are substituted (in this case, after further manipulation explained below) for the actual endogenous variable's values in a second-stage regression explaining outcomes. It is believed that this newly constructed IV will not be correlated with the disturbance term in the outcome regression (thereby avoiding omitted variable bias) or with other intervening endogenous variables (thereby avoiding multicollinearity).

The challenge of this method, of course, is identifying first-stage variables that reasonably meet the aforementioned correlation criteria. In the seminal example of instrumental variables applied to the neighborhood selection problem, Evans *et al.* (1992) used metropolitan-level variables for unemployment rate, median family income, poverty rate and percentage of adults completing college as identifying variables predicting the 'neighborhood variable': proportion of students in the local school who are economically disadvantaged. Analogously, Foster & McLanahan (1996) used citywide labor market conditions as identifying variables predicting neighborhood high school dropout rates. It is thought that this strategy for instrumenting not only neighborhood-level but individual-level variables with corresponding variables measured at larger geographic scales is fruitful, and it is used in the present study together with other identifying instruments, as explained below.

Data to be Analyzed and Key Measures

The Panel Study of Income Dynamics

A brief overview of the Panel Study of Income Dynamics (PSID) data analyzed is a prerequisite for understanding the particular instrumental variables approach used here. Beginning in 1967, the PSID began interviewing 5000 American families. In every year through 1996 and every other year since then, those families have been interviewed, as have all families subsequently formed by individuals in those families and by future spouses and children of those individuals. So, by 1999, the PSID was following nearly 10 000 families. While the PSID over-sampled poor households in order to obtain relatively large sample sizes for such households, the poverty over-sample was subsequently dropped in the 1990s. Consequently, the present analysis is limited to a sample designed to be nationally representative of the US population in 1967. Differential attrition over the course of the panel is accounted for by adjusting individuals' PSID sampling weights by the inverse of the reciprocal of the attrition rate of PSID sample members with the same race, gender and poverty status at birth. A PSID geo-matched file is employed, which appends the child's census tract identifier to each observation. Values of census tract variables are interpolated for observations between census years. Therefore it is possible to observe annually the household and (approximate) neighborhood environments in which the sample individuals spend their childhood.

The analysis focuses on the PSID cohort of children born during the period 1968–74 because it provides data on their first 18 years as well as a variety of outcomes measured in 1999 when they were young adults (ages 25–31) who most probably had completed their education and had ample opportunity to enter the labor force.[4] Here, as throughout, statistics weighted by PSID sampling weights are presented, adjusted for group-specific attrition.

A necessary condition for the precise measurement of neighborhood effects is that the widest possible array of characteristics of the children and their household while growing up are included as controls in the model (Ginther *et al.*, 2000). The authors believe that the work here has met this condition in a way superior to prior work. The study not only controls for a wide range of objective characteristics of the household but, unlike prior work, also controls for several attitudinal and behavioral characteristics of the head. Descriptive statistics for these numerous aspects of the sample of children that were analyzed—themselves, their households, the heads of their households, and their neighborhoods as they were growing up—are provided in Table 1.

Measures of Key Explanatory Variables and Outcomes

This paper considers a commonly used measure of a disadvantaged neighborhood environment: percentage of population with household incomes below the US federal poverty standard. In each case information from the census tract is used, an area of approximately 4000 inhabitants, tabulated in the decennial *Census of Population and Housing*, with values interpolated for inter-census years.[5] On average during their childhood, children in the sample experienced a census tract having a 10.5 per cent poverty rate, slightly below the national average during this era.

Several studies suggest that census tract data on socio-economic disadvantage may serve as reasonable (if admittedly imperfect) proxies for intra-neighborhood social processes through which neighborhood effects reasonably might transpire. Measures similar to neighborhood poverty rate have proven statistically related to: a multi-dimensional index of social processes (Cook *et al.*, 1997); unsupervised peer groups and organizational participation (Sampson & Groves, 1989); informal social control (Elliott *et al.*, 1996); collective efficacy (Sampson *et al.*, 1997); multiple dimensions of social capital (Sampson *et al.*, 1999); and perceived disorder (Coulton *et al.*, 1999; Kohen *et al.*, 2002).[6] However, it is recognized that neighborhood poverty is not a proximate measure of the underlying processes that may be responsible for neighborhood effects, and thus interpretation of regression results remains somewhat ambiguous, a topic which will be returned to in closing. Several potential causal mechanisms may underpin the correlations between neighborhood poverty during childhood and young adult fertility, education and earnings. These include: low-quality local schools and institutions; greater exposure

Table 1. Characteristics of sample individuals and their mean circumstances during ages 0–18

	Mean
Characteristics of individuals in 1999	
Black female [blackfem]	0.041
Black male [blackmale]	0.057
White female [whitefem]	0.331
Order of birth (1 = first, 2 = 2nd, etc.) [birthorder]	2.233
Age in years [age99]	28.74
Married [married]	0.481
Characteristics of their households (calculated over ages 0–18)	
Proportion of years lived in poverty [pro_live_under_poverty0to18]	0.069
Proportion of years when not changed residence [pro_stability_year0to18]	0.809
Proportion of years when head owned the home [pro_own0to18]	0.722
Proportion of years lived with two parents [pro_livew_2_parents0to18]	0.842
Proportion of years lived in metropolitan area [ave_smsa0to18]	0.731
Characteristics of their household heads (* = average during ages 0–18)	
Education of household head* [ave_education_head0to18]	13.24
Occupational prestige of household head* [ave_hdocc_pre0to18]	43.92
Proportion of years head was self employed [ave_self_employed0to18]	0.141
Proportion of years wife of head employed [ave_employed_wife0to18]	0.491
Annual hours head worked* [ave_annu_hrs_wkd0to18]	2123
Head self-identified as protestant, catholic, or jewish [religion]	0.901
Proportion of years head read newspaper every day [ave_readnewspaper]	0.802
Proportion of years head belonged to a union [ave_union]	0.285
Proportion of years head did not attend religious service weekly [ave_nochurch]	0.226
Proportion of years head never participated in social clubs [ave_no_socialclubs]	0.538
Proportion of years head 'planned his/her life ahead' [ave_plan_ahead]	0.581
Proportion of years head 'trusted most people' [ave_trust]	0.604
Head is a veteran [veteran]	0.392
Mother first gave birth as teen [momteen]	0.045
Head raised in large city (not suburb) [largecity]	0.419
Head raised in rural or small town (not suburb) [farm]	0.174
Characteristics of their neighborhood (calculated over ages 0–18)	
Average number of neighbors head knew by name [ave_num_neigh_known]	12.33
Proportion of years lived with family in walking distance [ave_relatives]	0.392
Average per cent population below poverty in census tract [ave_perc_inc_pov]	10.25

Note: Variable acronym used in Appendix 2 shown in square brackets.
Source: Authors' analysis of PSID data for select sample (see text); $n = 755$ (weighted)

to violence, subcultural social norms, lack of collective social controls, resource-poor interpersonal networks and spatial stigmatization.

The goal here is to relate a child's neighborhood poverty rate, controlling for all the other characteristics of the child's family and environment listed in Table 1, to three key outcomes: fertility prior to age 18, school attainment and earnings as of 1999. A total of 94 per cent of the sample children born between 1968–74 had not had a child prior to age 18. By 1999, 90 per cent of this cohort had graduated from high school or obtained a Graduate Equivalent Degree, and 20 per cent had graduated from a four-year college or university. The PSID only collects income information from respondents who have formed their own household and worked at some time during the previous year, so income statistics and regression results reported refer only to this subset of the cohort. However,

81 per cent of the cohort had formed a household and were employed by the time of the 1999 survey. On average in 1998, this cohort of household heads who were employed part- or full-time individually earned $17 348. Note that the analysis of earnings thus excludes all full-time students who were not employed during 1998.

Model and Estimation Procedure

Model Overview

Expressed symbolically, the model for outcomes of young adults is:

$$FER = f(N_c, HO_c, M_c, H_c, [X_6], [X_7], [X_8]) \tag{6}$$

$$HS = f(N_c, HO_c, M_c, H_c, [X_6], [X_7], [X_8], FER) \tag{7}$$

$$COL = f(N_c, HO_c, M_c, H_c, [X_6], [X_7], [X_8], FER) \tag{8}$$

$$INC = f(N_c, HO_c, M_c, H_c, [X_6], [X_7], [X_8], FER, HS, COL, HRS) \tag{9}$$

where:
 FER = 1 if reached age 18 without having a child, 0 otherwise
 HS = 1 if received a high school diploma or equivalency degree by 1999, 0 otherwise
 COL = 1 if received a college bachelor's (4-year) degree by 1999, 0 otherwise
 INC = natural logarithm of 1998 income from earnings (only for those who had formed a household and were employed some time during 1998)
 N_c = average poverty rate in census tract during ages 0–18
 HO_c = proportion of childhood years that household owned the dwelling occupied
 M_c = proportion of childhood years that the household moved between dwellings
 H_c = proportion of childhood years that the household earned less than poverty income
 $[X_{6c}]$ = exogenous characteristics of the individual in 1999; see Table 1 for listing
 $[X_{7c}]$ = exogenous characteristics of the household during childhood; see Table 1
 $[X_{8c}]$ = exogenous characteristics of the neighborhood during childhood (average number of neighbors the household knew by name and proportion of years when family members were within walking distance); see Table 1
 HRS = hours worked during 1998 and c subscripts indicate variables computed for the entire childhood period.

The coefficients of variables in the model above were estimated using ordinary least squares (OLS) when the outcome is continuous (Equation (9)) and logit when the outcome is dichotomous (Equations (6)–(8)). The sample for estimating these coefficients includes all children in the initial 1968–74 PSID cohort who have 'survived' in the sample to the point at which the outcome in question is observed, 1999. Equations for fertility, education and earnings outcomes have virtually identical right-hand sides measuring (exogenous or predetermined) characteristics of the individual and the individual's household and (endogenous) aforementioned childhood conditions; descriptive statistics of these last variables are presented in Table 1. For all of these variables in the model, proportional figures calculated over the first 18 years of the child's life (or for however many years data are available) are used.

It should be noted that the set of outcomes are modeled as causally interrelated, as shown in the right panel of Figure 1. Educational attainment is a function of fertility prior to age 18. Earnings are a function of fertility and education.

Instrumentation Procedure

It is suspected that N_c will be correlated with the disturbance terms in Equations (6)–(9) because of aforementioned selection and endogeneity issues. Therefore, the study experiments with instrumental variables. The approach for estimating IVs proceeds in the following three steps.

First, an OLS regression is estimated based on observations of individual child-years. In this regression the left-hand side is the observed value of the census tract poverty rate in a given child's neighborhood in a particular PSID year and the right-hand side contains observed values of every exogenous variable [X] in the system of Equations (1)–(5). These exogenous variables include contemporaneous values of 'countywide' characteristics corresponding to the N_c, HO_c, M_c, and H_c variables and dummy variables for calendar year. The complete listing is shown in Appendix 1. In this first step, the regression is estimated based on all observations from age 1 to 18 of each child in the sample. All observations of children having data for at least 10 years of their childhood were included. What is of prime importance here is how well the first-stage regressions predict the values of N_c, not their estimated parameters in and of themselves, since this will determine the power of the instrument (Murray, 2006). As a result, for this first stage OLS is used, not needlessly complicated panel estimation procedures.

In the second step of the approach, the aforementioned regression is employed to generate predicted values of neighborhood poverty for each of the first 18 years of each child's life, based on values of all exogenous variables appropriate for the given year. There must now be a switch from a child-year unit of observation to a child-childhood average unit of observation, which necessitates a step not normally required in two-stage least squares. In the third step the 'average' of these predicted values is computed over all observed years of childhood. These childhood averages of annual predicted values for each sampled individual become the IV measures for neighborhood poverty experienced during childhood N_c.

Identifying and Evaluating Instruments for Childhood Neighborhood Poverty Rate

In order to satisfy the rank condition in performing two-stage least squares, there must be at least as many exogenous variables excluded from each Equation (1)–(5) as there are endogenous variables included in each equation. This condition is met; indeed, the equation system (1)–(5) is over-identified.

Moreover, each equation must have one or more clearly exogenous variables that appear only in the given equation as strong predictors. In the case of childhood neighborhood poverty rate, the corresponding county-level value was employed as the unique identifying instrument.[7] Indeed, this proved highly predictive of the tract-level values (t statistic of 34), and typically was minimally correlated with other endogenous variables in the models.

Overall the first-stage regression for neighborhood poverty rate performed moderately well (the R^2 was 0.45). Moreover, because there were 12 500 child-year observations in this first-stage regression and only 31 regressors, confidence is high that the study substantially reduced the bias associated with using OLS coefficients (Han & Hausmann, 2005) and avoided the problem of weak instruments (Murray, 2006).[8]

Complicating Issues

Five technical issues require further discussion. The first of these is the operational definition of neighborhood. While imperfect, census tracts are employed as the preferred approximation to neighborhood, as is common in US studies. However, until 1990 rural areas were not divided into census tracts. In order to avoid the potential problems of (1) missing data and (2) mixing urban and rural scales of 'neighborhood', the analysis is confined to children who spent at least 12 of their first 18 years in tracted, metropolitan area neighborhoods.

Second, the attitudes and behaviors of the household head that are employed as controls (see Table 1) are not measured annually in the PSID. Indeed, for most variables the questions were asked only during the years 1968–72.[9] Each attitude and behavior employed as a control proved stable over time. Pair-wise correlations between responses to the question 'carry out plans' over the six points in time at which this question was asked ranged from 0.17 to 0.40. Cronbach's alpha, a measure of internal consistency, for a scale consisting of the sum of the responses to this question over the six years, was 0.70. Pair-wise correlations between responses to the question 'plan ahead' over the six points at which this question was asked ranged from 0.20 to 0.46; Cronbach's alpha was 0.77. Pair-wise correlations between responses to the question 'trust' over the five points in time at which this question was asked ranged from 0.40 to 0.54; Cronbach's alpha was 0.81.

Third, although the model provides unusually strong controls, the spectre of omitted variables must be considered nevertheless. There is no control in (6)–(9) for neighborhood characteristics or numerous personal characteristics of the young adult in 1999 (such as a variety of experiences, attitudes and behaviors). However, these omitted variables do not confound the basic estimates of childhood neighborhood effects. If these variables prove to be uncorrelated with N_c there will be no bias in its coefficient, even though the overall explanatory power of the outcomes regressions will be reduced. On the other hand, it may be that these omitted variables may be correlated because they are (partially) influenced by the childhood endogenous and exogenous characteristics specified in (6)–(9). In this case reduced-form estimates of childhood neighborhood poverty on young adult outcomes are essentially obtained, some of which may transpire through the omitted (but intervening) variables.

Fourth, given the conceptual model in Figure 1 it would have been desirable to simultaneously instrument for N_c but *all* the endogenous variables in (6)–(9): HO_c, M_c and H_c. This would have permitted the estimation of less-biased parameters for these variables as well. Unfortunately, in the preliminary experiments it proved challenging to identify instruments that uniquely identified all these variables. The result was that the resulting instruments for N_c, HO_c, M_c and H_c proved too inter-correlated to be meaningfully employed in the same regression.

Finally, as noted above, the instrumentation procedure involves estimates for N_c that are 'multi-year averages of predicted values of neighborhood poverty'. Given that the distribution of this new, 'average' instrument is not known, the standard errors yielded by conventional OLS or logit procedures cannot be interpreted in a straightforward fashion. Thus, as is standard practice under these circumstances, 'bootstrapped' parameter values will be reported, as estimated by STATA when examining the IV estimates.

Results

Overview and Discussion of Control Variables

Before turning to results for the neighborhood poverty variable of primary interest, the study briefly highlights some of the more interesting relationships involving other variables; details are presented in Appendix 2. As an overarching assessment, all four outcome equations evinced decent explanatory power according to the criteria appropriate for logit and OLS estimations (see Appendix 2). Moreover, there is strong support for the specification of recursive relationships between teen fertility, educational attainments and subsequent earnings. Not surprisingly, having a child before 18 clearly appears to reduce the chances of graduating from high school. Educational attainments, especially a college degree, are strongly related to earnings, in turn. Finally, there is strong support for the claim here that the intervening variables (that it is argued are mutually causal with neighborhood) are important predictors of young adult outcomes. Each of these intervening childhood conditions—time spent in a poor household, a two-parent household, an owner-occupant household, and a residentially stable household—proved predictive of one or more subsequent outcomes. This reinforces the contention here that models of neighborhood effects that do not control for these contexts probably suffer from severe omitted variables bias.

As for predictors of not having a child before age 18, growing up in a family that did not move often and whose head aspired to 'planning ahead' proved efficacious. Perhaps it is the case that residential stability both reduces the need of adolescents to make friends by engaging in risky behaviors and increases the likelihood that neighbors will provide both normative and supervisory sanctions against such behaviors. Future-oriented parents may be more prone to instill these attitudes in their children, thereby encouraging them to avoid future prospect-stunting actions such as teen childrearing. Older cohorts in the sample, those born in the late 1960s, were more likely to have a child as a teen. This might be attributable to radically shifting sexual mores during that period, although this is only speculation. It is also noted that women (both black and white roughly equally) are substantially less likely to reach age 18 without having a child, although part of this result is probably due to gendered response bias.

Consider next the educational attainment equations. Not surprisingly, having well-educated parent(s) was strongly correlated with greater chances of later graduating from high school and college. More surprising, the same pattern held for children raised by parents who knew more of the neighbors by name. There is uncertainty about why this greater degree of parental neighborhood social integration (controlling for mobility) seemingly translates into greater educational achievements, although it may be due to the implied intensification of neighbors' monitoring of children's behaviors, both pro- and anti-educational. This explanation would also be consistent for the finding that children of parents who never belonged to social organizations were less likely to graduate from high school. Children raised in homes owned by their parents had higher probabilities of completing high school and (especially) college. There are a number of developmental and behavioral reasons why this may be so, which are explored in depth in another paper (Galster *et al.*, forthcoming). Older members of the cohorts evinced higher achievements, probably because they had more time to obtain graduate equivalency exams and complete college coursework. Interestingly, blacks were more likely to graduate from high school than whites in the sample (black makes statistically significant more so), once the battery of parental and contextual characteristics were controlled. Other statistically significant relationships do not have obvious explanations. Children from homes where the head was more trusting of other people, a veteran or not a union member were less likely to graduate from high school. Children who were raised in a large city (instead of a suburb), and came from homes where both parents were not present were more likely to get a college degree.

Finally, in the wage earnings equation it was observed that children raised by a head who was more future-oriented earned more, all else equal. This suggests that these children have learned a set of attitudes and behaviors related to delayed gratification and longer-term strategizing that has substantial labor market payoffs. Children from households experiencing longer spells of poverty and/or single parenting earn less, consistent with the hypothesis that material and psychological deprivation associated with these circumstances creates developmental disadvantages with lasting earnings impacts. Older cohorts earn more, as is predicted from their typically longer tenure in the workforce. Employees earn more who are better-educated, white males and work more weeks annually, as expected. It is less clear why children raised in dual-parent homes with mothers who worked more earned more as young adults, though role modeling may be at work.

Of course, the results of primary interest relate to neighborhood poverty during childhood; these are reported in the columns denoted 'no-IV' in Table 2. As an overview, it is found that experiencing more neighborhood poverty on average as a child is associated in a statistically significant way (both directly and indirectly) with: (1) greater chances of having a child before age 18; (2) lesser chances of graduating from high school; and (3) earning lower wages as a young adult. Experiencing more neighborhood poverty as a child is also associated with a lower rate of college graduation, although the coefficient is only slightly larger than its standard error. The non-trivial magnitudes of these associations can be assessed as follows. For each one percentage-point higher average childhood poverty rate, the probability of the individual having a child before age 18 increases by 0.005, the probability of the individual graduating from high school decreases by 0.006 (both calculations conducted at the respective outcome means), and the individual's earnings decrease by 2.1 per cent.

Several features about these relationships warrant emphasis, which suggest that they are a lower-bound estimate. First, the earnings relationship is only estimated for those who have formed households and were employed in 1998, and thus does not count any potential impacts of childhood neighborhood poverty on likelihoods of forming households or being employed. Second, the earnings relationship does not consider any potential impacts of childhood neighborhood poverty on number of hours worked if employed. (However, in preliminary experiments it was not possible to identify any strong relationship between neighborhood poverty and either employment or hours worked.) Third, the relationships for education and earnings are only the direct effects, and do not consider the indirect paths from teen fertility to educational attainments to earnings.

Assessing Magnitude of Implied Impacts of Childhood Neighborhood Poverty

To explore this last aspect above further, simulations were conducted that utilized the entire recursive structure of the outcomes. Counterfactual changes were imposed to the value of average childhood neighborhood poverty rate to generate corresponding predicted values for the probability of reaching age 18 before having any children. Predicted changes in these fertility probabilities were then added as input into the models explaining educational attainments, along with initial changes in childhood neighborhood

Table 2. Estimated parameters for neighborhood poverty and intermediate outcome variables

Variable	No Child Pre-18		High School Graduate		College Graduate		ln (Earnings)	
	no IV	IV	no IV	IV	no IV	IV	no IV	IV
Neighborhood poverty rate	−0.104 [0.035]***	0.04 [0.074]	−0.059 [0.029]**	−0.04 [0.048]	−0.038 [0.031]	−0.015 [0.039]	−0.021 [0.012]*	−0.019 [0.014]
No child pre-age 18	N/A	N/A	1.208 [0.458]***	1.44 [0.368]**	−0.081 [0.559]	0.481 [0.610]	0.032 [0.214]	0.101 [0.140]
High school graduate +	N/A	N/A	N/A	N/A	N/A	N/A	0.111 [0.135]	0.234 [0.117]
College graduate	N/A	N/A	N/A	N/A	N/A	N/A	0.361 [0.107]***	0.261 [0.113]***
n	755	680	755	680	755	680	541	486

Note: Robust standard errors in brackets; estimated by bootstrap technique in case of IVs.
Parameters estimated by logit, except OLS for earnings.
*** $p < 0.01$; ** $p < 0.05$; * $p < 0.10$ (two-tailed tests).

poverty, yielding new estimates for these intermediate outcomes. Finally, predicted changes in fertility and educational attainments were then added as input into the model explaining earnings (as well as the direct effect of altered childhood neighborhood poverty). The conclusion is that realistic variations in average neighborhood poverty rates experienced by the 1968–74 cohort from ages 0 to 18 are associated with a substantial variation in their outcomes in 1999, all else equal. Take an admittedly extreme, although certainly plausible, difference in neighborhood environments. Compared with otherwise identical children raised by otherwise identical parents in a neighborhood with a low average poverty rate of 5 per cent (approximately half the sample mean), children experiencing an average 40 per cent rate (a conventional US benchmark for 'concentrated poverty' neighborhoods; Jargowsky, 1997) are predicted by the simulation to have a:

- 24 percentage-point (24 per cent of the mean) greater chance of having a child before age 18;
- 14 percentage-point (15 per cent of the mean) lower probability of graduating from high school;
- 10 percentage-point (70 per cent of the mean) lower probability of graduating from college; and
- $13 334 (54 per cent of the mean) lower annual earnings.

It is believed that these simulated values represent socio-economically significant differences. This evidence is supportive of the position that poverty neighborhoods in America create important limitations on the life chances of children who are raised there.

The Importance of Neighborhood Poverty Relative to Other Predictors

The prior simulation results beg the question of how important is neighborhood poverty compared to other characteristics of the child's household or residential environment. The answers are explored by employing a simulation process analogous to the one above, except that it is applied to selected variables besides neighborhood poverty that proved predictive in the models. To ease comparisons across multiple characteristics, the 10th, 25th, 50th, 75th and 90th percentile values for each are identified and the associated outcome value is computed when all other predictors are held at their sample means. In each case the 10th percentile represents the least desirable situations. The results are presented in Table 3. As a convenient summary means of comparing strength of relationships, the differences in the given outcome associated with changing the given predictor from the 10th to the 25th percentile and from the 25th percentile to the mean values are computed, as shown in the last two rows of each section of Table 3.

Consider initially the strength of childhood neighborhood poverty's relationships with young adult outcomes relative to the other aspects of context that are viewed here as endogenous. Neighborhood poverty proves stronger than: (1) residential stability for all outcomes; (2) family poverty for all outcomes except earnings; (3) family homeownership for all outcomes except college degree. Consider next the strength of childhood neighborhood poverty's relationships with young adult outcomes relative to two exogenous characteristics of parents that often proved predictive. Neighborhood poverty proves stronger than: (1) living with both parents for all outcomes except earnings; and (2) parental education for all outcomes except educational attainment. These results suggest

Table 3. Comparative effects of childhood neighborhood poverty and other variables

Non-IV results from Table 3 re-organized 1-07

	Neighborhood poverty	Family poverty*	Family owns home*	Residential stability	Lived with 2 Parental*
Probability of having no child by Age 18					
10th percentile	0.880	0.948	0.985	0.933	0.955
25th percentile	0.945	0.967	0.978	0.957	0.964
Mean	0.968	0.968	0.968	0.968	0.968
75th percentile	0.984	0.973	0.952	0.979	0.971
90th percentile	0.988	0.973	0.949	0.982	0.971
10th to 25th percentile	0.065	0.019	−0.007	0.024	0.009
25th percentile to mean	0.023	0.001	−0.010	0.011	0.004
Probability of High School Diploma by 1999					
10th percentile	0.891	0.905	0.925	0.958	0.946
25th percentile	0.935	0.951	0.941	0.955	0.951
Mean	0.953	0.953	0.953	0.953	0.953
75th percentile	0.969	0.964	0.963	0.949	0.955
90th percentile	0.973	0.964	0.964	0.947	0.955
10th to 25th percentile	0.044	0.046	0.016	−0.003	0.005
25th percentile to mean	0.018	0.002	0.012	−0.002	0.002
Probability of having College Degree by 1999					
10th percentile	0.041	0.101	0.032	0.063	0.178
25th percentile	0.055	0.068	0.047	0.065	0.093
Mean	0.067	0.067	0.067	0.067	0.067
75th percentile	0.085	0.057	0.097	0.069	0.045
90th percentile	0.093	0.057	0.103	0.070	0.045
10th to 25th percentile	0.014	−0.032	0.015	0.002	−0.085
25th percentile to mean	0.011	−0.002	0.020	0.001	−0.026

Table 3. *Continued*

Non-IV results from Table 3 re-organized 1-07

			Earnings of householders employed during 1998		
	Neighborhood poverty	Family poverty*	Family owns home*	Residential stability	Lived with 2 Parental*
10th percentile	12953	10494	19627	16254	9962
25th percentile	15468	16882	18416	16904	14467
Mean	17348	17348	17348	17348	17348
75th percentile	20139	20801	16321	18005	21495
90th percentile	21248	20801	16166	18286	21495
10th to 25th percentile	2516	6388	−1211	651	4505
25th percentile to mean	1880	466	−1067	444	2881

Note: 10th percentile = highest neighborhood and family poverty; lowest homeownership and stability; least time spent living with 2 parents; lowest parental education.

that the cumulative importance of childhood neighborhood poverty may be at least as great as many other family and contextual characteristics that have often been central to the child development discussion (e.g. Haveman & Wolfe, 1994).

Non-linear Effects of Neighborhood Poverty

There is considerable theoretical basis for arguing that the impact of neighborhood poverty in shaping the developmental context for children will be non-linear, and the US empirical evidence consistently supports this position (see reviews in Galster, 2002, 2003b). The current results add still more support. Although it is recognized that the logit and semi-logarithmic models necessarily involve some non-linearities, it is thought that the extent of such evinced in the estimated parameters is noteworthy. Table 3 provides the clearest presentation of this. The difference in the probability of having no child by age 18 between growing up in a neighborhood with the mean poverty rate (10 per cent) compared to the 25th percentile poverty rate (19 per cent) is estimated as 0.023; the comparable difference between neighborhoods with the 25th percentile poverty rate and 10th percentile poverty rate (28 per cent) is 0.065, almost three times as great. Similarly, the difference in the probability of graduating from high school between growing up in a neighborhood with the mean poverty rate compared to the 25th percentile poverty rate is estimated as 0.018; the comparable difference between neighborhoods with the 25th percentile poverty rate and 10th percentile poverty rate is 0.044, over twice as great. Qualitatively similar non-linearities are evinced in the case of earnings as well. The consequences of neighborhood poverty in deleteriously distorting the developmental environment for children thus appear especially pernicious when it passes roughly 20 per cent.

Comparing Results for Neighborhood Poverty With and Without IVs

Given the absolute and relative magnitudes of variation demonstrated by the prior simulations, the study explores the extent to which they probably reflect causal influences of neighborhood poverty instead of biases from selection and simultaneity issues. Therefore, this section presents parameters of the childhood neighborhood poverty rate estimated using IVs generated as per the procedures described above. These are shown in the right-hand member of each pair of columns of Table 2.

The main penalty from employing two-stage least squares estimators as IVs is an increase in the standard errors compared to OLS (Murray, 2006). The effort is doubly impaired by the need to estimate the standard errors via bootstrapping methods. Here these penalties have the effect of rendering all neighborhood poverty IV coefficients statistically insignificant. However, it is inappropriate to interpret this as the coefficients are zero, given the aforementioned difficulties with standard errors. Instead, the focus is on how the point estimates of the coefficients have changed.

In this regard, for all outcomes it can be seen that the magnitude of the childhood neighborhood poverty coefficient falls substantially when IVs are applied. The magnitude of decline varies by outcome: (1) no child before age 18 by 62 per cent; (2) high school graduate by 32 per cent; (3) college graduate by 61 per cent; and (4) earnings by 10 per cent. Moreover, the sign switches in the teen fertility equation, which suggests that there is no reliable evidence of an independent causal effect whereby neighborhood poverty leads to greater teen childbearing rates.

In sum, the IV evidence in Table 2 strongly supports the earlier concerns that neighborhood effect models that fail to confront the empirical challenges of selection and endogeneity will produce biased results. Nevertheless, although it is thought that OLS modeling overstates the causal impact of neighborhood poverty, it should be added that the application of IV techniques did not make the apparent effect of neighborhood poverty disappear. Indeed, it is thought that the totality of evidence supports the hypothesis of an independent, non-trivial impact of childhood neighborhood poverty on high school attainment and earnings, controlling for a wide range of parental and other background characteristics.

Comparing Alternative Estimates of Neighborhood Effects

It has been previously observed that there is little consensus in the literature on the magnitude of neighborhood effects (Earls & Carlson, 2001; Ginther *et al.*, 2000; Leventhal & Brooks-Gunn, 2000; Robert, 1999; Sampson *et al.*, 2002) and the present study adds yet more variance. Indeed, the implied magnitude of childhood neighborhood poverty impacts presented in Table 3 is greater than that measured by earlier studies using OLS with comparable neighborhood measures and outcomes: teen fertility (Hogan & Kitagawa, 1985; Brewster *et al.*, 1993; Brewster, 1994a, 1994b), educational attainment (Aaronson, 1998; Clark, 1992; Datcher, 1982; Duncan, 1994; Garner & Raudenbush, 1991), employment (Datcher, 1982; Vartanian, 1999) and earnings (Page & Solon, 1999).[10] One possible reason for this is that neighborhood poverty is measured averaged over childhood, not just for a shorter span, as most other studies have. Thus the study measures the 'cumulative impact' of this neighborhood condition.[11] Another reason is that a recursive relationship is modeled among various outcomes, thereby allowing both direct and indirect effects of neighborhood poverty.

Conclusions, Caveats and Next Steps

This paper represents the first attempt to estimate the cumulative effect of neighborhood poverty on several interrelated children's outcomes in later life in the context of a holistic model involving the simultaneous parental choice of neighborhood, mobility, and homeownership status. It has argued that an IV approach based on such a model is helpful for obtaining estimates of neighborhood effects that are purged from the twin confounding influences of selection and endogeneity. Using a cohort of children born 1968–74 and interviewed through the PSID in 1999, the IV estimates provided indications that these cumulative neighborhood poverty effects averaged over childhood have an independent, non-trivial causal effect on high school attainment and earnings. The IV evidence is not compelling with regard to teen fertility or college attainment.

As befits a prototype, the IV modeling experiments suggested that this approach can only reach its full potential if stronger and unique instruments for childhood neighborhood poverty rate can be identified. A reliance upon coincident county-level data as identifying instruments for census tract poverty rates proved only partially successful, even when combined with exogenous predictors found elsewhere in the system of equations. An intensified future search for 'uniquely' identifying instruments would also permit researchers to more fully operationalize hypothesized endogenous relationships between neighborhood choice, tenure choice, mobility and household head characteristics, as portrayed in Figure 1. The efforts here fell short in this regard, yielding instruments for many endogenous variables that were too collinear to be employed in modeling.

Of course, this study has identified statistical associations, not proven causal links. However, in the IV modeling care was taken to purge the measured association of the common confounding elements in a fashion that it is thought offers an important advance. Moreover, several, not-mutually exclusive hypotheses have been offered above that offer plausible causal mechanisms about how neighborhood poverty rates might provide an independent contribution to the environment in which children are raised.

More work is clearly needed at drilling below readily available census data to better uncover the underlying neighborhood processes at work here (Friedrichs, 1998; Gephart, 1997; Raudenbush & Sampson, 1999; Sampson et al., 2002). Measures for institutional infrastructure, organizational participation, collective supervision of youth, clarity and consensus regarding group norms, intra- and extra-neighborhood social networks for adults and children, and exposure to violence are especially salient. In addition, much more needs to be done to measure perceptions and stereotypes held by external actors that may affect opportunities of neighborhood residents and, thereby, their behaviors. Indeed, the mechanisms of how neighborhood effects transpire provide crucial information for guiding prospective policy responses aimed at deconcentrating poverty spatially (Galster, 2005, 2007, forthcoming)

But even without full understanding of the underlying causal processes, the findings here hold powerful implications for policy makers in their efforts to create neighborhoods that provide superior developmental environments for children. Numerous community development efforts are underway aimed at revitalizing distressed core neighborhoods in the US, often supported by municipalities and charitable foundations, such as the Annie E. Casey Foundation's Making Connections and the MacArthur Foundation's New Communities Programs. Similarly, several strands of the US Department of Housing and Urban Development's assisted housing policy have similar goals of enhancing developmental contexts by expanding residential options for the poor, such as the Moving To Opportunity (MTO) program involving rental voucher subsidies, public housing desegregation remedies in dozens of locales across the country, and redevelopment of distressed public housing as mixed-income communities through the HOPE VI program (Galster et al., 2003; Popkin et al., 2003; Rubinowitz & Rosenbaum, 2000). The results here imply that all of these initiatives should aim to deconcentrate extreme poverty, both by creating mixed-income developments in revitalized core neighborhoods and targeting locations for assisted housing developments or rental subsidies in other, low-poverty neighborhoods.

Acknowledgements

This research is supported by a grant from the Ford Foundation. The authors wish to thank Jorg Blasius, Jurgen Friedrichs, Harry Holzer, Alex Marsh and anonymous referees for their helpful suggestions on earlier drafts. Seminar participants at the Universities of Southern California, Cologne and Cambridge also provided constructive suggestions. The research assistance of Jackie Cutsinger and Ying Wang and clerical assistance of Caitlin Malloy is gratefully acknowledged. The opinions expressed herein are the authors', and do not necessarily reflect those of the Boards of Trustees of the Ford Foundation or our respective Universities.

Notes

[1] The direction of the bias has been the subject of debate, with Jencks & Mayer (1990) and Tienda (1991) arguing that neighborhood impacts are biased upwards, and Brooks-Gunn et al. (1997) arguing the opposite.

[2] While other studies have discussed this issue, it has been in the context of the reflection problem (Manski, 1995) of people in the neighborhood tautologically cause the aggregate neighborhood characteristics to be what they are as well as the neighborhood causes constituent residents' behaviors (Duncan & Raudenbush, 1999).

[3] Other recent research has employed natural experiments where the selection bias was minimized through geographic assignment of households through governmental housing program auspices (Aslund & Fredriksson, 2005; Edin et al., 2003; Oreopolis, 2003).

[4] Such a longitudinal analysis has been strongly recommended as the vehicle for overcoming the reflection problem (Duncan & Raudenbsuh, 1999; Manski, 1995).

[5] A database from Geolytics is used, the 'Neighborhood Change Database', that adjusts data in 1970, 1980 and 1990 tracts that have changed their boundary definitions over the years to values that would appertain had boundaries remained at their 1990 specifications.

[6] For details, see Galster (2003a).

[7] There are two exceptions to this. First, for those years in which the family lived in a rural area, the observed value of county characteristics is used. Second, for child age zero the observed value is used since a first-stage equation for year zero (due to unavailability of lagged variables) cannot be estimated.

[8] Details of the first-stage regressions are available upon request.

[9] However, some were asked again in 1975 and a question about union membership was collected from 1968 through to 1981.

[10] The estimates here also differ substantially from those finding no statistically significant impacts from neighborhood poverty and associated measures of disadvantage; e.g. see Corcoran et al. (1992); Ensminger et al. (1996); Plotnick & Hoffman (1999).

[11] Wheaton & Clarke (2003) find cumulative neighborhood conditions much more powerful in explaining various child developmental outcomes than contemporaneous conditions.

References

Aaronson, D. (1998) Using sibling data to estimate the impact of neighborhoods on children's educational outcomes, *Journal of Human Resources*, 33, pp. 915–946.

Aslund, O. & Fredricksson, P. (2005) Ethnic enclaves and welfare cultures: quasi-experimental evidence. Unpublished manuscript, Department of Economics, Uppsala University.

Barber, J. S. (2001) The intergenerational transmission of age at first birth among married and unmarried men and women, *Social Science Research*, 30, pp. 219–247.

Brewster, K. (1994a) Race differences in sexual activity among adolescent women: the role of neighborhood characteristics, *American Sociological Review*, 59, pp. 408–424.

Brewster, K. (1994b) Neighborhood context and the transition to sexual activity among young black woman, *Demography*, 31, pp. 603–614.

Brewster, K., Billy, J. O. & Grady, W. R. (1993) Social context and adolescent behavior: the impact of community on the transition to sexual activity, *Social Forces*, 71, pp. 713–740.

Brooks-Gunn, J., Duncan, G. J., Leventhal, T. & Aber, J. L. (1997) Lessons learned and future directions in research, in: J. Brooks-Gunn, G. J. Duncan & J. L. Aber (Eds) *Neighborhood Poverty: Vol. 1. Context and Consequences for Children*, pp. 279–298 (New York: Russell Sage Foundation).

Clark, R. (1992) Neighborhood Effects of Dropping Out of School Among Teenage Boys, *Working paper* (Washington DC: Urban Institute).

Cook, T., Shagle, S., Degirmencioglu, S., Coulton, C., Korbin, J. & Su, M. (1997) Capturing social process for testing mediational models of neighborhood effects, in: J. Brooks-Gunn, G. Duncan & L. Aber (Eds) *Neighborhood Poverty: Vol. II, Policy Implications in Studying Neighborhoods*, pp. 94–119 (New York: Russell Sage Foundation).

Corcoran, M., Gordon, R., Laren, D. & Solon, G. (1992) The association between men's economic status and their family and community origins, *Journal of Human Resources*, 27, pp. 575–601.

Coulton, C., Korbin, J. & Su, M. (1999) Neighborhoods and child maltreatment: A multi-level study, *Child Abuse and Neglect*, 23, pp. 1019–1040.

Datcher, L. (1982) Effects of community and family background on achievement, *The Review of Economics and Statistics*, 64, pp. 32–41.

Dietz, Robert D., Haurin, Donald R. & Weinberg, Bruce A. (2002) The impact of neighborhood homeownership rates: a review of the theoretical and empirical literature, *Journal of Housing Research*, 13(2), pp. 119–151.

Duncan, G. (1994) Families and neighbors as sources of disadvantage in the schooling decisions of white and black adolescents, *American Journal of Sociology*, 103, pp. 20–53.

Duncan, Greg J. & Raudenbush, Stephen (2001) Getting context right in quantitative studies of child development, in: A. Thornton (Ed.) *The well-being of children and families: Research and data needs*, pp. 356–383 (Ann Arbor, MA: University of Michigan Press).

Duncan, G. J., Connell, J. P. & Klebanov, P. K. (1997) Conceptual and methodological issues in estimating causal effects of neighborhoods and family conditions on individual development, in: J. Brooks-Gunn, G. J. Duncan & J. L. Aber (Eds) *Neighborhood Poverty: Vol. 1, Context and Consequences for Children*, pp. 219–250 (New York: Russell Sage Foundation).

Earls, F. & Carlson, M. (2001) The social ecology of child health and well-being, *Annual Review of Public Health*, 22, pp. 143–166.

Edin, P., Fredricksson, P. & Aslund, O. (2003) Ethnic enclaves and the economic success of immigrants: evidence from a natural experiment, *Quarterly Journal of Economics*, 113, pp. 329–357.

Elliott, Delbert S., Wilson, William Julius, Huizinga, David Amanda Elliott & Bruce Rankin (1996) The effects of neighborhood disadvantage on adolescent development, *Journal of Research in Crime and Delinquency*, 33(4), pp. 389–426.

Ellen, I. & Turner, M. (1997) Does neighborhood matter? Assessing recent evidence, *Housing Policy Debate*, 8, pp. 833–866.

Ellen, I. & Turner, M. (2003) Do neighborhoods matter and why?, in: J. Goering & J. Feins (Eds) *Choosing a Better Life? Evaluating the Moving To Opportunity Experiment*, pp. 313–338 (Washington DC: Urban Institute Press).

Ensminger, M., Lamkin, R. & Jacobson, N. (1996) School leaving: a longitudinal perspective including neighborhood effects, *Child Development*, 67, pp. 2400–2416.

Evans, W. N., Oates, W. & Schwab, R. (1992) Measuring peer group effects: a study of teenage behavior, *Journal of Political Economy*, 100, pp. 966–991.

Foster, E. M. & McLanahan, S. (1996) An illustration of the use of instrumental variables: do neighborhood conditions affect a young person's chance of finishing high school?, *Psychological Methods*, 1, pp. 249–260.

Freeman, R. B. (1991) Crime and the employment of disadvantaged youths. NBER Working Paper No. w3875, October (Cambridge, MA: NBER).

Friedrichs, J. (1998) Do poor neighborhoods make their residents poorer? Context effects of poverty neighborhoods on their residents, in: H. Andress (Ed.) *Empirical Poverty Research in a Comparative Perspective*, pp. 77–99 (Aldershot: Ashgate).

Friedrichs, J. & Blasius, J. (2003) Social norms in distressed neighborhoods: testing the Wilson hypothesis, *Housing Studies*, 18, pp. 807–826.

Friedrichs, J., Galster, G. & Musterd, S. (2003) Neighborhood effects on social opportunities: the European and American research and policy context, *Housing Studies*, 18, pp. 797–806.

Furstenberg, F. F., Jr., Levine, J. A. & Brooks-Gunn, J. (1990) The children of teenage mothers: patterns of early childbearing in two generations, *Family Planning Perspectives*, 22, pp. 54–61.

Furstenberg, F. F., Jr., Cook, T. D., Eccles, J., Elder, G. H. Jr. & Sameroff, A. (1999) *Managing to Make It: Urban Families and Adolescent Success* (Chicago: University of Chicago Press).

Galster, G. (2002) An economic efficiency analysis of deconcentrating poverty populations, *Journal of Housing Economics*, 11, pp. 303–329.

Galster, G. (2003a) Investigating behavioral impacts of poor neighborhoods: towards new data and analytical strategies, *Housing Studies*, 18, pp. 893–914.

Galster, G. (2003b) The effects of MTO on sending and receiving neighborhoods, in: J. Goering, T. Richardson & J. Feins (Eds) *Choosing a Better Life? A Social Experiment in Leaving Poverty Behind*, pp. 365–382 (Washington DC: Urban Institute Press).

Galster, G. (2005) *Neighborhood Mix, Social Opportunities and the Policy Challenges of an Increasingly Diverse Amsterdam* (Amsterdam: Department of Geography, Planning and International Development

Studies, University of Amsterdam). Available at http://www.fmg.uva.nl/amidst/object.cfm/objectid = 7 C149E7C-EC9F-4C2E-91DB7485C0839425.
Galster, G. (2007) Neighbourhood social mix as a goal of housing policy: a theoretical analysis, *European Journal of Housing Policy* (forthcoming).
Galster, G. (forthcoming) Should policy makers strive for neighborhood social mix? An analysis of the Western European evidence base, *Housing Studies* (forthcoming).
Galster, G., Santiago, A., Tatian, P., Pettit, K. & Smith, R. (2003) *Why NOT in My Back Yard? The Neighborhood Impacts of Assisted Housing* (New Brunswick, NJ: Rutgers University/Center for Urban Policy Research Press).
Galster, G., Marcotte, M., Mandell, M., Wolman, H. & Augustine, N. (forthcoming) The impacts of parental homeownership on children's outcomes during early adulthood, *Housing Policy*.
Garner, C. & Raudenbush, S. (1991) Neighborhood effects on educational attainment, *Sociology of Education*, 64, pp. 251–262.
Gephart, M. A. (1997) Neighborhoods and communities as contexts for development, in: J. Brooks-Gunn, G. Duncan & L. Aber (Eds) *Neighborhood Poverty: Vol. I. Context and Consequences for Children*, pp. 1–43 (New York: Russell Sage Foundation).
Ginther, D., Haveman, R. & Wolfe, B. (2000) Neighborhood attributes as determinants of children's outcomes: how robust are the relationships?, *Journal of Human Resources*, 35, pp. 603–642.
Gleason, P. M. & Vartanian, T. P. (1999) Do neighborhood conditions affect high school dropout and college graduation rates?, *Journal of Socio-Economics*, 28, pp. 21–41.
Goering, John, Feins, Judith D. & Richardson, Todd M. (2002) A cross-site analysis of initial moving to opportunity demonstration results, *Journal of Housing Research*, 13(1), pp. 1–30.
Gottschalk, P. (1996) Is the correlation in welfare participation across generations spurious?, *Journal of Public Economics*, 63, pp. 1–25.
Gottschalk, P., McLanahan, S. & Sandefur, G. (1994) The dynamics and intergenerational transmission of poverty and welfare participation, in: S. Danziger, G. Sandefur & D. Weinberg (Eds) *Confronting Poverty*, pp. 85–108 (Cambridge, MA: Harvard University Press).
Green, R. K. & White, M. J. (1997) Measuring the benefits of homeowning: effects on children, *Journal of Urban Economics*, 41, pp. 441–461.
Grogger, J. (1997) Incarceration-related costs of early childbearing, in: R. A. Maynard (Ed.) *Kids Having Kids: Economic Costs and Social Consequences of Teen Pregnancy*, pp. 95–143 (Washington DC: The Urban Institute Press).
Hahn, J. & Hausman, J. (2005) Instrumental variable estimation with valid and invalid instruments. Unpublished paper, Department of Economics, MIT, Cambridge, MA.
Haurin, R. J. (1992) Patterns of childhood residence and the relationship to young adult outcomes, *Journal of Marriage and the Family*, 54, pp. 846–880.
Haurin, D. R., Parcel, T. L. & Haurin, R. J. (2002a) Impact of home ownership on child outcomes, in: E. Belsky & N. P. Retsinas (Eds) *Low Income Homeownership: Examining the Unexamined Goal*, pp. 427–446 (Washington DC: Brookings Institution Press).
Haurin, D. R., Parcel, T. L. & Haurin, R. J. (2002b) Does home ownership affect child outcomes?, *Real Estate Economics*, 30, pp. 635–666.
Haveman, R. & Wolfe, B. (1994) *Succeeding Generations: On the Effects of Investments in Children* (New York: Russell Sage Foundation).
Hogan, D. & Kitagawa, E. (1985) The impact of social status, family, structure and neighborhood on the fertility of black adolescents, *American Journal of Sociology*, 90, pp. 825–855.
Holloway, S. & Mulherin, S. (2004) The effect of adolescent neighborhood poverty on adult employment, *Journal of Urban Affairs*, 26, pp. 427–454.
Jargowsky, P. (1999) Non-linear neighborhood effects and aggregate metropolitan outcomes. Unpublished manuscript, University of Texas-Dallas.
Jenks, C. & Mayer, S. E. (1990) The social consequences of growing up in a poor neighborhood, in: L. L. Lynn & M. McGeary (Eds) *Inner-city Poverty in the United States*, pp. 111–186 (Washington DC: National Academy Press).
Kohen, Dafna E., Brooks-Gunn, Jeanne, Leventhal, Tama & Hertzman, Clyde (2002) Neighborhood income and physical and social disorder in Canada: associations with young children's competencies, *Child Development*, 73(6), pp. 1844–1860.

Leventhal, T. & Brooks-Gunn, J. (2000) The neighborhoods they live in, *Psychological Bulletin*, 126, pp. 309–337.
Manski, C. F. (1995) *Identification Problems in the Social Sciences* (Cambridge, MA: Harvard University Press).
Manski, C. F. (2000) Economic analysis of social interactions, *Journal of Economic Perspectives*, 14, pp. 115–136.
Mayer, S. E. (1997) *What Money Can't Buy: Family Income and Children's Life Chances* (Cambridge, MA: Harvard University Press).
McLanahan, S. & Bumpass, L. (1988) Intergenerational consequences of family disruption, *American Journal of Sociology*, 94, pp. 130–152.
Moffitt, R. (1992) Incentive effects of the US welfare system: a review, *Journal of Economic Literature*, 30, pp. 1–61.
Murray, M. (2006) Avoiding invalid instruments and coping with weak instruments, *Journal of Economic Perspectives*, 20, pp. 111–132.
Oreopolis, P. (2003) The long-run consequences of living in a poor neighborhood, *Quarterly Journal of Economics*, 118, pp. 1533–1575.
Page, M. & Solon, G. (1999) Correlations between brothers and neighboring boys in their adult earnings. Unpublished manuscript, Department of Economics, University of Michigan, Ann Arbor.
Payne, J. (1987) Does unemployment run in families? Some findings from the General Household Survey, *Sociology*, 21, pp. 199–214.
Peeples, F. & Loeber, R. (1994) Do individual factors and neighborhood context explain ethnic differences in juvenile delinquency?, *Journal of Quantitative Criminology*, 10, pp. 141–157.
Pepper, J. V. (2000) The intergenerational transmission of welfare receipt: a nonparametric bounds analysis, *Review of Economics and Statistics*, 82, pp. 472–488.
Plotnick, R. & Hoffman, S. (1999) The effect of neighborhood characteristics on young adult outcomes: alternative estimates, *Social Science Quarterly*, 80, pp. 1–8.
Popkin, S., Galster, G., Temkin, K., Herbig, C., Levy, D. & Richter, D. (2003) Obstacles to desegregating public housing: lessons learned from implementing eight consent decrees, *Journal of Policy Analysis and Management*, 22, pp. 179–200.
Raudenbush, S. & Sampson, R. (1999) Ecometrics: Toward a science of assessing ecological settings, with application to the systematic social observation of neighborhoods, *Sociological Methodology*, 29, pp. 1–41.
Robert, S. A. (1999) Socioeconomic position and health: the independent contribution of community socioeconomic context, *Annual Review of Sociology*, 25, pp. 489–516.
Rubinowitz, L. & Rosenbaum, J. (2000) *Crossing the Class and Color Lines: From Public Housing to White Suburbia* (Chicago: University of Chicago Press).
Sampson, R. & Groves, W. B. (1989) Community structure and crime: Testing social disorganization theory, *American Journal of Sociology*, 94(4), pp. 774–802.
Sampson, R. J., Morenoff, J. D. & Earls, F. (1999) Beyond social capital: spatial dynamics of collective efficacy for children, *American Sociological Review*, 64, pp. 633–660.
Sampson, R. J., Morenoff, J. D. & Gannon-Rowley, T. (2002) Assessing 'neighborhood effects': social processes and new directions in research, *Annual Review of Sociology*, 28, pp. 443–478.
Sampson, Robert J., Raudenbush, Stephen W. Earls & Felton (1997) Neighborhoods and Violent Crime: A Multilevel Study of Collective Efficacy, *Science*, 277, pp. 918–924.
Sawhill, I. & Chadwick, L. (1999) *Children in cities: uncertain futures*. Working Paper, Center on Urban and Metropolitan Policy Survey Series (Washington DC: Brookings Institution).
Sullivan, M. L. (1989) *Getting Paid: Youth Crime and Work in the Inner City* (Ithaca, NY: Cornell University Press).
Tienda, M. (1991) Poor people and poor places: deciphering neighborhood effects of poverty outcomes, in: J. Haber (Ed.) *Macro-Micro Linkages in Sociology*, pp. 244–262 (Newbury Park, CA: Sage).
Vartanian, T. P. (1999) Childhood conditions and adult welfare use: examining neighborhood and family factors, *Journal of Marriage and the Family*, 61, pp. 225–237.
Wheaton, B. & Clarke, P. (2003) Space meets time: integrating temporal and contextual influences on mental health in early adulthood, *American Sociological Review*, 68, pp. 680–706.

Appendix 1

Exogenous and Predetermined Variables [X] from Equations (1)–(5) Used in First-Stage of Instrumentation Procedure for Neighborhood Poverty Rate*

1. Index of owner-occupied housing prices in metropolitan area (lag 1 year)
2. Index of owner-occupied housing prices in metropolitan area (lead 1 year)
3. Index of gross rents paid by renter occupants in metropolitan area (lag 1 year)
4. (3.) × renter status in prior year
5. Home mortgage interest rate for 30-year fixed-rate loan
6. (5.) × renter status in prior year
7. Ratio of costs of renting to owning in metropolitan area (lag 1 year)
8. (7.) × renter status in prior year
9. Whether family's oldest child reached age 5 in prior year (1 = yes; 0 = no)
10. Whether family's oldest child reached age 13 in prior year (1 = yes; 0 = no)
11. Whether any other child in family reached age 5 in prior year (1 = yes; 0 = no)
12. Whether any other child in family reached age 13 in prior year (1 = yes; 0 = no)
13. Age of household head
14. Household head received a lump-sum monetary payment since child's birth; e.g. inheritance (1 = yes; 0 = no)
15. (14.) × renter status in prior year
16. Difference in household's real income from prior to current year (if GT 0; 0 otherwise)
17. (16.) × renter status in prior year
18. Poverty rate of county (lag 1 year)
19. Household expects to move next year (lag 1 year)
20. Household owns home occupied (lag 1 year)
21. Logarithm of deflated household income (lag 1 year)
22. Year (denoted by a set of dummy variables, 1968 = excluded year)

*Note: First-stage procedure also uses all exogenous variables noted in Table 1

Appendix 2

Table A1. Estimated parameters for baseline model of neighborhood effects (no IVs)

	No child pre-18	HS graduate	College grad	ln(earnings)
Blackfem	−1.524	0.788	−0.145	0.151
	[0.700]**	[0.644]	[0.876]	[0.317]
blackmale	0.839	1.59	−0.958	0.404
	[0.908]	[0.763]**	[0.792]	[0.311]
whitefem	−1.708	0.183	−0.429	−0.36
	[0.528]***	[0.367]	[0.282]	[0.087]***
birthorder	−0.03	0.05	0.012	−0.083
	[0.105]	[0.102]	[0.097]	[0.040]**
age99	−0.203	0.157	0.411	0.074
	[0.099]**	[0.078]**	[0.066]***	[0.023]***
pro_live_under_poverty0to18	−1.162	−1.716	1.051	−1.142
	[1.262]	[1.097]	[1.657]	[0.434]***
pro_livew_2_parents0to18	0.538	0.188	−1.705	0.951
	[0.934]	[0.834]	[0.774]**	[0.255]***
pro_own0to18	−1.248	0.839	1.251	−0.232
	[0.931]	[0.679]	[0.690]*	[0.213]
pro_stability_year0to18	2.956	−0.636	0.228	0.211
	[1.357]**	[1.006]	[1.219]	[0.334]
ave_pert_inc_below_pov0to18	−0.104	−0.059	−0.038	−0.021
	[0.035]***	[0.029]**	[0.031]	[0.012]*
religion	−0.07	−0.57	−0.549	−0.035
	[0.703]	[0.506]	[0.557]	[0.156]
largecity	0.625	0.541	0.97	0.02
	[0.459]	[0.454]	[0.310]***	[0.110]
farm	0.309	−0.109	0.419	−0.027
	[0.531]	[0.450]	[0.423]	[0.121]
veteran	−0.481	−0.985	0.211	0.028
	[0.460]	[0.451]**	[0.285]	[0.104]
momteen	−0.637	0.866	−0.634	−0.489
	[0.631]	[0.556]	[0.869]	[0.302]
ave_education_head0to18	0.189	0.66	0.337	−0.03
	[0.214]	[0.290]**	[0.106]***	[0.043]
ave_hdocc_pre0to18	0.037	0.028	0.005	−0.008
	[0.027]	[0.033]	[0.017]	[0.007]
ave_self_employed0to18	−0.051	−0.247	0.523	0.181
	[0.973]	[1.356]	[0.555]	[0.240]
ave_employed_wife0to18	0.499	−0.617	0.662	−0.431
	[0.819]	[0.711]	[0.532]	[0.183]**
ave_smsa0to18	−0.389	−0.168	0.966	−0.04
	[0.641]	[0.472]	[0.502]*	[0.128]
ave_annu_hrs_wkd0to18	0.0003	0.00001	−0.0001	0.0001
	[0.0006]	[0.0005]	[0.001]	[0.0002]
ave_readnewspaper	−0.62	0.9	0.087	0.193
	[0.615]	[0.572]	[0.549]	[0.172]
ave_union	−0.875	0.942	−0.005	0.086
	[0.624]	[0.518]*	[0.460]	[0.135]
ave_nochurch	0.357	0.517	−0.675	0.084
	[0.690]	[0.636]	[0.588]	[0.179]

Table A1. *Continued*

	No child pre-18	HS graduate	College grad	ln(earnings)
ave_no_socialclubs	0.226	−1.172	0.879	0.014
	[0.667]	[0.160]*	[0.405]**	[0.119]
ave_relatives	−0.223	0.065	0.086	−0.074
	[0.559]	[0.547]	[0.374]	[0.124]
ave_num_neigh_known	0.02	0.055	0.044	0.01
	[0.032]	[0.033]*	[0.019]**	[0.006]
ave_plan_ahead	1.186	−0.096	0.599	0.268
	[0.585]**	[0.494]	[0.458]	[0.140]*
ave_trust	−0.738	−1.081	0.0002	−0.13
	[0.726]	[0.529]**	[0.438]	[0.109]
no_child_before_18	NA	1.208	-0.081	0.032
		[0.458]***	[0.559]	[0.214]
at_least_hs	NA	NA	NA	0.111
				[0.135]
collgrad	NA	NA	NA	0.36
				[0.107]***
married	NA	NA	NA	0.098
				[0.082]
annu_hrs_wkd99	NA	NA	NA	0.0001
				[0.00004]**
constant	5.194	−11.126	−19.622	8.183
	[4.181]	[4.075]***	[2.731]***	[1.053]***
N of Observations	755	755	755	541
Pseudo R-squared (R-Squared)	0.31	0.26	0.19	(0.31)
Wald Chi-squared	97***	26***	49***	NA

Note: Robust standard errors in brackets NA = Not Applicable;
***p < .01; **p < .05; *p < .10 (two-tailed tests).

Internal Heterogeneity of a Deprived Urban Area and its Impact on Residents' Perception of Deviance

JÖRG BLASIUS & JÜRGEN FRIEDRICHS

Introduction

During the last two decades, the number of publications on neighbourhood effects has increased and has resulted in cumulative evidence, if the first systematic review by Jencks & Mayer (1990) is compared to the more recent ones (Dietz, 2002; Leventhal & Brooks-Gunn, 2000; Sampson *et al.*, 2002). Irrespective of the large number of empirical studies, only a few have addressed the problem of internal heterogeneity of the neighbourhoods. The two strains of research, neighbourhood contexts effects and social mix were only recently brought together (Atkinson, 2005; Ostendorf et al., 2001). However, the concept of social mix or social balance is closely related to the discussion of neighbourhood effects, since the concept of social mix implicitly rests upon the explicit and central assumption of neighbourhood effects.

In neighbourhood effect studies, typically, census tracts are used as units for neighbourhoods, thus ignoring the question of artificial borders such as streets and internal differentiation. In the field of segregation studies the heterogeneity of census tracts has been discussed for a long time (Cowgill & Cowgill, 1951) and even blocks might be heterogeneous because one group might reside in alleyways whereas the other resides on street-fronts (for example, Duncan & Duncan, 1955); more appropriate borders between neighbourhoods are given by natural areas (Zorbaugh, 1926). (However, there are areas in the city that are known or labelled as rich, others as poor.) But are these so-called homogeneous areas homogeneous, are all residents in poor areas poor and are all residents in rich areas rich? The existing evidence indicates the implicit assumption of neighbourhood homogeneity to be questionable.

It is this problem, the extent and consequences of heterogeneity within an area known as a homogeneous one that the paper wishes to address. The aim is to assess the internal heterogeneity of an urban area designated as 'deprived', assuming that deprived neighbourhoods too are not homogeneous. Moreover, the paper wishes to study the impact of social mix, i.e. heterogeneity by different indicators within the total area and within the neighbourhoods, assuming the extent of heterogeneity results in different perceptions of deviance of their residents.

First, the study asks how heterogeneity can be measured and how the total deprived area can be decomposed into sub-areas, which are denoted as neighbourhoods. Second, the empirical consequences of neighbourhood heterogeneity are analyzed, an obvious consequence of internal differentiation being that neighbourhood effects may vary by neighbourhood and their social structure. The research questions are as follows:

(1) Which extent of variance of social status can be found in the deprived area?
(2) How much variance of the total area can be explained between the neighbourhoods and how much variance do we find within the neighbourhoods?
(3) Do the extent of heterogeneity and the amount of social capital of a neighbourhood have an effect on perceived disorder and on perception of deviant norms?
(4) Are there different forms of deviant norms (as another indicator for social mix in the whole area) in the neighbourhoods, for example, in one neighbourhood there is a high observation of deviant behaviour of youth, in the other there is a high perception of disorder?

These questions will be answered on the basis of data collected in Cologne, Germany, in 2004, in an area that is known to be 'deprived'. This area has been divided twice into neighbourhoods, one with four cases and the other with six.

The substantive aims of the paper are linked to a methodological issue: how to assess the effects of the neighbourhood, if the decomposition of the total area yields only a small number of neighbourhoods, such as four or six as in the given study? Multi-level analysis usually applied in neighbourhood effects studies cannot be applied due to the small number of cases, since estimates of standard errors are unstable (Hox, 2002; Snijders & Bosker, 1999), To overcome this constraint, it is suggested that correspondence analysis should be applied to separate context from individual effects.

Theory

The assumption that the composition of a neighbourhood has a context effect on the residents already underlies the first publications on planned New Towns, such as the Cadbury new town 'Bournville', established in 1879, followed by all planning programmes for New Towns in England, as documented by the detailed historical reviews (Sarkissian, 1976; Sarkissian *et al.*, 1990). The concept—tenure and income diversification—is still central to urban planning in Great Britain following the Housing Act 1988 and the recent National Strategy for Neighbourhood Renewal (Goodchild & Cole, 2001, pp. 108–109; Manzi & Bowers, 2003; Page, 2000; Scottish Homes, 2006; SEU, 2000; Tunstall, 2003, p. 158), The Netherlands (Ostendorf *et al.*, 2001), the US (e.g. Brophy & Smith, 1997; Schwartz & Tajbakhsh, 1997), or Australia (Adelaide City Council, 2002, p. 3; Arthurson & Anaf, 2006; Johnston, 2002). The Housing Strategy of the City of Melbourne 2001–04 explicitly requests "building diverse and inclusive communities" (Adelaide City Council, 2002, p. 20). As Kleinhans (2004, p. 367) remarked, the concept is "at the core of urban planning".

The question of social mix or socially balanced communities was addressed in a seminal paper by Gans (1961). Discussing the potential outcomes of different extents of social mix, he concluded a 'moderate heterogeneity' to be most favourable for the residents of a given neighbourhood, although he did not suggest any percentages or thresholds. Further, it may be questioned whether the impact of homogeneity in upper-income areas is the same as in low-income areas. Since the literature on social mix almost exclusively pertains to low-income areas, it is not possible to give an empirical answer to the question of different impacts.

Social mix is ascribed to have many positive effects, i.e. context effects: on the residents of a neighbourhood. Sarkissian (1976, pp. 231–234) has listed 10 of such desired outcomes, other authors have presented similar sets of effects (Arthusson & Anaf, 2006; Kleinhans, 2004, p. 368; Sarkissian *et al.*, 1990). Many of these repeatedly occur in even the recent programmes for urban regeneration, e.g. in the assumed outcomes of mixed-income housing Brophy & Smith (1997, p. 6) list. The most important assumed and desired outcomes of social mix are:

- to 'upgrade' the standards of lower classes (cf. Gans, 1961, p. 179);
- encourage job search, or "managing the transition from welfare to work" (Page, 2000, p. 12);
- demand from middle-class households will increase the range and quality of services;
- social stability will increase, e.g. because of lower rates of in- and out-moves;
- local participation is encouraged due to the stronger interest of middle-class households;
- new social capital will be created, social cohesion increased;
- to mitigate the stigma often attributed to the area;
- deviant behaviour will be reduced.

In brief, as Sarkissian (1976, p. 232) states, "equality of opportunity" and "social harmony" are expected to increase. Of these diverse outcomes, the present study will only investigate deviant behaviour.

Irrespective of the impressive number of studies on social mix, the evidence is not conclusive. There is a gap between planners' beliefs in the positive social mix outcomes and the empirical evidence for such effects. However, as Atkinson (2005) states, "Social diversity ... 'is good' has been repeated so often that it has been considered to be a kind of truth" (p. 2).

Three crucial questions remain largely unsolved (cf. Goodchild & Cole, 2001, p. 103):

(1) Which is the spatial unit social mix refers to?
(2) Which are the fruitful indicators of social mix?
(3) Which outcome is expected for which group for which outcome variables?

Question 1: Both empirical studies and planning programmes pertain to different spatial units: floor, building, street, neighbourhood, a group of adjacent neighbourhoods. Sarkissian's (1976) comment is still relevant: "remarkably little attention has been paid to the vital question of scale. What is the unit which mixers propose to mix?" (p. 243). In a study of a mixed-income project, Lake Parc Place in Chicago, Rosenbaum *et al.* (1998) conducted 198 interviews with residents one year after a new group had moved in, most of them with higher incomes than the initial residents. Here, incomes were mixed at the floor level of the two 15-storey buildings. This proved to be successful with regard to perceived safety, enforcement of management rules, and satisfaction with management. In most of these respects, evaluations of the new residents turned out to be more positive than those of the initial residents. The main conclusion to be drawn from the findings is that the larger the spatial unit, the smaller are the effects of social mix (Kleinhans, 2004, p. 378; cf. Page & Boughton, 1997). Findings of a study of 10 mixed neighbourhoods and 1000 interviews by Jupp (1999) show mixture on the level of streets to be more meaningful than on the estate level.

Question 2: A wide range of indicators of social mix are suggested in the literature, such as income, tenure status, ethnicity, employment status, household size, position of household in lifecycle. However, even these studies vary by an important condition: social mix is either planned for a new neighbourhood (new project) or it is introduced in an existing, in most cases low-income, neighbourhood. An example for the second strategy is the Right to Buy policy in the UK, established under successive Housing Acts (Goodchild & Cole, 2001, p. 113).

Tenure mix and income mix are not independent. In most cases, tenure mix is to be achieved by raising the rate of homeownership. As several studies have shown, homeowners differ significantly from private renters and from social renters in several characteristics, among them income (Friedrichs & Blasius, 2006; Harkness & Newman, 2002; Haurin *et al.*, 2003). This raises the question of how to disentangle the effects of tenure from those of income. Several authors find homeowners maintain their homes better, and the theory of social mix assumes that the 'better' behaviour patterns of the homeowners will spread to the renters and to lower-income households.

The findings with regard to the impact of ethnic heterogeneity are mixed. McCulloch (2001) reports positive impacts on social and on residential stability, whereas ethnic homogeneity is associated with feelings of belonging. In contrast, Sampson & Groves (1989) find higher rates of deviant behaviour in areas with ethnic mix. Manzi & Bowers

(2003) report from a survey of 180 households in an estate in outer West London. A heterogeneous ethnic composition means high rates of anti-social behaviour and strong feelings, which result in the residents living in an unsafe environment. Mixed results are also obtained in studies of the impact of social heterogeneity on fear of crime (Atkinson, 2005, p. 12). Nyden et al. (1998) report results from a study of 14 stable and ethnically diverse neighbourhoods in nine US cities. 'Diversity' was defined as being close to the city's ethnic composition. From the case studies, they concluded that diversity could be preserved if community leaders viewed diversity as an intentional goal and if there was a "continuing process of community stabilization" (p. 7).

Question 3: It is evident that different types of social mix can have different effects on neighbourhood social groups, such as youth, the unemployed or renters. Most of the studies particularly refer to tenure mix as a device to increase social mix in lower-income neighbourhoods. However, as Tunstall (2003) has stated: "most existing studies do not attempt to control for potential intervening factors or distinguish neighbourhood tenure effects from possible cumulative effects due to social composition" (p. 157).

Mechanisms

As in the literature on context effects, contributions to the social mix debate seek to determine which mechanisms are responsible for any transfer of middle-class habits to lower classes. Two such mechanisms are suggested, both prominent as well in the neighbourhood-effects literature: role models (Tunstall, 2003) and social interaction. Unemployed residents see other residents go to work regularly, this is supposed to enhance their efforts to apply for a job and reduces the impact of negative role models of unemployed persons or those who have given up seeking employment.

Thus, the basic assumption underlying most of the social mix literature is that middle-income families serve as positive role models for low-income families. (Interestingly, the opposite effect, a negative impact of low- on middle-income families is not discussed in the literature, except for the propensity of middle-income families to move out of the mixed area, e.g. Ostendorf et al., 2001, p. 379.)

Evidently, both income and tenure mix do not per se result in the expected positive outcomes. The diffusion of positive role models or 'mainstream' social behaviour (Wilson, 1987) depends on social interaction. It should be noted that attributing social interaction to be the crucial mechanism in the diffusion of middle-class norms (what basically all programmes wish to achieve) implies that (a) pure observation of other residents' behaviour is much less relevant than interaction and (b) spatial proximity promotes the interaction between different social groups in the neighbourhood.

With regard to contacts, Sarkissian (1976, p. 244) asked "Does residential propinquity actually lead to greater interaction among dissimilar people and greater tolerance for social differences?" Spatial propinquity is assumed to foster social contacts among the different income of employment groups. This assumption is supported by findings from the contact-prejudice literature. In a meta-analysis of 515 studies, Pettigrew & Tropp (2006) found consistent evidence for the positive effect of contact on the reduction of prejudice. Generalizing his results to a wider range of attitudes, as Pettigrew & Tropp proposed, this part of the social mix hypothesis seems empirically justified. The prerequisite of contacts is to get into contact. Further, the evidence from network studies clearly shows that contacts depend on sharing similar characteristics, such as age, education or religion (cf. Jackson, 1977; Laumann, 1966). This tendency (termed 'homophily' by Lazarsfeld & Merton, 1954, p. 23) obstructs contacts with non-similar persons, even if they are spatially available. In this context, social mix studies indicate that mixing renters and owners does not lead to a higher proportion of contacts or social relations between these groups.

In a mail survey of 3000 adults in the West of Scotland, Hiscock (2001) studied the impact of tenure mix on social capital. She concluded that "mixing tenures has more than a dilution effect" and that residents are "more neighbourly in mixed tenure areas". However, with regard to social contacts, she finds little interaction between owners and social renters. "More interaction takes place when owners and renters have similar characteristics, especially when they have children" (Hiscock, 2001, p. 6).

Whereas Jupp (1999, p. 45) finds that the closer owners and renters live to each other, the more frequent contacts are, Kleinhans (2004, p. 378) concludes from his review of the literature, "patterns of social life vary by tenure and, in general, yield little social interaction between owner-occupiers and tenants". A moderating condition fostering contacts seems to be a good management of the neighbourhood.

In their study of seven mixed-income communities in the US, Brophy & Smith (1997, pp. 8, 15) found positive impacts of social mix, but only a minimal interaction of residents. Similar results were obtained by Atkinson & Kintrea (2000, 2001). Based on 49 diaries of households, the authors studied the impact of tenure mix in three estates in Scotland. They report only little contact between renters and owners.

To test the impact of mixed housing, Ostendorf *et al.* (2001) conducted a survey based on a random sample of 4000 residents in Amsterdam. A persons' residence was coded into a 100 × 100 m grid with at least 25 persons per unit. Contrary to their proposition of a curvilinear relationship between the proportion of owner-occupied dwellings or private dwellings and the proportion of underprivileged, the data revealed a linear relationship. Hence, social mix by tenure does not reduce the number of underprivileged (p. 377).

In a study of three deprived areas in Britain, using discussion groups, expert interviews and community workshops, Page (2000, p. 24) found a "culture of low attainment that ... mocked educational success" and concluded: "The 'estate effect' influences the attitude of respondents to welfare, work, crime, drugs and education". Further, he found a "toleration of a level of 'non-personal' crime within 'acceptable' limits which had less to do with the law and more to do with an acceptance that low-level criminal activity was a useful source of additional income for some people living locally" (p. 39).

As outlined above, the assumption that social mix or the extent of *internal* heterogeneity of a neighbourhood has an impact on the attitudes and behaviour of the residents rests upon implicit propositions on the social mechanisms relating the macro level variable 'heterogeneity' to the micro level outcomes. But how is it possible to specify such 'social mechanisms' (Hedstrom, 2005; Mayntz, 2003; Opp, 2004)? It is evident that a mechanism is an elaborated set of propositions linking at least two phenomena or observations. The present study has to specify how different compositions of a neighbourhood are related to residents' perceptions of behaviour in the area. In the authors' view, the model suggested by Sampson & Groves (1989) and Sampson, Raudenbush & Earls (1999) serves this intention. This framework will be adapted for this purpose, as explained below.

Sampson & Groves (1989) specified the relevant variables and grouped them into three blocks. The first block represents macro variables and comprises what Leventhal & Brooks-Gunn (2000) had termed 'neighbourhood organization': economic status of the neighbourhood, ethnic heterogeneity, residential mobility, percentages of family disruptions and degree of urbanization. The third block consists of the dependent variable(s) at the micro level, typically indicators of deviant behaviour, such as crime and delinquency. The intermediate block specifies intervening variables, constructed from variables measured at the individual level, but interpreted as characteristics of the meso level, such as local networks, unsupervised teenage peer groups, and low organizational participation. Sampson et al. (1999) revised the model from Sampson & Groves (1989) slightly, first by reducing variables in the first block and second, and more importantly, by replacing the middle block variables by the concept of collective efficacy. In a broader sense of socio-economic theory, this concept represents the ability of residents to create collective goods (Olson, 1965).

Sample and Data

The data come from a survey in Cologne, Germany, conducted in 2004. The study area, Vingst-Hoehenberg, is an administrative district in the Eastern part of the city with approximately 23 000 inhabitants. According to percentage receiving public assistance and expert judgements, it belongs to the poorest areas in Cologne. Table 1 shows some basic data of the area compared to Cologne totals.

A random sample of residents aged 16–85 was drawn from the Cologne Population Register. Face-to-face interviews were conducted with a standardized questionnaire. The questionnaire was based on a previous study (Friedrichs & Blasius, 2000, 2003) and group discussions with experts from the Cologne Health Department, Youth Department, professors of the Advanced School of Social Work, neighbourhood police, school directors and a priest of a local church.

A total of $n = 707$ interviews were obtained; the response rate was 46.7 per cent. This is a good result for a survey in a deprived area of a large city in Germany, since surveys in such areas usually obtain much lower values; even most surveys of the entire population in Germany have response rates close to only 50 per cent (cf. Reuband & Blasius, 1996).

Operationalization

Neighbourhoods

The first aim was to delineate the neighbourhoods of Vingst-Hoehenberg methodologically, i.e. neighbourhoods accounting for a maximum amount of explained variance of given dependent variables, such as observed deviant behaviour. Furthermore, variance within neighbourhoods should be minimal compared to a maximal variance between neighbourhoods.

Table 1. Basic characteristics of the study area (31 December 2002)

Characteristic	Vingst-Hoehenberg	Cologne
Population	23293	1 020 116
% Change 1990–2002	−8.4	+3.2
% Foreign-born	20.7	17.8
% Unemployed	20.3	12.3
% Public assistance	10.4	6.4

The literature on human and social ecology has addressed the delineation problem by the concept of 'natural areas' (Zorbaugh, 1926). The term refers to areas (or neighbourhoods) of relative social homogeneity and distinct physical borders, such as railway tracts, traffic arteries or industrial land use. As is well known, delineations for natural areas are often arbitrary. Furthermore, Reber (1993) has shown that residents of Cologne's sub-areas indicate very different delineations of their neighbourhood; hence, borders drawn by residents differ and cannot be aggregated in a straightforward manner to a coherent delineation of neighbourhoods. Since statistical data for census tracts (for some cities they are defined by natural areas) are only available from the population register, almost all research on neighbourhood effects relies upon administratively defined areas.

For the current study, two delineations of neighbourhoods were chosen: one based upon the perceptions of residents and one based upon objective criteria. The subjective one was achieved by asking the residents "Are there parts in this neighbourhood you would not like to go to alone after dark?" Respondent replies were coded into four categories by the frequency a given street or part of the street was mentioned. This classification of neighbourhoods is termed 'Dangerous Areas' (DA): If a certain street, part of the street or a place had been mentioned less than four times, this part was classified as 'not dangerous', if it had been named between 4 and 10 times, it was classified as 'low dangerous', 11 to 30 times was classified as 'strong' and more than 30 times as 'very strong'. Note that these neighbourhoods are not clearly separated by physical borders; they contain a number of parts of streets and places that have a certain degree of perceived danger in common. The advantage of this subdivision is that there are no arbitrary borders such as streets, in contrast to census tracts (and natural areas), opposite dwellings of a certain street belong to the same 'Dangerous Area'.

A second internal differentiation was derived from a collaboration with the Cologne Statistical Office and the Institute of Geography at the University of Cologne. They developed a differentiation of the 85 Cologne districts into 269 neighbourhoods that was based on objective criteria, e.g. on social homogeneity and the similarity of the building structures (Warmelink & Zehner, 1996), similar to the Chicago School criteria for natural areas. This classification is referred to as natural areas (NA), shown in Figure 1. Thus, there are two classifications of the internal differentiation in the study area: a subjective (DA) and an objective one (NA).

The NA delineation yields six neighbourhoods for which statistical data from the population register are available, such as percentage receiving public assistance, percentage unemployed, percentage foreign born, proportion of single-headed households, fluctuation rate (or residential mobility), defined as the sum of in- and out-migration, divided by the total number of residents, and persons per room. These data correspond to the macro level variables as suggested by Leventhal & Brooks-Gunn (2000), Sampson *et al.* (1999), and by Sampson *et al.* (2002), which will be discussed later.

Table 2 presents a subdivision of the study area into six natural areas that are ranked according to poverty, measured by the percentage of persons receiving social assistance, ranging from low (SV) to high (HS). First, census data are listed for the six neighbourhoods, followed by a set of data from the survey. As a measure for the variation in the neighbourhoods, Simpson's (1949) Index of Diversity was used, which is defined as $D = \frac{\sum_i n_i(n_i-1)}{N(N-1)}$ with $n_i = $ number of residents in each group i (with $i = 1, 2, 3$ in the cases of educational level) of the neighbourhood and $N = $ number of residents in the neighbourhood. To gain an intuitive

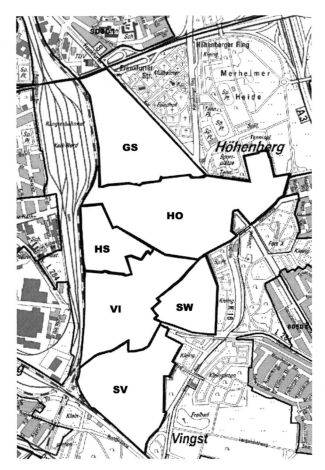

Figure 1. Study area and six neighbourhoods. Key: GS = Germania Settlement, SW = Sweden Settlement, HO = Hoehenberg, VI = Vingst, HS = Hoehenberg South, SV = Settlement Vingst

interpretation, $1 - D$ were calculated; thus the index values range from zero (low diversity, e.g. all residents have the same educational level) to one (high diversity, e.g. all residents have different educational levels) in the same group.

As can be seen, census data show that fluctuation (in- and out-moves) rates do not follow the rank order established by social assistance, for example, the highest fluctuation rate is observed in the neighbourhood with the third lowest percentage of households receiving social assistants (HO). With regard to migration rates, all but the last natural area (SW) correspond to the initial order.

With regard to the sample data, the wording of the question and categorization of responses to the variable 'willingness-to-move out of the area' follows Rossi (1955) who distinguished mere desires to move from activities. This variable has three categories: (1) no intention; (2) intention, but no activities; (3) intention with activities, e.g. reading or placing advertisements, viewing of dwellings, and consultation of real estate agents.

Table 2. Census and sample characteristics of the six natural areas (%)

Characteristic	Natural area					
	SV	GS	HO	VI	HS	SW
Census data (2004)						
Social assistance	7.1	9.1	10.5	13.5	15.8	19.0
Fluctuation rate	4.2	6.9	15.4	7.6	10.5	8.3
Migrants	21.0	22.2	27.4	32.9	48.9	32.4
Sample data						
Transfer income	17.6	13.9	15.8	26.5	32.7	21.4
Single-headed households	18.2	10.9	8.5	9.0	12.2	14.5
Willingness to move out	18.7	16.3	20.9	22.4	26.5	21.4
Perceived risk (no – high risk)	34.4	44.4	38.3	32.3	40.8	16.1
Education[a]						
9 years	43.1	47.0	42.2	55.7	54.8	78.2
10 years	21.6	24.0	31.9	16.7	26.2	10.9
12 years and more	35.3	29.0	25.9	27.6	19.0	10.9
Heterogeneity	*0.648*	*0.644*	*0.657*	*0.589*	*0.600*	*0.372*
Equivalent Income[b]						
Up to € 500.-	8.8	9.1	15.2	9.3	17.9	5.9
€ 500.– to € 749.-	12.7	17.0	8.0	17.9	15.4	15.7
€ 750.– to € 999.-	18.6	12.5	14.5	22.2	30.8	19.6
€ 1000.– to € 1249.-	21.6	15.9	15.9	12.3	7.7	21.6
€ 1250.– to € 1499.-	19.6	25.0	20.3	17.9	15.4	25.5
€ 1500.– and more	18.6	20.5	26.1	20.4	12.8	11.8
Heterogeneity	*0.849*	*0.825*	*0.818*	*0.826*	*0.825*	*0.824*
Age groups[c]						
16–25	11.5	18.3	14.2	10.4	10.2	7.1
26–35	13.1	9.6	17.0	12.0	12.2	5.4
36–45	21.3	13.5	17.0	16.7	18.4	5.4
46–55	23.8	17.3	13.1	21.9	18.4	26.8
56–64	15.6	13.5	11.9	17.7	16.3	10.7
65 and older	14.8	27.9	26.7	21.4	24.5	44.6
Heterogeneity	*0.828*	*0.821*	*0.824*	*0.827*	*0.838*	*0.719*
Tenure status[d]						
Social renter	28.5	18.3	7.9	28.3	46.9	69.6
Private renter	31.7	56.7	71.8	59.2	36.7	28.6
Owner	39.8	25.0	20.3	12.6	16.3	1.8
Heterogeneity	*0.665*	*0.588*	*0.440*	*0.557*	*0.631*	*0.441*
n (max)	123	104	177	192	49	56

Notes: [a]Chi^2 = 35.5, df = 10, $p < .001$, Cramer's V = 0.17 ($n = 653$).
[b]Chi^2 = 33.8, df = 25, n. s. ($n = 580$).
[c]Chi^2 = 43.9, df = 25, $p < .05$, Cramer's V = 0.11 ($n = 699$).
[d]Chi^2 = 145.5, df = 10, $p < .001$, Cramer's V = 0.32 ($n = 700$).

From the question of the propensity to move out of the neighbourhood, those respondents who answered with 'yes' *and* had already undertaken some activity were selected. Again, the order of the proportion of respondents that are willing-to-move out of the neighbourhood does not follow the order according to the percentage of residents receiving social assistance.

Further, the responses were used from the question about whether a person felt insecure or perceived risk in the neighbourhood. The variable 'perceived risk' is defined by responses to the question to estimate the risk of becoming victimized in the neighbourhood (with categories 'none', 'yes, some', 'yes, strong'). To obtain a single value, the differences in the percentages between the responses of 'no risk' and 'high risk' (the higher the value, the less the perceived risk) were used. Although this classification is highly subjective, it is known that such perceptions shape the attitudes and actions of individuals. Note, the variable 'perceived risk' is different from DA: the former is the resident's expression of risk in the neighbourhood, the latter residents' evaluation of single parts of the deprived area as dangerous.

Finally, age groups, income and educational level were included in Table 2. The most deprived neighbourhood (according to the proportion of residents receiving social assistance) clearly has the oldest population, the differences are significant on the 5 per cent level; in SW the highest proportion of residents are found with the lowest level of formal education. Apart from these differences, there are clear differences between the neighbourhoods; all of them consist of old and young residents, different levels of formal education and different equivalent incomes (this variable is not significant on the 5 per cent level).

With regard to social mix (comparing the D-values in Table 2), the lowest heterogeneity is found in the most distressed neighbourhood (SW), and the values for age and education in particular are clearly below average. This neighbourhood can be described as having a high proportion of old and less educated inhabitants, living relatively seldom in their own properties. The highest amount of social mix is found in the less distressed neighbourhood (SV). However, there is no clear relationship between the extent of social mix and the proportion of residents receiving social assistance.

In general, none of the micro level data and none of the other macro level data mirror the order given by social assistance. The values do not vary systematically with poverty level and different indicators do not result in different rank orders of poverty. This is a first indicator that poverty areas are internally heterogeneous. Furthermore, also within the neighbourhoods a large amount of variation is found. These findings are in accord with the main proposition that poverty areas are internally heterogeneous.

In analogy to traditional multi-level studies, the focus here is on the variation to be explained by the neighbourhoods within the total area. For deciding which sub-classification, DA or NA, is more appropriate, first both variables are cross-tabulated. As Table 3 shows, both classifications are highly associated (Cramer's $V = 0.50$), which is obvious in all categories. As expected, residents of sub-areas with a high rate of poverty also have a high fear of crime. Given this association between these two classifications, the question arises about which of these two classifications is 'better'. This question will be discussed later.

Scales

The basic model to be applied is adopted from the Sampson *et al.* (2002) model, which makes the study comparable to the North American methodology and findings. The model is displayed in Figure 2.

Table 3. 'Dangerous Areas' by natural areas, (%)[a]

'Dangerous Area'	Natural area						Total
	SV	GS	HO	VI	HS	SW	
None	57.9	53.1	0.0	0.0	0.0	0.0	122
Low	38.0	27.6	53.7	7.8	24.5	53.6	225
Strong	4.1	19.4	46.3	75.0	71.4	30.4	302
Very strong	0.0	0.0	0.0	17.2	4.1	16.1	44
Total	121	98	177	192	49	56	693

Notes: $\text{Chi}^2 = 516.3$; df $= 15$; $p < 0.001$; Cramer's V $= 0.50$.
[a]None: area mentioned 0–3 times, low: mentioned 4–10 times, strong: 11–30 times, very strong: 31 times and more.

The first block comprises four non-global variables (in the terminology of Lazarsfeld & Menzel, 1969), i.e. constructed from characteristics of individuals and aggregated to the macro level. In the present case, this block was measured on the level of the six natural areas, the variables being: percentage foreign-born, percentage receiving social assistance, percentage single-headed households and fluctuation rate. It should be noted that the fluctuation rate (measured on the level of census data) as well as the willingness-to-move out of the neighbourhood (measured on the level of sample data) could be interpreted as independent and as dependent variable. Fluctuation is an independent variable if it is assumed—in the tradition of the early Chicago School—that it leads to heterogeneity of social norms and thus to low informal social control. In contrast, fluctuation (or the willingness-to-move out) is a dependent variable if the social conditions in a neighbourhood instigate residents to move out, resulting in a rise of the fluctuation rate. Nonetheless, this variable was used in the analyses in order to replicate the prior studies. Three of the four variables were also measured on the level of sample data: transfer income, single-headed households, and propensity to move out of the neighbourhood (for categories, see Table 7).

The second block refers to the meso level by specifying intervening variables. Here, the variables mentioned by Leventhal & Brooks-Gunn (2000) can be replaced by two concepts suggested by Sampson & Groves (1989) and Sampson *et al.* (1999): 'collective efficacy' and 'intergenerational closure'. Collective efficacy is a composite measure of social

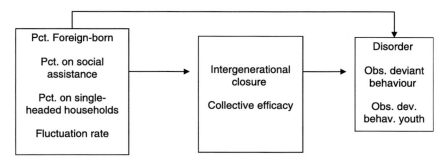

Figure 2. The Cologne study model

cohesion and informal control that seems to be very powerful (Sampson *et al.*, 2002). The concept 'collective efficacy' is supposed to measure the social capital of a neighbourhood by combining two dimensions: trust and informal control. This scale has also been used by Oberwittler (2004a, 2004b) in the above mentioned German study. His items were used (cf. Table A1 in the Appendix) and they were measured on a four-point scale, ranging from 'fully agree' to 'fully disagree'. The items from the scale 'intergenerational closure' are supposed to measure the amount of supervision or surveillance of children by their parents and neighbours. As several studies have shown, supervision of children turns out to be one of the decisive factors of neighbourhood quality. If this form of control is lacking, peers will have a dominant influence on younger residents, this in turn fosters deviant behaviour of teenagers (e.g. Haynie, 2001; Oberwittler, 2004a, 2004b).

Both sets of items were analyzed for their underlying constructs. Since Principal Components Analysis (PCA) requires metric data, Categorical (or Nonlinear) Principal Components Analysis (CatPCA) was used. In CatPCA only the ordering of the successive categories is retained or at least not disrupted, the distances between the successive categories are calculated within an iterative procedure. Since the order of categories is retained, the minimum value between two (or more) successive categories is zero; in this case the categories are tied. In contrast to PCA, CatPCA solutions are not nested, i.e. the number of dimensions has to be determined in advance. The final solution of CatPCA can be interpreted as traditional PCA; the method also provides eigenvalues and their explained variances, factor loadings and factor scores (Gifi, 1990; de Leeuw, 2006).

Applying CatPCA to the five items measuring collective efficacy, the one-dimensional solution yields an explained variance of 60.8 per cent with a high internal consistency of Cronbach's alpha $= 0.84$; all items load highly on the scale (cf. Table A1 of the Appendix). The interpretation of the scale is straightforward: the higher the value, the higher the collective efficacy. The scale 'intergenerational closure' (INTCLOS) is also constructed by using the one-dimensional CatPCA solution; it is presented in Table A2 of the Appendix. It explains half of the total variance and has a Cronbach's alpha $= 0.75$; again, all items are highly associated with the scale. The higher the scale value, the higher the intergenerational closure, i.e. the better the respondents know the children in the neighbourhood.

The third block comprises the micro-level measurements of dependent variables: disorder, observed deviance in general and observed deviance of youth. The 11 four-point items from the scale DISORDER were adopted from Ross *et al.* (2001). Applying CatPCA to these 11 items, a one-dimensional solution was estimated, which explains 35 per cent of the total variation with Cronbach's alpha $= 0.82$. Except for the items 'People in my neighbourhood take good care of their houses and apartments' and 'I am always ...' all loadings on the first dimension are satisfying (cf. Table A3 of the Appendix). Ross *et al.* (2001) do not report a similar test on dimensionality. Therefore, it cannot be judged whether the two items have low loadings on the first dimension in the US sample as well, and the same holds true for the scales collective efficacy, intergenerational closure and observed deviance of youth. As for the other scales, higher scale values indicate higher reported disorder in the neighbourhood.

To measure the observed deviance of residents (adults), a scale that was originally developed by Friedrichs & Blasius (2000, 2003) was used and it was applied in a study on four deprived neighbourhoods in Cologne. The results of CatPCA for the present study are shown in Table A4 of the Appendix. The one-dimensional solution (OBSDEV) has a satisfactory Cronbach's alpha of 0.67 and an explained variance of 30.4 per cent. This latent variable shows that higher values indicate a higher degree of observed deviance.

Finally, a scale was included on observed deviant behaviour of youngsters (OBSYOUTH), adopted from the German version by Oberwittler (2003, and in this issue). Again, the CatPCA yields a single dimension that accounts for 57.8 per cent of the total variation. Cronbach's alpha for this scale is 0.63 (cf. Table A5 of the Appendix). Again, the higher the value, the higher the degree of observed deviance of youth. All five scales are standardized to means of zero and standard deviations of one.

The correlations between the five scales are all in the predicted direction (Table 4). Some are comparatively low, indicating that they measure different phenomena. Relatively high correlation coefficients are found between the three scales of observed deviance, observed youth deviance and disorder. Furthermore, disorder and the two Sampson-scales intergenerational closure and collective efficacy are negatively correlated. Although some of these associations were expected to be even higher, they clearly support the results obtained in North American studies.

Findings

The analysis proceeds in three steps. First, differences among the neighbourhoods are explored by analyses of variance (NA and DA classification). Second, an assessment is made of the effects of neighbourhood and intermediate variables on the dependent variables of observed deviant behaviour, observed deviant behaviour of youth and disorder by multiple regressions. Third, context and individual effects are separated by the application of correspondence analysis.

In the theory section, it was argued that neighbourhoods designated as 'poverty' or 'deprived' are not homogeneous. Data presented in Tables 5 and 6 (means of the neighbourhoods, F- and eta-values for the five scales) clearly indicate that this is the case in the present study area. Both for the NA and the DA classification, significant differences are found in neighbourhoods with regard to the indicators of perceived deviance, collective efficacy and intergenerational closure.

Although all mean differences are highly significant, the explained variance is relatively low (with a maximum of little more than 6 per cent in INTCLOS, see Table 5 and Table 6, column Eta). Further, the standard deviations (standardized for all variables to 1) are quite similar for all natural areas and for all Dangerous Areas. It can be concluded that there are differences within and between the neighbourhoods and as already shown, neither the whole area nor the natural areas are homogeneous (cf. Table 2).

With regard to observed deviant behaviour and the NA classification, the highest values are found in HS and SW, the natural areas that were classified as most deprived. In the case

Table 4. Inter-correlation of scales (Pearson's r)

	OBSDEV	DEVYOUTH	DISORDER	COLLEFF
OBSDEV	–			
DEVYOUTH	0.44	–		
DISORDER	0.35	0.49	–	
COLLEFF	−0.25	−0.19	−0.37	–
INTCLOS	−0.17	−0.21	−0.33	0.56

Table 5. Analysis of Variance of Scales, by natural areas; mean values, F and Eta, standard deviations in italics

Scale	Natural area						F	Eta
	SV ($n = 123$)	GS ($n=104$)	HO ($n = 177$)	VI ($n = 192$)	HS ($n = 49$)	SW ($n = 56$)		
OBSDEV	0.00	−0.01	−0.18	0.03	0.40	0.40	4.1*	0.17
DEVYOUTH	0.09	−0.29	−0.25	0.13	0.49	0.22	8.0*	0.23
DISORDER	−0.03	−0.42	−0.07	0.20	0.47	−0.05	7.8*	0.23
COLLEFF	0.27	0.31	−0.21	−0.10	−0.39	0.13	7.7*	0.23
INTCLOS	0.41	0.26	−0.13	−0.21	−0.40	0.00	9.4*	0.25
OBSDEV	*1.13*	*1.06*	*0.88*	*1.05*	*1.11*	*1.26*		
DEVYOUTH	*1.04*	*0.98*	*0.92*	*1.00*	*0.90*	*1.09*		
DISORDER	*0.97*	*1.04*	*0.96*	*0.97*	*0.81*	*1.23*		
COLLEFF	*1.02*	*0.88*	*1.02*	*0.97*	*0.84*	*1.12*		
INTCLOS	*1.08*	*1.01*	*1.02*	*0.91*	*1.02*	*1.00*		

Notes: *$p < 0.001$.
All variables standardized to mean of 0 and standard deviation of 1.

of observed deviant behaviour of youth, the two most deprived natural areas again have the highest values, but they are interchanged; in the case of disorder, HS again has the highest value whereas the value of SW (-0.05) is even slightly below average (see the negative value in the respective row, Table 5). The lowest values for these indicators are found in the three less deprived natural areas, GS has particularly very low values. The lowest values in collective efficacy and intergenerational closure are in the second most deprived area (HS), the highest values have the two less deprived areas SV and GS. It should be noted that all mean differences are highly significant, which supports the assumption of the heterogeneity within an area that was assigned as homogeneously deprived. However,

Table 6. Analysis of Variance of Scales, by 'Dangerous Area', mean values, F and Eta, standard deviations in italics

Scale	Dangerous Area				F	Eta
	None ($n = 122$)	Low ($n = 226$)	Strong ($n = 302$)	Very strong ($n = 44$)		
OBSDEV	−.06	.02	.01	.38	1.9	.09
DEVYOUTH	−.26	−.03	.06	.44	6.0*	.16
DISORDER	−.29	−.06	.10	.45	7.7*	.18
COLLEFF	.42	−.02	−.12	−.34	10.4*	.21
INTCLOS	.55	−.05	−.18	−.23	16.3*	.26
OBSDEV	*1.10*	*1.06*	*0.99*	*1.44*		
DEVYOUTH	*1.03*	*1.03*	*0.95*	*1.08*		
DISORDER	*0.95*	*1.05*	*0.96*	*1.08*		
COLLEFF	*0.94*	*1.05*	*0.96*	*1.05*		
INTCLOS	*1.08*	*0.97*	*0.98*	*1.02*		

Notes: *$p < 0.001$. All variables standardized to mean of 0 and standard deviation of 1.

there are quite large differences in the order of the natural areas, i.e. the order in the level of distress varies by the measurement. Combining the five scales of micro and meso level data seems to support the ordering in level of deprivation derived from the macro data (percentage of households receiving social assistance). These facts will be explained in the final section when correspondence analysis is applied.

ANOVA was also applied to the four Dangerous Areas (DA classification). With one small interchange in OBSDEV (between 'low' and 'strong'), the order in Dangerous Areas perfectly reflects the order in the five scales: the higher the level of assigned danger, the higher the observed deviant behaviour, the higher the observed deviance of youth, the higher the disorder, the lower the collective efficacy, and the lower the intergenerational closure. From this point of view, both DA and NA classifications are suitable for further analysis. Since both indicators are highly associated (see Table 3) and since the eta-coefficients for the DA classification are lower than those for the NA classification, only the NA delineation is considered in the following.

Multiple Regression Analyses

To assess the effects of natural areas and the explanatory variables taken from the model of Sampson *et al.* (2002), multiple regression analyses are used for three dependent variables: observed deviance, observed deviance of youth and disorder. Independent variables are the six natural areas (coded as dummy variables), with SW serving as reference category. (According to the percentages of residents receiving social assistance, SW has the highest extent of distress. Therefore, the effects of the other natural areas on the dependent variables are expected to be negative.) The variables 'transfer' and 'move' are also constructed as dummies, indicating persons receiving transfer payment and persons willing-to-move out the neighbourhood with some activity undertaken (as proxy for 'fluctuation rate'). Further, 'single headed' was included as a proxy for the macro-variable 'percentage single-headed households'.

In the regression analyses that follow, two models are used for each dependent variable: the first considers only neighbourhood effects for the assessment of the extent of variation caused by natural areas. In the second model, the effects of the meso-level and micro-level variables crucial to the model are included: collective efficacy, intergenerational closure, propensity to move out, living on transfer income and single-headed household. (These multiple regressions were also ran for Dangerous Areas. All analyses point in the same direction, but as in the case of ANOVA, natural areas explain more variance.)

The most general measure of perceived deviance is the disorder scale (Ross *et al.*, 2001). Model 1 shows little impact on explained variance when including natural areas only. As already shown, when applying ANOVA (Table 5) disorder is highest in HS, and lowest in GS. Including the variables collective efficacy, intergenerational closure, transfer income, single-headed households, as well as willingness-to-move out in the analysis, and comparing models 1 and 2, shows that natural areas do not have any significant effect upon perceived disorder, once these attributes are controlled. In contrast, both collective efficacy (-0.20) and intergenerational closure (-0.16) have significant effects, as posited in the theoretical model. Further, living alone with children has a significant effect, whereas depending on transfer payments has no effect. The resulting adjusted $R^2 = 0.23$ is fairly satisfying.

In contrast to the dependent variable disorder, significant effects of natural areas are also found in the extended models for both observed deviance and observed deviance of youth. Turning to observed deviance and the effects of natural areas only, Table 7 documents that four of them have significant effects (compared to SW), but explain almost no variation.

In Model 2, only two of the four initial (although low) effects (HO and VI) are still present. The natural area HO has a highly negative effect (b = −0.61), indicating low deviance, followed by VI with b = −0.38. Further, collective efficacy has a high negative effect, but also variables of neighbourhood composition: the propensity to move out, transfer income, and the status of a single-headed household. However, explained variance for observed deviance (R^2 = 0.13) is much lower than for disorder.

With regard to observed deviance of youth, again the natural areas have only a little impact, but a little higher than for observed deviance. Note that the neighbourhood HS is worse than the reference neighbourhood SW; the lowest observed crime is found among youth in GS and HO. The inclusion of the five other independent variables raises the explained variance to 14 per cent. In this case, collective efficacy is partialled out, while the effect of intergenerational closure remains. In addition, significant effects are found of propensity to move and, to a minor extent, single-headed household. Further, the extent of (perceived) intergenerational closure has a negative effect (as expected).

The different effects of collective efficacy and intergenerational closure on the three dependent variables are explained by positing that the effects depend on the variable which is regressed. In the case of observed deviant behaviour it is collective efficacy, in the case of observed deviance behaviour among youth it is intergenerational closure, and in the case of disorder both of them are highly significant.

Table 7. Multiple regressions on Disorder, Observed Deviance (OBSDEV), and Observed Deviance of Youths (DEVYOUTH), given are the unstandardized coefficients (b)

Variable	DISORDER		OBSDEV		DEVYOUTH	
	Model 1	Model 2	Model 1	Model 2	Model 1	Model 2
Constant	−0.05	−0.51*	0.40**	−0.39*	0.22	−0.46**
SV	0.02	0.14	−0.39*	−0.32	−0.13	−0.02
GS	−0.37*	−0.25	−0.40*	−0.29	−0.51**	−0.40**
HO	−0.02	−0.12	−0.58***	−0.61***	−0.47**	−0.48***
VI	0.26	0.20	−0.36*	−0.38**	−0.09	−0.11
HS	0.52*	0.28	0.01	−0.20	0.27	0.10
SW (ref.)	–	–	–	–	–	–
COLLEFF		−0.20***		−0.17***		−0.03
INTCLOS		−0.16***		−0.05		−0.14***
Transfer income		−0.01		0.33***		0.18
Single-headed hh.		0.23*		0.32**		0.26*
Willingness-to-move		0.27***		0.21***		0.25***
Adj. R^2	0.05	0.23	0.02	0.13	0.05	0.14

Notes: *p < 0.05; **p < 0.01; ***p < 0.001. Coding of variables: transfer income: yes = 1; single-headed household; yes = 1; willingness-to-move out: none = 1, yes, without activity = 2, yes, with activity = 3.

Although not systematically, all variables included in the model have significant effects on the dependent variables of observed deviance, observed deviance of youth and observed disorder. Hence, the study supports the model derived from Sampson *et al.* (2002). More specifically, collective efficacy and intergenerational closure proved to have predictive power for various types of disorder, not only in the North American studies, but also in the German context, as previously documented by Oberwittler (2004a, 2004b) for youth.

Correspondence Analysis

In the next step, the paper explores the relations among the characteristics at the macro, meso and micro levels (census characteristics, sample characteristics and scales, see Tables 3 and 6) corresponding to the six natural areas. Since it is not possible to perform multi-level analysis due to the small number of cases at the macro level, a multivariate method is used that allows for such a subdivision: correspondence analysis.

Correspondence analysis (CA) is a multivariate method for exploring any data table with non-negative entries and converting such tables into graphical displays, called 'maps'. It is intended to reveal structures in the data rather than to confirm or reject hypotheses about the underlying processes that generated the data. In the given example, first a table is constructed combining items from different levels, i.e. items from the survey with indicators from the Statistical Office. For including the information from the macro level, different types of individual data have to be aggregated to the level of natural areas. The final analysis has to consider data from different levels: percentages from the macro level, percentages from the micro level and standardized numerical data (with means of zero and standard deviations of one). To apply CA, a stacked table has to be constructed, with variables in the rows and natural areas in the columns.

The variables included in the final model are:

- Three variables from the population register: fluctuation rate (in percentage per year), percentage of receiving social assistance, and percentage of foreign-born (see Table 2). The percentage of single-headed households from the population register was not included because residents will not change their behaviour and their attitudes according to the rate of single-headed households in the neighbourhood.
- Four manifest variables from the survey data: perceived risk (responses to the question, to estimate the risk to become victimized in the neighbourhood, with categories 'no', 'yes, some', 'yes, high'; for receiving a single value, the difference in the percentages was estimated between 'no risk – high risk', the higher the value, the less the perceived risk), willingness-to-move out (from this question the proportion of those respondents who answered with 'yes' and who already undertook some activities to move out were selected), percentages of receiving transfer income and single-headed households (see Table 2).
- Five latent variables constructed from the variables discussed above (see Appendix 1 to 5), with mean value 0 and standard deviation 1: observed deviance, observed deviance of youth, collective efficacy, intergenerational closure and disorder. From these variables the means of the natural areas are considered.

Since the variables are scaled differently, they have to be standardized to the same range; values from 0 to 1 were chosen (the lower value has to be 0 because the variables must also be centred, cf. Greenacre, 1993, ch. 19). In the process of standardization and to exclude effects from the direction of the variables, the items have to be doubled (the scales). Thereby, the doubled value of each item (or scale) is defined as the difference between 1 (the maximum value of the standardized item/scale) and the standardized value of the original item or scale. A high value of the original variable (which will be called 'images') indicates that the corresponding neighbourhood has a high proportion of this indicator. A high value of the doubled scale (which will be called 'anti-images'; the sum of 'image' and 'anti-image' for every variable in every natural area is equal to 1) indicates that the corresponding neighbourhood has a low proportion of this indicator. Figure 3 the graphical solution of the CA displays. When connecting the images and their corresponding anti-images with straight lines, these lines go through the centroid of the presentation (these lines are not included in Figure 3). This is because the construction of the table of input data, images and anti-images are associated 100 per cent negative; in the CA solution they are located exactly opposite in all dimensions (for more details, see Blasius, Friedrichs & Galster, this issue).

The first dimension, which explains 58.3 per cent of the total variation, contrasts the images and anti-images of disorder, willingness-to-move out, migrants, transfer income and the percentage of social assistance. Thereby, all categories that can be labelled as indicators of a good neighbourhood (e.g. low disorder, low number of persons receiving transfer income, low number of persons willing-to-move out) are on the left side, the ones that reflect a relative critical view of the neighbourhood (for example, high disorder) are

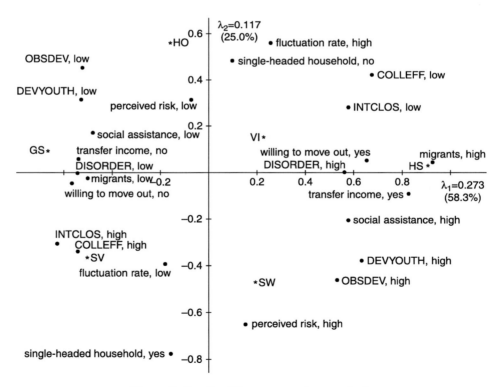

Figure 3. Results of the correspondence analysis

on the right side. Thus, the first dimension can be regarded as a general indicator for 'deprivation', it particularly contrasts the attitudes towards the descriptors mentioned above: the more a position tends to the left, the lower the disorder in the neighbourhood, the lower the intention to leave the neighbourhood, the lower the number of persons receiving transfer money and the lower the number of migrants. Since CA does not include assumptions about causality, it is not possible to decide whether the migrants cause disorder or respondents report high disorder because they interpret high percentages of migrants as indication of disorder.

The second dimension explains an additional 25.0 per cent of the total variation; thus, 83.3 per cent of the total variation is explained within the two-dimensional solution. Whereas the first dimension reflects a general type of deprivation, the second dimension (ordinate axis) mainly reflects the perceived risk, the proportion of single-headed households as well as (but to a lesser degree) the fluctuation rate. The more positive a value on the second dimension, the less is the perceived risk, the lower the number of single-headed households, but the higher the fluctuation rate and, as expected, the lower both the collective efficacy and intergenerational closure.

Between these two dimensions are observed deviant behaviour and observed deviant behaviour of youth. On the one hand, low values for deviant behaviour and low values for deviant behaviour of youth are positively associated with low values for perceived risk, on the other hand with low values for disorder. It follows that the perception of risk is quite independent from reporting disorder in the neighbourhood; further, the observation of deviant behaviour in general and deviant behaviour of youth is positively associated with both indicators (perceived risk and disorder). Nearly independent of both forms of deviant behaviour, but negatively associated with disorder, are intergenerational closure and collective efficacy. The higher collective efficacy and intergenerational closure, the lower is the disorder.

In the next step, the six natural areas are assigned to the groups of indicators. Here, only the distances between the indicators as well as between the natural areas can be interpreted as Euclidean distances, bearing in mind that only 83.3 per cent of the variation is displayed. Categories that are close together are similar with regard to the natural areas (the profiles of the respective categories are similar); categories that are far away from each other are dissimilar in this respect. Although the distances between the natural areas and the indicators are not defined, it is possible to interpret their similarities via common factor loadings on the same axes. For the geometry of CA solutions and the interpretation of CA maps, see Greenacre (1993) and Blasius & Greenacre (2006).

GS is relatively close to the negative part of dimension 1 and therefore characterized by a low value on transfer income, on migrants, on households willing-to-move out (compare also Table 2) and by a low value on disorder (also compare Table 5); or in general, GS can be seen as less deprived in the whole deprived area. Opposite to GS there is HS; this natural area can be described just as the opposite: high disorder, high number of migrants, high number of respondents receiving transfer income, and high number of households willing-to-move out. In other words, according to the whole set of indicators HS is the most deprived neighbourhood (according to the census indicator 'percentage of households receiving social assistance' it was SW). HO is close to the positive part of dimension 2: here a low number of single-headed households and a high fluctuation rate can be found, the perceived risk is low. In contrast, SW is described by the opposite of HO, having the highest rate of perceived risk (cf. Table 2). Again different is SV, which is mainly characterized by a high intergenerational closure and a high collective efficacy. Finally, the natural area VI is located close to the centroid of the presentation, i.e. objective and subjective distress in VI are close to average.

The CA solution corroborates the results of the multiple regression analyses. There is heterogeneity within the deprived area; in the given case the natural areas can be clearly differentiated. However, the differentiation is not that simple as the literature may suggest, i.e. perceived risk and disorder are almost uncorrelated, the same holds for observed deviance which is only weakly correlated to intergenerational closure and collective efficacy.

As already shown, the correlations between the indicators are in the expected direction, although lower than assumed (cf. Table 4). Diverging solutions were further received from ANOVA (cf. Table 5) and from the regression analyses (cf. Table 7), the rank order of deprived neighbourhoods with regard to the variables of interest. The reason for these findings is that there are different expressions of 'deprived neighbourhood': in terms of perception of deviant behaviour in general and perception of deviant behaviour of youth, HO and GS have the best values (i.e. the residents in HO and GS reported the lowest values in perception of deviant behaviour), followed by SV and VI; SW and HS show the worst values, i.e. the highest values on perception of deviant behaviour. To follow this interpretation, a super-dimension has to be included in the figure; starting at the top left between 'OBSDEV, low' and 'DEVYOUTH, low', going through the centroid of the figure, i.e. the cross of the axes, to bottom right, then project the six natural areas in right angles onto this super-dimension and read off the order of them (cf. also Table 5).

A second method of classifying 'deprived neighbourhoods' is based on the proportion of intergenerational closure and collective efficacy. Including once more a super-dimension in Figure 3, here it starts at bottom left and goes via the centroid to top right, and provides the following rank order of natural areas: SV and GS with relatively low values, followed by SW, which is also located in the negative part of this super-dimension. HO and VI are in the middle of the scale, HS is clearly separated in the part where low collective efficacy and low intergenerational closure are found (cf. also Table 5). However, there is a third type to differentiate natural areas, in terms of perceived risk. Including a third super-dimension into the given solution, which is close to dimension 2, yields a rank order where HO has the lowest value, i.e. the lowest level of perceived risk, and where SW has clearly the highest value. Describing the natural areas by perceived risk, SW will be far away on the last position.

With regard to social mix within the neighbourhoods, the natural area SW has the lowest values and SV has the highest values on the socio-demographic characteristics and housing tenure, the other neighbourhoods were somewhere in between. In the graphical presentation of the CA, the only two neighbourhoods that are clearly distinct by this concept are neither far away from each other nor close together. Since the closeness of SW to 'high perceived risk' might be explained by the high proportion of elderly residents in this neighbourhood, it could only be theorized that a high social mix might serve as an indicator for a relatively high social capital (compare the closeness of SV to high collective efficacy and intergenerational closure). However, it should be followed that according to this solution the extent of social mix within the neighbourhoods is not a fruitful indicator for the level of distress of a neighbourhood.

Summary and Discussion

The aim of the paper was to assess the internal heterogeneity of a larger deprived urban area and to study the variation of perceived deviance within and between its neighbourhoods. The results clearly support the assumption of internal heterogeneity in the total deprived area; the differentiation into four and six neighbourhoods proved to be fruitful. Neighbourhoods differ with regard to three indicators of deviance: disorder, observed deviance and observed deviance of youth. A subjective delineation of neighbourhoods by Dangerous Areas is highly correlated with an 'objective' delineation based on natural areas according to administrative statistics.

From the data a much differentiated picture of internal heterogeneity emerges. This supports the findings in the literature and accounts for the difficulty to assess the impact of single social mix variables on the residents. As expected, the total deprived area is found to be heterogeneous. It can be decomposed into four or six neighbourhoods. Two methods to delineate these neighbourhoods, by objective indicators as natural areas, or by a subjective indicator, result in similar findings. Thereby, the natural area decomposition has the advantages that it explains more variance and provides us with census data.

Also in accord with the assumptions, the six neighbourhoods exhibit high internal heterogeneity. However, the extent and pattern of internal heterogeneity of the whole distressed area differs from neighbourhood to neighbourhood according to the indicators. These findings support the conclusion drawn from the existing studies in the Theory section. There is no overall impact of social mix on several (desired) outcomes; instead, the effects vary by the indicators. Ordering in the level of distress is different when using tenure status, percentage receiving social assistance, level of disorder, perceived risk or observed deviance. However, an overall ordering of neighbourhoods led to a tentative order of distress: SW/HS, followed by VI/HO and GS/SV.

The two least distressed neighbourhoods, SV and GS, have low proportions of migrants, a low fluctuation rate and low percentage of residents wishing to move out, in addition SV has a high proportion of owners. In these neighbourhoods, more collective efficacy and intergenerational closure are reported. The two most distressed neighbourhoods, HS and SW, have high proportions of persons receiving transfer incomes, high proportions of migrants and high proportions of persons willing-to-move out. In these areas the observed deviance and extent of disorder are comparatively high.

Some dependent variables that were expected to be highly correlated explain little variance. Further, both indicators of social capital, collective efficacy and intergenerational closure, are only weakly related to observed deviance. Surprisingly, disorder and perceived risk are almost uncorrelated. Thus, in the sample, perceptions such as vandalism, crime or drug use are not related to the perceived personal risk. It seems that the observations of manifest disorder and deviance have little impact on the (more attitudinal) evaluations of social capital and of personal risk.

From these results it must be concluded that disorder is something different than observed deviant behaviour and that both are different from perceived risk. This means crime or deviance is not a homogeneous concept, it is a mixture of different types of behaviour and their perceptions, and therefore explanatory variables have different effects on different measures of crime.

The intervening variables in the model, collective efficacy and intergenerational closure exert significant effects on the extent of deviance. Thus, the model in Figure 2 is supported by the findings here and corroborates the North American findings: the impact of collective efficacy and intergenerational closure varies by neighbourhood.

Thus, the scales collective efficacy and intergenerational closure have a different status than variables transfer income, single-headed households and propensity to move out of the neighbourhood. The former refer to latent variables based on resident perceptions of the neighbourhood and may be attributed to the meso level, whereas the latter are individual characteristics attributed to the micro level. From multiple regressions it is concluded that neighbourhood perception data explain neighbourhood disorder better than categories delineating neighbourhoods.

Applying CA makes it possible to describe and differentiate the natural areas and also by including material from different sources to analyze these data simultaneously, in the given case micro, meso and macro level data. The possibility of visualizing the complex structure of the data, and in particular the application of the method when the number of macro-level categories is limited, should make CA an appropriate alternative to multi-level analysis. Since the philosophy of CA is that "the model has to follow the data and not vice versa" (cf. Benzécri et al., 1973; cf. Blasius & Greenacre, 2006, p. 6), it is possible to detect structures that were otherwise not revealed before.

Further, CA shows that neighbourhoods are clearly separated within the two-dimensional space, indicating a highly differentiated structure of the whole deprived area. Moreover, the analysis shows that the neighbourhoods exhibit different types of distress or perceived deviant behaviour. 'Clusters' of distress, can be found, which are associated with different indicators of residential structure, e.g. high disorder with transfer payments and a high propensity to move out of the neighbourhood, or the close link between high perceived risk and single-headed households.

These findings lead to a tentative conclusion. Social mix, if conceptualized as social status heterogeneity, is not a decisive explanation of (perceived) deviant behaviour. Instead, the dominance of residents with specific characteristics, such as single-headed or willingness-to-move out, can (better) account for the variation of the dependent variables. If this proposition holds true, it could explain the low impact of social mix Musterd & Andersson (2005) reported from their empirical study.

To explain such findings it has to be considered that there are two overlapping effects. The first refers to the increase of social mix, e.g. by increasing the proportion of homeowners. The second refers to the impact this increase has on the (average) attitudes on all residents in the neighbourhood. To show the positive effect of social mix would require panel data allowing separation of the effects of the higher proportion of homeowners from the change in the attitudes of neighbours due to the increase of homeowners in the neighbourhood.

Policy Implications

These findings have several policy implications. First, social mix per se might be desirable, but the dimension of mix has to be specified, e.g. tenure status, income, ethnicity or household composition—the different outcomes depend on these indicators. Second, the effects of different dimensions of social mix presumably interact and therefore yield inconclusive outcomes. Third, decomposing larger areas into smaller neighbourhoods may improve the social mix effect, but the present study indicates that even in the natural-area based delineation the neighbourhoods still exhibit large internal variation. Finally, the social mix effects are context effects and should not be overestimated. The study corroborates the evidence from other studies (e.g. Friedrichs *et al.*, 2003; Leventhal & Brooks-Gunn, 2000) that these context or neighbourhood effects hardly exceed 8 per cent of the explained variance of a given outcome; they are low compared to individual-level effects. With regard to the question of indicators and outcomes of social mix, the findings indicate that different forms of heterogeneity produce different outcomes. Hence, it is concluded heterogeneity has to be measured and analyzed by different indicators (in the same study).

If social mix is multi-dimensional, it must be assessed which combination of proportions, e.g. tenure status and ethnicity, produces which outcomes. Since even now the evidence solely for the variable tenure mix is inconclusive and "neither uniform nor neatly meshed with current nostrums" (Galster *et al.*, 2000, p. 719) or even just a euphemism for privatization (Tunstall, 2003, p. 158), both have to be done to evaluate and conceive policies and projects in a much more differentiated way.

References

Adelaide City Council (2002) *What Sort of Goods are Neighbours? Social Mix and Sustainable Residential Community in Adelaide*, Green Paper for the City Living Summit, 26 February, Adelaide, Australia.

Arthurson, K. & Anaf, J. (2006) Social mix and disadvantaged communities: clarifying the links between policy, practice and the evidence base. Paper presented at the ENHR Conference, Cambridge, 2–6 July.

Atkinson, R. (2005) Neighbourhoods and the impacts of social mix: crime, tenure diversification and assisted mobility. CNR Paper 29 (University of Tasmania, Housing and Community Research Unit). Available at www.neighbourhoodcentre.org.uk.

Atkinson, R. & Kintrea, K. (2000) Owner-occupation, social mix and neighbourhood impacts, *Policy and Politics*, 28, pp. 93–108.

Atkinson, R. & Kintrea, K. (2001) Disentangling area effects: evidence from deprived and non-deprived neighbourhoods, *Urban Studies*, 38, pp. 2277–2298.

Benzécri, J.-P. et al. (1973) *L'Analyse des données. L'Analyse des correspondances* (Paris: Dunod).

Blasius, J. & Greenacre, M. J. (2006) Correspondence analysis and related methods in practice, in: M. J. Greenacre & J. Blasius (Eds) *Multiple Correspondence Analysis and Related Methods*, pp. 3–40 (Boca Raton, FL: Chapman & Hall).

Brophy, P. C. & Smith, R. N. (1997) Mixed-income housing: factors for success, *Cityscape*, 3, pp. 3–31.

Cowgill, D. O. & Cowgill, M. (1951) An index of segregation based on block statistics, *American Sociological Review*, 16, pp. 825–831.

De Leeuw, J. (2006) Nonlinear principal component analysis and related techniques, in: M. Greenacre & J. Blasius (Eds) *Multiple Correspondence Analysis and Related Techniques*, pp. 107–133 (Boca Raton, FL: Chapman & Hall).

Dietz, R. (2002) Estimation of neighborhood effects in the social sciences: an interdisciplinary approach, *Social Science Research*, 31, pp. 539–575.

Duncan, O. D. & Duncan, B. (1955) A methodological analysis of segregation indexes, *American Sociological Review*, 20, pp. 210–217.

Friedrichs, J. & Blasius, J. (2000) *Leben in benachteiligten Wohngebieten (Living in Distressed Areas)* (Opladen: Leske + Budrich).

Friedrichs, J. & Blasius, J. (2003) Social norms in distressed neighbourhoods. Testing the Wilson hypothesis, *Housing Studies*, 18, pp. 807–826.

Friedrichs, J. & Blasius, J. (2006) Attitudes of owners and renters in a deprived neighbourhood. Paper presented at the ENHR Conference, Ljubljana, Slovenia, 2–5 July. Available at http://enhr2006-ljubljana.uirs.si/publish/W12_Friedrichs_Blasius.pdf.

Friedrichs, J., Galster, G. & Musterd, S. (2003) Editorial. Neighbourhood effects on social opportunities: the European and American research and policy context, *Housing Studies*, 18, pp. 797–806.

Galster, G., Quercia, R. G. & Cortes, A. (2000) Identifying neighborhood thresholds: an empirical exploration, *Housing Policy Debate*, 11, pp. 699–730.

Gans, H. J. (1961) The balanced community: homogeneity or heterogeneity in residential areas?, *Journal of the American Institute of Planners*, 27, pp. 176–184.

Gifi, A. (1990) *Nonlinear Multivariate Analysis* (Chichester: Wiley).

Goodchild, B. & Cole, I. (2001) Social balance and mixed neighbourhoods in Britain since 1979: a review of discourse and practice in social housing, *Environment and Planning D: Society and Space*, 19, pp. 103–121.

Greenacre, M. (1993) *Correspondence Analysis in Practice* (London: Academic Press).

Harkness, J. & Newman, S. J. (2002) Homeownership for the poor in distressed neighborhoods: does this make sense? *Housing Policy Debate*, 13, pp. 597–630.

Haurin, D. R., Dietz, R. D & Weinberg, B. A. (2003) The impact of neighborhood homeownership rates: a review of the theoretical and empirical literature, *Journal of Housing Research*, 13, pp. 119–151.

Haynie, D. L. (2001) Delinquent peers revisited: does network structure matter? *American Journal of Sociology*, 106, pp. 1013–1057.

Hedstrom, P. (2005) *Dissecting the Social. On the Principles of Analytical Sociology* (Cambridge: Cambridge University Press).

Hiscock, R. (2001) Are mixed tenure estates likely to enhance the social capital of their residents? Paper presented at the Housing Studies Association Conference, Cardiff, 3–4 September. Available at http://www.cf.ac.uk/cplan/conferences/hsa_sept01/hiscock-r.pdf#search=%22Notting%20Hill%20Housing%20-Trust%20%22Mixed%20Tenure%20Housing%22%22.

Hox, J. (2002) *Multilevel Analysis: Techniques and Applications* (Newbury Park: Sage).

Jackson, R. M. (1977) Social structure and process in friendship choice, in: S. C. Fischer & L. McCallister (Eds) *Networks and Places*, pp. 59–78 (New York and London: Free Press).

Jencks, C. & Mayer, S. E. (1990) The social consequences of growing up in a poor neighbourhood, in: L. E. Lynn & M. G. H. McGeary (Eds) *Inner-City Poverty in the United States*, pp. 111–186 (Washington DC: National Academy Press).

Johnston, C. (2002) Housing policy and social mix: an exploratory paper (Sydney: Shelter WSW). Available at http://www.shelternsw.infoxchange.net.au/docs/rpt02socialmix-sb.pdf.

Jupp, B. (1999) *Living Together. Community Life on Mixed Tenure Estates* (London: Demos).

Kleinhans, R. (2004) Social implications of housing diversification in urban renewal: a review of recent literature, *Journal of Housing and the Built Environment*, 19, pp. 367–390.

Laumann, E. O. (1966) *Prestige and Association in an Urban Community. An Analysis of an Urban Stratification System* (Indianapolis and New York: Bobbs-Merrill).

Lazarsfeld, P. F. & Merton, R. K. (1954) Friendship as a social process: a substantive and methodological analysis, in: M. Berger, T. Abel & C. H. Page (Eds) *Freedom and Control in Modern Society*, pp. 18–66 (Toronto: van Nostrand).

Lazarsfeld, P. F. & Menzel, H. (1969) On the relation between individual and collective properties, in: A. Etzioni (Ed.) *A Sociological Reader on Complex Organizations*, revised and enlarged, pp. 422–440 (New York: Holt, Rinehart & Winston).

Leventhal, T. & Brooks-Gunn, J. (2000) The neighborhoods they live in: the effects of neighborhood residence on child and adolescent outcomes, *Psychological Bulletin*, 126, pp. 309–337.

Manzi, T. & Smith Bowers, B. (2003) Developing unstable communities? The experience of mixed tenure and multi-landlord estates. Paper presented at the Housing Studies Association Conference, Bristol, 9–10 September.

Mayntz, R. (2003) Mechanisms in the analysis of social macro-phenomena, *Philosophy of Social Sciences*, 34, pp. 237–259

McCulloch, A. (2001) Ward-level deprivation and individual social and economic outcomes in the british household panel study, *Environment and Planning A*, 33, pp. 667–684.

Musterd, S. & Andersson, R. (2005) Housing mix, social mix and social opportunities, *Urban Affairs Review*, 40, pp. 761–790.

Nyden, P., Lukehart, J., Maly, M. T. & Peterman, W. (1998) Neighborhood racial and ethnic diversity in US cities, *Cityscape*, 4, pp. 1–17.

Oberwittler, D. (2003) Die Messung und Qualitätskontrolle kontextbezogener Befragungsdaten mit Hilfe der Mehrebenenanalyse—am Beispiel des Sozialkapitals von Stadtvierteln (Measurement and quality control of context-related survey data by multi level analysis—an example of social capital of neighbourhoods), *ZA-Information*, 53, pp. 11–41.

Oberwittler, D. (2004a) Sozialstruktur, Freundeskreise und Delinquenz. Eine Mehrebenenanalyse zu sozialökologischen Kontexteffekten auf schwere Jugenddelinquenz (Social structure, friendships and delinquency. A multi level analysis of social-ecological context effects on severe youth delinquency), in: D. Oberwittler & S. Karstedt (Eds) *Soziologie der Kriminalität (Sociology of Crime)*, pp. 135–170 (Wiesbaden: VS Verlag).

Oberwittler, D. (2004b) A multilevel analysis of neighbourhood contextual effects on serious juvenile offending, *European Journal of Criminology*, 1, pp. 201–235.

Olson, M. (1965) *The Logic of Collective Action* (Cambridge, MA: Harvard University Press).

Opp, K.-D. (2004) Erklärungen durch Mechanismen: Probleme und Alternativen. (Explanations by mechanisms: problems and alternatives), in: R. Kecskes, M. Wagner & C. Wolf (Eds) *Angewandte Soziologie (Applied Sociology)*, pp. 361–379 (Wiesbaden: VS Verlag).

Ostendorf, W., Musterd, S. & de Vos, S. (2001) Social mix and the neighbourhood effect. Policy ambitions and empirical evidence, *Housing Studies*, 16, pp. 371–380.

Page, D. (2000) *Communities in the Balance. The Reality of Social Exclusion on Housing Estates* (York: Joseph Rowntree Foundation).

Page, D. & Boughton, R. (1997) *Mixed Tenure Housing Estates: A Study Undertaken for Notting Hill* (London: Notting Hill Housing Association).

Pettigrew, T. F. & Tropp, L. R. (2006) A meta-analytic test of intergroup contact theory, *Journal of Personality and Social Psychology*, 90, pp. 751–783.

Reber, P. (1993) *Heimat in der Großstadt (Home in the Large City)* (Köln: Geographisches Institut).

Reuband, K.-H. & Blasius, J. (1996) Face-to-face, telefonische und postalische Befragungen: Ausschöpfungsquoten und Antwortmuster in einer Großstadt-Studie (Face-to-face, telephone and mail surveys: response rates and response patterns in an urban study), *Kölner Zeitschrift für Soziologie und Sozialpsychologie*, 48, pp. 296–318.

Rosenbaum, J. E., Stroh, L. K. & Flynn, C. A. (1998) Lake Parc Place: a study of mixed-income housing, *Housing Policy Debate*, 9, pp. 703–740.

Ross, C. E., Mirowski, J. & Pribesh, S. (2001) Powerlessness and the amplification of threat: neighborhood disadvantage, disorder, and mistrust, *American Sociological Review*, 66, pp. 568–591.

Rossi, P. H. (1955) *Why Families Move* (Glencoe, IL: Free Press).

Sampson, R. J. & Groves, W. B. (1989) Community structure and crime: testing social-disorganization theory, *American Journal of Sociology*, 94, pp. 774–802.

Sampson, R. J., Raudenbush, S. W. & Earls, F. (1999) Neighborhoods and violent crime: a multilevel study of collective efficacy, pp. 336–350, in: I. Kawachi, B. P. Kennedy & R. G. Wilkinson (Eds) *The Society and Population Health Reader. Vol 1: Income Inequality and Health* (New York: New Press) (Originally published in: *Science,* 277 (1998), pp. 918–924).

Sampson, R. J., Morenoff, J. D. & Gannon-Rowley, T. (2002) Assessing 'neighborhood effects': social processes and new directions in research, *Annual Review of Sociology*, 28, pp. 443–478.

Sarkissian, W. (1976) The idea of social mix in town planning: an historical review, *Urban Studies*, 13, pp. 231–246.

Sarkissian, W., Forsyth, A. & Heine, W. (1990) Residential social mix: the debate continues. *Australian Planner*, March. Available at www.sarkissian.com.au/sap/pdfs/Residential_social_mix_the_debate_continues_by_Wendy_Sarkissian.pdf.

Schwartz, A. & Tajbakhsh, K. (1997) Mixed-income housing: unanswered questions, *Cityscape*, 3, pp. 71–92.

Scottish Homes (2006) Tenure mix and neighbourhood regeneration. *PRECiS* No. 127. Available at www.scot-homes.gov.uk/pdfs/pub.

SEU (Social Exclusion Unit) (2000) *National Strategy for Neighbourhood Renewal: A Framework for Consultation* (London: Cabinet Office). Available at http://www.socialexclusionunit.gov.uk/downloaddoc.asp?id=48.

Simpson, E. H. (1949) Measurement of diversity, *Nature*, 163, p. 688.

Snijders, T. A. B. & Bosker, R. J. (1999) *Multilevel Analysis. An Introduction to Basic and Advanced Multilevel Modeling* (London: Sage).

Tunstall, R. (2003) Mixed tenure policy in the UK: privatisation, pluralism or euphemism?, *Housing, Theory and Society*, 20, pp. 153–159.

Warmelink, F. & Zehner, K. (1996) Sozialräumliche Verteilungen in der Großstadt. Eine faktorökologische Untersuchung von Stabilität und Wandel städtischer Quartiere am Beispiel Kölns (Socio-spatial distributions

in the city: a factorial ecological study of stability and change of neighbourhoods in Cologne), in: J. Friedrichs & R. Kecskes (Eds) *Gentrification*, pp. 41–54 (Opladen: Leske + Budrich).
Wilson, W. J. (1987) *The Truly Disadvantaged* (Chicago: The University of Chicago Press).
Zorbaugh, H. W. (1926) The natural areas of the city, *American Sociological Society*, 20, pp. 188–197.

Table A1. Scale, Collective Efficacy (COLLEFF)*, factor loadings and explained variances, $n = 707$

People in the neighbourhood...	D_1	%
... help each other	0.80	63.5
... know each other well	0.68	45.8
... are trustworthy	0.83	68.9
... get along well	0.84	70.7
... respect law and order	0.74	54.8
Eigenvalue	3.04	
Explained variance	60.8%	
Cronbach's alpha	0.84	

Note: *Adapted from Sampson & Groves (1989); Oberwittler (2003).

Appendix

Table A2. Scale, Intergenerational Closure (INTCLOS)*, factor loadings and explained variances, $n = 703$

Item	D_1	%
Adults in this neighbourhood know who the local children are	0.68	45.8
Parents in this neighbourhood know their children's friends	0.78	61.5
Parents in this neighbourhood care for what their children do	0.79	62.1
This is a good place for children to grow up	0.72	51.8
There are adults in this neighbourhood that children can look up to	0.53	28.0
Eigenvalue	2.49	
Explained variance	49.9%	
Cronbach's alpha	0.75	

Note: *Adapted from Sampson & Groves (1989); Oberwittler (2003).

Table A3. Scale Observed Neighbourhood Disorder (DISORDER)*, factor loadings and explained variances, $n = 706$

Item	D_1	%
There is a lot of graffiti in my neighbourhood	0.43	18.7
My neighbourhood is noisy	0.60	35.6
Vandalism is common in my neighbourhood	0.73	53.3
My neighbourhood is clean	−0.62	38.6
People in my neighbourhood take good care of their houses and apartments	−0.29	8.4
There are too many people hanging around on the streets near my home	0.58	33.5
There is a lot of crime in my neighbourhood	0.77	58.5
There is too much drug use in my neighbourhood	0.72	51.7
There is too much alcohol use in my neighbourhood	0.69	47.7
I'm always having trouble with my neighbours	0.29	8.2
My neighbourhood is safer	−0.59	34.5
Eigenvalue	3.89	
Explained variance	35.3%	
Cronbach's alpha	0.82	

Note: *Adapted from Ross *et al.* (2001).

Table A4. Observed Deviant Behaviour (OBSDEV)*, factor loadings and explained variances, $n = 707$

Item	D_1	%
Neighbour shouts at children	0.49	23.8
Sexual molestation	0.45	20.1
Elderly woman steels cheese	0.55	30.0
Youngsters shout at foreign-born woman	0.69	47.5
Neighbour beats his children	0.61	37.6
Public assistance fraud	0.56	30.9
Teenage pregnancy	0.47	22.1
Drunk in public	0.56	31.6
Eigenvalue	2.44	
Explained variance	30.4%	
Cronbach's alpha	0.67	

Note: *Adapted from Friedrichs & Blasius (2000).

Table A5. Scale Observed Deviant Behaviour of Youngsters (OBSYOUTH)*, factor loadings and explained variances, $n = 707$

Item	D_1	%
A group of youngsters make a lot of noise	0.77	59.1
Youngsters damage something on purpose	0.77	58.7
Youngsters beat up each other and one is injured	0.74	55.0
Eigenvalue	1.73	
Explained variance	57.8%	
Cronbach's alpha	0.63	

Note: *Adapted from Oberwittler (2003).

The Effects of Neighbourhood Poverty on Adolescent Problem Behaviours: A Multi-level Analysis Differentiated by Gender and Ethnicity

DIETRICH OBERWITTLER

Introduction

Current Research on Neighbourhood Contextual Effects on Children and Adolescents

Despite the recent upsurge of interest in the social consequences of poverty and social exclusion for the development of children and adolescents, empirical knowledge remains sparse, especially in Europe, and particularly with regard to the question of neighbourhood contextual effects on individual behaviour. Theoretical reasoning as well as common sense have for a long time suggested that living in areas of concentrated poverty restricts the opportunities of residents and aggravates individual disadvantage, fostering subcultural orientations and problem behaviours especially among children and adolescents

(Booth & Crouter, 2001; Friedrichs, 1998; Friedrichs et al., 2003; Jencks & Mayer, 1990; Leventhal & Brooks-Gunn, 2000; Murie & Musterd, 2004; Sampson et al., 2002; Wilson, 1987). In most European countries, the issue of poverty and social segregation is inextricably linked to the issue of migration and ethnicity. Among the outcomes most often studied are educational and labour market success, health behaviour and crime. Yet, few European studies have given empirical support to the notion of neighbourhood contextual effects because results are often inconclusive. One direction of research, often following an ethnographic approach, typically focuses on just one or few disadvantaged neighbourhoods. Studies by French sociologists on adolescents' experiences of daily life in the *banlieues* are a prominent example (Body-Gendrot, 2005; Dubet & Lapeyronnie, 1992; Wacquant, 1996). While they have produced important and in-depth knowledge, a methodological problem of these case studies is that the basic assumption about exacerbating effects of spatially concentrated poverty on social problems is taken for granted, and not put to an empirical test because data from poverty areas cannot be compared to data from non-poverty areas. Yet, it is by no means self-evident that the social opportunities, behaviour or psychological well-being of residents in poverty areas are different from other people, once individual characteristics are taken into account. A contextual effect means, for example, that a child whose parents are unemployed but lives in an affluent neighbourhood has better prospects than a similar child whose parents are unemployed *and* lives in a deprived neighbourhood (Duncan & Raudenbush, 2001).

Another, quantitative direction of research following this idea samples all or at least a large variation of different neighbourhoods from a city or a larger geographical area, sometimes using existing national-representative samples, and tries to disentangle the effects of individual factors from the effects of concentrated poverty at the neighbourhood level often using multi-level analysis, also called hierarchical linear modelling (Hox, 2002; Raudenbush & Bryk, 2002; Snijders & Bosker, 1999). Looking at the length of welfare dependency, a recent German study (Farwick, 2004) supports the 'poverty trap' hypothesis whereas a similar Dutch study (Musterd et al., 2003) does not. Likewise, two Swedish studies on the labour market success of young adults come to contradictory conclusions (Brännström, 2004, 2005; Hedström et al., 2003). Self-report surveys on adolescent crime conducted in Rotterdam in the Netherlands (Rovers, 1997), Peterborough in England (Wikström & Butterworth, 2006) and Antwerp in Belgium (Pauwels, 2007) found no evidence of neighbourhood effects, whereas the present study in two German cities (Oberwittler, 2004a, 2004b) found strong evidence for such effects, but only for certain subgroups of adolescents. Finally, a Dutch national-representative study reports a considerably increased risk of children's psychosocial problems in the most disadvantaged neighbourhoods (Reijneveld et al., 2005).

Although this is not a complete review of current research, it seems fair to conclude that European studies on neighbourhood effects are much sparser, and find less support for the 'concentration hypothesis' than studies conducted in the US. For example, a few recent US studies found evidence for higher crime involvement of adolescents living in high poverty areas net of individual risk factors (Bellair et al., 2003; Bingenheimer et al., 2005; Sampson et al., 2005).

While it seems plausible to link these differences to the much higher scale of social exclusion and spatial segregation in the US (especially as most European studies are from countries with better welfare provisions), it is much too early to draw conclusions. For many relevant social, psychological or health outcomes and in many parts of Europe as Germany and the Romanic-speaking countries, research on neighbourhood effects has just begun or is still completely lacking. Furthermore, existing research, in Europe as well in the US, has hardly addressed the questions of social mechanisms which translate structural disadvantage into individual behaviour, nor has it sufficiently looked to the interactions between contextual and individual characteristics and the factors influencing resilience or susceptibility to adverse ecological conditions (Elliott et al., 2006; Furstenberg et al., 1999; Luthar, 2003; Massey, 2001). The intention of this paper is to add to this research by looking to the differential impact of neighbourhood disadvantage on boys and girls, as well as for native adolescents and those with immigrant backgrounds. By looking to the spatial relationship between residential neighbourhood and school, and by exploring the role of peer contacts in moderating the impact of neighbourhood conditions, the present study adds to the knowledge on social mechanisms of ecological context effects on adolescents.

Theoretical and Methodological Considerations

The basic assumption of research on neighbourhood poverty is that the spatial concentration of social disadvantage aggravates social ills, such as unemployment, psychosocial and health problems or crime. There are two main branches of hypotheses about the social mechanisms of this macro-level effect on individual behaviour. One branch concentrates on social interactions between people and the reciprocal influence these interactions bear on them. Jonathan Crane's (1991) study on adolescent problem behaviour in US ghettos is a prime example of this approach. He assumes that "social problems are contagious and are spread through peer influences" (Crane, 1991, p. 1227). This approach can be seen as an application of social learning theories and is supported by other research on peer influences for example on delinquency (Haynie, 2002; Haynie & Osgood, 2005; Warr, 2002). In addition to peer influences, William J. Wilson (1987) pointed to the lack of positive role models for adolescents in neighbourhoods where most adults are unemployed. A second branch rather focuses on the role of neighbourhood social capital for preventing or intervening into problem behaviour, especially crime. This approach evolved from the classic theory of social disorganization (Shaw & McKay, 1969) and centres around the concept of 'collective efficacy' (Sampson et al., 1997, 1999). In addition, it is argued that social opportunities of residents of disadvantaged neighbourhoods are impaired by stigmatization processes (Wacquant, 1996), and that disadvantaged neighbourhoods experience a spiral of 'disorder and decline' fuelled by visible signs of disorder and low-level incivilities (Kelling & Coles, 1996; Skogan, 1990). Conclusive empirical evidence for a specific social mechanism translating concentrated poverty into problem behaviour has been very rare to date which is mainly due to the complexity of data and statistical methods necessary to test macro-micro-links on human behaviour, and partly to the lack of alternative hypothesis testing. For example, empirical studies following the 'collective efficacy' approach often do not look to possible peer influences (cf. Oberwittler, 2004a).

One of the major theoretical and methodological challenges to research into neighbourhood effects is the problem of self-selection or 'endogenous membership'. If certain properties of individuals have been causative both for their residing in poverty areas and at the same time for the outcome, and are not accounted for in the multivariate model, then the neighbourhood effect is likely to be overestimated. Duncan & Raudenbush (2001, p. 13) give the example of parents who are less caring about their children and therefore do not consider leaving or avoiding to move to a 'bad' neighbourhood. If parenting style is omitted from the explanatory model, the neighbourhood effect on adolescent problem behaviour would be overestimated. This is even truer for the selection of adolescents into schools; previous problem behaviour or poor academic achievement may be causative for an adolescent to be admitted to a 'bad' school; it would be a mistake to attribute the adolescent's subsequent behaviour to school influences alone. Obviously, cross-sectional studies are particularly ill-equipped to avoid this danger. Longitudinal studies are much better suited to analyze the development of attitudes or behaviour controlling for a baseline level at the beginning of observations, and therefore to make inferences about causation. It is important to stress that the results of the present cross-sectional study, too, cannot be interpreted as evidence for causation, but more modestly as evidence for potential neighbourhood effects.

A second challenge for research on neighbourhood effects is the fact that residents of disadvantaged areas are not isolated from the outside world, but may have varying degrees of social contacts with people and institutions outside their neighbourhood. Although it is often assumed that the daily routines and social interactions of children and adolescents are closely focused on their immediate environment, it will be shown in the empirical part of this paper that this is hardly the case. Peer groups and routine activities may or may not spread across neighbourhood boundaries, and the spatial orientation of adolescents is again a matter of self-selection (Kiesner *et al.*, 2003). In particular, the school constitutes an overlapping but independent ecological context for the younger age groups. Unfortunately, different strands of research have kept neighbourhood and school research mostly separate, focusing solely on the one and ignoring the respective other context. The question of how both contexts compete or interact with each other has been largely ignored in recent research. The advance of more sophisticated statistical techniques as cross-classified multi-level analysis will hopefully render integrative approaches to ecological context effects easier to pursue (Browne *et al.*, 2001). Some preliminary results of cross-classified models integrating neighbourhood and school contexts will be reported at the end of the paper.

Finally, research on neighbourhood effects in its early phase has neglected the fact that individuals react differently to external influences, and instead has looked to the behaviour of residents in an aggregate and 'collectivistic' fashion. The main research question initially was whether there is an *overall* increase of crime, teenage pregnancies, school dropouts etc. in disadvantaged neighbourhoods (e.g. Crane, 1991), not whether and why some residents are more vulnerable than others to the threats of the neighbourhood context. The latter perspective calls for an interactional approach which takes individual differences in reacting to neighbourhood conditions seriously (Conger & Donnellan, 2007; Massey, 2001; Wikström, 2006). In consequence, if contextual conditions do not affect all residents equally, estimating an 'average' effect would actually *under*estimate the true strength of the contextual effect for vulnerable subgroups of the population. Therefore, it is an important task for neighbourhood research to identify individual factors which amplify or attenuate the risks of concentrated disadvantage, and to look for subgroups which tend to be vulnerable or resilient to these risks. This paper will focus on gender and ethnicity as two fundamental dimensions in research on adolescent problem behaviour. Ethnicity is of particular relevance here because social and ethnic segregation are closely linked phenomena.

Data and Measures

For the present study, two West German cities, Cologne and Freiburg, and some rural communities adjacent to Freiburg have been selected (Oberwittler, 2003b for details).

Cologne is Germany's fourth largest city with a population of 1 million. With a 20 per cent proportion of non-German citizens, Cologne ranks among the ethnically most diverse cities in Germany. The largest ethnic minority is Turkish, numbering approximately 80 000. Cologne's economic and social structure is very diverse including traditional and declining manufacturing industries but also many electronic media and the country's second largest university. Both unemployment and welfare rates are above the national average. The extent of poverty—within the context of the well-developed German welfare system—and the degree of social and ethnic diversity make Cologne a well-suited example for studies on segregation and neighbourhood effects.

On the other hand, Freiburg is a rather small city (200 000 inhabitants) with little industry and is dominated by administration and the university. Both unemployment and welfare rates are lower than in Cologne. The purpose of comparing these two cities is to see whether empirical findings can be reproduced in different urban settings. The purpose of including a rural area is to enhance the variety of ecological settings beyond the urban-rural divide.

For reasons of feasibility, in Cologne a sample of about one-third of all small administrative units had to be drawn. For simplicity, these small units will be called 'census tracts' which is not a technical expression in Germany. The distribution of structural conditions of the sampled tracts almost completely matches the distribution of all Cologne tracts (Oberwittler, 2003b, p. 16). For the purpose of multi-level analysis, adjacent census tracts have been merged to a total of 61 generic 'neighbourhoods' with an average population of 11 200 based on socio-demographic similarity in order to have enough respondents in each aggregate unit and to reduce the unequal sizes of tracts. As this merger of small units was driven by data needs, the question arises whether these generic neighbourhoods represent meaningful residential units. This question is difficult to answer. In many cases census tracts are small subdivisions of historically meaningful parts of the city, and when respondents were asked to name their neighbourhood, they often referred to these larger units rather than to smaller census tracts. In addition, a comparison of Gini coefficients for measures of spatial inequality on both levels of aggregation reveals that the generic neighbourhoods retain most of the cities' social heterogeneity (Oberwittler, 2003b, p. 14).

Socio-demographic information on neighbourhoods has been provided by the statistical offices of both cities and rural districts. Most of the official data refer to the years 1999 or 2000. The rate of welfare recipients under 18 years ('child welfare rate') will be used as the key indicator of poverty.

Data on perceptions, attitudes and self-reported delinquency of adolescents come from a self-administered classroom survey of about 6400 8th to 10th grade students (age range ca. 13 to 16 years) conducted in 1999 and 2000 (Oberwittler & Blank, 2003). At the end of the interviews, the student's addresses were geocoded by the interviewers to ensure they had exact information on their places of residence. Approximately 5300 of the respondents live within the defined survey neighbourhoods, whereas the rest are scattered widely across other areas and have to be omitted from neighbourhood-focused (but not necessarily from school-focused) analyses. Of the 5300 respondents, ca. 4850 reside in the 61 generic neighbourhoods used in multi-level models. The correlation of a combined factor score measuring the socio-economic status (SES) of respondents and a factor score based on official data on children and adolescents is $r = 0.96$ in Cologne and $r = 0.90$ in Freiburg.[1]

Whereas the official definition of ethnicity and migration status is citizenship, and most migrants in Germany in fact do not hold German citizenship (with the important exception of ethnic Germans from Eastern Europe and the former Soviet Union), the survey asked for the parents' countries of origin. If both parents have been born abroad, the adolescent is defined as having an 'immigrant background'; if one or both parents have been born in Germany, he or she is categorized as 'native'. The parents' socio-economic status (SES) consists of both the educational status (university degree yes/no) and the occupational status which is based on ISCO'68 codes transformed to values on Wegener's (1988) 'Magnitude Prestige Skala'.[2]

The key concepts for the analyses presented in this paper are measured by a number of survey questions. 'Relative deprivation' is a scale consisting of four items as "Often I have to do without something because my parents cannot afford it" (Cronbach's alpha 0.72). 'External locus of control' is a 4-item scale (Cronbach's alpha 0.54) reflecting a fatalistic view of the respondent's future ("It's not worth striving for a goal because I will probably not achieve it anyway"). 'Alienation by the police' is a single item answering the question "Do you feel you are treated fairly, not better or worse than any other youth, by the police?" 'Violence tolerance' is a 3-item scale (Cronbach's alpha 0.72) measuring attitudes on the use of violence in interpersonal conflicts (e.g. "It is quite normal to hit somebody if provoked").

The delinquency scale consists of 14 items describing punishable offences and truancy (Oberwittler *et al.*, 2002). These items cover common types of juvenile offending from shop-lifting, graffiti spraying, drug consumption to the theft of motor bikes, wounding and burglary. For each offence, the respondents were asked whether and how often they committed it during the last 12 months. The open frequencies of self-reported offences were recoded to five ordinal categories from 0 (no offence) to 4 (10 or more offences), and total and offence-specific subscales for violence, serious property offences etc. were constructed by computing unweighted means of the recoded items. The resulting indices reflect both the frequency and versatility of offending which are known to be highly intercorrelated (Klein, 1984). Whereas 55 per cent of respondents have reported at least one offence of the total delinquency scale during the previous year, 28 per cent have reported a violent or serious property offence.

In addition, there are questions on the delinquency of friends and whether respondents belong to a stable group of friends who often get into fights and behave aggressively ('delinquent youth gang'). The assessment of the peer group's delinquent tendency is based on a 4-item scale (Cronbach's alpha 0.82) tapping the extent of arguments and fighting with rival youth groups (e.g. "Sometimes we have fights with other adolescents not belonging to our neighbourhood"). Respondents with scores higher than median are defined as members of a delinquent youth gang. The term 'gang' is used cautiously because these groups should not be likened with US-style criminal gangs (Esbensen & Weerman, 2005; Klein *et al.*, 2006).

Results

The Extent of Urban Poverty and Segregation

There is a lack of reliable data on poverty in Germany, especially for small area analyses. At the time of this study, 14 per cent of children and adolescents in Cologne were welfare recipients. In addition, many families received some form of unemployment benefit. 9.5 per cent of the total population in Cologne and nearly 14 per cent of children under

14 lived in census tracts with a high concentration of poverty, defined by a child welfare rate of 25 per cent or more. In Freiburg, only one of 40 neighbourhoods met this definition, yet it was home to 7 per cent of the child population; the city-wide child welfare rate was 10.5 per cent in 1999. Figure 1 illustrates the close link between social and ethnic segregation in Cologne; results for Freiburg are not presented here due to space limitations. Whereas the native German child population is relatively evenly distributed across more affluent and poorer neighbourhoods, and roughly one-third of them live in the poorest third of neighbourhoods, almost 60 per cent of children with an immigrant background are concentrated in the poorest areas of Cologne, and only 5 per cent of them live in the most affluent one-third of neighbourhoods. As a result of this, the proportion of immigrant children rises from less than 10 per cent to 45 per cent from the richest to the poorest decile of neighbourhoods. If the recently immigrated ethnic German families from the Soviet Union were added to this figure, the percentage of children with an immigrant background would surpass 50 per cent.

Recent research has highlighted the role of street violence as one dimension of neighbourhood disadvantage that endangers positive child and adolescent development (Bingenheimer et al., 2005). Based on police data on the spatial distribution of violence, Figure 2 shows that a much higher proportion of immigrant than native children live in the more violent neighbourhoods of Cologne, and are potentially much more exposed to violence (and will also contribute to this violence themselves when they grow older).

Little Evidence for Increased Psychological Strain in Disadvantaged Neighbourhoods: Some Exploratory Results

One of the key tasks for quantitative research on urban poverty is to disentangle the effects of neighbourhood poverty from the effects of individual poverty. Before turning to more complex multi-level models in the second step, the paper first presents a number of line

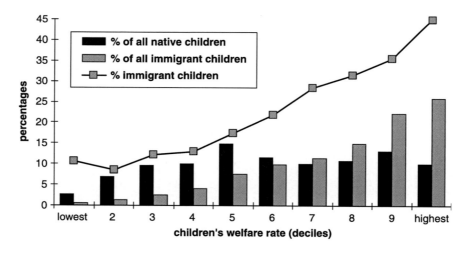

Figure 1. Distribution of native and immigrant children (0–14 years) in neighbourhoods by neighbourhood child welfare rates (Cologne, 2000, official data). *Note:* native: German nationality; immigrant: other nationalities. *Source:* Statistical Office, City of Cologne

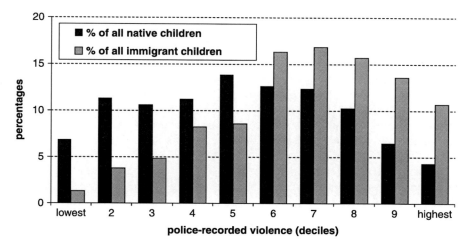

Figure 2. Distribution of native and immigrant children (0–14 years) in neighbourhoods by police-recorded violence rates (Cologne, 2000, official data). *Note:* native: German nationality; immigrant: other nationalities. *Source:* Statistical Office, City of Cologne; Cologne Police Headquarters

plots which are intended to explore some of the possible neighbourhood effects on attitudes and perceptions of adolescents often linked to concentrated poverty. Theory and common sense suggests that adolescents living in concentrated poverty will experience more strain, feel more deprived, less optimistic and more alienated than other adolescents. In the following figures, the survey respondents are divided into five groups of ca. 1300 each according to the neighbourhood child welfare rate (Table 1). However, the lowest and the highest of these quintiles are smaller (ca. 650 respondents) representing the very extreme ends of the neighbourhood distribution with welfare rates of less than 3 per cent and more than 24.5 per cent respectively in order to boost possible non-linear effects. The line plots compare respondents whose families are or are not individually affected by unemployment or welfare dependency for a period of at least 6 months,[3] and in addition, the sample is split into native and immigrant respondents. Because few adolescents of immigrant background live in affluent neighbourhoods, the sample size is very small for this particular subgroup rendering statistical significance difficult to achieve. For example, some effects seem to be stronger for welfare recipients than for other respondents, but due to the small sample size fail to achieve statistical significance. However, native and

Table 1. Survey sample by quintiles of neighbourhood welfare rates (MPI Youth Survey 1999/2000, Cologne and Freiburg)

		Welfare rate (under 18 years), quintiles with extreme groups					
		lowest (< 3%)	2	3	4	highest (> 24.5%)	Total
Background	Immigrant	50	115	341	527	320	1353
	Native	593	1233	1016	797	325	3964
Total		643	1348	1357	1324	645	5317

160 *Quantifying Neighbourhood Effects*

immigrant respondents are equally represented in the highest quintile of neighbourhoods (ca. 320 each), as official demographics would predict.

Figures 3a and 3b report the levels of relative deprivation. As expected, adolescents individually affected by poverty score higher on this scale than others, yet the differences are not pronounced. Immigrant respondents do not report higher relative deprivation than native respondents, nor do any of the groups living in high poverty areas. In fact, the only marked and significant neighbourhood effect is for native welfare recipients living in 'affluent' neighbourhoods. This result makes sense, as the concept of 'relative' deprivation implies that the psychological strain of being poor is more intense in an environment where most others are affluent.

Another adverse effect ascribed to concentrated poverty is a fatalistic or bleak view of the future, measured by the scale 'external locus of control'. The results reported in Figures 3c and 3d are even less pronounced than the previous ones. For native adolescents, there is a very slight increase, with neighbourhood poverty for those individually affected by poverty but not for the others. For immigrant adolescents, the effect is reversed: respondents not affected by poverty score slightly higher in concentrated poverty, and those affected by individual poverty show rather the reverse trend. However, the latter effect is non-significant and should be treated even more cautiously than the others.

Results are more clear-cut for the question of whether adolescents feel alienated by the police. Tensions between immigrant adolescents and the police, and violent anti-police riots are a recurrent problem in many European countries, especially in France, and have wide and serious repercussions for integration policies. The main and surprising message of Figures 3e and 3f is that there is absolutely no difference in alienation between native and immigrant adolescents. This important result is supported by the absence of riots by immigrant youths in Germany. For both native and immigrant respondents, there is a combined effect of individual-level and neighbourhood-level poverty to increase feelings of alienation.

Noticeable Neighbourhood Effects on Delinquency Restricted to Native Adolescents

As a crucial dimension of adolescent adjustment to social disadvantage, delinquency and crime is a frequently analyzed topic, and is also the main concern of the present study. Does the concentration of poverty cause adolescents to become more delinquent? Figures 4a to 4d allow a first, exploratory look to the data. These graphs are similarly organized as the previous ones, but this time the sample is split up by gender, and the lines now represent immigration status. The frequency of overall offending by boys increases slightly (but not significantly) with neighbourhood disadvantage for both native and immigrant respondents (Figures 4a and 4b). While girls with an immigrant background show a slight *decrease* of delinquency with neighbourhood poverty, native girls who live in the poorest neighbourhoods report much more delinquency than the others. The latter effect is highly significant and non-linear. There will be a return to these gender differences later.

Similar, but more pronounced results can be seen in Figures 4c and 4d for the percentage of respondents who are members of a delinquent 'youth gang' (overall prevalence is 10 per cent). The share of 'gang members' increases with neighbourhood poverty for native as well as for immigrant adolescents, although steady and more pronounced for the former subgroup; for native girls, the proportion increases dramatically in the most deprived neighbourhoods, while immigrant girls show a reverse tendency, *declining* with

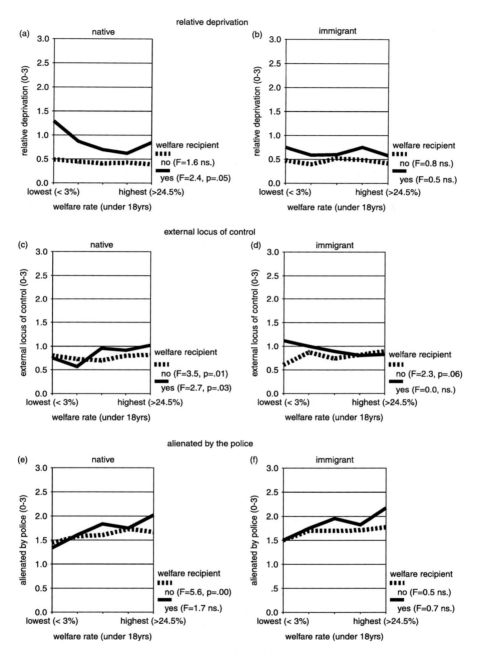

Figure 3a–3f. Psychological strain of adolescents affected by individual and neighbourhood poverty by immigrant background (MPI Youth Survey 1999/2000, Cologne and Freiburg, $n = 5317$)

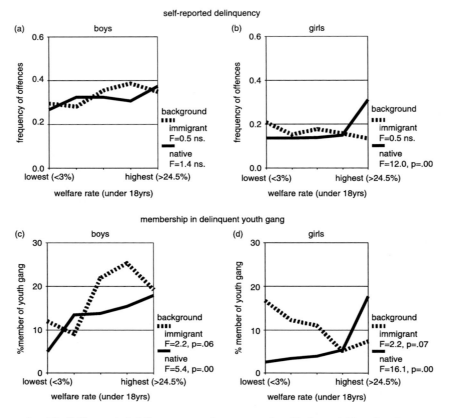

Figure 4a–4d. Self-reported delinquency and gang membership by neighbourhood poverty, sex and immigration status (MPI Youth Survey 1999/2000, Cologne and Freiburg, $n = 5317$)

neighbourhood poverty. In general, delinquency of adolescents with immigrant backgrounds seems to be less strongly associated with neighbourhood poverty levels than delinquency of native adolescents. For immigrant girls, the effects are contrary to expectation—their delinquency tends to be lower in the more disadvantaged neighbourhoods. Clearly, these preliminary findings need further and more elaborated analyses.

As a fairly recent statistical innovation, multi-level analysis, or hierarchical linear modelling, allows for the integration of individual- and context-level perspectives on social phenomena by simultaneously estimating multiple regression equations on both levels without violating important assumptions of conventional regression analysis (DiPrete & Forristal, 1994). Thus it becomes possible, in principle, to estimate the contextual effects of neighbourhoods (or other contexts) on adolescents' behaviour net of individual influences, which may also vary between contexts. In multi-level modelling, usually the first step of analysis is to compute the so-called 'empty model' with no explanatory variables in order to examine whether a significant proportion of variance is attributable to the context level, comparable to a conventional ANOVA. The intraclass correlation coefficient (ICC) computed from the variance components shows how large (as a percentage of total variance) a possible contextual effect is. If an ICC is non-significant, contextual effects are unlikely to exist.

Applying this technique to the delinquency scales in the present survey sample, some of the previous findings are confirmed (Table 2). Native adolescents generally have much higher ICCs than immigrant adolescents, indicating a higher potential for neighbourhood effects compared to adolescents with migration backgrounds. For example, the ICC for serious property offences of native boys is 5.0 per cent, and only 0.6 per cent for immigrant boys. The only significant, but very modest, ICC of immigrant adolescents is for serious property offences by girls (1.5 per cent). Consequently, it does not make sense to build more complex multi-level models for the group of immigrant respondents as the results do not suggest significant neighbourhood effects on delinquency.

How can these unexpected results be explained? Scholarly opinion has, from the early days of the Chicago School, assumed that higher crime involvement of adolescents from ethnic minority or immigrant groups can partly be explained by the additional disadvantage of living in the most disadvantaged neighbourhoods (Krivo & Peterson, 2000; Sampson & Wilson, 1995; Shaw & McKay, 1969). Most recently, the longitudinal Project on Human Development in Chicago Neighbourhoods (PHDCN) has empirically confirmed this hypothesis by estimating that difference between the higher level of violence among black compared to white adolescents is reduced by 38 per cent when neighbourhood contexts are taken into account (Sampson et al., 2005). However, the present case study implies that immigrant adolescents outside poverty areas are nearly as delinquent as or (in the case of girls) even more delinquent than their peers inside poverty areas. The current study can only offer some tentative and exploratory observations from the survey data that may help to explain this finding.

Even if they live in more affluent neighbourhoods, immigrant adolescents do not seem to 'profit' to the same extent from the advantage connected with their place of residence. Their families' individual socio-economic situation remains vulnerable even if

Table 2. Share of neighbourhood-level variance (intraclass correlation coefficients) of serious delinquency by immigration status, sex and location of friends (MPI Youth Survey 1999/2000, Cologne and Freiburg, $n = 5317$ in $n = 61$ neighbourhoods)

	Offence type	
Intraclass correlation coefficient (ICC)	Violent[c]	Serious property[d]
Native adolescents		
Boys	1.2	5.0
Girls	6.2	4.6
Friends from own neighbh.[a]	8.1	7.9
Friends from different neighbh.[b]	*0.0*	1.1
Immigrant adolescents		
Boys	0.8	*0.6*
Girls	*0.3*	1.5
Friends from own neighbh.[a]	*0.9*	*1.8*
Friends from different neighbh.[b]	*2.3*	*2.6*

Notes: 'empty models' computed in HLM 6. Italics: non-significant ($p > 0.05$); all others: $p < 0.05$.
  [a] 'all' or 'many' of friends live in respondent's neighbourhood (54.0% of sample).
  [b] 'few' or 'none' of friends live in respondent's neighbourhood (46.0% of sample).
  [c] assault, robbery, threatening/extortion.
  [d] theft of motor vehicles, car breaking in, burglary.

they live in a more affluent neighbourhood, as can be seen from the relatively high proportion (13 per cent) of immigrant respondents living in welfare-dependent households (including unemployment benefit) (Figure 6a), whereas this rate is down to 3 per cent for native respondents in the most affluent neighbourhoods. As can be seen in Figure 6b, immigrant youths generally live in multiple apartment buildings more often than native youths, rendering the difference between neighbourhoods less pronounced than for the native adolescents. As a result of this, differences in social status and living conditions between native and immigrant adolescents are actually much more pronounced outside poverty areas, possibly rendering integration opportunities in these areas even more difficult. When asked about their perceptions of social problems in their neighbourhood, reports of immigrant adolescents did not vary across levels of neighbourhood poverty contrary to expectation, whereas native adolescents report significantly less violence and signs of economic subculture in affluent neighbourhoods (Figures 7a and 7b). This implies that although natives and immigrants live in the same neighbourhoods, their social experiences and 'life worlds' remain partly separated. However, the present data allow for raising these important questions rather than answering them. Clearly, more research is needed on social living conditions and behaviour of immigrant youths particularly *outside* poverty areas.

Strong Neighbourhood Effect on Violence for Native Girls

Returning to results reported in Table 2, native girls display a much larger ICC than native boys for violent offences (6.2 per cent vs. 1.2 per cent), reflecting the results in Figures 4c and 4d, whereas the ICC of serious property offences is slightly higher for boys than for girls. The range of ICCs between 5 per cent and 6 per cent indicates quite substantial room

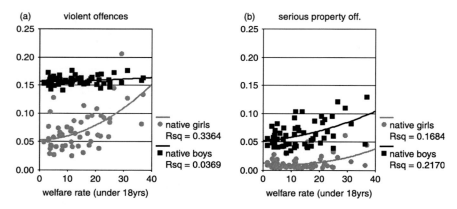

Figure 5a–5b. Self-reported offending by neighbourhood poverty adjusted for individual socio-demographic composition (Youth Survey 1999/2000, Cologne and Freiburg, $n = 3580$ native respondents in $n = 57$ neighbourhoods).[a] *Notes:* [a]predicted neighbourhood-level values from linear multi-level models adjusted for parental SES, family structure, unemployment/welfare dependence (empirical Bayes estimates, dependent variable log-transformed). 3 neighbourhoods in rural communities near Freiburg excluded because most respondents commute to Freiburg, 1 neighbourhood excluded as outlier

for neighbourhood effects. In a second step of multi-level analysis, relevant socio-demographic characteristics of respondents are introduced at the individual level to control for compositional effects. The results of these models are graphically displayed in Figures 5a and 5b which represent the estimated neighbourhood-level delinquency rates adjusted for socio-demographic composition as predicted from multi-level regression models (models not reported). Figure 5a shows that once individual socio-demographic composition is accounted for, native boys in the poorest neighbourhoods are hardly more violent than native boys in other neighbourhoods. For native girls, in contrast, the non-linear increase of violence with neighbourhood poverty remains considerable even after controlling for social composition, becoming very strong at the high end of neighbourhood disadvantage (cf. Oberwittler, 2003). In the most disadvantaged neighbourhoods, native girls almost completely catch up with native boys in terms of self-reported violence. Whereas violence is probably no accepted form of behaviour for native girls in general, a local subculture in the most disadvantaged neighbourhoods seems to promote female violence. Violence by boys, in contrast, is not restricted to the disadvantaged neighbourhoods but much more universal, reflecting traditional differences in gender roles. On the other hand, serious property offences such as burglaries and car break-ins are much more frequent among boys than among girls in all types of neighbourhoods, and are considerably associated with neighbourhood poverty. It seems plausible to assume that boys need a subcultural environment and opportunity structure in order to commit these more sophisticated property crimes, and that this environment is more readily available in the most disadvantaged neighbourhoods.

Neighbourhood Effects Depend on Local Friendship Circles

One of the most remarkable results of the present study is that the spatial orientation of peer contacts determines the existence of potential neighbourhood effects on delinquency (see Oberwittler, 2004b for a more extensive analysis). In Table 2, the sample is split by the locality of friendship circles which turns out to have a dramatic effect on ICCs. For

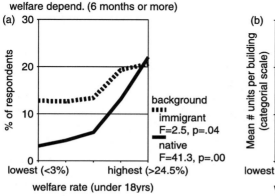
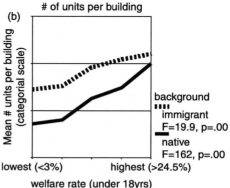

Figure 6a–6b. Individual social conditions by neighbourhood poverty and migration status (MPI Youth Survey 1999/2000, Cologne and Freiburg, $n = 5317$)

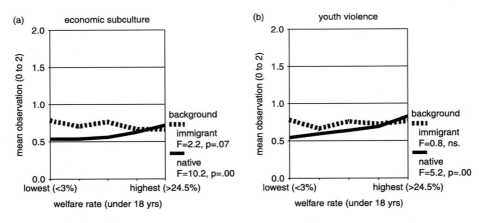

Figure 7a–7b. Observations of neighbourhood social problems by neighbourhood poverty and migration status (MPI Youth Survey 1999/2000, Cologne and Freiburg, $n = 5317$)

those of the native respondents who say that none or few of their friends live in their own neighbourhood, the share of neighbourhood-level variance is negligible, whereas for those who say that many or all friends live in their own neighbourhood, the ICC is around 8 per cent for both violent and serious property offences. This hints at the conclusion that if friends come from the same neighbourhood, the neighbourhood context is important for native adolescents; if not, the neighbourhood context is not important—at least the residential neighbourhood that is mostly assumed in multi-level analysis. This dramatic difference in ICCs seems to lend strong support to differential association and learning theories that stress the role of delinquent peers for the transmission of delinquent behaviour (Akers & Jensen, 2003).

The crucial importance of the location of friends for the existence of potential neighbourhood effects merits some further analyses. At all levels of neighbourhood poverty, between 40 per cent and 50 per cent of respondents say that their best friends predominantly are not from their own neighbourhood. This figure contradicts assumptions about a Ghetto-like situation of inescapable spatial exclusion. It is fair to assume that the spatial choice of friends is influenced by many factors, among them the location of schools. There is a clear negative correlation between the distance to school and the proportion of friends who reside in the respondent's neighbourhood. There will be a return to the role of schools in the final part of this paper.

Of course, there are more factors influencing the spatial orientation of friendship networks (see Oberwittler, 2004b, 2004c for a more extensive discussion). Further analyses of the survey data showed that apart from factors over which adolescents have no control (e.g. parental status, moving home in recent years), there is clearly an element of choice and self-selection of adolescents into neighbourhood contexts. Particularly in the most disadvantaged neighbourhoods, adolescents seem to be divided into two groups. Some youths who tend to have higher educational aspirations are dissatisfied with and feel uncomfortable in their neighbourhood and prefer to choose their friends from and spend their free time in other neighbourhoods. Other youths who tend to have low educational aspirations and often show a taste for unsupervised street life seem quite content with their social environment and spend most time in their neighbourhood together with their local friends.

In sum, there are some indications that adolescents make choices about the location of their friendship networks and their routine activities. By doing so, they actively decide upon the relevance of their own neighbourhood context for their behaviour. Consequently, the residential social segregation is supplemented and even reinforced by a self-directed segregation of adolescents' social networks and routine activities. In this perspective, Arum (2000) claims "that an individual's community is actually both created and defined by an individual's specific social relationships" (p. 402). On the methodological side, the impact of ecological contexts is therefore a rather inextricable mixture of self-selection and reinforcement which also makes it even more risky to interpret contextual effect as causal effects.

Neighbourhoods and Schools as Overlapping but Independent Contexts

As already mentioned, the spatial location of schools has a strong impact on the spatial distribution of friendship circles. An adolescent who attends a school far away from home inevitably meets and befriends more peers from other neighbourhoods than an adolescent who attends a local school. As an ecological context in its own right, the school, its teachers and its social 'climate' may influence the attitudes and behaviour of children and adolescents quite independently from the residential neighbourhood context. In the Cologne sample, only one-fifth of respondents attend a school in their own neighbourhood, and for around half of the respondents, the distance between home and school is more than 2 km.

The choice of schools and resulting spatial relations between home and school are, of course, very much dependent on educational policies and the legal framework set at the national level. In the German case, the secondary school system is highly selective based on academic achievement at the end of primary school age, and because academic achievement has been shown to be closely associated with social class in Germany (Baumert *et al.*, 2001), the traditional three-tier system of lower, intermediate and higher-level schools very much reflects the stratification of German society. However, within this selective three-tier system, parents in big cities at least have a choice between schools and are not strictly bound to catchment areas as, for example, in the UK where secondary schools are officially non-selective but where parents struggle to move into the catchment areas of 'good' schools, thereby probably fuelling residential segregation (Croft, 2004). As a result of this framework, there is a considerable variation between neighbourhood-level and school-level social composition to which adolescents are exposed, as can be seen from Figure 8. This Figure illustrates how respondents from different levels of neighbourhood poverty are allocated to schools of different levels of 'school poverty', both measured identically by the respondents' average parental SES. Half of respondents living in a very low SES neighbourhood (first quartile) also attend a school with a very low mean parental SES, but about a quarter of them attend schools with an above average mean SES. Especially those students from the middle quartiles of neighbourhood poverty are almost equally distributed across various degrees of social disadvantage on the school level. Due to the high social selectivity of the German school system, the social segregation of adolescents is more extreme on the school level than on the neighbourhood level, as Figure 9 reveals. Fewer adolescents from a low parental SES background manage to get into schools with a higher mean parental SES than reside in neighbourhoods with higher mean parental SES.

The important research question is whether this higher segregation between affluence and poverty, between low and high social status in schools translates into different ecological contexts shaping the behaviour and psychosocial development of adolescents. Figure 10 is a first descriptive answer to this question. Using the same definitions as in the previous graphs, the association between social context and serious adolescent delinquency is much stronger on the school level (eta-square 0.34) than on the neighbourhood level (eta-square 0.16). On the school level, the group of respondents in the lowest quintile of mean parental SES report more crime, and those in the highest quintile of mean parental SES report less crime, than the respective neighbourhood-level groups. Of course, this could just be a compositional effect, reflecting the higher levels of segregation.

In order to shed more light on this question and to answer the question of relative importance of neighbourhood and school context, tentative results are presented of a so-called cross-classified multi-level model in which individuals are nested into two contexts simultaneously, and the influence of each context is estimated while controlling for the respective other context (Table 3). This recent statistical innovation is well suited to deal with social conditions in which individuals are placed in and potentially influenced by two contexts at the same time. Because the single-context multi-level models reported above did not produce evidence of potential neighbourhood effects on immigrant adolescents, it does not make sense to run cross-classified models for this subgroup, and hence the following models are restricted to native respondents.[4] The first of the models controls for socio-demographic composition and 'violence tolerance', an attitude scale known to be closely related to self-reported offending. The bottom part of Table 3 reports how much the ICCs for neighbourhood and school contexts are reduced by controlling for these individual variables, compared to the empty model. Only a small proportion of the neighbourhood-level variance (3 per cent) but a huge part of the school-level variance

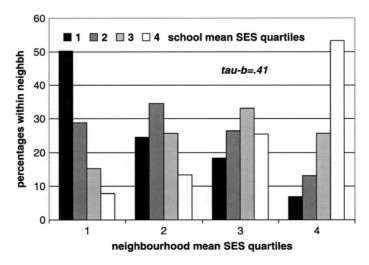

Figure 8. Allocation of adolescents to schools by school and neighbourhood average parental SES (MPI Youth Survey 1999/2000, Cologne, $n = 2862$)

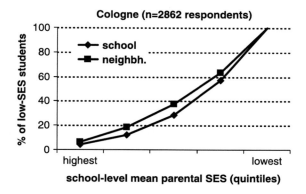

Figure 9. Concentration of adolescents of low parental SES on quintiles of schools/neighbourhoods ordered by parental SES (MPI Youth Survey 1999/2000)

(72 per cent) is accounted for by the socio-demographic composition and the attitude to violence of respondents. In effect, this means that the larger part of school differences in delinquency reported above is due to a compositional, not to a 'true' contextual effect. However, the potential school effect on delinquency is double the size of the potential neighbourhood effect (0.0131 vs. 0.0061).

In the second model, poverty indicators are introduced for both contexts in order to try to explain neighbourhood and school differences in delinquency by the concentration of poverty. Both predictors are significant and explain half of the remaining neighbourhood-level and almost all of the remaining school-level variance, suggesting the existence of both neighbourhood and school contextual effects on adolescent delinquency. Again, the school poverty predictor indicates a stronger school effect compared to the neighbourhood effect, but considering the limitations of this cross-sectional study and especially the issue of selection bias, these results should be treated with caution. It is also noteworthy that poverty is rendered insignificant on the individual level after context-level poverty is introduced to the model. This lends support to the hypothesis that poverty does not affect

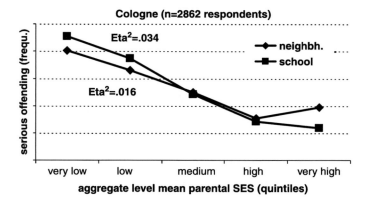

Figure 10. Neighbourhood vs. school-level association between mean parental SES and serious offending (MPI Youth Survey 1999/2000)

Table 3. Multi-level cross-classified linear model of serious offending in neighbourhood and school contexts (MPI Youth Survey 1999/2000, Cologne and Freiburg, $n = 3212$ native respondents in $n = 61$ neighbourhoods)

	Model 1			Model 2		
	Unstand. B-coeff.	t-value	Sign.	Unstand B-coeff.	t-value	Sign.
Fixed effects: L1 (n = 3212 native respondents)						
Incomplete family	0.032	4.9	***	0.031	4.7	***
Parental SES	−0.002	−0.5	n.s.	0.006	1.6	n.s.
Unemployed/welfare recip. > 6 months	0.023	2.0	*	0.016	1.4	n.s.
Violence tolerance (scale 0–3)	0.109	28.5	***	0.107	28.1	***
Constant	0.044	4.0	***	0.053	5.5	***
Fixed effects: neighbh. level (n = 61)						
Welfare rate (under 18 years)[a,b]	—			0.013	3.0	**
Fixed effects: school level (n = 68)						
Mean parental SES[a]	—			−0.032	−7.0	***
Random effects	Var. comp.	Reduction of var. vs. empty model		Var. comp.	Reduction of var. vs. model 1	
Level 1 – respondents	0.02520	19.8%		0.02541	19.1%	
Level 2 – neighbourhoods	0.00061	3.2%		0.00032	49.2%	
Level 2 – schools	0.00131	71.9%		0.00011	91.7%	

Notes: [a]z-transformed; [b]official data. ***$p < 0.001$; **$p < 0.01$; *$p < 0.05$.

delinquency directly, on the individual level, but works through macro-level social processes (Sampson & Wilson, 1995).

Conclusion and Outlook

This paper has presented empirical evidence for the existence of potential neighbourhood as well as school contextual effects on adolescent delinquency. Due to the cross-sectional nature of the data, the results should be treated with caution and interpreted as potential rather than actual effects.

These findings are somewhat at odds with other European studies that rarely found strong evidence of contextual effects of concentrated poverty on adolescents, and are instead comparable to studies from the US that did find such evidence. Considering the much higher degree of social inequality and urban segregation in the US compared to most European countries, it is not a surprise to see such differences across the Atlantic. On the other hand, studies from related fields have shown that social inequality and structural disadvantage may have a stronger impact on behavioural outcomes in Germany than in other European countries. The international PISA study on school performance found that Germany had the highest slope of parental SES on educational achievement of all participating countries, including the US (Baumert *et al.*, 2001, p. 388). It is an important challenge for future research to explain this apparent ineffectiveness of the German welfare system.

The analyses revealed differential effects by gender and ethnicity, as well as hinting strongly about the role of peer relations as a decisive social mechanism translating the concentration of poverty into problem behaviour. Adolescents who spend much of their free time outside their own neighbourhood together with friends from other neighbourhoods are apparently not affected by conditions in their resident neighbourhoods. Therefore, the interesting question is what, apart from the location of schools which have proven to be an overlapping but independent context, influences these spatial choices and preferences of adolescents. It can be assumed that parental influences are important. In addition, if routine activities of adolescents extend beyond their residential neighbourhoods, new strategies of data collection are needed to capture these 'activity fields' as, for example, network studies (Snijders & Baerveldt, 2003) or time budget studies (Wikström & Sampson, 2003).

Finally, the unexpected result that immigrant adolescents are not affected by neighbourhood contexts in a similar way that native adolescents are, and in part even report higher rates of problem behaviour *outside* poverty areas, calls for further research into the social conditions of ethnic minority families inside and outside disadvantaged neighbourhoods. Again, if these findings were confirmed in further research, this would raise serious questions about integration policies. More research, and particularly more comparative multi-level research is needed to enhance our knowledge about the complex interactions between adolescents and their behavioural contexts.

Acknowledgements

This research has been supported by the Deutsche Forschungsgemeinschaft (Ob 134/3-1,2). The author was a Marie-Curie Intra-European Fellow at the Institute of Criminology, University of Cambridge (UK) during 2004 to 2006. The author would also like to thank the organizers and participants of the conference Inside Poverty Areas, the editors and anonymous reviewers of this special issue and Per-Olof Wikström for their useful comments.

Notes

[1] Survey factor score: percentage immigrant background, percentage unemployed or welfare recipient > 5 months; mean parents' highest occupational prestige, percentage university degree of parents, mean household goods; official factor score: percentage non-German < 14 years, percentage welfare recipients < 18 years, mean dwelling floor space per person.

[2] In ca. one-third of cases, no sufficient information was available for assigning an ISCO code; however, a rough categorization to a four-point ordinal scale yielded valid information for 95 per cent of the sample, using the highest status of either father or mother (Oberwittler & Blank, 2003 for details).

[3] This survey question suffers from a relatively high item non-response (3.4 per cent), which implies that some respondents decided not to report their parents' unemployment or welfare dependency due to social desirability concerns. It seems possible that these respondents also under-reported on related scales such as relative deprivation, thus causing a systematic bias to wrongly accept the null hypothesis.

[4] Single-context models of potential school effects on delinquency yield significant ICCs for both native (8.9 per cent) and immigrant respondents (5.6 per cent) (conditional models controlling for socio-demographic composition).

References

Akers, R. L. & Jensen, G. F. (Eds) (2003) *Social Learning Theory and the Explanation of Crime: A Guide for the New Century* (New Brunswick, NJ: Transaction).
Arum, R. (2000) Schools and communities: ecological and institutional dimensions, *Annual Review of Sociology*, 26, pp. 395–418.
Baumert, J. Klieme, E. & Neubrand, M. (2001) *PISA 2000: Basiskompetenzen von Schülerinnen und Schülern im internationalen Vergleich* (Opladen: Leske + Budrich).
Bellair, P. E., Roscigno, V. J. & McNulty, T. L. (2003) Linking local labor market opportunity to violent adolescent delinquency, *Journal of Research in Crime and Delinquency*, 40, pp. 6–33.
Bingenheimer, J. B., Brennan, R. T. & Earls, F. J. (2005) Firearm violence exposure and serious violent behavior, *Science*, 308, pp. 1323–1326.
Body-Gendrot, S. (2005) Deconstructing youth violence in French cities, *European Journal of Crime, Criminal Law and Criminal Justice*, 13, pp. 4–26.
Booth, A. & Crouter, A. C. (Eds) (2001) *Does it Take a Village? Community Effects on Children, Adolescents, and Families* (Mahwah, NJ: Erlbaum).
Brännström, L. (2004) Poor places, poor prospects? Counterfactual models of neighbourhood effects on social exclusion in Stockholm, Sweden, *Urban Studies*, 41, pp. 2515–2537.
Brännström, L. (2005) Does neighbourhood origin matter? A longitudinal multilevel assessment of neighbourhood effects on income and receipt of social assistance in a Stockholm birth cohort, *Housing, Theory and Society*, 22, pp. 169–195.
Browne, W. J., Goldstein, H. & Rasbash, J. (2001) Multiple Membership Multiple Classification (MMMC) models, *Statistical Modelling*, 1, pp. 103–124.
Conger, R. D. & Donnellan, M. B. (2007) An interactionist perspective on the socioeconomic context of human development, *Annual Review of Psycholgy*, 58, pp. 175–199.
Crane, J. (1991) The epidemic theory of ghettos and neighborhood effects on dropping out and teenage childbearing, *American Journal of Sociology*, 96, pp. 1226–1259.
Croft, J. (2004) Positive choice, no choice or total rejection: the perennial problem of school catchments, housing and neighbourhoods, *Housing Studies*, 19, pp. 927–945.
DiPrete, T. A. & Forristal, J. D. (1994) Multilevel models: methods and substance, *Annual Review of Sociology*, 20, pp. 331–357.
Dubet, F. & Lapeyronnie, D. (1992) *Les quartiers d'exil* (Paris: Seuil).
Duncan, G. J. & Raudenbush, S. W. (1999) Assessing the effect of context in studies of child and youth development, *Educational Psychologist*, 34, pp. 29–41.
Duncan, G. J. & Raudenbush, S. W. (2001) Neighborhoods and adolescent development: how can we determine the links?, in: A. Booth & A. C. Crouter (Eds) *Does it Take a Village? Community Effects on Children, Adolescents, and Families*, pp. 105–136 (Mahwah, NJ: Erlbaum).
Elliott, D. S., Menard, S., Rankin, B. H., Wilson, W. J. & Huizinga, D. (2006) *Good Kids from Bad Neighborhoods. Successful Development in Social Context* (Cambridge: Cambridge University Press).

Esbensen, F.-A. & Weerman, F. M. (2005) Youth gangs and troublesome youth groups in the United States and the Netherlands. A cross-national comparison, *European Journal of Criminology*, 2, pp. 5–37.
Farwick, A. (2004) Segregierte armut: zum einfluss städtischer wohnquartiere auf die dauer von armutslagen, in: H. Häußermann, M. Kronauer & W. Siebel (Eds) *An den Rändern der Städte. Armut und Ausgrenzung*, pp. 286–314 (Frankfurt: Suhrkamp).
Friedrichs, J. (1998) Do poor neighborhoods make their residents poorer? Context effects of poverty neighborhoods on residents, in: H.-J. Andreß (Ed.) *Empirical Poverty Research in a Comparative Perspective*, pp. 77–98 (Aldershot: Ashgate).
Friedrichs, J., Galster, G. & Musterd, S. (2003) Neighbourhood effects on social opportunities: the European and American research and policy context, *Housing Studies*, 18, pp. 797–806.
Furstenberg, F. F. J., Cook, T. D., Eccels, J., Elder, G. H. J. & Smeroff, A. (1999) *Managing to Make It. Urban Families and Adolescent Success* (Chicago: University of Chicago Press).
Haynie, D. L. (2002) Friendship networks and delinquency: the relative nature of peer delinquency, *Journal of Quantitative Criminology*, 18, pp. 99–134.
Haynie, D. L. & Osgood, D. W. (2005) Reconsidering peers and delinquency: how do peers matter?, *Social Forces*, 84, pp. 1009–1130.
Hedström, P., Kolm, A.-S. & Aberg, Y. (2003) Social interactions and unemployment. Working Paper No. 15 (Uppsala Institute for Labour Market Policy Evaluation).
Hox, J. (2002) *Multilevel Analysis. Techniques and Applications* (Mahwah, NJ: Erlbaum).
Jencks, C. & Mayer, S. E. (1990) The social consequences of growing up in a poor neighborhood, in: L. E. Lynn & L. McGeary (Eds) *Inner-City Poverty in the United States*, pp. 111–186 (Washington DC: National Academy Press).
Kelling, G. L. & Coles, C. M. (1996) *Fixing Broken Windows: Restoring Order and Reducing Crime in Our Communities* (New York: Free Press).
Kiesner, J., Poulin, F. & Nicotra, E. (2003) Peer relations across contexts: individual-network homophily and network inclusion in and after school, *Child Development*, 74, pp. 1328–1343.
Klein, M. W. (1984) Offence specialisation and versatility among juveniles, *British Journal of Criminology*, 24, pp. 185–194.
Klein, M. W., Weerman, F. M. & Thornberry, T. P. (2006) Street gang violence in Europe, *European Journal of Criminology*, 3, pp. 413–437.
Krivo, L. J. & Peterson, R. D. (2000) Structural context and homicide: accounting for racial differences in process, *American Sociological Review*, 65, pp. 547–559.
Leventhal, T. & Brooks-Gunn, J. (2000) The neighborhoods they live in: the effects of neighborhood residence on child and adolescent outcomes, *Psychological Bulletin*, 126, pp. 309–337.
Luthar, S. S. (Ed.) (2003) *Resilience and Vulnerability. Adaption in the Context of Childhood Adversities* (Cambridge: Cambridge University Press).
Massey, D. (2001) The prodigal paradigm returns: ecology comes back to sociology, in: A. Booth & A. C. Crouter (Eds) *Does it Take a Village? Community Effects on Children, Adolescents, and Families*, pp. 41–48 (Mahwah, NJ: Erlbaum).
Murie, A. & Musterd, S. (2004) Social exclusion and opportunity structures in European cities and neighbourhoods, *Urban Studies*, 14, pp. 1441–1459.
Musterd, S., Ostendorf, W. & de Vos, S. (2003) Neighbourhood effects and social mobility: a longitudinal analysis, *Housing Studies*, 18, pp. 877–892.
Oberwittler, D. (2003a) Geschlecht, Ethnizität und sozialräumliche Benachteiligung—überraschende Interaktionen bei sozialen Bedingungfaktoren von Gewalt und schwerer Eigentumsdelinquenz von Jugendlichen, in: S. Lamnek & M. Boatca (Eds) *Geschlecht—Gewalt—Gesellschaft*, pp. 269–294 (Opladen: Leske + Budrich).
Oberwittler, D. (2003b) *Das stadtviertel- und gemeindebezogene Stichprobendesign—Anlage und empirische Ergebnisse*, Working paper des Projekts 'Soziale Probleme und Jugenddelinquenz im sozialökologischen Kontext' / Nr. 9.
Oberwittler, D. (2004a) A multilevel analysis of neighbourhood contextual effects on serious juvenile offending. The role of subcultural values and social disorganization, *European Journal of Criminology*, 1, pp. 201–235 (see (2005) Correction of results, *European Journal of Criminology*, 2, pp. 93–97).
Oberwittler, D. (2004b) Stadtstruktur, freundeskreise und delinquenz. Eine mehrebenenanalyse zu sozialökologischen konteffekten auf schwere jugenddelinquenz, in: D. Oberwittler & S. Karstedt (Eds) *Soziologie der Kriminalität*, pp. 135–170 (Wiesbaden: VS Verlag für Sozialwissenschaften).

Oberwittler, D. (2004c) Which context? Conditional impacts of neighbourhoods, schools and spatial friendship patterns on serious juvenile offending. Paper presented at the Annual Meeting of the American Society of Criminology, Nashville, 14 November.

Oberwittler, D. & Blank, T. (2003) *Methodenbericht MPI-Schulbefragung 1999*, Technical paper of the project 'Social Problems and Juvenile Delinquency in Ecological Perspective', No. 1.

Oberwittler, D., Köllisch, T. & Würger, M. (2002) Selbstberichtete delinquenz bei jugendlichen, in: A. Glöckner-Rist (Ed.) *ZUMA-Informationssystem. Elektronisches Handbuch sozialwissenschaftlicher Erhebungsinstrumente* (Mannheim: Zentrum für Umfragen, Methoden und Analysen).

Pauwels, L. (2007) *Buurtinvloeden en jugenddelinquentie. Een toets van de Sociale Desorganisatietheorie* (The Hague: Boom Juridische uitgevers).

Raudenbush, S. & Bryk, A. (2002) *Hierarchical Linear Models: Applications and Data Analysis Methods (2.A.)* (Thousand Oaks: Sage).

Reijneveld, S. A., Brugman, E., Verhulst, F. C. & Verloove-Vanhorick, P. (2005) Area deprivation and child psychosocial problems. A national cross-sectional study among school-aged children, *Social Psychiatry and Psychiatric Epidemiology*, 40, pp. 18–23.

Rovers, B. (1997) *De Buurt een Broeinest? Een onderzoek naar de invloed van woonomgeving op jeugdcriminaliteit* (Nijmegen: Ars Aequi Libri).

Sampson, R. J. & Wilson, W. J. (1995) Towards a theory of race, crime, and urban inequality, in: J. Hagan & R. Peterson (Eds) *Crime and Inequality*, pp. 37–54 (Stanford, CA: Stanford University Press).

Sampson, R. J., Raudenbush, S. W. & Earls, F. J. (1997) Neighborhoods and violent crime: a multilevel study of collective efficacy, *Science*, 277, pp. 918–924.

Sampson, R. J., Morenoff, J. D. & Earls, F. (1999) Beyond social capital: spatial dynamics of collective efficacy for children, *American Sociological Review*, 64, pp. 633–660.

Sampson, R. J., Morenoff, J. D. & Gannon-Rowley, T. (2002) Assessing 'neighborhood effects': social processes and new directions in research, *Annual Review of Sociology*, 28, pp. 443–478.

Sampson, R. J., Morenoff, J. D. & Raudenbush, S. W. (2005) Social anatomy of racial and ethnic disparities in violence, *American Journal of Public Health*, 95, pp. 224–232.

Shaw, C. & McKay, H. D. (1969 [1942]) *Juvenile Delinquency and Urban Areas* (Chicago: Chicago University Press).

Skogan, W. G. (1990) *Disorder and Decline. Crime and the Spiral of Decay in American Neighbourhoods* (New York: Free Press).

Snijders, T. & Bosker, R. (1999) *Multilevel Analysis. An Introduction to Basic and Advanced Multilevel Analysis* (London: Sage).

Snijders, T. & Baerveldt, C. (2003) A multilevel network study of the effects of delinquent behavior on friendship evolution, *Journal of Mathematical Sociology*, 27, pp. 132–151.

Wacquant, L. (1996) Red belt, black belt: racial division, class inequality, and the state in the French urban periphery and the American ghetto, in: E. Mingione (Ed.) *Urban Poverty and the Underclass: A Reader*, pp. 234–274 (Oxford and New York: Basil Blackwell).

Warr, M. (2002) *Companions in Crime: The Social Aspects of Criminal Conduct* (Cambridge: Cambridge University Press).

Wegener, B. (1988) *Kritik des Prestiges* (Opladen: Westdeutscher Verlag).

Wikström, P.-O. H. (2002) *Adolescent Crime in Context*, Report to the Home Office.

Wikström, P.-O. H. (2006) Individuals, settings and acts of crime. Situational mechanisms and the explanation of crime, in: P.-O. H. Wikström & R. J. Sampson (Eds) *Crime and its Explanation: Contexts, Mechanisms and Development* (Cambridge: Cambridge University Press).

Wikström, P.-O. H. & Butterworth, D.A. (2006) *Adolescent crime. Individual differences and lifestyles* (Cullompton: Willan).

Wikström, P.-O. H. & Sampson, R. J. (2003) Social mechanisms of community influences on crime and pathways in criminality, in: B. B. Lahey, T. E. Moffitt & A. Caspi (Eds) *The Causes of Conduct Disorder and Serious Juvenile Delinquency*, pp. 118–148 (New York: Guilford Press).

Wilson, W. J. (1987) *The Truly Disadvantaged: The Inner City, the Underclass, and Public Policy* (Chicago: Chicago University Press).

The Socio-cultural Integration of Ethnic Minorities in the Netherlands: Identifying Neighbourhood Effects on Multiple Integration Outcomes

MÉROVE GIJSBERTS & JACO DAGEVOS

Introduction

Non-Western ethnic minorities have traditionally been concentrated in the densely populated west of the Netherlands, and especially in the four largest cities Amsterdam, Rotterdam, The Hague and Utrecht. This concentration has increased in recent years. The proportion of non-Western ethnic minorities in some neighbourhoods and districts has increased more than might be expected on the basis of the organic population growth. In these neighbourhoods, not only are problems of decay and safety an issue, but also a lack of social cohesion. In the public and political debate ethnically segregated neighbourhoods are seen as an important obstacle to the integration of ethnic minorities. However, some Dutch authors question this line of reasoning. As a consequence of modern modes of transportation and communication, they argue that place of residence loses its importance for finding a job as well as maintaining social contacts (see, e.g. Bolt, 2004; Ostendorf & Musterd, 2005). This argument could well apply to the socio-economic position of ethnic minorities. The influence of the neighbourhood on socio-economic integration is, as has been shown in earlier Dutch research, rather small (for an overview Veldboer & Duyvendak, 2004). However, for several aspects of socio-cultural integration it is too early to draw this conclusion. First, amazingly little research has been done, either in the Netherlands or abroad, on the consequences of ethnic concentration for socio-cultural integration. Second, the research that has been done in the Netherlands points to the existence of neighbourhood effects. These effects are especially profound in explaining inter-ethnic contacts between ethnic minorities and indigenous Dutch: in neighbourhoods with many ethnic minority residents, inter-ethnic contacts less frequently occur (Tesser et al., 1995; Van der Laan Bouma-Doff, 2005).

This paper aims to contribute to the discussion on the impact of ethnic concentration on elements of socio-cultural integration. Socio-cultural integration is concerned with the question of whether ethnic minority groups become part of the receiving society or whether these groups remain distinct from the host country. In other words, socio-cultural integration is concerned with the social and cultural distance between ethnic minorities and the indigenous majority. This paper is restricted to specific aspects of socio-cultural integration. First, it looks at the social contacts between ethnic minorities and the Dutch majority in their daily lives. A second aspect is the command of the Dutch language by members of ethnic minority groups. Finally, it examines inter-ethnic attitudes: what do ethnic minorities and the indigenous Dutch think about one another?

For many decades the four largest ethnic groups—Turks, Moroccans, Surinamese and Antilleans (Arubans included)—dominated the immigration picture in the Netherlands, but in the 1990s the arrival of asylum-seekers began to change this (Van Praag, 2003). The emphasis in this report consequently lies both on the four largest non-Dutch ethnic groups plus the 'new' or refugee groups, in particular the five largest refugee groups: (former) Yugoslavs, Iraqis, Afghans, Iranians and Somalis. Previous analyses (SCP/WODC/CBS, 2005) have revealed that these 'new' immigrant groups (with the exception of Somalis) are generally better integrated in a socio-cultural respect than Turks and Moroccans. It is unclear whether this is due to the higher education level of these groups or is a consequence of their living scattered throughout the country. This paper addresses this issue. Moreover, it also explicitly addresses the implications of ethnic concentration for contacts and attitudes of the 'indigenous Dutch' with and towards ethnic minorities. The position of the Dutch remains largely unaddressed in the public debate, whereas it is very important in diagnosing social contacts that are almost by definition reciprocal.

Research into neighbourhood effects has become extremely popular in recent years. The harmful effects of living in high-poverty areas often with large concentrations of ethnic minorities have been evident for a long time. Living in these areas has been shown to have negative effects on labour market success, education and criminal behaviour (Wilson, 1987). A large number of studies have been carried out on the relationship between the characteristics of a neighbourhood and phenomena such as social exclusion (Buck, 2001), various aspects of people's living situation such as labour market position, income and health (McCulloch, 2001), and crime (Sampson *et al.*, 1997; Van Wilsem *et al.*, 2006). An extensive overview of studies on neighbourhood effects may be found in Sampson *et al.* (2002).

The research question the authors set out to answer in this paper is whether autonomous neighbourhood effects can be observed on several indicators of socio-cultural integration in the Netherlands. To determine these neighbourhood effects it is important to make sure no composition effects are at work. For example, if more immigrants with a lower education level live in a neighbourhood, the educational composition alone could be a reason for a lower level of socio-cultural integration. Therefore, the analyses control for important individual variables. Multi-level analysis is performed to adequately test the theoretical expectations.

Theoretical Expectations on Effects of Ethnic Concentration

Ethnic Concentration and Inter-ethnic Contacts

Although heavily criticized, assimilation theories offer important leads for research on the integration of ethnic minorities. Assimilation theories (Gordon, 1964; Park, 1928) emphasize time as a crucial variable for the integration of ethnic minorities. Integration processes demand a succession of generations. While first-generation immigrants are forced into the lowest areas of the stratification system, second-generation offspring increasingly become part of the receiving society, mainly as a consequence of educational participation. Integration proceeds as even newer generations appear. However, other authors have stressed that improving one's socio-economic position does not necessarily imply losing one's cultural roots (e.g. Portes & Zhou, 1994). Moreover, a succession of generations does not by definition imply an improvement in socio-economic position, as the situation of the Afro American population in the US has shown. This deprivation is often explained by pointing to the neighbourhood (Wilson, 1987). The neighbourhood in which members of ethnic minorities live can cause a further deterioration in their position. One possible explanation is that living in an ethnically segregated situation isolates these groups from the majority population and thus from essential contacts that have been proven useful for finding jobs and housing. Granovetter (1973) has emphasized the strength of 'weak ties' that are able to bridge distances between different population groups. Weak ties are especially important in improving a person's living situation. As a result of ethnic concentration different ethnic groups hardly mix, and consequently weak ties do not appear to work out for ethnic minority groups. Based on the above line of reasoning, it was hypothesized that ethnic concentration diminishes social contacts of ethnic minorities with the indigenous Dutch.

For the indigenous majority, too, ethnic concentration can be expected to exert a negative influence on contacts with minority groups. Mechanisms of ethnic competition are likely to play a role. Earlier research has repeatedly suggested that negative attitudes towards minority groups are more prevalent among the less privileged groups in society (e.g. Billiet *et al.*, 1996). Many explanations, psychological as well as sociological, have been put forward for this. An important theoretical tradition seeks an explanation in the competition between ethnic groups. Central to this 'ethnic competition theory' is the idea that ethnic groups have opposing interests in attaining scarce goods (such as a job, a house and social benefits). Consequently, competition between these groups arises, which is also experienced as such (Blalock, 1967; Bobo, 1988; Taylor, 1998). Those social categories that experience more competition from ethnic out-groups will have a more negative view of these other groups. Since ethnic minorities generally occupy the lower social strata in society (Dagevos *et al.*, 2003; Kiehl & Werner, 1998), it can be expected that indigenous persons in the same social positions will feel the most threatened. Indigenous groups who live in ethnically segregated neighbourhoods could see the presence of many ethnic minorities as a threat to their own position (Olzak, 1992; Quillian, 1995). As a consequence of this perceived ethnic threat, people are less prone to engage in contact with ethnic minorities. Thus, the hypothesis would be that also for the ethnic majority ethnic concentration diminishes contacts with ethnic minority groups. More specifically, this is expected to be so *because* residents of ethnically concentrated areas perceive higher ethnic threat.

On the other hand, it might well be the case that the indigenous Dutch maintain more social contacts with ethnic minorities in ethnically concentrated neighbourhoods simply because there are more opportunities to meet (assuming that social contacts among other things occur within the neighbourhood). This would imply that the effect of ethnic concentration on contacts of the Dutch with ethnic minorities is positive, at least to a certain extent. Possibly, a 'tipping point' can be expected. Many authors have discussed this issue, mainly related to the issue of residential segregation in the US and the preference for moving out of the neighbourhood after a certain maximum amount of minority residents is reached (e.g. Clark, 1986, 1993; Goering, 1978). This tipping point hypothesis would mean that a non-linear effect of ethnic concentration on social contacts is to be expected in the analyses, i.e. the influence of the presence of ethnic minorities on contacts of the Dutch with minority groups is expected to be positive until a certain turning point. When even more minority people are living in the neighbourhood the effect will turn negative and perceptions of ethnic threat will start to play a larger role (see Galster & Zobel (1998) for a discussion of non-linear neighbourhood effects on individual outcomes).

The pace of the influx of new minority groups in a neighbourhood can also be important. Olzak (1992) for instance has shown that the degree of ethnic collective action in American cities is not only affected by the level of immigration, but also by the percentage of change in immigration levels (see also Coenders & Scheepers, 1998). In the past few years the proportion of non-Western citizens in several Dutch neighbourhoods has increased dramatically. This development could have an additional negative effect on the contacts maintained by the Dutch with minority groups. Thus, contacts of indigenous Dutch with ethnic minorities are expected to reduce if the ethnic population of a neighbourhood increases within a short space of time.

A final possible hypothesis is that neighbourhood characteristics are not important at all and that it is simply a matter of the composition of the population in the neighbourhood: in ethnically concentrated neighbourhoods more indigenous Dutch have lower levels of education and previous research has revealed that people with low levels of education maintain fewer inter-ethnic contacts.

Ethnic Concentration and Second-language Proficiency

Previous research has shown that second-language proficiency depends on two different but related factors: the 'investments' that people are prepared to make in order to learn a language, and the 'opportunities' they have to speak this language (Chiswick & Miller, 2001; Van Tubergen & Kalmijn, 2005). The influence of these factors may differ between individuals. People who migrated for purposes of work or study for example may need to invest in their second language, simply to be able to function in their new situation (Carliner, 2000). However, this new situation (a job or study) also enables them to learn the language, since the opportunity to speak it is greater than for migrants who stay at home: the more intensively immigrants are exposed to the new language, the better they speak this language (see, e.g. Jasso & Rosenzweig, 1990).

Investments and opportunities may not only operate at the individual level, but also at higher levels of aggregation. The general view that ethnic concentration hinders the integration of ethnic minorities is based on both factors and accordingly has both a forced and a voluntary component. In the first instance, the expectation is that ethnic concentration has a negative impact on language proficiency, because it diminishes the opportunity for contacts with the majority population. In ethnically concentrated neighbourhoods, meeting opportunities between ethnic minority groups and the indigenous Dutch are lower than in mixed neighbourhoods. On the other hand, the necessity to *invest* in the language of the destination country is also smaller when more members of an individual's own ethnic group live in the neighbourhood. In ethnically concentrated neighbourhoods it is after all easier to manage in the mother tongue.

The expectation here that ethnic concentration slows down the process of learning the second language is thus based on the assumption that ethnic concentration hinders social contacts with the indigenous population. Other authors call this the 'language-contact thesis' (Driessen *et al.*, 2003) or the 'isolation thesis' (Van der Laan Bouma-Doff, 2005). According to this line of reasoning, social contacts are expected to intervene in the negative relationship between living in an ethnically concentrated neighbourhood and second-language proficiency. This intervening relationship will be examined in the paper.

Ethnic Concentration and Inter-ethnic Attitudes

An open question is whether a relationship can be hypothesized on theoretical grounds between the ethnic concentration in a neighbourhood and inter-ethnic attitudes. Again, this relationship may be expected to exist based on ethnic competition theory. Negative outgroup attitudes are likely to vary with the amount of (perceived) competition in a neighbourhood (Olzak, 1992; Quillian, 1995). The level of competition may be related to conditions where an increasing number of people are competing for approximately the same amount of scarce resources. Majority groups living in neighbourhoods with large concentrations of ethnic minorities can be expected to perceive this presence as a threat to their own position. As a consequence of this perceived threat, indigenous residents of these neighbourhoods may well hold more negative views about ethnic out-groups.

Moreover, a change in the proportion of ethnic minorities in a neighbourhood may exert an influence (see, e.g. Coenders & Scheepers, 1998). In recent years, many neighbourhoods have witnessed quite dramatic increases in the proportion of ethnic minority residents. Based on ethnic competition theory, this trend is expected to have an additional negative effect on attitudes of the indigenous majority towards ethnic minorities.

If a negative relationship is found between (increases in) ethnic concentration and inter-ethnic attitudes, the question still remains as to why this should be so. As indicated above, a first expectation is based on ethnic competition theory and predicts that a concentration of ethnic minorities in a neighbourhood has a negative influence on the attitudes of the majority group *because* they feel more threatened by those minorities (Olzak, 1992; Quillian, 1995; Taylor, 1998). Perceived ethnic threat thus is hypothesized to mediate the relationship between (increases in) ethnic concentration and negative out-group attitudes.

To date, most research has been aimed at finding determinants that cause or reinforce exclusionist tendencies. However, there is also a strand of research that examines which factors reduce negative out-group attitudes. An important hypothesis in this regard is the 'contact hypothesis', which posits that more contacts between different ethnic groups will enhance mutual understanding and acceptance, and consequently reduce negative out-group attitudes (Forbes, 1997; Hamberger & Hewstone, 1997; Brown & Hewstone, 2005; Pettigrew & Tropp, 2006). Particularly in ethnically concentrated neighbourhoods, the opportunities for such contacts are fewer. In this case, social contacts can again be hypothesized to mediate the relationship between ethnic concentration and negative out-group attitudes: people in ethnically concentrated neighbourhoods hold more negative views of out-groups *because* contacts with these out-groups are fewer than in neighbourhoods that are less ethnically concentrated.

The negative influence of ethnic concentration in different societal contexts (such as neighbourhoods or countries) on out-group attitudes has been established for majority attitudes over and over again (Gijsberts *et al.*, 2004; Quillian, 1995; Scheepers *et al.*, 2002). For minority groups, much less is known about the possible correlation between living in an ethnically concentrated neighbourhood and out-group attitudes. However, as indicated in a previous section, the current study expected to find a negative relationship between ethnic concentration and inter-ethnic contacts: in ethnically concentrated neighbourhoods there will be fewer social contacts between minority and majority groups. Based on contact theory, the absence of inter-ethnic contact in ethnically concentrated neighbourhoods is expected to work out negatively on attitudes of minority groups towards the ethnic majority. More generally, the less ethnically concentrated the neighbourhood minority groups reside, the more social contacts with the indigenous population there will be.

The Issue of Causality

A final remark concerns the issue of causality. Theoretically, in this paper as in many previous studies, the main idea is that contextual, neighbourhood characteristics influence various individual outcomes (Sampson *et al.*, 2002; Van Tubergen & Kalmijn, 2005). However, these relationships will also operate in the reverse direction. Ethnic minorities living in neighbourhoods where not many other minorities live will presumably have more frequent contacts with the indigenous population and consequentially attain a better command of the language of the destination country. However, better socio-cultural integration will also induce these people to move out of segregated neighbourhoods. This could cause a potential problem of selection effects, i.e. the better integrated move out of ethnically concentrated neighbourhoods, while the less integrated stay in these neighbourhoods. Most families have at least some degree of choice over where they live. So, the correlation between individual outcomes and neighbourhood characteristics may reflect causal effects but may also be (partly) reflecting self-selection bias (see, e.g. Johnson *et al.*, 2002). Since most studies on this subject (including the present one) are based on data gathered at one moment in time, the causality of the hypothesized relations cannot be tested. Strictly speaking, it is not possible to speak of causal effects, but rather of circular or mutual effects.

Data and Methods

Data Sources

For information on minority groups this study used the most important dataset in the Netherlands on the position of ethnic minorities: the Social Position and Use of Provisions by Ethnic Minorities (2002). This is a large-scale survey that has been conducted at four-yearly intervals since 1988 and which contains extensive information on the four largest minority groups in the Netherlands: Turks, Moroccans, Surinamese and Antilleans. The data used for this paper were collected in 2002 in face-to-face interviews with people aged 15 years and over. A household sample was drawn resulting in about 1000 cases for each ethnic group. Turkish and Moroccan respondents were interviewed by bilingual interviewers, using translated questionnaires. Surinamese and Antilleans were questioned using questionnaires in Dutch, but mostly by interviewers from their own ethnic groups. A Social Position and Use of Provisions by Ethnic Minorities Survey was also carried out (in 2003) among the five largest refugee groups in the Netherlands: Afghans, Iraqis, Iranians, (former) Yugoslavs and Somalis. This survey used the same methodology as the survey among the four largest immigrant groups and largely covers the same issues. Both surveys were used in this paper.

To give some background on the scale of the minority population into the Netherlands, there are approximately 1.6 million non-Western citizens living in the Netherlands of which well over 300 000 are Turks, Moroccans and Surinamese and 130 000 Antilleans. Refugee groups are much smaller, varying between approximately 20 000 Somalis to 75 000 people from the former Yugoslavia.

Data on the indigenous Dutch stem from a survey of 3000 Dutch respondents that was carried out in 2002, the Attitudes towards Minorities Survey. This survey sample is representative of the indigenous Dutch population and contains extensive information on all important aspects in this paper. The questions posed to respondents are largely identical to those in the Social Position and Use of Provisions by Ethnic Minorities Survey. All datasets used are weighted using a number of demographic characteristics (for more information on the datasets see Dagevos *et al.*, 2003). Item non-response of the variables used in this paper turns out to be low.

Indicators of Integration

Social contacts. Measures of social contacts differ between ethnic minority groups and the indigenous Dutch. Social contacts of ethnic minorities with the indigenous Dutch are measured in the Social Position and Use of Provisions by Ethnic Minorities Survey. Respondents in this survey were asked whether they engage in their free time mainly with members of their own ethnic group, maintain more contacts with members of the indigenous population or have a mixed circle of friends and acquaintances. The variable used therefore comprises three categories: more contact with members of one's own ethnic group, ethnically mixed circle of friends and acquaintances, and more contact with the indigenous population. For the analyses this variable has been dichotomized: (0)

ethnically mixed social contacts or predominantly contacts with indigenous people; (1) social contacts predominantly within own ethnic circle. This measurement is available for both the four largest immigrant groups (2002) and the five refugee groups (2003).

For data on the social contacts of indigenous Dutch people with ethnic minorities the Attitudes towards Minorities Survey is used. In this survey, contacts with minority groups are measured by combining two items: (1) the degree of contact with minority groups in the respondent's own neighbourhood, and (2) the degree of contact with minority groups in daily life. This scale was transformed into an increasing scale from 0 to 100; the higher the value on the scale, the more social contact there is (Cronbach's alpha $= 0.61$).

Language proficiency. To obtain an insight into the language proficiency of the main ethnic minority groups in the Netherlands (both the four largest and the five refugee groups) the study uses the Social Position and Use of Provisions by Ethnic Minorities Surveys carried out in 2002 and 2003. Measures of language proficiency are constructed by combining the respondent's own estimation of his or her command of the Dutch language with an estimation by the interviewer. Both estimates correlate quite highly (0.7), thus implying reasonably reliable estimates. Since the response categories of both questions differ, the answers have been transformed into a uniform scale from 0 to 100. The higher the score, the better the command of the Dutch language. Cronbach's alpha of the resulting scale is 0.82.

Stereotypical attitudes. Indigenous respondents were able to indicate on four-point scales to what extent they believed a number of characteristics apply to Turks, Moroccans and Surinamese. For the sake of clarity, and since attitudes towards these different groups stand in the same relationship with the independent variables (see Gijsberts & Dagevos, 2005), only the attitudes of the majority group towards Moroccans are presented here. Minority group respondents could indicate the extent to which they felt the same characteristics apply to the indigenous Dutch. This measurement is only available for Turks, Moroccans, Surinamese and Antilleans (not for refugee groups). A scale was constructed based on eight items that measure the ascribing of 'stereotypical characteristics'. The characteristics presented to respondents were: easygoing, honest, polite, hospitable, respectable, tolerant, helpful and friendly. Item scores were transformed to a scale from 0 to 100: the higher the score, the more positive the feeling about the other group. Cronbach's alpha was 0.77 for stereotypical views of ethnic minorities about the indigenous Dutch and 0.89 for the reverse situation.

Individual Background Controls

Individual characteristics that were measured in similar ways in both surveys were used in the analyses. Independent variables in both datasets are gender, age, education, employment and income. Gender is a dichotomous variable ($0 =$ female, $1 =$ male). Age is available from 17 years and older. Education is measured in several categories, from no education to higher education. People who are still at school are assigned the level of the education they are currently following. Employment is measured in some analyses as a dummy variable ($0 =$ not employed, $1 =$ employed). There is also a more extensive categorization including occupational level and types of non-employment (unemployed, housewife, disabled). In some analyses, income is also included. Income is measured as net household income in euros per month and divided into six categories.

For minority groups a 'migration type' variable was also constructed incorporating both the history of migration and the length of stay in the host society. First, based on the age at migration a distinction was made between migrants and their descendants. Descendants are those who were below the age of 18 when entering the Netherlands and those who were born in the Netherlands. This category is subdivided into two subcategories: people who were born in the Netherlands or who moved there before the age of six are classed as the second generation; those who migrated between the ages of 6 and 18 are labelled the in-between generation. The first generation is subdivided into three categories: early first-generation migrants (who migrated in or before 1980), later first-generation migrants (migrated after 1980) and marriage migrants. This latter category consists of migrants who migrated to the Netherlands in order to marry a member of their own ethnic group already living there. Each respondent is coded into one of these five categories.

For the indigenous Dutch a variable measuring 'perceived ethnic threat' could be identified. Perceived ethnic threat is operationalized in the analysis by constructing a scale based on the following four items: 'The presence of other cultures threatens our way of life'; 'The presence of minority groups is a source of crime and lack of safety'; 'Ethnic minorities abuse our system of social security'; 'The arrival of foreigners in the Netherlands threatens our welfare'. Cronbach's alpha of the resultant scale is 0.81. This scale was transformed to a scale from 0 to 100, where a high value stands for a higher perceived threat.

Neighbourhood Characteristics

To test hypotheses on the effects of ethnic concentration within neighbourhoods, we used postcode data obtained from Statistics Netherlands, which were pooled with the survey data. These postcode data contain information on all the almost 4000 postcode areas in the Netherlands, including information on the percentage of citizens of non-Western origin. In the Netherlands these postcode areas are commonly used to analyze the effects of neighbourhood variables, since they allow matching with individual-level data. These postcode areas do vary in size, depending on the density of the housing units in the area. In the larger cities a postcode area on average consists of 3000 dwellings.

Since the survey data were collected at the end of 2002 and in early 2003, the study uses the 'percentage of non-Western citizens' for each neighbourhood as at 1 January 2003. In the Netherlands, unlike in other societies like the US, inter-ethnic neighbourhoods are almost always multi-ethnic, i.e. consisting of many different ethnic groups. Table 1 presents the distribution of the different ethnic groups by percentage of non-Western citizens in the neighbourhood concerned (for this Table presented in four categories: 0–10 per cent; 10–25 per cent; 25–50 per cent; and more than 50 per cent).

Ethnic minorities much more often live in neighbourhoods with high ethnic concentrations as compared to the indigenous Dutch; 8 per cent of whom live in a neighbourhood with at least 25 per cent non-Western citizens, this applies for 64 per cent of Turks and no fewer than 76 per cent of Moroccans. Of the Antilleans and Surinamese, 46 per cent and 57 per cent, respectively, live in a neighbourhood with a more than 25 per cent minority population. Of all ethnic groups in the Netherlands, the refugee groups are least likely to live in ethnically concentrated neighbourhoods (between 10 and 15 per cent). These proportions could be somewhat overestimated, since the data were collected among ethnic minorities in urban areas. However, since the vast majority of

Table 1. Distribution of ethnic minority groups by proportion of non-Western citizens in a neighbourhood, 1 January 2003 (percentages)

	0–10%	10–25%	25–50%	50–100%
Turks	6	30	31	33
Moroccans	4	20	38	38
Surinamese	12	31	37	20
Antilleans	17	37	31	15
Afghans	11	38	39	12
Iraqis	12	44	31	12
Iranians	15	47	30	9
(former) Yugoslavs	16	46	26	13
Somalis	6	38	40	16
Indigenous Dutch	70	22	7	1

ethnic minorities in the Netherlands live in the (large) cities, this overestimation is likely to be modest.

Not only the proportion of non-Western citizens in a neighbourhood, but also an increase in that proportion in recent years may be relevant in determining mutual attitudes. Including this variable in the analyses makes it possible to examine whether a sudden increase in the proportion of ethnic minorities in a neighbourhood influences the opinion of the other groups. This change is measured by taking the difference in the percentage of non-Western citizens between 1998 and 2003 (see Table 2). A few (recently built) neighbourhoods did not exist in 1998. For these neighbourhoods the proportion of non-Western citizens is estimated to be equal to that of 2003. For the sake of presentation only, the difference scores have been subdivided into four categories in Table 2, reflecting the degree of change. Again the difference between the majority group and the ethnic minority groups attracts attention. The indigenous Dutch mainly live in neighbourhoods where the percentage of ethnic minorities increased only moderately (up to 2 percentage points), while ethnic minorities more often live in neighbourhoods where these proportions increased much more strongly (by at least 5 percentage points). Moroccans and Somalis in particular have seen a relatively rapid rise in the proportion of non-Western citizens in their own neighbourhood.

Table 2. Distribution of ethnic minority groups by change in proportion of non-Western citizens in a neighbourhood between 1998 and 2003 (percentages)

	Slight decrease	increase 0–2 pp	increase 2–5 pp	increase >5 pp
Turks	2	16	35	47
Moroccans	3	13	27	57
Surinamese	5	18	34	43
Antilleans	8	22	28	43
Afghans	3	18	32	47
Iraqis	3	20	28	49
Iranians	4	21	35	41
(former) Yugoslavs	4	23	39	34
Somalis	2	10	24	63
Indigenous Dutch	9	60	20	10

Note: pp = percentage points.

Multi-level Modelling

To examine the relationship between ethnic concentration and multiple integration outcomes, individual characteristics should be related to the percentages of non-Western citizens in neighbourhoods. A multi-level design makes it possible to examine whether the effects of ethnic concentration are organic or merely the result of compositional effects at individual level. If, for example, many lower-educated people live in a certain neighbourhood, and there is a correlation between education level and integration outcomes (as has been suggested in much previous research), this composition alone can be a reason for less well-integrated groups of inhabitants of this neighbourhood. Furthermore, a rapid increase in the proportion of non-Western citizens in the neighbourhood will correlate with socio-cultural integration. By subsequently adding intervening variables into the analyses, such as inter-ethnic contacts and perceived ethnic threat, possible explanatory mechanisms can be examined to clarify the relationship between ethnic concentration and integration outcomes. For this reason the study presents hierarchical models, to test the additional contribution made by a (group of) variable(s) to the explanation.

Multi-level analyses allow simultaneous modelling of individual-level and contextual neighbourhood-level effects and their interactions. A multi-level analysis takes account of the hierarchical structure of the data: individuals are 'nested' within neighbourhoods. Neglecting the error terms at the neighbourhood level underestimates the standard errors of the parameters. This in turn could lead to incorrect confirmation of hypotheses concerning neighbourhood effects. This technique provides information about the variation in the dependent variable at neighbourhood level (see Bryk & Raudenbusch, 1992; Snijders & Bosker, 1999). By including neighbourhood characteristics in the analyses it is possible to ascertain which part of the variation in integration outcomes is explained by characteristics of the neighbourhood, while including individual characteristics allows us to control for compositional effects of the individual-level variables.

Findings

Social Contacts of Ethnic Minorities with the Indigenous Dutch

Of the ethnic minority groups studied here, people of Turkish origin have the strongest orientation towards their own ethnic group; two out of three Turks living in the Netherlands have a predominantly Turkish circle of friends and acquaintances (Table 3). This holds to a slightly lesser extent for Moroccans, although a large majority of this group mainly have contact with members of their own group in their free time. People of Surinamese and Antillean origin have a much more ethnically mixed circle of friends and acquaintances. The same applies for the majority of refugee groups, a striking finding given their much shorter period of residence in the Netherlands. Nationals of Iran and (former) Yugoslavia, in particular, have frequent contact with the indigenous population. Somalis, by contrast, predominantly have contact with members of their own group. The fact that, across the board, refugees relatively frequently socialize with the native population is related among other things to their relatively high education level, the small size of these groups and their dispersal throughout the country.

The analysis shows that the observed social distance has a great deal to do with the residential segregation of different population groups. Contact with the indigenous population is lowest in neighbourhoods containing large numbers of ethnic minorities.

Table 3. Social contacts within own ethnic circle[a]: total proportion and proportion by ethnic composition of the neighbourhood (in percentages)

	Total	<10%	10–25%	25–50%	≥50%
Turks	70	52	65	71	77
Moroccans	61	49	55	60	67
Surinamese	38	20	32	40	56
Antilleans	31	23	24	35	47
Afghans	35	20	32	39	45
Iraqis	43	23	43	45	53
Iranians	25	17	26	27	31
(former) Yugoslavs	27	23	23	33	37
Somalis	50	41	43	54	61

Notes: [a]This is a dichotomous variable: (0) ethnically mixed social contacts or predominantly contacts with indigenous people; (1) social contacts predominantly within own ethnic circle.

This applies in particular for Amsterdam, Rotterdam and The Hague, where one in three residents is now of non-Western origin (Gijsberts, 2004). By way of illustration, if virtually no ethnic minorities live in a neighbourhood, half the Turkish and Moroccan community have contacts predominantly with members of their own ethnic group (Table 3). This proportion increases sharply if more than half the residents in the neighbourhood are of non-Western origin, then at least two out of three Turks and Moroccans mainly have contact with members of their own group. One in five people of Surinamese and Antillean origin who live in a neighbourhood with less than 10 per cent non-Western residents have contact predominantly with their own ethnic group; this applies for half of those living in neighbourhoods with more than 50 per cent non-Western residents. Homogeneous neighbourhoods thus reinforce ethnically homogeneous contacts. Therefore, at first sight the neighbourhood is a significant factor in the contacts between different population groups.

The multi-level analysis showed that the neighbourhood effects remain even after controlling for individual characteristics (Table 4). This analysis also explored the effect of the proportion of non-Western minorities in the cities (i.e. a three-level-analysis in this case). It was found that in cities with more than 30 per cent of non-Western ethnic minorities—as is the case in Amsterdam, Rotterdam and The Hague—there is a greater likelihood that their circle of friends and acquaintances will consist of members of their own ethnic group. The ethnic profile of the city and neighbourhood thus determines the probability of contacts with members of one's own ethnic group. It was also found that second-generation members of ethnic minorities have the fewest contacts with members of their own group, while first-generation minorities often stick to their own groups. Another important finding is that a high education level and good labour market position correlate with contacts with the indigenous population. Structural and social integration thus go hand-in-hand. This is an important finding for government policy: promoting a good education and labour market position for ethnic minorities also fosters their contacts with members of the host society.

Social Contacts of the Dutch with Ethnic Minorities

The identified social distance is due not only to the fairly strong orientation of Turks and Moroccans towards their own ethnic group, but also to the low level of contacts by the

Table 4. Multi-level logistic regression analysis of social contacts within own ethnic circle[a] by relevant individual and neighbourhood characteristics, ethnic minority groups[bc]

	Model 1	Model 2	Model 3
Ethnic group (Turks = ref. cat.)			
Moroccans	−0.43	−0.50	−0.53
Surinamese	−1.46	−1.28	−1.25
Antilleans	−1.69	−1.70	−1.64
Afghans	−1.44	−1.87	−1.80
Iraqis	−1.13	−1.55	−1.46
Iranians	−1.98	−2.21	−2.10
(former) Yugoslavs	−1.84	−2.04	−1.94
Somalis	−0.87	−1.34	−1.25
Migration type (second generation = ref. cat.)			
in-between generation		0.63	0.64
marriage migrants		1.01	1.04
first generation > 1980		1.18	1.16
first generation ≤ 1980		0.85	0.83
Gender (male = ref. cat.)		n.s.	n.s.
Age		n.s.	n.s.
Education level (max. prim. school = ref. cat.)			
lower secondary		−0.40	−0.39
higher secondary		−0.40	−0.39
higher education		−0.57	−0.54
Working (non-working = ref. cat.)			
Housewife		0.24	0.24
Disabled		n.s.	n.s.
Student		−0.54	−0.53
Other		n.s.	n.s.
Unemployed		n.s.	n.s.
Elementary occupation level		−0.23	−0.21
Low occupation level		−0.51	−0.49
Middle occupation level		−0.48	−0.45
High occupation level		−0.76	−0.71
% non-Western in neighbourhood (<10% = ref. cat.)			
10–25% non-Western in neighbourhood			0.31
25–50% non-Western in neighbourhood			0.51
≥ 50% non-Western in neighbourhood			0.84
% non-Western in city (<20% = ref. cat.)			
20–30%			n.s.
≥ 30%			0.24
Intercept	0.21	0.80	n.s.

Notes: [a]This is a dichotomous variable: (0) ethnically mixed social contacts or predominantly contacts with indigenous people; (1) social contacts predominantly within own ethnic circle.
[b]The effects of a change in % of non-Western citizens in the neighbourhood are not statistically significant and therefore not included in the Table.
[c]In this instance, a three-level-analysis has been performed in which individuals are level 1 units, neighbourhoods level 2 and cities level 3.

native population with ethnic minorities. Findings from the Attitudes towards Minorities Survey reveal that only one in three indigenous Dutch people maintain contacts with members of ethnic minorities in their free time (Gijsberts & Dagevos, 2005). The neighbourhood is a significant factor for the native population in the contacts between different population groups. Indigenous Dutch people come into contact with members of minorities more often if they live in a mixed neighbourhood. In these neighbourhoods there is more opportunity for contact. Table 5 presents the results of the analysis on contacts by the indigenous Dutch with ethnic minorities. In the analyses a dichotomous variable was added to control for the fact that a proportion of the questionnaires (16 per cent) were filled in after the murder of Pim Fortuyn, a populist Dutch politician. This political murder led to a great deal of political and social turmoil in the Netherlands just before the General Election in May 2002. Pim Fortuyn and his political party LPF made the issue of integration a central plank of their electoral campaign. Their position in the polls before the election was very strong, mainly because they mobilized the dissatisfaction about the multi-ethnic society felt by many members of the Dutch majority. Even after his murder (by a left-wing animal activist) many people still voted for him.

Table 5 reveals that older people maintain fewer social contacts with minority groups, while people with a higher education and working people have more contacts with ethnic minorities (see model 1). However, the direction of the income effect differs: the higher a person's income, the less contact there is. This may be connected with the higher incidence of income segregation in the Netherlands; both at work and in their free time, and also when in their own residential setting, people with high incomes have fewer contacts with ethnic minorities.

Although individual characteristics do matter in the explanation of differences in these contacts, the variance between neighbourhoods does not decrease when these characteristics are added (the neighbourhood-level variance in the (empty) intercept model is 43.81). This implies that differences between neighbourhoods in inter-ethnic contacts are not due to differences in the composition of these neighbourhoods in socio-demographic or socio-economic terms. However, these differences do depend on the proportion of non-Western citizens in the neighbourhood (model 2). The findings still hold

Table 5. Multi-level regression analysis of social contacts with ethnic minorities (0 to 100, 100 = intensive contacts) by relevant individual and neighbourhood characteristics, indigenous Dutch[a]

	Model 1	Model 2	Model 3
Intercept	29.41	22.37	37.55
Gender (female = ref. cat.)	–	–	–
male	n.s.	n.s.	n.s.
Age[b]	−0.17	−0.20	−0.22
Education level	0.86	n.s.	n.s.
Working (non-working = ref. cat.)	–	–	–
working	9.31	9.22	8.75
Household income	−1.10	−0.64	−0.80
% non-Western in neighbourhood		1.27	1.23
(% non-Western in neighbourhood)^2		−0.01	−0.01
Change in % non-Western in neighbourhood		−0.68	−0.55
Perceived ethnic threat			−0.23
Variance components			
between neighbourhoods	54.98	9.60	7.16
(% explained compared to previous model)	0%	83%	25%
between individuals	482.35	481.16	465.75

Notes: [a]Significance at $p < 0.05$; italic = significance at $p < 10$; n.s. = no significance.
[b]Containing a quadratic term for age in the model is not significant, so the effect of age is linear.

if contacts in a person's own neighbourhood are left out of consideration and only the degree of contact in daily life is considered. The more non-Western citizens there are living in a neighbourhood, the more contact indigenous Dutch people maintain with ethnic minorities. This implies that it has something to do with greater opportunities to meet in ethnically concentrated neighbourhoods. The variance between neighbourhoods decreases sharply (by more than 80 per cent) when neighbourhood characteristics are fed into the model. This means that differences between neighbourhoods in the extent of contact can be largely attributed to the presence of ethnic minorities in the neighbourhood. As noted earlier, for minority groups it works symmetrically: the more ethnic minorities there are in the neighbourhood, the fewer contacts they have with indigenous Dutch people, since meeting opportunities with the other group are low in this instance.

However, the study also found a curvilinear effect of the degree of ethnic concentration in a neighbourhood: the quadratic term is statistically significant (Table 5). This means that there is a limit to the effect of the presence of ethnic minorities in a neighbourhood. The findings suggest that if more than half the residents are members of non-Western ethnic minorities, contact by the native Dutch with ethnic populations in fact generally declines. This is more clearly visible in Figure 1. The tipping point is at 50 per cent non-Western citizens, the situation in which contacts are most frequent. Given the limited numbers in this sample, some qualification is necessary here. As this was a general sample drawn from the Dutch population, only a small proportion live in 'concentration neighbourhoods'. Further research targeting these neighbourhoods specifically would be needed to verify the relationship established empirically here. Nonetheless, sensitivity analyses performed on the models reported here suggest that the results found are stable (the *Cook's distance* has a maximum value of 0.05).

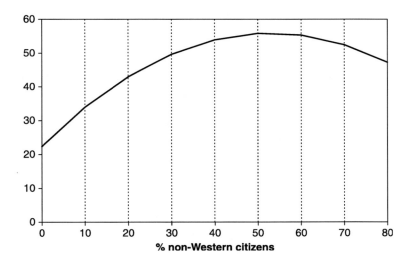

Figure 1. Relationship between proportion of non-Western citizens in a neighbourhood and degree of social contact of indigenous Dutch with ethnic minorities (0 to 100, 100 = intensive contacts).[a]
Note: [a]This relationship is controlled for other individual and neighbourhood characteristics.

When a majority of the inhabitants of a neighbourhood is of non-Western origin, the indigenous Dutch more often stay into their own circle. This may be related to several characteristics of ethnically concentrated neighbourhoods. First, the multi-ethnic nature of these neighbourhoods in Dutch neighbourhoods may obstruct social cohesion. Second, previous research has shown that people move house more often in ethnically concentrated neighbourhoods. The ethnic minority groups in these neighbourhoods in particular move frequently, mostly from one ethnically concentrated neighbourhood to another (Uunk & Dominguez Martinez, 2002). This results in a rather unstable composition of the population, with presumably negative consequences on contacts between different population groups.

The influence of a change in the proportion of non-Western citizens in a neighbourhood (between 1998 and 2003) was also examined. A rapid influx of non-Western ethnic minorities also turns out to have a negative impact; if the ethnic population of a neighbourhood increases within a short space of time, contacts between the indigenous population and ethnic residents of their neighbourhood or town are lower (model 2). The question is how this can be explained. The analysis shows that it is connected with the fact that an increasing presence of ethnic minorities in a neighbourhood is 'perceived as threatening' by the indigenous residents, causing them to withdraw more and more into their own ethnic group (model 3). In this respect the growing concentration of ethnic minorities in the large cities has a negative impact, since it will lead to even fewer contacts. 'Perceived ethnic threat' is measured on a scale from 0 to 100, where a high value stands for a higher perceived threat. Perceptions of ethnic threat explain part of the effect of the change in the proportion of non-Western citizens on inter-ethnic contacts (compare model 3 with model 2). People who live in a neighbourhood experiencing a dramatic change in ethnic composition feel more threatened by minority groups. This perceived ethnic threat is a reason, as the analyses show, to withdraw from other ethnic groups.

Other Consequences of Concentration and Contact

Inter-ethnic contact important for command of Dutch language. Of all ethnic groups living in the Netherlands, Moroccans and especially Turks have the poorest command of the Dutch language, while most of the Antilleans and, in particular, Surinamese speak Dutch well (Gijsberts & Dagevos, 2005). The command of the Dutch language of most refugee groups is somewhere in between these two extremes, with Iranians and Yugoslavs speaking Dutch much better than Afghans, Iraqis and Somalis. Considering the shorter length of stay of these refugee groups, their language proficiency is strikingly better than that of Turks and Moroccans.

Multi-level analysis of differences in language proficiency show that this proficiency differs between neighbourhoods, but these differences are mainly due to compositional effects (Table 6). Accounting for the composition of individual characteristics such as ethnic group, migration type and education leaves hardly any initial differences between neighbourhoods (see the decrease in the neighbourhood-level variance in models 1 and 2). Individual differences in language proficiency are thus considerable and, as can be seen from Table 6, correlate strongly with migration type, age, education and activity. Members of the older first generation of immigrants have a much poorer command of the Dutch language than the second generation and the in-between generation (those who moved to the Netherlands between the ages of 6 and 18). Young people have significantly less

Table 6. Multi-level regression analysis of second-language proficiency (0 to 100, 100 = excellent command of Dutch language) on relevant individual and neighbourhood characteristics[a]

	Model 1	Model 2	Model 3	Model 4
Intercept	54.52	58.84	60.55	53.28
Ethnic group (Turks = ref. cat.)	–	–	–	–
Moroccans	15.02	14.51	14.67	13.82
Antilleans	38.39	33.22	32.95	29.65
Surinamese	42.40	34.63	34.47	32.54
Afghans	17.02	15.82	15.47	12.50
Iraqis	14.82	14.72	14.27	11.92
Iranians	27.62	23.34	22.87	18.97
(former) Yugoslavs	28.49	23.69	23.28	19.81
Somalis	18.54	18.55	18.23	16.14
Migration type (second generation = ref. cat.)		–	–	–
in-between generation		n.s.	n.s.	n.s.
marriage migrants		−18.42	−18.42	−17.01
first generation >1980		−13.42	−13.28	−11.11
first generation ≤1980		−6.49	−6.34	−4.70
Gender (female = ref. cat.)		–	–	–
male		n.s.	n.s.	n.s.
Age		−0.44	−0.44	−0.45
Education level[b]		6.84	6.81	6.50
Working (non-working = ref. cat.)		–	–	–
unemployed		2.27	2.26	2.41
low occupational level		10.68	10.70	10.30
middle occupational level		13.44	13.41	12.89
higher occupational level		10.43	10.33	9.56
% non-Western in neighbourhood			−0.06	n.s.
Change in % non-Western in neighbourhood			n.s.	n.s.
Contacts with indigenous Dutch				4.82
Variance components				
between neighbourhoods	29.09	15.56	15.18	15.71
(% explained compared to previous model)	58%	25%	2%	0%
between individuals	726.98	544.24	543.87	531.77

Notes: [a] Significance at $p < 0.05$; n.s. = no significance.
[b] Education is measured in four categories, from no education/maximum primary school to higher education.

difficulty with Dutch. It is also striking that marriage migrants have a great deal of difficulty with the Dutch language. The language problems confronting older Turks and the Moroccans in particular have a great deal to do with their predominantly very low education level. A sizeable proportion of these older immigrants have in fact never been to school at all, and this makes it difficult for them to learn another language. Table 6 makes clear that persons from ethnic minorities who have a higher education level and a job (at whatever level) have a much better command of the Dutch language than lower-educated persons and members of ethnic minorities who do not participate in the labour market. Education and employment are thus of enormous importance for the acquisition of a second language. However, it should be noted that there is an issue of causation here. Education and employment will improve second-language proficiency, but it also works the other way around. Those with better language skills will also be more able to participate in higher education and have a better chance of finding a good job.

Now the study has controlled for individual differences in language proficiency, the question remains as to whether any additional effects can be traced to the ethnic concentration in the neighbourhood. The proportion of ethnic minorities in the neighbourhood is indeed found to have an independent though slight effect on the degree of language proficiency (model 3). This means that the more members of non-Western ethnic minorities live in a neighbourhood, the poorer will be the command of the Dutch language. There is thus a concentration effect, although this neighbourhood effect is small. This echoes findings in earlier research (Tesser *et al.*, 1995; Van der Laan Bouma-Doff, 2005). Moreover, the change in the proportion of ethnic minorities has no additional effect.

What also becomes clear is that the small effects of ethnic concentration disappear in the analyses when the degree of contact with the indigenous population is fed into the model (model 4). In this analysis, contacts with indigenous people were measured by combining two items: contacts with indigenous people in leisure time and visits of indigenous friends or neighbours. This results in a reliable scale running from 0 to 100, where 0 is no contact at all and 100 is intensive contact (Cronbach's alpha $= 0.83$). The finding means that social contacts play a role in the relationship between ethnic concentration and language proficiency. In neighbourhoods with high proportions of non-Western ethnic minorities, the minorities have a weaker command of the Dutch language, because they have fewer contacts with the indigenous Dutch.

The analysis also reveals that members of ethnic minorities who have a good deal of contact with indigenous Dutch people have a substantially better command of Dutch, after controlling for all the other characteristics, than those who have little or no contact with native Dutch-speakers. The correlation between contact frequency and language proficiency is moreover strong, roughly comparable with the correlation between education level and language proficiency. Once again, the qualification must be made here that it is impossible to make any statements about causality. If ethnic minorities have more contacts with the indigenous population, their proficiency in Dutch will improve, but having a better command of Dutch naturally also means that contacts are (or can be) more readily initiated.

As stated earlier, it is striking that refugees, despite their relatively short period in the Netherlands, already speak Dutch so well. Based on the analysis performed here, something more can be said about the reasons for this. The most important factor is found to be the higher education level of these groups. This applies for all refugee groups except Somalis, who have a predominantly low education level (comparable with Turks and Moroccans). Approximately 40 per cent of the lead in the command of Dutch by Afghans, Iraqis and Iranians over the group with the weakest command of the language, the Turkish group, is attributable to the higher education level of these groups. The fact that education level explains part of the differences between groups in terms of their command of the Dutch language can be seen from the declining effects of ethnic origin between models 1 and 2. In addition, the better language proficiency of refugees, as well as of Antilleans and Surinamese, is connected to the fact that compared with Turks and Moroccans they have more contacts with the indigenous population. This can be seen from the declining effects of ethnic origin between models 3 and 4 when social contacts are incorporated in the model. However, differences in education level have a bigger effect.

Finally, the analyses make clear that the degree of ethnic concentration in a neighbourhood hardly plays any role in explaining the differences in language proficiency between the traditional and new groups. This can be seen from the only small decreases in the effects of ethnic origin when the percentage of non-Western residents is included into the model (compare model 2 with model 3 in Table 6). In other words, the fact that refugee groups speak Dutch better than the traditional immigrant groups has nothing to do with the fact that refugees live in less concentrated neighbourhoods.

Inter-ethnic contact important for mutual acceptance. Tables 7 and 8 present findings on stereotypical attitudes. First, attitudes of the indigenous Dutch towards minority groups, in this case Moroccans (Table 7) are discussed. The findings reveal that men as well as the lower-educated hold significantly more negative views about characteristics of Moroccans. Young people also hold more negative views (model 1). However, this is not a linear effect (see the quadratic effect of age): older persons hold negative views to roughly the same extent as the young. The middle-aged population embraces more positive stereotypes about Moroccans than either the young or the elderly.

The percentage of non-Western citizens in a neighbourhood does not affect negative stereotypes (model 2). In addition, no curvilinear effect of the proportion of non-Western inhabitants could be observed (the quadratic term is not statistically significant). This implies that it is not the case that attitudes are most negative in neighbourhoods with a large minority of non-Western citizens, while they are more positive in 'white' or 'black' neighbourhoods. However, the change in the percentage of non-Western citizens does exert an influence: the greater the increase in the proportion of non-Western citizens in a neighbourhood, the more negative attitudes towards Moroccans tend to be. The question is how this can be explained. Comparing model 2 with model 3 reveals that it can hardly be attributed to the fact that indigenous people in rapidly changing neighbourhoods maintain

Table 7. Multi-level regression analysis of stereotypical attitudes towards Moroccans (0 to 100, 100 = very positive) by relevant individual and neighbourhood characteristics, indigenous Dutch[a]

	Model 1	Model 2	Model 3	Model 4
Intercept	36.19	36.94	35.77	73.26
Gender (female = ref. cat.)	–	–	–	–
male	−3.37	−3.36	−3.16	−1.63
Age	0.73	0.73	0.71	0.45
(Age)^2	−0.01	−0.01	−0.01	−0.01
Education level[b]	1.57	1.56	1.49	n.s.
Working (non-working = ref. cat.)	–	–	–	–
working	n.s.	n.s.	n.s.	n.s.
Household income	n.s.	n.s.	n.s.	−0.59
% non-Western in neighbourhood		n.s.	n.s.	n.s.
Change in % non-Western in neighbourhood		−0.58	−0.53	n.s.
Contacts with ethnic minorities			0.14	0.08
Perceived ethnic threat				−0.50
Variance components				
between neighbourhoods	9.17	8.00	6.48	2.34
(% explained compared to intercept model)	(14%)	(25%)	(40%)	(78%)
between individuals	391.35	391.03	383.33	305.35

[a]Significance at $p < .05$; n.s. = no significance.
[b]Education is measured in seven categories, from no education/maximum primary school to higher education.

Table 8. Multi level regression analysis of stereotypical attitudes towards indigenous Dutch (0 to 100, 100 = very positive) by relevant individual and neighbourhood characteristics, ethnic minorities[a]

	Model 1	Model 2	Model 3	Model 4
Intercept	73.08	73.73	75.58	70.04
Ethnic group (Surinamese = ref. cat.)	–	–	–	–
Turks	−8.58	−9.29	−9.22	−7.57
Moroccans	n.s.	n.s.	n.s.	n.s.
Antilleans	−2.38	−2.45	−2.55	−2.70
Migration type (second generation = ref. cat.)		–	–	–
in-between generation		n.s.	n.s.	n.s.
marriage migrants		n.s.	n.s.	n.s.
first generation >1980		n.s.	n.s.	n.s.
first generation ≤1980		n.s.	n.s.	n.s.
Gender (female = ref. cat.)		–	–	–
male		1.46	1.39	1.36
Age[b]		n.s.	n.s.	n.s.
Education level[c]		n.s.	n.s.	−0.45
Working (non-working = ref. cat.)		–	–	–
working		n.s.	n.s.	n.s.
Household income		n.s.	n.s.	n.s.
% non-Western in neighbourhood			n.s.	n.s.
Change in % non-Western in neighbourhood			*−0.17*	n.s.
Contacts with indigenous Dutch				0.09
Variance components				
between neighbourhoods	10.46	10.39	9.46	8.33
(% explained compared to intercept model)	(9%)	(10%)	(18%)	(27%)
between individuals	219.15	218.12	218.06	212.75

Notes: [a]Significance at $p < 0.05$; italic: significance at $p < 0.10$; n.s. = no significance.
[b]There is no quadratic effect of age in this analysis.
[c]Education is measured in seven categories, from no education/maximum primary school to higher education.

fewer social contacts with ethnic minorities. Of much greater importance is the higher degree of perceived ethnic threat: this variable entirely explains the effect of the change in the proportion of non-Western inhabitants in the neighbourhood (model 4). People living in neighbourhoods where the ethnic composition has changed dramatically feel more threatened by the presence of ethnic minorities. As a consequence, they hold more negative opinions about characteristics of ethnic minorities (in this case Moroccans).

Perceptions of ethnic threat also explain the effect of education level on negative stereotypes (see Table 6). The lower-educated are more negative in their views about Moroccans, because they feel more threatened by ethnic minorities than the better educated. Differences between men and women and between age groups also vanish after controlling for perceived ethnic threat.

In short, mechanisms of ethnic competition play an important role in fostering negative stereotypes of ethnic minorities. However, the analyses also support the contact hypothesis. As the paper has shown, maintaining social contact with ethnic minority groups has a substantial effect on stereotypes; people who maintain more intensive contact with members of ethnic minority groups hold much more positive views on (in this case) Moroccans. In this respect the expression 'unknown, unloved' can be said to hold. In fact this relationship is probably more one of reciprocity than of one-way causality. Maintaining social contacts with ethnic out-groups will cause attitudes towards these groups to become more positive, while thinking more positively about other ethnic groups will also induce people to establish more friendly relations with members of those groups.

A final comment on Table 7 concerns the changes in the variance components between neighbourhoods when individual and neighbourhood characteristics are included (see the variance components in Table 7). Including individual characteristics leads to a slight decrease in the variance between neighbourhoods (model 1). This means that differences in stereotypes between neighbourhoods are only partly due to differences in the composition of the population in those neighbourhoods (e.g. education level, etc.). The inclusion of contextual neighbourhood characteristics (in this case the change in the proportion of ethnic minorities in the neighbourhood), as well as the extent of inter-ethnic contacts and perceived ethnic threat, reduces the variance at the contextual level even further (models 2 to 4). What does this mean? The existence of negative stereotypes about Moroccans in a neighbourhood depends on several factors: (1) the socio-economic composition of the neighbourhood; (2) the change in the proportion of members of non-Western ethnic minorities in the neighbourhood in the past few years; (3) the smaller number of contacts between the majority and minority groups in the neighbourhood; and (4) the higher perceived threat from ethnic minorities in this neighbourhood. To put these findings into perspective, it should be noted that the variation in attitudes at the individual level is by far larger than at the neighbourhood level: differences in stereotypical attitudes between neighbourhoods are thus much less relevant than individual differences.

So far the paper has looked at the attitudes of the indigenous majority towards minority groups; but how do these minority groups feel about the indigenous Dutch? First, there is a look at to what extent stereotypical attitudes on the part of members of ethnic minority groups depend on individual and neighbourhood characteristics (Table 8). As can be seen, Turks apply the most negative stereotypes to the indigenous Dutch, followed by Antilleans. No significant differences were found between the attitudes of the Surinamese and Moroccans. In contrast to the findings for the indigenous Dutch, here demographic and socio-economic characteristics have hardly any effect on stereotypical attitudes. Moreover, the effect of gender is the opposite of that found among the indigenous Dutch: women from ethnic minority groups think more negatively about the indigenous Dutch than men. Moreover, there is little generational change in the perception of the indigenous Dutch: the stereotypical attitudes of the second generation of immigrants are no different from those of the first generation.

The proportion of non-Western citizens in a neighbourhood does not influence the stereotypical ideas of minorities about the indigenous Dutch. However, recent changes in these proportions do. The greater the increase in the proportion of non-Western citizens in a neighbourhood, the more negative are the opinions of the indigenous Dutch, but this effect is weak (only significant at the 10 per cent level). The question of why this effect appears can be found in the last model in Table 8, where social contacts with indigenous Dutch are included into the model. For reasons of comparability with the analysis on the second-language proficiency of ethnic minorities and the analysis on attitudes among the indigenous Dutch, contacts with indigenous people were measured by combining the two items: contacts with indigenous people in leisure time and visits of indigenous friends or neighbours (scale running from 0 to 100, where 0 is no contact at all and 100 is intensive contact). Again, the contact hypothesis holds: ethnic minorities who maintain more social contacts with indigenous Dutch citizens uphold fewer negative stereotypes. Once more the saying 'unknown, unloved' applies. Moreover, inter-ethnic contacts mediate the relationship between a change in the percentage of non-Western citizens and negative stereotypes (a comparison of models 3 and 4 shows that the relationship becomes insignificant). From this it is inferred that ethnic minorities in a rapidly changing neighbourhood (in terms of proportion of non-Western citizens), are less positive in their views of the indigenous Dutch because they maintain fewer contacts with them.

Previous research has shown that the effects of individual characteristics on prejudice vary with the proportion of ethnic minorities at the contextual level (Kunovich, 2004; Scheepers et al., 2002). These varying effects can be expected to occur particularly in the relationship between social contacts and inter-ethnic attitudes between majority and minority groups. Therefore, the study also examined whether the effects of social contacts vary between neighbourhoods (a random slope model, not shown in the table but available from the authors on request). This random effect turned out to be present for stereotypical attitudes of ethnic minorities towards the indigenous Dutch (no variation in effects was found in the opposite direction). To explain these varying effects, an interaction is included in the model between the proportion of non-Western citizens in a neighbourhood and the amount of contact at the individual level (a 'cross-level interaction effect'). This interaction effect turned out to be small, but statistically significant. This means that although more inter-ethnic contacts lead to less negative stereotypes, this effect loses its importance at high levels of ethnic concentration: in ethnically concentrated neighbourhoods inter-ethnic contacts are less relevant in determining the attitudes of ethnic minorities towards the indigenous Dutch.

A final counter-intuitive finding is that the effect of education turns positive as soon as social contacts are brought into the model (model 4). The previous finding, namely that earlier models in Table 8 show no educational effect is striking in itself, especially since research in the field of prejudice has always suggested strong educational effects for majority groups (e.g. Quillian, 1995): the better educated are generally less prejudiced than the lower-educated. However, this general finding does not appear to hold for ethnic minorities in the Netherlands. Moreover, when inter-ethnic contacts are taken into account the effect of education actually operates in the reverse direction from that among the indigenous Dutch: better-educated members of ethnic minorities are more negative about the indigenous Dutch than the lower-educated. This is known as a 'suppressor effect': the effect of education was suppressed in previous models because social contacts were not taken into account. These social contacts with indigenous Dutch are more prevalent among better-educated members of minorities than among their lower-educated group members (and the correlation between education level and inter-ethnic contact is substantial for ethnic minority groups).

Finally, there is a closer look at changes in the variances between neighbourhoods as a consequence of including individual and neighbourhood characteristics (see the variance components in Table 8). This reveals that differences between neighbourhoods in negative stereotypes held by ethnic minority groups are not explained by the demographic and socio-economic composition of the neighbourhood (model 2). However, differences between neighbourhoods in negative stereotypes do correlate with changes in the proportion of non-Western citizens in the past five years (model 3), as well as with differences in inter-ethnic contacts between different neighbourhoods (model 4).

However, a large part of the differences between neighbourhoods remains unexplained (more so than among the indigenous Dutch).

Conclusions

This paper has shown that the observed social distance between different ethnic groups in the Netherlands has a great deal to do with the residential segregation of different population groups. Contact of ethnic minorities with the indigenous population is lowest in neighbourhoods containing large numbers of ethnic minorities. This applies in particular for Amsterdam, Rotterdam and The Hague, where one in three residents is now of non-Western origin. Homogeneous neighbourhoods thus reinforce ethnically homogeneous contacts. Therefore, the neighbourhood is a significant factor in the contacts between different population groups. The identified social distance is due not only to the fairly strong orientation of Turks and Moroccans, in particular, towards their own ethnic group, but also to the low level of contacts by the native population with ethnic minorities. Among other things this has to do with the residential segregation of the ethnic and native communities. Indigenous Dutch people come into contact with members of minorities more often if they live in a mixed neighbourhood. Where there is the opportunity for contact, as in mixed neighbourhoods, this is also more likely to take place. However, there is a limit to the effect of the presence of ethnic minorities in the neighbourhood. The findings here suggest a tipping point at 50 per cent: if more than half the residents are members of non-Western ethnic minorities, contact by the native Dutch with ethnic populations in fact generally declines.

One development is that in the last 10 years the frequency of social contact with the native population by Turks and Moroccans has declined, while among Surinamese and Antilleans it has stabilized (Gijsberts & Dagevos, 2005). The social distance from the native population is thus not reducing. This development is linked to the steady rise in the numbers of ethnic minorities living in the large cities. This alone has greatly increased the chances that ethnic minorities will meet members of their own group. A further factor is the continuing high influx of Turkish and Moroccan 'marriage migrants' who, as other studies have shown, remain largely ensconced in their own community. If the observed correlation is indicative of an independent causal effect of the neighbourhood, this naturally exacerbates the problem of, in this instance voluntary, social segregation.

Table 9 summarizes the main findings of this paper. Three things are immediately apparent. First, high concentrations of ethnic minorities in a neighbourhood have consequences mainly for the degree of contact between the indigenous and ethnic populations. Moreover, a rapid change in these concentrations is seen as negative by indigenous residents (affecting both their contacts with and their views on ethnic minorities). Finally, the Table highlights the importance of inter-ethnic contact for command of the Dutch language among ethnic minority groups and for mutual acceptance between ethnic minorities and the Dutch.

To a large extent, the correlation between ethnic concentration and language depends on the contacts between the ethnic and indigenous populations. The concentrations of ethnic minorities in certain neighbourhoods are an obstacle to contacts between minorities and natives, and it is precisely these contacts that are important for gaining a rapid and good command of the Dutch language. Ethnic minorities with frequent contacts with indigenous Dutch citizens have a significantly better command of Dutch than those who have little or no contact with native Dutch-speakers. The fact that Turks have the poorest command

Table 9. Summary of the relations found between the concentrations of ethnic minorities in a neighbourhood, the change in those concentrations, the degree of inter-ethnic contact and the dependent variables (contacts, language and attitudes)

	% minorities in neighbourhood	Change in % minorities in neighbourhood	Inter-ethnic contact
Ethnic minorities			
inter-ethnic contact	−	0	
command of Dutch language	(−)	0	+
stereotypical attitudes	0	(−)	+
Indigenous population			
inter-ethnic contact	+	−	
stereotypical attitudes	0	−	+

Notes: + = positive effect; − = negative effect; (−) = slight negative effect; 0 = no (significant) effect; empty cell = relationship not studied.

of Dutch of all ethnic minority groups, for example, has much to do with the strong orientation of Turks towards their own ethnic group; stronger than among any other minority group living in the Netherlands, as the analyses have shown. A poor command of the language also naturally presents a considerable obstacle to contacts with the indigenous population and is therefore an important hindrance to the integration of minorities into Dutch society.

This paper shows that contacts between the ethnic and indigenous population are also important in promoting mutual acceptance. A greater social distance between population groups is accompanied by negative stereotyping. A rapid influx of ethnic minorities into a neighbourhood leads the ethnic and native populations to form a more negative image of each other. This is because indigenous people living in these neighbourhoods feel more threatened by the presence of ethnic minorities than residents of neighbourhoods where the ethnic mix has not changed so quickly. It also has to do with the fact that there are fewer contacts between the native and ethnic population groups in neighbourhoods where the ethnic population has increased rapidly. It is precisely these social contacts which tend to mitigate the mutual views; the more time indigenous and ethnic minority people spend with each other in their free time, and the more they visit each other at home and in their neighbourhood, the more positive are their views of each other. Familiarity thus does indeed breed mutual acceptance, an important finding in the present social debate in which tensions between ethnic groups appear to becoming ever more visible.

Finally, the importance of education for the integration of minorities is emphasized. Despite the relatively short time they have spent in the Netherlands, the fact that refugees have established so many contacts with the indigenous population and often already have a good command of the Dutch language, has a great deal to do with the fact that their education level is generally higher. All manner of analyses reaffirm the central role of education in the social and cultural integration of minorities (Dagevos *et al.*, 2003; Hagendoorn *et al.*, 2003). Therefore, the importance of education as a driver of integration cannot be stressed often enough. A good education is not only important in enabling immigrants to attain a good socio-economic position, but also benefits their socio-cultural integration; better-educated members of ethnic minorities have more contacts with the native population, speak the Dutch language better and have a positive influence on their children's command of the language. However, the better-educated members of ethnic minorities turned out to be more negative about the indigenous Dutch than the lower educated. This finding about negative views among the more educated can be interpreted as an indication of stagnating integration. Better education might get someone into the labour market and give them a better command of the Dutch language, but they might end up liking the indigenous Dutch less. It may be connected with the fact that the higher educated more than anyone experience discrimination and other barriers in their social careers. Moreover, they are probably more aware than the lower-educated members of minorities of the recent hardening of attitudes in the media coverage and political debate on ethnic minorities. This interpretation deserves more research.

The findings in this paper also underline the relevance of the neighbourhood for the socio-cultural integration of immigrants. Continuing the recently initiated restructuring of neighbourhoods in the Netherlands with the aim of mixing different population groups therefore offers opportunities in this regard. The pressure on the major cities is likely to increase further in the years ahead due to the influx of low-opportunity newcomers and the move of the indigenous and, to an increasing extent, ethnic middle class out of the cities. The term 'ethnic flight' has already been used in this connection. The above findings are a stark illustration that maximum efforts should be made to persuade the high-potential middle class, both indigenous and ethnic minority, to stay in the large cities. Better-educated members of ethnic minorities generally have a much stronger orientation towards Dutch society. Conversely, the better-educated members of the native Dutch population generally have more contact with members of ethnic minorities and also have a more positive image of them. Precisely these groups can stimulate mutual contacts between different ethnic groups.

Acknowledgements

This paper recapitulates a more extensive study published (in Dutch) by the Social and Cultural Planning Office in 2005, entitled 'Love thy Neighbour? The Influence of Ethnic Concentration on Integration and Inter-ethnic Attitudes' (translated from Dutch).

References

Billiet, J., Eisinga, R. & Scheepers, P. (1996) Ethnocentrism in the low countries, a comparative perspective, *New Community, European Journal on Migration and Ethnic Relations*, 3, pp. 401–416.
Blalock, H. M. (1967) *Toward a Theory of Minority Group Relations* (New York: John Wiley and Sons).
Bobo, L. (1988) Group conflict, prejudice and the paradox of contemporary racial attitudes, in: P. Katz & D. Taylor (Eds) *Eliminating Racism. Profiles in Controversy* (New York: Plenum Press).
Bolt, G. (2004) Over spreidingsbeleid en drijfzand (On dispersion policy and quicksand), *Migrantenstudies*, 20, pp. 60–73.
Brown, R. & Hewstone, M. (2005) An integrative theory of intergroup contact, in: M. P. Zanna (Ed.) *Advances in Experimental Social Psychology*, Vol. 37 (Amsterdam: Elsevier).
Bryk, A. & Raudenbusch, S. (1992) *Hierarchical Linear Models: Application and Data Analysis Methods* (Newbury Park: Sage).
Buck, N. (2001) Identifying neighbourhood effects on social exclusion, *Urban Studies*, 12, pp. 2251–2275.
Carliner, G. (2000) The language ability of US immigrants: assimilation and cohort effects, *International Migration Review*, 34, pp. 158–182.
Chiswick, B. R. & Miller, P. W. (2001) A model of destination-language acquisition: application to male immigrants in Canada, *Demography*, 38, pp. 391–409.
Clark, W. A. V. (1986) Residential segregation in American cities: a review and interpretation, *Population Research and Policy Review*, 5, pp. 95–127.

Clark, W. A. V. (1993) Neighborhood tipping in a multiethnic/racial context, *Journal of Urban Affairs*, 15, pp. 161–172.

Coenders, M. & Scheepers, P. (1998) Support for ethnic discrimination in the Netherlands 1979–1993, effects of period, cohort and individual characteristics, *European Sociological Review*, 4, pp. 405–422.

Dagevos, J., Gijsberts, M. & Van Praag, C. (Eds) (2003) *Rapportage Minderheden 2003 (Report on Ethnic Minorities 2003)* (The Hague: Social and Cultural Planning Office).

Driessen, G., Doesborgh, J., Ledoux, G., Van der Veen, I. & Vergeer, M. (2003) *Sociale Integratie in het Primair Onderwijs (Social Integration in Primary Education)* (Amsterdam: SCO-Kohnstamm Instituut/Nijmegen: ITS).

Forbes, H. D. (1997) *Ethnic Conflict, Commerce, Culture and the Contact Hypothesis* (New Haven, CT: Yale University Press).

Galster, G. & Zobel, A. (1998) Will dispersed housing programmes reduce social problems in the US?, *Housing Studies*, 13, pp. 605–622.

Gijsberts, M. (2004) *Ethnic Minorities and Integration. Outlook for the Future* (The Hague: Social and Cultural Planning Office).

Gijsberts, M. & Dagevos, J. (2005) *Uit Elkaars Buurt. De Invloed van Etnische Concentratie op Integratie en Beeldvorming (Love thy Neighbour? The Influence of Ethnic Concentration on Integration and Interethnic Attitudes)* (The Hague: Social and Cultural Planning Office).

Gijsberts, M., Hagendoorn, L. & Scheepers, P. (Eds) (2004) *Nationalism and Exclusion of Migrants. Cross-National Comparisons* (Aldershot: Ashgate).

Goering, J. M. (1978) Neighborhood tipping and racial transition: a review of social science evidence, *Journal of the American Institute of Planners*, 44, pp. 68–88.

Gordon, M. (1964) *Assimilation in American Life. The Role of Race, Religion and National Origins* (New York: Oxford University Press).

Granovetter, M. S. (1973) The strength of weak ties, *American Journal of Sociology*, 78, pp. 1360–1380.

Hagendoorn, L., Veenman, J. & Vollebergh, W. (Eds) (2003) *Integrating Immigrants in the Netherlands. Cultural versus Socio-Economic Integration* (Aldershot: Ashgate).

Hamburger, J. & Hewstone, M. (1997) Inter-ethnic contact as a predictor of blatant and subtle prejudice: test of a model in four West European nations, *British Journal of Social Psychology*, 36, pp. 173–190.

Jasso, G. & Rosenzweig, M. R. (1990) *The New Chosen People: Immigrants in the United States* (New York: Russell Sage Foundation).

Johnson, M. P., Ladd, H. F. & Ludwig, J. (2002) The benefits and costs of residential mobility programmes for the poor, *Housing Studies*, 17, pp. 125–138.

Kiehl, M. & Werner, H. (1998) *The Labour Market Situation of EU and of Third Country Nationals in the European Union. Labour Market Topics No. 32* (Nurnberg: Institut fur Arbeitsmarkt- und Berufschforschung der Bundesanstalt fur Arbeit).

Kunovich, R. (2004) Social structural position and prejudice: an exploration of cross-national differences in regression slopes, *Social Science Research*, 33, pp. 20–44.

McCulloch, A. (2001) Ward-level deprivation and individual social and economic outcomes in the British Household Panel Study, *Environment and Planning*, 33, pp. 667–684.

Olzak, S. (1992) *The Dynamics of Ethnic Competition and Conflict* (Stanford: Stanford University Press).

Ostendorf, W. & Musterd, S. (2005) Segregatie en integratie. Feiten en visies (Segregation and integration. Facts and views), in: P. Brassé & H. Krijnen (Eds) *Gescheiden of Gemengd. Een Verkenning van Etnische Concentratie op School en in de Wijk* (Utrecht: Forum).

Park, R. E. (1928) Human migration and the marginal man, *American Journal of Sociology*, 33, pp. 81–117.

Pettigrew, T. & Tropp, L. R. (2006) A meta-analytic test of intergroup contact theory, *Journal of Personality and Social Psychology*, 90, pp. 751–783.

Portes, A. & Zhou, M. (1994) Should immigrants assimilate?, *Public Interest*, 18, pp. 116–125.

Quillian, L. (1995) Prejudice as a response to perceived group threat: population composition and anti-immigrant and racial prejudice in Europe, *American Sociological Review*, 60, pp. 816–860.

Sampson, R. J., Raudenbusch, S. & Earls, F. (1997) Neighbourhoods and violent crime: a multilevel study of collective efficacy, *Science*, 277, pp. 918–924.

Sampson, R. J., Morenoff, J. D. & Gannon-Rowley, T. (2002) Assessing 'neighbourhood effects': social processes and new directions in research, *Annual Review of Sociology*, 28, pp. 443–478.

Scheepers, P., Gijsberts, M. & Coenders, M. (2002) Ethnic exclusionism in European countries. Public opposition to civil rights for legal migrants as a response to perceived ethnic threat, *European Sociological Review*, 18, pp. 17–34.
SCP/WODC/CBS (2005) *Jaarrapport Integratie 2005 (Annual Report on Integration 2005)* (The Hague: Social and Cultural Planning Office/WODC/Statistics Netherlands).
Snijder, T. & Bosker, R. (1999) *Multilevel Analysis: An Introduction to Basic and Advanced Multilevel Modelling* (London: Sage).
Taylor, M. C. (1998) How white attitudes vary with the racial composition of local populations: numbers count, *American Sociological Review*, 63, pp. 512–535.
Tesser, P. T. M., Van Praag, C. S., Van Dugteren, F., Herweijer, L. J. & Van der Wouden, H. C. (1995) *Rapportage Minderheden 1995. Concentratie en Segregatie (Report on Ethnic Minorities 1995. Concentration and Segregation)* (Rijswijk/The Hague: Social and Cultural Planning Office).
Uunk, W. & Dominguez Martinez, S. (2002) *Wijken in Beweging. Migratie in en uit Concentratiewijken (Neighbourhoods in Motion. Migration into and out of Concentration Neighbourhoods)* (Assen: Van Gorcum).
Van der Laan Bouma-Doff, W. (2005) *De Buurt als Belemmering? (The Neighbourhood as an Obstacle?)* (Assen: Van Gorcum).
Van Praag, C. (2003) Demografie (Demography), in: J. Dagevos, M. Gijsberts & C. Van Praag (Eds) *Rapportage Minderheden 2003. Onderwijs, Arbeid en Sociaal-Culturele Integratie (Report on Ethnic Minorities 2003. Education, Labour Market and Socio-Cultural Integration)* (The Hague: Social and Cultural Planning Office).
Van Tubbergen, F. & Kalmijn, M. (2005) Destination-language proficiency in cross-national perspective: a study of immigrant groups in nine Western countries, *American Journal of Sociology*, 110, pp. 1412–1457.
Van Wilsem, J., Wittebrood, K. & De Graaf, N. D. (2006) Socioeconomic dynamics in the neighborhoods and the risk of crime victimization. A multilevel study of improving, declining, and stable areas in the Netherlands, *Social Problems*, 53, pp. 226–247.
Veldboer, L. & Duyvendak, J. W. (2004) Wonen en integratiebeleid: een gemengd beeld (Housing and integration policy: a mixed picture), *Sociologische Gids*, 51, pp. 36–52.
Wilson, W. J. (1987) *The Truly Disadvantaged. The Inner City, the Underclass and Public Policy* (Chicago/London: University of Chicago Press).

Intergenerational Neighborhood-Type Mobility: Examining Differences between Blacks and Whites

THOMAS P. VARTANIAN, PAGE WALKER BUCK & PHILIP GLEASON

Introduction

The issue of neighborhood effects has been a focus of much social science enquiry over the last decade, spurred largely by the work of Wilson (1987). He argues that neighborhood disadvantage plays a vital role in preventing low-income blacks from getting good jobs and escaping poverty, with chronic unemployment and social isolation from the mainstream economy causing a breakdown of social function. These types of poor neighborhood conditions have been hypothesized to have deleterious effects on virtually all forms of human and social capital and other outcomes, including education, income, welfare use, health outcomes, social support networks and civic engagement (Jencks & Mayer, 1990; McClintock *et al.*, 2005; Wilson, 1987). While most of this literature focuses on child and adolescent outcomes, there is also evidence that neighborhoods have effects on adults. For example, Mendenhall *et al.* (2005) find that the level of neighborhood resources affects women's welfare receipt and employment. Others find that neighborhood conditions affect annual hours of work (Weinberg *et al.*, 2004) and health outcomes (McClintock *et al.*, 2005; Borrell *et al.*, 2003), often linking high crime rates and poor housing conditions to these outcomes.

One important question that arises from this literature is what childhood factors lead people to live in these types of disadvantaged neighborhoods as adults. More specifically, how likely is it that children who grow up in poor neighborhoods will end up in the same types of neighborhoods as adults? Drawing on existing work (Duncan & Raudenbush, 2001; Galster & Killen, 1995; Jencks & Mayer, 1990; Sampson & Wilson, 1995; Wilson, 1987), the paper hypothesizes that the experience of childhood residential context influences adult neighborhood outcomes by conditioning and often constraining the choice of where one lives as an adult. In part, this occurs through the accumulation, or lack thereof, of social and human capital, which stems from the quality of child neighborhoods including educational, occupational and cultural resources. In addition, adult residential choice is a function of the preferences and perceptions that are shaped by the social processes of childhood neighborhood experiences.

Previous Literature

While there are no studies on intergenerational neighborhood quality in particular, this study is located within research on intergenerational socio-economic mobility, residential mobility and neighborhood effect theories. Intergenerational socio-economic mobility has been the long-standing focus of much scholarly work, prompted initially by Blau & Duncan's (1967) seminal work, *American Occupational Structure*. Studies have estimated intergenerational income correlations in the range of 0.35 to 0.49 (Chadwick & Solon, 2002; Lee & Solon, 2005; Zimmerman, 1992), earnings correlations as high as 0.60 (Mazumder, 2003), and wealth correlations before bequests of 0.37 (Charles & Hurst, 2003). The extent to which the intergenerational transmission of economic success is a function of neighborhood mobility is an area that has received little attention in the economic mobility literature (Bowles & Gintis, 2002). Sociologists have studied the probability of 'escaping' distressed neighborhoods in adulthood (Crowder & South, 2005; Massey *et al.*, 1994; Quillian, 1999), however no studies have examined the intergenerational nature of neighborhood mobility. The ability to move out of a distressed neighborhood may well be a factor in predicting one's economic mobility.

Theories of residential mobility suggest that the ability to move to a more desirable neighborhood is a function of three primary factors: human capital, life-cycle development and place stratification (Verma, 2003). Human and other forms of capital, including education, income and stable employment, as well as life-cycle factors such as age, marital status and fertility are often considered to be the foundations of residential mobility. Whereas increases in socio-economic status (SES) have been found to promote mobility into advantaged neighborhoods (Rossi, 1980; South & Crowder, 1997), welfare receipt, public housing (Kasarda, 1988), and homeownership (South & Crowder, 1997) have been found to be limiting. However, these frequently cited factors do not operate equally across races. Blacks, for example, are less likely to translate human capital into residential mobility (South & Deane, 1993) due to what some suggest is place stratification (South & Crowder, 1997). That is, neighborhoods are sorted along racial and ethnic lines, such that minorities end up living in the most disadvantaged areas because of social preferences, hierarchies, and discrimination (Logan & Alba, 1993). Compared with whites, blacks live in significantly worse neighborhoods with fewer resources available to them (Crowder & South, 2005; Massey et al., 1994; Quillian, 2003; Timberlake, 2002). Residential segregation is further maintained in large part by the fact that whites overwhelmingly avoid predominantly black and racially mixed neighborhoods (Massey & Denton, 1993; Quillian, 2002), and are more able and more likely to move out of poor neighborhoods (South & Crowder, 1997). However, while considering both individual and structural factors in the study of residential mobility, none of this research takes into account the impact of childhood residence on adult neighborhoods. Net of individual and structural level factors, to what degree does childhood neighborhood quality affect where one lives as an adult?

It is suggested that child neighborhood context influences adult neighborhood residence by conditioning and constraining the choices that adults can make about where they live. Previous literature suggests that this operates through mechanisms of residential advantage. The theory of neighborhood advantage (Vartanian & Buck, 2005) is a combination of several theories originally defined by Jencks & Mayer (1990): collective socialization, social isolation and institutional resources. It suggests that the greater the resources and other advantages of good neighborhoods during childhood, including exposure to positive role models and institutional resources, the better the adult outcomes. At the same time, negative neighborhood conditions resulting from social isolation from such positive role models and community resources, coupled with a higher exposure to crime, have negative intergenerational effects (Aaronson, 1998; Mendenhall et al., 2005). The epidemic theory of neighborhood disadvantage (Crane, 1991) suggests that when conditions reach a certain level of disadvantage, the negative effects become highly contagious. The resulting effect of these factors is that adult residential choice is a function of the accumulation of social and human capital, which stems in part from the quality of child neighborhoods.

The choice of adult neighborhoods may also be conditioned and constrained by one's childhood residential experience if neighborhoods are understood as "cognitive landscapes" through which children develop "ecologically structured social perceptions" (Sampson & Wilson, 1995, p. 46). In this sense, neighborhood characteristics shape the way in which people perceive their general life opportunities. This may be especially true for those living in the most disadvantaged neighborhoods and probably occurs through perceptions of group status, a theory supported by the work of Bobo & Zubrinsky (1996). The present paper argues that living in highly disenfranchised neighborhoods as a child not only affects human and social capital accumulation, but also shapes attitudes and preferences about where one can and should live as an adult based on perceptions of group status.

Knowing the extent to which adult neighborhood quality is a function of where one lives as a child has the potential to add an important new dimension to existing work on neighborhood effects and SES mobility in the US. In particular, this knowledge may provide insight into the mechanisms through which residential experiences produce inequality. Here, neighborhood quality in childhood is measured as a proxy for the experience of these social processes and mechanisms.

In this regard, the study seeks to answer three primary questions. First, is there an intergenerational component to neighborhood quality whereby the type of neighborhood a person lives in as a child influences the type of neighborhood he or she lives in as an adult? Second, does the relationship between child and adult neighborhood quality vary by race? Third, is this relationship non-linear? More specifically, is there any evidence of the epidemic theory of neighborhood effects, with those in the worst neighborhoods most strongly influenced by these neighborhood conditions?

Methods

Estimating causal inference in neighborhood studies is confounded by the related issues of simultaneity, omitted variable bias, and endogenous membership (Leventhal & Brooks-Gunn, 2000; Duncan & Raudenbush, 2001; Dietz, 2002). The challenge is that individuals and households are not exogenously placed in particular neighborhoods, but live there either out of choice or because of their characteristics. As described below, a fixed effects (FE) model is used to address this challenge.

The following equation shows a model of the determinants of adult neighborhood conditions:

$$Y_{ij} = \alpha_j + \beta_1 FP_j + \beta_2 FIV_{ij} + \gamma N_{ij} + \mu_{ij}$$

Here, FP_j represents a set of observed permanent characteristics of family j, FIV_{ij} represents a set of time varying characteristics of family j and individual i, N_{ij} represents characteristics of the neighborhood that individual i lived in as a child, μ_{ij} is the error term, β_1, β_2, and γ are coefficients to be estimated, and α_j is the family-specific intercept. This intercept, or a fixed family effect, represents unobserved time invariant family characteristics that influence adult neighborhood conditions. The dependent variable in the model, Y_{ij}, is a measure of the quality of the neighborhood that individual i from family j lives in as an adult. The key parameter that we will be estimating in this model is γ, the neighborhood effect.

Under the assumption that there are no family fixed effects (in other words, that $\alpha_j = \alpha$), this model can be estimated using ordinary least squares (OLS) with robust standard errors. However, if family fixed effects are correlated with an individual's childhood neighborhood, OLS estimates of the neighborhood effect will be biased. To estimate this fixed effects model, data are used from individuals in families with more than one child, and the family mean values are subtracted from each individual sibling's observation, as shown by:

$$Y_{ij} - Y_{\cdot j} = (\alpha_j - \alpha_j) + \beta_1 (FP_j - FP_{\cdot j}) + \beta_2 (FIV_{ij} - FIV_{\cdot j}) + \gamma (N_{ij} - N_{\cdot j}) + (\mu_{ij} - \mu_{\cdot j})$$

Because the fixed effect does not vary across siblings, it drops out of the model, and it is possible to effectively control for this fixed effect even though it is unobserved. The observed permanent family characteristics also drop out of the model. Neighborhood effects in this model are identified by variation in neighborhood characteristics across siblings. Almost all families in the sample show some variation in their neighborhood variables during childhood, either because the family moves or the neighborhoods in which they live change over time.

This model does not deal with the potential issue of unobserved time-varying differences between siblings that are both related to their childhood neighborhood conditions and that influence the outcome of interest (Aaronson, 1998; Vartanian & Buck,

2005). Differences may arise from differences in parental aspirations for their children or changes in parents' emotional states. It may also be that parenting is a learned process (Aaronson, 1998) whereby younger children may benefit from parental experience. Alternatively, parents may favor one child over another or use scarce resources for the benefit of the most promising child (Conley, 2004), which could influence both the type of neighborhood the child lives in and the later outcome for that child. To partly address this issue, numerous control variables are included in the models, including the birth order of the child.

In the model described above, childhood neighborhood conditions are entered into the model linearly. The study also estimates models in which childhood neighborhood conditions are allowed to influence adult neighborhood conditions non-linearly, through quadratics and splines for the childhood neighborhood index variable. Spline regressions fit a regression equation into a series of linear segments, and each segment may have a different slope (Galster et al., 2000).[1]

Childhood neighborhood characteristics might influence adult neighborhood conditions directly, or indirectly, through a preliminary impact on outcomes such as education or work experience. For example, bad neighborhood characteristics in childhood could lead to fewer years of education and ultimately leading to living in more disadvantaged neighborhoods as an adult. To assess whether the estimated relationship between childhood and adult neighborhood conditions is direct or indirect, the basic model is estimated both with and without control variables that reflect adult outcomes other than neighborhood conditions. In the models that exclude these adult outcomes, overall neighborhood effects are estimated, both direct and indirect. In the models that include these other adult outcomes, only direct neighborhood effects are estimated. Separate models are estimated for blacks and whites because of the vastly different types of neighborhoods they experience as children.

Data and Variables

Data from the 2001 Panel Study of Income Dynamics (PSID) are used, a nationally representative dataset that originally included approximately 5000 families in 1968 and included over 7400 families by 2001. The heads of the original households, or heads of households that have split off from the original households, have been interviewed annually from 1968 to 1997, and biannually since then. Among the original households, the poor and blacks were oversampled, with weights used to account for this oversampling and attrition.

A secondary source of data is the PSID Geocode File, which allows for the linking of decennial census data with PSID respondents. Census data are the source of information on the characteristics of PSID respondents' neighborhoods, operationally defined as their census tracts. This file contains 1970, 1980, 1990 and 2000 census data on factors such as the poverty rate and the proportion of households receiving public assistance income for the census tract in which each PSID respondent lived during each year of the survey.

To be included in the sample, respondents and their sibling(s) must have at least four years of childhood (age 0 to 18) data and at least one year of adult (over age 24) data. In some cases all 18 years of childhood data are examined, while in others it is only four. Kuntz et al. (2003) found that because childhood neighborhood characteristics are highly correlated across childhood years, even having a single year of neighborhood information produces only small errors-in-variables bias. Respondents must have at least one year of adult data, although some have more than 20. In all cases, childhood and adult variables are averaged over the period of observation to minimize the effects of single-year outliers. In models that include adult variables, the maximum age as an adult (including its quadratic) is included to control for the effects that work history, experience and earnings potential could have on the ability to live in a more affluent neighborhood. The white sample consists of 2265 observations and the black sample consists of 1863 observations. All observations have siblings in the sample in order to make the fixed effect and OLS models comparable. Models that also included children without siblings ($n = 2887$ for whites and $n = 2274$ for blacks) showed similar results to the OLS models.

The measure of neighborhood adult quality, both in childhood and adulthood, is comprised of several neighborhood variables. These variables include the neighborhood poverty rate, the percentage of households receiving public assistance income, the percentage of households headed by females, the percentage of households with income below $15 000 (in 2001 dollars), the percentage of households with income above $60 000 (in 2001 dollars), the percentage of households with income above the respondent's average family income, the percentage of households with income at the same level of income as the respondent's average family income, and the percentage of white residents. The selection of neighborhood income variables is based on previous research that shows both absolute and relative neighborhood income levels matter in assessing child and adult outcomes (Brooks-Gunn *et al.*, 1993; Duncan *et al.*, 1994; Ginther *et al.*, 2000; Vartanian & Buck, 2005). The proportion of white families is used as a proxy for the level of racial diversity in the neighborhood. Children who grow up in racially segregated neighborhoods may be less likely to live in areas with people of other races when they become adults (Ginther *et al.*, 2000). Ginther *et al.* find that the percentage of white families in the neighborhood affects such outcomes as completed schooling and non-marital births. Some studies (Brooks-Gunn *et al.*, 1993; Ginther *et al.*, 2000; Vartanian & Buck, 2005) also find that the proportion of female headed families in the neighborhood during childhood affects pre-adult and adult outcomes such as non-marital births, high school completion and income.

To serve as summary indicators of neighborhood quality, index variables are created through principal components analysis for both childhood and adulthood neighborhood quality. Each index takes into account information from the seven neighborhood variables for all observations. Details of the construction of the neighborhood quality index are shown in the Appendix Table A1. High quality neighborhoods, both in childhood and adulthood, have a high proportion of residents with high income, a low proportion of residents with low income, a low poverty rate, few households receiving public assistance, a high proportion of whites and primarily two-parent households. Because of the way both the childhood and adult neighborhood index variables are created, low values of the index represent high quality neighborhoods, and vice versa.

The dependent variable is the index of adult neighborhood conditions at age 25 and beyond. It is created using neighborhood values from all observations and is then examined in separate white and black samples (see Appendix Table A1). The key independent variable in the model is a similarly constructed index of childhood neighborhood conditions.

Other independent variables in the model include controls for factors such as region of the country, marital status, the log of family income-to-needs, gender, number of years as a child in the sample, and the percentage of years the family moved residence. (See Appendix Table A2 for a complete list of control variables and the models in which they are used.) Each variable is measured as the average value of the characteristic over the childhood years. However, among those children who moved away from their parents before age 19, only the years that they lived with their parents are used in this calculation. In the first set of multivariate models, only childhood variables are included. In a second set of multivariate regressions, variables from the respondents' adult years are included in order to control for a number of personal, educational and economic outcomes. It is important to emphasize that in the FE models, individual differences from the mean for the family's neighborhood quality are regressed on the individual differences from the mean for the family for all other variables.

To help interpret the estimation results and illustrate the implications of these results, a series of simulations were conducted. These simulations are designed to address a set of hypothetical questions with regard to how a given individual's adult neighborhood conditions might be expected to change if they had experienced different neighborhood conditions while growing up. See Appendix A for a description of the simulation methods used in the analyses.

Results

The results are presented in three parts. First, types of neighborhoods in which black and white sample members live, both as children and as adults are described. Second, the results of the multivariate regression analyses are presented, showing the estimates of the relationship between childhood and adult neighborhood characteristics separately by race. This presentation includes examining differences between the model specifications, such as OLS and fixed effects models, as well as linear versus non-linear specifications. The results from the FE models are then used in simulation models that further illustrate the implications of our model estimates.

Table 1 shows the weighted distribution of neighborhood types for black and white sample members in both childhood and adulthood. Neighborhood type is defined according to the distribution of the neighborhood index variables across the full sample (including both black and white sample members). For example, a child is defined as living in the top decile of neighborhoods if the neighborhood index for that child is among the top 10 per cent of all sample members.

Table 1. Weighted percentage of sample living in neighborhoods by overall-type

Neighborhood type	Top 10%	11–25	26–50	51–75	76–90	Bottom 10%
As children:						
White	19.57	29.40	35.73	13.07	2.00	0.23
Black	0.00	0.91	12.40	38.17	30.39	18.14
As adults:						
White	18.73	25.19	34.78	18.17	2.61	0.52
Black	0.94	2.64	12.99	32.82	28.78	21.84

Note: Overall percentiles are calculated for the entire sample ($n = 4128$). As noted in other Tables, some neighborhood percentiles are calculated separately by race ('race-specific') due to the small number of blacks in the most advantaged neighborhoods and the low number of whites in the most disadvantaged neighborhoods.

Table 2. Weighted cross-tabulation of adult neighborhood types and childhood neighborhood quality (percentiles calculated using *overall* neighborhood values)

Neighborhood quality	Grew up in top 10%	11–25	26–50	51–75	76–90	Grew up in bottom 10%
Whites						
Live in top 10% as adult	31.47	26.36	11.06	5.74	6.05	0
11–25	35.24	32.51	20.22	10.13	10.56	0
26–50	29.00	31.28	44.04	28.93	18.23	0
51–75	4.29	9.26	22.11	44.59	37.81	52.62
76–90	0	0.38	2.29	8.85	26.63	9.39
Live in bottom 10% as adult	0	0.21	0.29	1.76	1.72	37.98
$n = 2265$	413	608	859	325	55	5
Blacks						
Live in top 10% as adult	0	13.72	2.95	0.60	0.63	0.14
11–25	0	8.69	7.45	1.53	2.68	1.29
26–50	0	21.86	18.22	14.73	12.26	6.55
51–75	0	13.21	46.99	34.78	33.75	18.55
76–90	0	2.21	18.68	29.53	29.81	33.67
Live in bottom 10% as adult	0	40.31	5.70	18.83	20.87	39.81
$n = 1863$	0	11	173	708	563	408

Blacks and whites live in very different types of neighborhoods. Whites are very unlikely to live in the most disadvantaged neighborhoods while blacks are very unlikely to live in the most advantaged neighborhoods, both in childhood and as adults. For example, almost half of all whites (49 per cent) live in the most advantaged quartile of neighborhoods during childhood, while less than 1 per cent of blacks live in such neighborhoods. During adulthood, whites have around a 44 per cent chance of living in the most advantaged quartile of neighborhoods while blacks have a 4 per cent chance of living in such neighborhoods. The opposite patterns emerge in the most disadvantaged neighborhoods. Whites have a 3 per cent chance of living in the most disadvantaged quartile of neighborhoods during adulthood, while blacks have a 51 per cent chance of living in such neighborhoods.

Table 2 shows the simple relationship between childhood and adult neighborhood characteristics by race. The columns represent the types of neighborhoods children grow up in, and within each column, the rows show the distribution of neighborhood conditions that this group of children experience as adults. The initial column shows, for example, that among white children who grow up in the top decile of neighborhood quality, 31 per cent are in the top decile of neighborhoods as adults, while 35 per cent are in the next best category of neighborhoods (11th to 25th percentiles), 29 per cent are in the next category (26th to 50th percentiles), and 4 per cent are in a neighborhood with an index value below the median.

There is a modest relationship between childhood and adult neighborhood conditions. Among both blacks and whites, children who grow up in relatively good neighborhoods are more likely to end up in relatively good neighborhoods as adults than those who grow up in lower quality neighborhoods. However, interpreting this Table is challenging because white sample members are concentrated almost entirely in the top half of the distribution while black sample members are concentrated in the bottom half.

Table 3. Weighted cross-tabulation of adult neighborhood types and childhood neighborhood quality (percentiles calculated using *race-specific* neighborhood values)

Neighborhood quality	Grew up in top 10%	11–25	26–50	51–75	76–90	Grew up in bottom 10%
Whites						
Live in top 10% as adult	22.03	16.81	12.19	5.65	3.82	2.64
11–25	27.31	24.19	18.90	10.07	6.18	4.85
26–50	24.67	32.45	31.45	26.15	16.18	8.37
51–75	21.15	18.88	25.27	32.33	24.71	18.94
76–90	3.52	5.31	8.13	17.67	33.53	24.23
Live in bottom 10% as adult	1.32	2.36	4.06	8.13	15.59	40.97
$n = 2265$	413	608	859	325	55	5
Blacks						
Live in top 10% as adult	25.81	13.98	9.01	7.71	4.30	4.84
11–25	22.58	20.07	14.81	10.92	14.34	11.29
26–50	27.96	25.81	28.54	27.41	19.00	15.59
51–75	14.52	22.94	26.82	26.98	29.03	22.58
76–90	4.30	12.90	13.95	18.42	15.77	22.04
Live in bottom 10% as adult	4.84	4.30	6.87	8.57	17.56	23.66
$n = 1863$	0	11	173	708	563	408

To address this issue, separate white and black neighborhood quality indexes were used. The index created using the white sample defines neighborhood quality only as it is experienced by white children and adults, while the index created using the black sample captures neighborhood conditions experienced by black children and adults. While 10 per cent of white children have values in the bottom decile of the white childhood index and 10 per cent of black children have values in the bottom decile of the black index, the actual neighborhood conditions represented by the bottom decile of the white and black indexes are very different from one another.

Table 3 shows the relationship between childhood and adult neighborhood quality using these race-specific neighborhood indexes. For both groups, those who grow up in the most advantaged neighborhoods have a high likelihood of staying in those neighborhoods as adults. This pattern also holds for those who grow up in average and more disadvantaged neighborhoods, though there are differences between whites and blacks. Among whites who grow up in the most disadvantaged decile of neighborhoods (based on the white neighborhood index), 41 per cent end up in that type of neighborhood as an adult. For blacks, the analogous likelihood is 24 per cent. These results give some evidence that blacks are less likely to be 'trapped' in the most disadvantaged race-specific neighborhoods. However, if bad neighborhoods were defined by using the white (or overall) neighborhood index for the black sample, the vast majority of blacks are in bad neighborhoods as both children and adults.

Table 4 shows the weighted characteristics of the residents of different race-specific neighborhood-types during childhood. Differences in income levels are notable. Even in the most advantaged neighborhoods (for black sample members), black income levels are on average only 70 per cent above the poverty line, compared to whites who have incomes that are on average 278 per cent above the poverty line in the best neighborhoods among white sample members. Looking at these income discrepancies another way, it is found

Table 4. Weighted means and standard deviations using *race-specific* neighborhood values

	Blacks top 10%	Whites top 10%	Blacks 11–25%	Whites 11–25%	Blacks 26–50%	Whites 26–50%
Family and location variables						
Family income-to-needs	1.69 (0.97)	3.78 (2.20)	1.15 (0.62)	3.59 (2.13)	1.13 (0.64)	2.61 (1.09)
Big city (pop. of 50 000+)	42 (0.57)	0.76 (0.44)	0.44 (0.50)	0.49 (0.50)	0.45 (0.50)	0.26 (0.44)
Rural (pop. of 10 000–24 999, outside of SMSA)	0.00 (0.08)	0.00 (0.06)	0.05 (0.22)	0.00 (0.05)	0.02 (0.14)	0.08 (0.27)
Very rural (pop. of under 10 000, outside of SMSA)	0.03 (0.18)	0.00 (0.04)	0.14 (0.35)	0.02 (0.14)	0.25 (0.43)	0.08 (0.27)
Neighborhood variables						
During childhood						
Child Nbhd Index	−0.91 (0.58)	−3.47 (0.28)	0.23 (0.24)	−2.76 (0.19)	1.12 (0.28)	−1.96 (0.24)
In poverty (%)	11.76 (3.15)	2.77 (1.14)	18.30 (4.43)	4.35 (1.66)	24.66 (6.19)	7.32 (2.66)
Public assistance (%)	5.44 (2.77)	1.65 (0.89)	7.91 (2.77)	2.47 (1.22)	11.24 (3.66)	3.50 (1.82)
White (%)	66.70 (20.11)	98.72 (2.04)	48.79 (23.43)	97.86 (2.99)	40.37 (23.52)	97.31 (3.67)
During adulthood						
Adult Nbhd Index	0.28 (2.09)	−1.90 (0.69)	1.00 (1.99)	−1.81 (0.79)	1.39 (2.00)	−1.63 (0.79)
In poverty (%)	16.56 (9.94)	7.55 (4.98)	19.94 (9.66)	8.03 (4.78)	22.08 (9.90)	9.15 (5.17)
Public assistance (%)	10.21 (7.96)	4.48 (2.33)	12.18 (7.76)	4.77 (2.73)	13.83 (8.26)	5.23 (2.90)
White (%)	50.86 (25.95)	88.96 (8.70)	44.93 (25.87)	88.63 (9.43)	42.77 (25.06)	89.19 (9.19)

	Blacks 51–75%	Whites 51–75%	Blacks 76–90%	Whites 76–90%	Blacks bottom 10%	Whites bottom 10%
Family and location variables						
Family income-to-needs	0.42 (0.49)	0.15 (0.36)	0.52 (0.50)	0.19 (0.40)	0.49 (0.50)	0.15 (0.35)
Big city (pop. of 50 000+)	0.05 (0.23)	0.13 (0.34)	0.01 (0.08)	0.13 (0.34)	0.02 (0.15)	0.21 (0.41)
Rural (pop. of 10 000–24 999, outside of SMSA)	0.21 (0.41)	0.20 (0.40)	0.04 (0.19)	0.39 (0.49)	0.06 (0.25)	0.37 (0.48)
Family income-to-needs	0.99 (0.62)	2.28 (1.16)	0.97 (0.60)	2.00 (1.08)	0.83 (0.36)	1.81 (1.46)
Neighborhood variables						
During childhood						
Child Nbhd Index	2.05 (.30)	−1.22 (0.23)	3.41 (0.47)	−0.27 (0.34)	5.45 (0.92)	1.19 (0.71)
In poverty (%)	30.07 (6.18)	11.47 (3.55)	38.75 (8.18)	18.35 (4.59)	51.05 (7.27)	30.27 (7.11)
Public assistance (%)	15.20 (5.41)	5.26 (2.60)	21.00 (6.75)	8.29 (3.47)	31.90 (8.98)	12.37 (5.30)
White (%)	28.90 (21.04)	95.66 (6.05)	15.20 (14.46)	90.96 (9.54)	8.70 (10.60)	75.39 (21.29)

During adulthood					
Adult Nbhd Index	1.72 (2.16)	−1.21 (0.97)	2.20 (2.32)	−0.81 (1.01)	3.02 (3.13)	−0.13 (1.36)
In poverty (%)	23.93 (10.39)	11.70 (6.52)	25.76 (12.01)	14.35 (6.26)	29.66 (16.12)	17.96 (7.90)
Public assistance (%)	15.58 (9.30)	6.14 (3.66)	16.57 (9.40)	7.34 (3.97)	19.40 (12.52)	9.74 (5.15)
White (%)	38.77 (24.69)	89.28 (10.14)	34.11 (23.08)	87.63 (10.37)	30.67 (24.74)	79.07 (18.22)

that whites living in the most disadvantaged white-type neighborhoods have income levels (81 per cent above the poverty line) that are comparable to the income levels of blacks living in the most advantaged black-type neighborhoods.

Neighborhood conditions for whites and blacks also vary considerably for those living in the most advantaged white-sample and black-sample neighborhoods. For example, the poverty rate in the best white-sample neighborhoods is under 3 per cent, compared with around 12 per cent in the best black-sample neighborhoods. The poverty rate for white-sample neighborhoods does not reach 12 per cent until the 51st to 75th percentile. In addition, blacks living in the most disadvantaged neighborhoods tend to live in highly populated areas, whereas whites who live in the most disadvantaged neighborhoods tend to live in rural areas. For example, 58 per cent of whites who live in the lowest decile of neighborhoods live in cities/towns outside of standard metropolitan statistical areas (SMSAs), with populations of less than 25 000 people. Comparatively, only 8 per cent of blacks live in these rural types of areas.

Multivariate Regression Results

Key results are presented from linear and non-linear specifications of the fixed effect models for blacks and whites in the first two columns of Table 5. Among both white and black sample members, the results of the FE models for the spline and quadratic models are substantially different than the results of the OLS models (not shown), suggesting that the unobserved permanent family characteristics controlled in the FE models, but not in the OLS models, are important. Thus, only the results of the FE models are presented here. In interpreting these results, it should be noted that higher values of the neighborhood index represent more disadvantaged neighborhood conditions (higher poverty rates, fewer two-parent families, etc.). Thus, the 91st to 100th percentile of the childhood neighborhood index shown in the spline specification represents the worst 10 per cent of neighborhood conditions. In the regression models, positive neighborhood effects indicate that the more disadvantaged the neighborhood in childhood, the more disadvantaged the neighborhood in adulthood (ceteris paribus). Because the neighborhood index can take on both positive and negative values, two squared terms are included in the quadratic specification, one for those who have positive (worse) neighborhood index values as children and one for those who have negative (better) neighborhood index values as children.[2] The top panel of results in the Table excludes variables representing adult outcomes, such as educational attainment, that could mediate the effects of childhood neighborhood conditions on adult neighborhood conditions.

For whites, childhood neighborhood quality has a positive and significant effect in the linear model on adult neighborhood quality. In both of the non-linear models evidence of neighborhood effects is also found. For the spline results, these effects are positive and statistically significant only for those who grew up in the bottom decile of neighborhoods. These spline results suggest that a marginal improvement in neighborhood conditions among those who grew up in the worst neighborhoods could lead to a substantial improvement in adult neighborhood conditions. The quadratic FE results for whites are consistent with these spline results.

For blacks, the linear specification suggests a positive relationship between childhood and adult neighborhood conditions. Although evidence is also found of effects in the spline models, the estimates are difficult to interpret. In particular, there is evidence of both

Table 5. Fixed effects regression analyses for the adult neighborhood index for all blacks and whites, and poor blacks

	White b (SE)	Black b (SE)	Poor Blacks b (SE)
Childhood controls included			
Linear			
Child Nbhd Index	0.273 (0.095)***	0.265 (0.102)**	0.317 (0.174) +
Within R^2	0.0391	0.0407	0.0538
Quadratic			
Child Nbhd Index	0.026 (0.170)	0.335 (0.233)	0.061 (0.374)
Child Nbhd Index (squared – positive)	0.448 (0.113)***	−0.007 (0.034)	0.047 (0.057)
Child Nbhd Index (squared – negative)	−0.018 (0.046)	0.356 (0.354)	0.473 (1.031)
Within R^2	0.0509	0.0415	0.0554
Spline			
0–10: (top 10%)	0.162 (0.364)	−0.467 (0.626)	−0.453 (1.363)
11–25	0.088 (0.331)	0.778 (0.539)	0.230 (0.908)
26–50	0.121 (0.269)	0.272 (0.344)	0.500 (0.554)
51–75	0.292 (0.275)	0.798 (0.330)*	0.683 (0.454)
76–90	−0.065 (0.217)	−0.670 (0.287)*	−0.384 (0.385)
91–100: (bottom 10%)	1.007 (0.261)***	0.780 (0.269)**	0.932 (0.434)*
Within R^2	0.0454	0.0511	0.0605
Childhood and adulthood controls included			
Linear			
Child Nbhd Index	0.277 (0.095)***	0.182 (0.097) +	0.207 (0.166)
Within R^2	0.0539	0.1472	0.1639
Quadratic			
Child Nbhd Index	0.049 (0.170)	0.327 (0.221)	0.080 (0.355)
Child Nbhd Index (squared – positive)	0.426 (0.113)***	−0.020 (0.033)	0.023 (0.054)
Child Nbhd Index (squared – negative)	−0.015 (0.046)	0.377 (0.335)	0.216 (0.980)
Within R^2	0.0647	0.1481	0.1643
Spline			
0–10: (top 10%)	0.169 (0.364)	−0.466 (0.593)	−0.116 (1.294)
11–25	0.076 (0.330)	0.665 (0.511)	0.102 (0.862)
26–50	0.138 (0.269)	0.326 (0.327)	0.521 (0.525)
51–75	0.319 (0.276)	0.640 (0.313)*	0.634 (0.430)
76–90	−0.047 (0.217)	−0.718 (0.272)**	−0.571 (0.365)
91–100: (bottom 10%)	0.970 (0.260)***	0.624 (0.255)**	0.721 (0.412) +
Within R^2	0.0597	0.1567	0.1710
Average no. of siblings in sample	2.8	3.4	3.7
n	2265	1863	1037

Note: See Appendix Table A2 for a full list of control variables used in each of the models.
***$p < 0.001$; **$p < 0.01$; *$p < 0.05$; +$p < 0.10$, all for two-tailed tests.

positive and negative significant marginal effects as neighborhoods become more disadvantaged.

Similar results are found when other adult outcomes are controlled (marital status, years married, family size, educational status, region of residence, SMSA residence), but the estimated neighborhood effects are somewhat attenuated from models without these controls (Table 5, bottom panel). This suggests that the neighborhood effects shown in the top panel are not primarily a function of the types of adult outcomes included in the model in the bottom panel. These estimated effects are either direct effects of childhood neighborhood conditions on adult neighborhood conditions, or they operate through other factors not included in the model.

An additional set of models was estimated for black sample members with incomes at or below the poverty line (the third column of Table 5). (Sample size was too small to run a similar model for whites.) In the FE spline model, effects are found only for those blacks who grew up in the most disadvantaged neighborhoods. Positive linear effects ($p < 0.10$) are found in the childhood only FE model.

Simulation Models

In order to better understand the size of the effects of child neighborhood quality on adult neighborhood-type, a number of simulations are run using the FE estimates from the spline regression models, using the estimates from models that control childhood variables only. Because the results are similar for the quadratic and spline models, only results from the spline specification are reported. The first set of simulations examines the likelihood of living in different types of neighborhoods as an adult given childhood neighborhood circumstances. The second set of simulations examines how black children would have fared if they grew up in the types of neighborhoods in which white children grew up, and how white children would have fared if they grew up in the types of neighborhoods in which black children grew up.

Table 6 shows a set of simulation results where the childhood neighborhood index is based on the race-specific measure, and the adult neighborhood types are defined according to a neighborhood index constructed from all sample members. As in the fixed effects model results, the relationship between childhood neighborhood quality and adult neighborhood quality reflected in this Table shows strong non-linear neighborhood effects for whites and slightly weaker effects for blacks. For example, whites who grow up in the top 90 per cent of neighborhoods have between an 84 per cent and a 73 per cent chance of being in the top 50 per cent of neighborhoods as adults. This probability drops off precipitously after we reach the 91st percentile of childhood neighborhoods. For blacks, we see a wide range of predicted values for living in the top 50th percentile as an adult and then a drop off once the 91st percentile is reached.

Table 7 indicates what adult neighborhoods would be like if the childhood neighborhood characteristics were exchanged, black for white and vice versa.[3] The results for these 'exchanged' simulations are presented alongside the results of simulations in which an individual's actual childhood neighborhood index is used.[4]

The top portion of Table 7 reveals the dramatic effects of this simulation for whites. The likelihood of ending up in the 10 per cent most disadvantaged white-sample neighborhoods goes from 10 per cent in the baseline simulation to 46 per cent in the simulation in which it is assumed that these individuals had grown up in the same type

Table 6. Simulation results using spline models for all observations. The likelihood of living in overall-type neighborhoods as adults given childhood neighborhood quality. Percentiles for adult neighborhoods calculated using *overall* neighborhood values

Childhood neighborhood	Whites					Blacks				
	Likelihood of living in overall-type neighborhoods as an adult					Likelihood of living in overall-type neighborhoods as an adult				
	Bottom 5%	Bottom 10%	Top 50%	Top 10%	Top 5%	Bottom 5%	Bottom 10%	Top 50%	Top 10%	Top 5%
99: worst	0.00	0.01	0.15	0.00	0.00	0.28	0.50	0.02	0.00	0.00
95	0.00	0.00	0.50	0.03	0.02	0.13	0.31	0.09	0.01	0.01
91	0.00	0.00	0.69	0.11	0.08	0.09	0.21	0.15	0.03	0.03
90	0.00	0.00	0.73	0.14	0.09	0.08	0.19	0.17	0.04	0.03
85	0.00	0.00	0.72	0.13	0.09	0.10	0.25	0.12	0.02	0.02
75	0.00	0.00	0.70	0.12	0.08	0.15	0.34	0.07	0.01	0.01
50	0.00	0.00	0.78	0.17	0.13	0.09	0.21	0.15	0.03	0.03
25	0.00	0.00	0.81	0.21	0.15	0.07	0.18	0.19	0.04	0.03
10	0.00	0.00	0.83	0.23	0.17	0.05	0.12	0.29	0.09	0.07
5	0.00	0.00	0.84	0.25	0.18	0.06	0.14	0.24	0.06	0.05
1: best	0.00	0.00	0.84	0.25	0.18	0.07	0.18	0.19	0.04	0.03

Table 7. (Exchanged) simulation results, using spline models for all observations. The likelihood of adult neighborhood type if whites and blacks grew up in the other's neighborhood-type (e.g. whites who grew up in the bottom 5th percentile of white-type neighborhoods take on the neighborhood characteristics of the bottom 5th percentile of black-type neighborhoods). Percentiles for adult neighborhoods calculated using *race-specific and overall* neighborhood values

Adult Neighborhood	White-type adult neighborhoods		Black-type adult neighborhoods		Overall-type adult Neighborhoods	
Whites	Childhood values: Black	Childhood values: White	Childhood values: Black	Childhood values: White[b]	Childhood values: Black	Childhood values: White
Bottom 5%	0.35	0.04[a]	0.02	0.00	0.05	0.00
Bottom 10%	0.46	0.10[a]	0.04	0.00	0.11	0.00
Top 50%	0.18	0.47[a]	0.73	0.98	0.38	0.75
Top 10%	0.04	0.13[a]	0.27	0.61	0.05	0.18
Top 5%	0.02	0.10[a]	0.16	0.44	0.03	0.12
Blacks	Childhood values: White	Childhood values: Black[b]	Childhood values: White	Childhood values: Black[c]	Childhood values: White	Childhood values: Black[b]
Bottom 5%	0.60	0.62	0.03	0.04[a]	0.08	0.10
Bottom 10%	0.71	0.73	0.07	0.09[a]	0.19	0.23
Top 50%	0.11	0.09	0.51	0.49[a]	0.19	0.16
Top 10%	0.04	0.03	0.14	0.12[a]	0.05	0.04
Top 5%	0.03	0.02	0.10	0.08[a]	0.04	0.03

Note: Probabilities are determined by using the spline regression results from the fixed effect models.
[a] These values should add up to the particular percentage on the left but do not because of randomized error values.
[b] This column uses the coefficient estimates for the neighborhood index for whites.
[c] This column uses the coefficient estimates for the neighborhood index for blacks.

of neighborhoods in which black sample members grew up. In this same simulation, white sample members would have only an 18 per cent chance of ending up in the top 50 per cent of white-sample neighborhoods as adults. Using the overall (non-race-specific) measure of adult neighborhoods, whites' chances of living in the bottom decile of adult neighborhoods rise from 0 per cent in the baseline model to 11 per cent in the simulation in which they are assigned blacks' childhood neighborhood values, and fall from a 75 per cent to a 38 per cent chance of living in the top 50 per cent of all neighborhoods. Table 7 shows that if black children had grown up in the same types of neighborhoods as white children, this would result in only marginal improvements in adult outcomes. For example, blacks would have a 23 per cent likelihood of being in the bottom decile of overall neighborhoods if they grew up with white neighborhood characteristics, compared to a 19 per cent likelihood with their own childhood neighborhood characteristics.[5]

Discussion and Conclusions

The results of this study on the intergenerational nature of neighborhood quality suggest that the effects of childhood neighborhood characteristics on adult residential outcomes vary by place. Support is found for the theory that place matters in the maintenance and promotion of SES inequality through intergenerational patterns of residence. By exploiting the unique nature of a longitudinal, geocoded sibling dataset, sibling fixed effects modeling was used to minimize the endogenous effects of neighborhood choice in an examination of intergenerational neighborhood residence — to the authors' knowledge, the first study to investigate this relationship. While the results should be viewed with some caution due to the inherent risk of measurement error in fixed effect models, the results suggest that place-based strategies aimed at promoting SES mobility should be considered.

The study finds that there are enormous differences between the types of neighborhoods in which blacks and whites live both as children and as adults. Approximately half of all black children live in the bottom 25 per cent of overall neighborhoods, compared to only 2 per cent of white children. Similarly, only 1 per cent of black children live in the top 25 per cent of overall neighborhoods, compared to over 50 per cent of white children. Based on existing literature on the limited nature of black residential mobility (Crowder & South, 2005; Gramlich et al., 1992; Quillian, 2003), the study expected to find that these stark racial differences were due, in part, to the fact that neighborhood quality is highly intergenerational, especially for blacks. However, the findings suggest otherwise. In fact, it is found that the non-linear effects of childhood neighborhoods are somewhat stronger, although not significantly so, for whites who live in the most disadvantaged white neighborhoods relative to blacks who live in the most disadvantaged black neighborhoods. These results show the important role that place plays for all those who live in the most disadvantaged neighborhoods. It lends support to theories of epidemic disadvantage (Crane, 1991; Wilson, 1987) which suggest that there is a tipping point after which poor neighborhood quality has stronger influence on adult residential outcomes. While it is not possible to directly measure the mechanisms by which these processes occur, past theoretical work can be used to hypothesize about the impact that neighborhood quality has on social and human capital accumulation as well as on perceptions of residential opportunities.

However, to roughly equate levels of intergenerational neighborhood mobility between blacks and whites is problematic in the context of the tremendously high levels of racial stratification found in the samples. While blacks in the most disadvantaged neighborhoods are similarly immobile as whites, they are trapped in far worse neighborhoods. Furthermore, blacks in general are only mobile within an extremely limited set of neighborhoods. Even if neighborhood conditions for blacks improve between childhood and adulthood, they will not improve so much that blacks end up living in the types of neighborhoods in which whites live. In other words, those whites who may be trapped in disadvantaged neighborhoods still live in better neighborhoods than the vast majority (over 70 per cent) of blacks.

Given prevailing assumptions about SES mobility, whites may have been expected to be more intergenerationally mobile than blacks because they grow up in far better neighborhoods. However, if the theories of cognitive landscaping and social group status are considered, it is plausible to understand how disadvantaged whites are just as 'trapped' as disadvantaged blacks because both groups arguably suffer from similar types of status group disenfranchisement. Living in distressed neighborhoods may well shape perceptions about where one can and should live as an adult by the mere fact of being at the lowest end of the relative social spectrum.

Combined with the role that neighborhood quality plays in the accumulation of social and human capital, we can begin to understand how these mechanisms might shape adult residential choice—part conditioning, part constraint. Further work is needed to truly appreciate exactly how these neighborhood processes operate and under what conditions. However, by relying on theoretical work that has been done with regional data on social processes in neighborhoods (Sampson *et al.*, 1997), the study is an important first step. Its longitudinal perspective makes it possible to suggest that the study of intergenerational socio-economic mobility will benefit from consideration of the intergenerational nature of neighborhood quality.

Acknowledgements

A version of this paper was presented at the Association for Public Policy Analysis and Management meetings in November 2005.

Notes

[1] Cutoff points have been set such that the spline function includes different linear segments for the top 10 per cent of neighborhoods, the 11th to the 25th percentiles, the 26th to the 50th percentiles, the 51st to 75th percentiles, the 76th to the 90th percentiles, and at the 91st to 100th percentiles. There would be evidence for the epidemic theory if the poorest neighborhoods (i.e. 91st to 100th percentile) were to have the most detrimental effects on future neighborhood conditions. In estimating the spline specification, each section of the spline function is entered into the model separately. In this specification, the overall effect of the neighborhood index—that is, the overall contribution of childhood neighborhood conditions to adult neighborhood conditions—is cumulative, in that it depends on the coefficients associated with each of the previous pieces of the spline function. However, the marginal effect of a change in childhood neighborhood conditions depends only on the coefficient associated with the part of the spline function in which a particular sample member is located. For example, if the coefficient on the piece of the spline function representing the 91st to 100th percentile is negative, then going from the 91st to the 95th percentile will have a negative effect on adult neighborhood outcomes, regardless of the coefficient on the segment of the spline function representing the 76th to 90th percentile.

[2] The neighborhood index takes on a roughly equal number of positive and negative values across the full sample. However, among white sample members the index is negative for most sample members, indicating better neighborhood conditions. Conversely, most black samples have positive values of the neighborhood index, indicating more disadvantaged conditions.

[3] Childhood neighborhood values are exchanged by percentile. For example, if the childhood neighborhood index value at the 50th percentile is -2 for whites and $+1$ for blacks, white sample members at that percentile would be given a childhood neighborhood value of $+1$ and black sample members a value of -2, keeping all other characteristics the same.

[4] The purpose of this simulation is to provide a baseline from where it is possible to compare the results of the simulation in which black and white childhood neighborhood conditions are exchanged. If the baseline simulations worked perfectly, it would be found that 5 per cent of white sample members were simulated to live in the top 5 per cent of neighborhoods (using the race-specific neighborhood index) as adults. However, the actual baseline simulation results do not quite achieve this goal, particularly at the extremes of the neighborhood distribution. These discrepancies between the actual baseline simulation value and its expected value arise because of differences between the true value of a given sample member's error term and its simulated value. The simulated value is based on a random draw from a normal distribution, and could be different from the actual value either because of the random nature of its selection or from the assumption that the error term has a normal distribution across sample members.

[5] An important caveat in interpreting this last set of simulations is that they are based on out-of-sample inferences. In particular, because a large proportion of black children live in neighborhoods worse than almost all of the neighborhoods in which white sample members live, there is no direct empirical evidence as to how white children would react to living in those very bad neighborhoods. Instead, this effect is inferred based on the relationship between childhood and adult neighborhood conditions that are observed.

References

Aaronson, D. (1998) Using sibling data to estimate the impact of neighborhoods on children's educational outcomes, *Journal of Human Resources*, 33, pp. 915–946.

Blau, P. & Duncan, O. (1967) *The American Occupational Structure* (New York: Wiley).

Bobo, L. & Zubrinsky, C. L. (1996) Attitudes toward residential integration: perceived status differences, mere in group preferences, or racial prejudice?, *Social Forces*, 74, pp. 883–909.

Borrell, L. N., Diez Roux, A. V., Rose, K., Catellier, D. & Clark, B. L. (2003) Neighborhood characteristics and mortality in the atherosclerosis risk in community studies, *International Journal of Epidemiology*, 33, pp. 398–407.

Bowles, S. & Gintis, H. (2002) The inheritance of inequality, *Journal of Economic Perspectives*, 16(3), pp. 3–30.

Brooks-Gunn, J., Duncan, G. J., Klebanov, P. K. & Sealand, N. (1993) Do neighborhoods influence child and adolescent development?, *American Journal of Sociology*, 99, pp. 353–395.

Chadwick, L. & Solon, G. (2002) Intergenerational income mobility among daughters, *American Economic Review*, 92, pp. 335–344.

Charles, K. K. & Hurst, E. (2003) The correlation of wealth across generations, *Journal of Political Economy*, 111, pp. 1155–1182.

Conley, D. (2004) *The Pecking Order: Which Siblings Succeed and Why* (New York: Pantheon Books).

Crane, J. (1991) The epidemic theory of ghettos and neighborhood effects on dropping out and teenage childbearing, *American Journal of Sociology*, 96, pp. 1226–1259.

Crowder, K. & South, S. J. (2005) Race, class, and changing patterns of migration between poor and nonpoor neighborhoods, *American Journal of Sociology*, 110, pp. 1715–1763.

Dietz, R. D. (2002) The estimation of neighborhood effects in the social sciences: an interdisciplinary approach, *Social Science Research*, 31, pp. 539–575.

Duncan, G. J. & Raudenbush, S. W. (2001) Neighborhoods and adolescent development: how can we determine the links?, in: A. Booth & A. C. Crouter (Eds) *Does it Take a Village? Community Effects on Children, Adolescents, and Families*, pp. 105–136 (Mahwah, NJ: Lawrence Erlbaum).

Duncan, G. J., Brooks-Gunn, J. & Klebanov, P. K. (1994) Economic deprivation and early childhood development, *Child Development*, 65, pp. 296–318.

Galster, G. & Killen, S. (1995) The geography of metropolitan opportunity: a reconnaissance and conceptual framework, *Housing Policy Debate*, 6, pp. 7–43.

Galster, G. C., Quercia, R. G. & Cortes, A. (2000) Identifying neighborhood thresholds: an empirical exploration, *Housing Policy Debate*, 11, pp. 701–732.

Ginther, D., Haveman, R. & Wolfe, B. (2000) Neighborhood attributes as determinants of children's outcomes: how robust are the relationships?, *Journal of Human Resources*, 35, pp. 603–642.

Gramlich, E., Laren, D. & Sealand, N. (1992) Moving into and out of poor urban areas, *Journal of Policy Analysis and Management*, 11, pp. 273–287.

Jencks, C. & Mayer, S. E. (1990) The social consequences of growing up in a poor neighborhood, in: L. E. Lynn & M. G. H. McGeary (Eds) *Inner-City Poverty in the United States*, pp. 111–186 (Washington DC: National Academy Press).

Kasarda, J. D. (1988) Jobs, migration, and emerging urban mismatches, in: M. G. H. McGeary & L. E. Lynn (Eds) *Urban Change and Poverty*, pp. 148–198 (Washington DC: National Academy Press).

Kuntz, J., Page, M. E. & Solon, G. (2003) Are point-in-time measures of neighborhood characteristics useful proxies for children's long-run neighborhood environment?, *Economic Letters*, 79, pp. 231–237.

Lee, C. & Solon, G. (2006) Trends in intergenerational income mobility, NBER Working Paper No. W12007.

Leventhal, T. & Brooks-Gunn, J. (2000) The neighborhoods they live in: the effects of neighborhood residence on child and adolescent outcomes, *Psychological Bulletin*, 126, pp. 309–337.

Logan, J. R. & Alba, R. D. (1993) Locational returns to human capital: minority access to suburban community resources, *Demography*, 30, pp. 243–268.

Massey, D. S. & Denton, N. A. (1993) *American Apartheid: Segregation and the Making of the Underclass* (Cambridge, MA: Harvard University Press).

Massey, D. S., Gross, A. B. & Shibuya, K. (1994) Migration, segregation, and the concentration of poverty, *American Sociological Review*, 59, pp. 425–445.

Mazumder, B. (2003) Revised estimates of intergenerational income mobility in the United States, FRB of Chicago Working Paper No. 2003–16.

McClintock, M. K., Conzen, S. D., Gehlert, S., Masi, C. & Funmi, O. (2005) Mammary cancer and social interactions: identifying multiple environments that regulate gene expression throughout the lifespan, *The Journals of Gerontology*, 60B, pp. 32–41.
Mendenhall, R., DeLuca, S. & Duncan, G. (2005) Neighborhood resources, racial segregation, and economic mobility: results from the Gautreaux program, *Social Science Research*, available online.
Quillian, L. (1999) Migration patterns and the growth of high-poverty neighborhoods, 1970–1990, *American Journal of Sociology*, 105, pp. 1–37.
Quillian, L. (2002) Why is black–white residential segregation so persistent? Evidence on three theories from migration data, *Social Science Research*, 31, pp. 197–229.
Quillian, L. (2003) How long are exposures to poor neighborhoods? The long-term dynamics of entry and exit from poor neighborhoods, *Population Research and Policy Review*, 22, pp. 221–249.
Rossi, P. H. (1980) *Why Families Move* (New York: Free Press).
Sampson, R. J. & Wilson, W. J. (1995) Toward a theory of race, crime, and urban inequality, in: J. Hagan & R. D. Peterson (Eds) *Crime and Inequality* (Stanford, CA: Stanford University Press).
Sampson, R. J., Raudenbush, S. & Earls, F. (1997) Neighborhood and violent crime: a multilevel study of collective efficacy, *Science*, 277, pp. 918–924.
South, S. J. & Deane, G. D. (1993) Race and residential mobility: individual determinants and structural constraints, *Social Forces*, 72, pp. 147–167.
South, S. J. & Crowder, K. D. (1997) Escaping distressed neighborhoods: individual, community, and metropolitan influences, *American Journal of Sociology*, 102, pp. 1040–1084.
Timberlake, J. M. (2002) Separate, but how unequal? Ethnic residential stratification, 1980 to 1990, *City & Community*, 1, pp. 251–266.
Vartanian, T. P. & Buck, P. W. (2005) Childhood and adolescent neighborhood effects on adult income: using siblings to examine differences in OLS and fixed effect models, *Social Service Review*, 78, pp. 60–94.
Verma, N. (2003) Staying or leaving lessons from jobs-plus about the mobility of public housing residents and implications for place-based initiatives. Working Paper, MDRC.
Weinberg, B. A., Reagan, P. B. & Yankow, J. J. (2004) Do neighborhoods affect work behavior? Evidence from the NLSY79, *Journal of Labor Economics*, 24, pp. 891–924.
Wilson, W. J. (1987) *The Truly Disadvantaged: The Inner City, the Underclass, and Public Policy* (Chicago: University of Chicago Press).
Zimmerman, D. J. (1992) Regression toward mediocrity in economic stature, *American Economic Review*, 82, pp. 409–429.

Appendix A

Two types of simulations are conducted. The first type of simulation examines how the average sample member would be affected by growing up in different types of neighborhoods. For example, if the average white child grew up in a very bad neighborhood (such as the worst 1 per cent of neighborhoods of white children in the sample), what would be the likelihood that the child would, as an adult, live in an equally bad neighborhood? What would be the likelihood that he or she would live in very good neighborhood as an adult (say, a neighborhood at the top 5 per cent of the distribution)? Conversely, a simulation could be conducted that would place that same child in the best of all neighborhoods while growing up, and the same set of questions could be asked about the type of neighborhood he or she would likely live in as an adult. If there is no relationship between childhood and adult neighborhood conditions, the answers to the questions about the likelihood of living in a very good neighborhood as an adult will be the same regardless of the type of childhood neighborhood into which the simulations placed the child. If there is a strong positive relationship, on the other hand, then the likelihood of living in a very good adult neighborhood will be much higher for the child simulated to have grown up in a very good neighborhood.

The second type of simulation conducted addresses the implications of neighborhood segregation. As described below, white children and black children currently grow up in very different types of neighborhoods. To assess how this influences the types of neighborhoods these groups live in as adults, the following thought experiment is performed. Suppose that white children grew up in the very same neighborhoods that black children now grow up in. How would this influence the types of neighborhoods that the white children lived in as adults? What would happen if black children grew up in the same neighborhoods that white children grow up in?

These simulations were conducted using the following five-step procedure:

(1) Generate estimates of the model parameters, or coefficients.
(2) For each individual in the sample, multiply those coefficients by the individual's values of all the associated variables in the model, except for the individual's childhood neighborhood quality index. Instead of multiplying the individual's value of this variable by its associated coefficient, use the simulated childhood neighborhood index. Sum the products of the variables in the model and their associated coefficient estimates to generate a predicted value of the outcome variable (the adult neighborhood index) under this simulation.
(3) Simulate a value of the error term for each individual by selecting a random draw from a normal distribution with a mean of 0 and variance of sigma squared (σ^2) (the error variance obtained from the model estimation).
(4) Sum the predicted value of the outcome variable under this simulation (#2) and the simulated error term (#3) for each individual. This is the simulated value of the adult neighborhood index for each individual.
(5) Calculate statistics based on the distribution of this simulated neighborhood index across all individuals in the sample.

The procedures for conducting the first and second types of simulations differ only in terms of how the simulated childhood neighborhood index value is created. In the first type of simulation, a single neighborhood index value is picked and used for all sample members. For example, in order to simulate the implications of all children growing up in very bad neighborhoods, a childhood neighborhood index value might be chosen that is in the worst percentile of the distribution and each individual in the sample is assigned that index value.

In the second type of simulation, the simulated childhood neighborhood index value varies across children. In particular, for the simulation in which white children in the neighborhood are assigned conditions experienced by black children, white children living in the very worst neighborhoods (among whites) are assigned the neighborhood index value of the corresponding black children living in the very worst neighborhoods among blacks. For example, all white children in the bottom 5 per cent of the distribution of the childhood neighborhood index among whites are assigned the 2.5th percentile of the neighborhood index among black children. Conversely, white children living in the best neighborhoods are assigned the neighborhood index values of the corresponding black children living in the best neighborhoods. Because few whites live in the poorest black-sample neighborhoods and few blacks live in the most advantaged white-sample neighborhoods, the simulation results for these 'out-of-sample' groups should be viewed with caution.

Table A1. Principal components analysis

Eigenvectors	Childhood variables		Adulthood variables		Childhood NB variance	
	Eigenvector	Correlation w/index	Correlation w/index	Eigenvector	Correlation w/index	Eigenvector
Poverty rate	0.417	0.936	0.420	0.953	0.469	0.869
% receiving public assist	0.381	0.855	0.400	0.908	0.456	0.844
% fem headed hh	0.386	0.866	0.407	0.923	0.479	0.887
% w/income < $15k (2001$)	0.409	0.918	0.419	0.951	−0.024	−0.044
% w/income > $60k (2001$)	−0.409	−0.919	−0.384	−0.871	0.471	0.873
% w/income above family's	0.124	0.278	0.038	0.087	0.033	0.061
% in same income category	−0.210	−0.472	0.209	0.475	−0.066	−0.122
% white	−0.370	−0.830	−0.361	−0.819	0.339	0.627
Eigenvalue	4.397		4.532		3.429	
% of variance explained	62.81		64.74		42.87	

Note: n = 4128.

Table A2. Control variables used in Tables 6 and 7

	No adult variables		Adult variables included	
	OLS	Fixed effect	OLS	Fixed effect
Family variables:				
Childhood neighborhood index	✓	✓	✓	✓
Childhood neighborhood variance	✓	✓	✓	✓
Years moved (%)	✓	✓	✓	✓
Income variance (000)	✓	✓	✓	✓
Log of family income-to-needs ratio (FMNS)	✓	✓	✓	✓
Years on AFDC (%)	✓	✓	✓	✓
Age of the head	✓	✓	✓	✓
Has work limitations	✓	✓	✓	✓
Owns home	✓	✓	✓	✓
Home value (000)	✓	✓	✓	✓
Married (all years)	excluded	excluded	excluded	excluded
Never married (all years)	✓	✓	✓	✓
Separated or divorced (all years)	✓	✓	✓	✓
Widow(er) (all years)	✓	✓	✓	✓
Got married	✓	✓	✓	✓
Got separated/divorced	✓	✓	✓	✓
Got widowed	✓	✓	✓	✓
No. children in family	✓	✓	✓	✓
Average age of youngest child	✓	✓	✓	✓
High school dropout	✓	...	✓	...
High school graduate	✓	...	✓	...
Attended some college	✓	...	✓	...
College graduate	excluded	...	excluded	...
Lives in South	✓	...	✓	...
Big city (population of 50 000 +)	✓	✓	✓	✓
City 2 (population of 100 000–499 999)	✓	✓	✓	✓
City 3 (population of 50 000–99 999)	✓	✓	✓	✓
City 4 (population of 25 000–49 999)	✓	✓	✓	✓
Rural (population of 10 000–24 999, outside of SMSA)	excluded	excluded	excluded	excluded
Very rural (population of under 10 000, outside of SMSA)	excluded	excluded	excluded	excluded
Child-specific variables:				
Birth order	✓	✓	✓	✓
Years in child sample	✓	✓	✓	✓
Began sample age 0–4	✓	✓	✓	✓
Began sample age 5–8	✓	✓	✓	✓
Began sample age 9–13	✓	✓	✓	✓
Began sample age 14–18	excluded	excluded	excluded	excluded
Young head/wife (< 19)	✓	✓	✓	✓

Table A2. *Continued*

	No adult variables		Adult variables included	
	OLS	Fixed effect	OLS	Fixed effect
Age at the end of the sample	✓	✓	✓	✓
Age at the end of the sample (squared)	✓	✓	✓	✓
Female	✓	✓	✓	✓
Entered sample in 1968–72	✓	✓	✓	✓
Adult-specific variables:				
Is a wife	…	…	✓	✓
Years married (%)	…	…	✓	✓
Family size	…	…	✓	✓
High school dropout	…	…	✓	✓
High school graduate	…	…	✓	✓
Attended some college	…	…	✓	✓
College graduate	…	…	excluded	excluded
Student after age 25	…	…	✓	✓
Lives in the South	…	…	✓	✓
Lives in a SMSA	…	…	✓	✓

Note: A ✓ indicates that the variable is included in the model. SMSA = standard statistical metropolitan area; AFDC = Aid to Families with Dependent Children.

Index

adult neighbourhood quality: modelling 205-6; variables 207-8
affluent neighbours, impact of 16
age, and deprivation 134
Amsterdam 129, 186, 197
analyses, multi-level 162
anti-social behaviour 37-8, 40-1, 55, 128
Aronson, D. 70
Arum, R. 167
assimilation theories 177
Atkinson, R. 42; & Kintrea, K. 39, 42, 72, 129

balanced communities 35, 46, 61, 126; *see also* mixed communities
Berube, A. 42
Blau, P. & Duncan, O. 203
Boehm, T. P. & Schlottman, A. M. 70
Bournville 126
Bramley, G.: & Karley, N. K. 76; & Morgan, J. 72
Brewster, K. 16
Britain: balanced community focus 35, 43; deprived areas study 129; deprived neighbourhoods 66; income profile of owner occupation 71; *see also* UK
Brooks-Gunn, J. *et al.* 16
Brophy, P. & Smith, R. 42, 129

CA (correspondence analysis) 9-10, 126, 137, 139, 141-4, 146
CatPCA, (Categorical Principal Components Analysis) 136-7
census tract data, usefulness 103
census tracts: heterogeneity 125; as neighbourhood unit 125, 156
child welfare rate, as poverty indicator 156, 158-9
childhood neighbourhood conditions, modelling 205-6
children and adolescents, current research 152-4
cognitive landscapes, neighbourhoods as 204
cohesion, social 14, 126, 176, 190
collective efficacy (COLLEFF) 29, 72, 103, 130, 135-41, 143-6, 150, 154
Cologne, Germany 116, 125, 130-1, 135, 155-9, 167-8, 170

competition theory 13, 14, 179
contact hypothesis 128, 180, 194, 196
contagion effects 13
contraception 16
Corcoran, M. *et al.* 15
Crane, J. 16, 154-5, 204, 218
crime 151; countering 72; desired improvements 50; the 'estate effect' 129; and homeownership 56; influence of local 13; intergenerational effects of exposure to 204; and minority groups 183; and mixed community living 40, 52-3; and mixed community policy 42; as neighbourhood problem 7, 49, 50, 53, 55, 66, 168; in outcomes literature 96, 153, 160; and peer-pressure 42; perceptions of 49; and poverty 42; and social capital 154; studies of adolescent 153
Crowder K. 16, 203-4, 218
cultural capital 40

Dawkins, C.J. *et al.* 16
delinquency: and friendship networks 165-6; and gender 164-5; and immigration status 160-5; measuring 157; poverty indicators 169; *see also* poverty and delinquency study
deprivation, relative 13, 38, 157, 160
deprived neighbourhoods: characteristics 66; classification methods 144
Dietz, R. & Haurin, D. 70
dilution strategies 38-9
DiPasquale, D. & Glaeser, E. 70, 72
dispersal strategies 39
diversity strategies 39
dogs 49, 52-6
Dolton, P. & Vignoles, A 73
Duncan, G.J. 15, 203

earnings 2, 12, 16, 17, 21, 29, 96-7, 103-6, 109-11, 113-15, 122-3, 207
earnings-neighbourhood characteristics study, *see* tenure-mixing study
education: and deprivation 134, 177; and ethnic prejudice 194, 196; and inter-ethnic contacts 178
educational attainment 15; factors affecting

67-72; race and 108; and school resources 68; and social exclusion 69, 70; and young adult outcomes 108
educational attainment study: data sources 76; measurements 76; methodology 73-6; model structure 74-6; modelling strategy 73-4; results 77-90; conclusions 90-2
employment effects, of housing mobility 42
Encouraging Mixed Communities (Social Exclusion Unit) 36
endogenous neighbourhood effects 13, 14
Ensminger, M.E. *et al.* 16
estate effect 129
ethnic concentration: causality issues 180-1; contact hypothesis 180; and inter-ethnic attitudes 179-80; and inter-ethnic contacts 177-8; and perception of threat 178, 179-80; and second-language proficiency 178-9; theoretical expectations on effects of 177-81
ethnic concentration study: conclusions 197-9; controls 182-3; data sources 181, 183; educational effects 196; findings 185-97; indigenous-ethnic social contact 185-90, 192; integration indicators 181-2; language proficiency 182, 190-3; model 185; neighbourhood characteristics 183-4; perception of threat 183; refugee groups 185, 192-3; stereotypical attitudes 182, 193-6
ethnic heterogeneity, impacts of 127-8
ethnic minorities: integration indicators 182; integration processes 177
ethnic threat, perception of 178, 180, 183, 185, 188, 190, 193-5
ethnicity: and delinquency 155; and deprivation 158, 160; and poverty 153; and violence 158-9
ethnographic approach, of contextual effects research 153
Europe: children and adolescents research 153-4; implications of mixed tenure research 43; programmatic strategies 12
exogenous neighbourhood effects 14

fear of crime: impact of social heterogeneity on 128; and poverty 134
female violence, and deprivation 165
financial exclusion, and educational attainment 70
fluctuation 132, 135
France 1, 160
free school meals (FSM) 69, 74, 77, 79, 81-3, 85, 88-90
Freiburg 156, 164; Germany 155, 159, 161-6
Friedrichs, J. & Blasius, J. 43, 127, 130, 136, 151

friendship networks, and school location 167

Galster, G. 7, 37, 42-3, 61-2, 70, 147, 206
Galster, G. *et al.* 7
gang membership 157, 160, 162
Gans, H.J. 126
Gatreaux Assisted Housing Programme (US) 39, 42
gender: and delinquency 155, 160, 162-3, 165; and ethnic perceptions 195; in mixed communities 15, 16; and social status impacts 16
Germany 116, 125, 130-1, 135, 153, 155-60, 167-8, 170
Ginther, D. *et al.* 16, 207
graffiti 7, 49, 52-6, 61, 151
Granovetter, M.S. 177
Green, R. & White, M. 70

Harkness, J. & Newman, S. J. 70-1, 127
Haurin, D.R. *et al.* 70
Haveman, R. 15, 96, 114
Haveman, R. & Wolfe, B 15, 114
heterogeneity 125, 129, 133, 135, 138, 144, 147; impacts of ethnic 127-8; *see also* homogeneity; social mix
Hiscock classification system 45-6, 50, 129
HLM (Hierarchical Linear Modelling) 8-9, 153, 162-3
home maintenance standards, impact on children's development 70
homeownership: and behaviour patterns 127; and collective efficacy 72; effects on educational attainment 70-1; and mobility expectations 99; and residential mobility 203; school attainment study findings 77-8, 81-2, 87-8, 90-2; Scottish findings 90; social benefits 70-2; and sustainability 36; and young adult outcomes 99; *see also* owner occupation
homogeneity 14, 125-7, 131; social 14; *see also* heterogeneity; social mix
homophily 129
HOPE VI programme (US) 12, 39, 116
household composition, previous research 15
household mix, Swedish study findings 29-30
housing tenure, changes in English 50

ICCs (intraclass correlation coefficients) 162-6, 168
immigrants: metropolitan concentration 21; and relative deprivation 159-60
income-neighbourhood characteristics study, *see* tenure-mixing study

institutional resources: access to 15; and young adult outcomes 204
integration: education as driver of 198; indicators of 181-2
integration processes 177
intergenerational closure (INTCLOS) 135-41, 143-6, 150
intergenerational mobility and race study: data and variables 206-8; discussion and conclusions 217-19; methodology 205-6; multivariate regression results 213-15; results 208-17; simulation methods 221-5; simulation models 215, 217

Jencks, C. & Mayer, S. 204
Jupp, B. 43, 127, 129

Kearns & Mason 7
Kleinhans, R. 35, 43, 126, 129
Kuntz, J. *et al.* 206

labour market outcomes 16
Lake Parc Place, Chicago 127
language proficiency 178-9, 190-1, 195
leisure facilities 50
Leventhal, T. & Brooks-Gunn, J. 129, 131, 135
litter 49, 52-6, 61

Manzi, T. & Smith Bowers, B. 127
McCulloch, A. 127
mechanisms: correlated 14-15; endogenous 13-14; exogenous 14
Meen, G. *et al.* 38, 47
Mendenhall, R. *et al.* 203
migration 92, 131-2, 153, 156, 160, 162-3, 165-6, 176, 178, 183, 187, 190-1, 194
mixed community policies: benefits and mechanisms 39-42; community effects 41; extant research 15, 16, 42-3; overview 35-9; policy instruments 38-9; questions about 37-8; research, *see* tenure-mixing studies; resource effects 40-1; role model effects 41; transformation effects 41-2; *see also* tenure-mixing studies
mixed housing survey, Amsterdam 129
mixed-income housing, US development 12
mobility, and race *see* intergenerational mobility and race study
Morenoff, J.D. *et al.* 72
Movement to Opportunity programme (US) 39, 42, 101, 116
multi-level analysis 8; *see also* HLM
Murie, A. & Musterd, S. 14
Musterd, S. & Andersson, R. 37

natural areas 10, 125, 131, 133, 135, 137-41, 143-6
neighbourhood organization 129
neighbours 13-16, 40-1, 49, 52-6, 136, 146, 151, 192, 195
Netherlands 1, 29, 43, 126, 129, 175-7, 181-6, 188, 190, 192, 196-9
New Deal for Communities (NDC) 36
New Towns, planning concept 126
noise 49, 52-6, 61, 151
non-linearity 30, 46-7, 62, 67, 73, 78, 85, 91, 114, 160, 178, 205-6, 208, 213, 215, 218

Oberwittler, D. 136
Observed Deviant Behaviour of Youngsters (OBSYOUTH) 136-7, 139-41, 151
Olzak, S. 178
Ostendorf, W. *et al.* 129
owner occupation: and educational attainment 76; in England 50-1; growth in English 50; Hiscock classification system 45-6, 50, 129; impact of 43, 52-3, 55-8, 86; income profile of 71; in NDC areas 36; *see also* homeownership

Page, D. 129; & Boughton, R. 42
parks 50
Parsons, C. 69
PCA (Principal Components Analysis) 9, 10, 83, 136
peer group effects 13, 42, 72, 97, 103, 130, 136, 154-5, 163, 165, 171
perception of ethnic threat 178, 180, 183, 185, 188, 190, 193-5
perception of risk 133-4, 141, 143-6
Pettigrew, T.F. & Tropp, L.R. 128
poverty: and educational attainment 69; and fear of crime 134; Townsend's definition of 69
poverty and delinquency study: conclusion and outlook 171; data sources 155-7; friendship networks 165-7; native delinquency 160-5; results 157-71; scales 157; schools context 167, 171; theoretical and methodological considerations 154-5; welfare rates 157-8
poverty and young adult outcomes study: conclusions caveats and next steps 115-16; data sources 96, 102-3; instrumental variables approach 102; instrumentation procedure 106-7; IV vs non-IV approach 114-15; key outcomes 104; measurement challenges 100-2; model 98-100, 105-6; other predictors 111-14; results 108-15; scales 103-6; technical issues 107; variables 102, 105-8
predictors, statistical literature on 96

private renting 7, 20, 45, 50-2, 55, 57-8, 60-1, 127, 133
propinquity, positive effects of 128
PSID (Panel Study of Income Dynamics) 96, 102-7, 115, 206
public housing 12, 203
public services 15, 48, 73
public transport 50

race: and educational attainment 108; and intergenerational mobility *see* intergenerational mobility and race study; and social status impacts 16; and teen pregnancy 16
racial harassment 49, 52-6, 61
refugee groups 176, 181-3, 185, 190, 192-3, 198
regression analysis 7-8; methodological problems 7
relative deprivation 13, 38, 157, 160
residential mobility: primary factors 203; and race 203-4; scholarly interest 203
resource effects 40-1
Right to Buy policy 127
risk, perception of 133-4, 141, 143-6
role model effects 13, 41, 43, 72, 128, 154, 204
Rosenbaum, J.E. *et al.* 127
Ross, C.E. *et al.* 136, 151
Rossi, P.H. 132
Rutter, M. 68

Sampson, R. & Groves, W. B. 127, 129-30, 135
Sampson, R. *et al.* 130-1, 134-5, 139, 141
Sampson, R. J., Raudenbush, S. W. & Earls, F. 129
SAMS classification scheme 19-21, 29
Sarkissian, W. 127-8
Scandinavia 43
school attainment study, *see* educational attainment study
second-language proficiency 178-9, 191, 195
SEH (Survey of English Housing) 3, 44-6, 49, 51
SEU (Social Exclusion Unit) 36, 69
Shannon-Weaver Equitability Index 45
social capital: impact of home ownership 67, 70-1, 91-2; impact of tenure mixing 41, 126, 129; indicators of 145; and intergenerational mobility 71, 204; and neighbourhood poverty 103; role of 154
social class, and educational attainment 68
social cohesion 14, 126, 176, 190
social exclusion 37, 40, 69, 70, 72, 152-3, 176
social heterogeneity 128
social homogeneity 14, 131
social housing 37, 41, 71

social inclusion 36-8
social mix: association between housing mix and 37; assumed and desired outcomes 126-7; and behaviour patterns 127; concept analysis 124-5; context effects 126; Glans' discussion 126; impact of a broad 36; impact of different types of 128; indicators 125, 127; mechanisms research 128-30; and school performance 85; and size of spatial unit 127; spatial unit 127
social mix impacts study: correspondence analysis 141-4; data sources 130; findings 137-44; model 134; multiple regression analyses 139-41; policy implications 146-7; scale 136; scales 136-7; study area 130-4; summary and discussion 145-7; variables 135-7
social networks 13, 41-2, 71, 167
social renting 45-7, 51-3, 55-8, 60-2, 70-1
social status, and hours of work 16
socialization effects 13
socio-economic mix, Swedish study findings 29-30
South, S. & Crowder, K. 16
Sparkes, J. & Glennerster, H. 68
spatial mismatch 15
spatial unit, implications of size 127
spline regression 8, 215, 217
stigma 40-2, 72, 91, 126
stigmatization: and educational attainment 72; of neighbourhoods 15
supervision of children 136
sustainable communities, definition of 36
Sweden 1, 12, 15, 17-21, 29, 34, 37
Swedish tenure mixing study, *see* tenure-mixing studies

teen pregnancy 16, 96, 108, 151, 155
teen sexual activity 16
tenure mix, achieving 127
tenure mixing, UK context 37
tenure mixing studies 37; aims & objectives 43-4; conclusions and caveats 29-30, 60-2; data sources 17, 44; econometric issues 29; limitations 48; measurement systems 45-6; methodologies 17-21, 44, 48; models 17-19, 46-7; multivariate regression results 23-8; neighbourhood mix patterns 21, 50-1; regression results 34, 58-60; results 21-9, 48-60; sampling units 45; Scotland 129; variables 19-21, 44-5; *see also* mixed community policies
Thomas, S. & Smees, R. 68
Townsend, P. 69
traffic 49, 52-6, 61

Tunstall, R. & Fenton, A. 37

UK: implications of mixed tenure research 43; mixed community policy 35; schools and residential segregation 167; *see also* Britain
urban development 36, 48, 116
urban planning 1, 126
urban renewal 43
Urban Task Force, UK 35
US: adolescent crime studies 153; children and adolescents research 153; consensus on neighbourhood indicators 11; ghetto research 154; housing mobility research 42; implications of mixed tenure research 43; programmatic strategies 12

Van der Klaauw, B. & Van Ours, J. C. 16
vandalism 7, 49, 50, 52-6, 61, 72, 145, 151
violence: and deprivation 165; and ethnicity 158-9; female adolescent 164-5; and gender 165; measuring attitudes 157

Weinberg, B.A. *et al.* 16
welfare dependency 153, 159, 164
Wilkinson, R. 38
willingness-to-move 132, 134-5, 139-42, 146
Wilson, W.J. 154, 202

young adult outcomes, influencing factors 97; *see also* poverty and outcomes study
young adult outcomes literature 96; reviews 96; shortcomings of existing 96, 98